Africa In Perspective

Hayden Series in Social Studies

Africa In Perspective

F. SETH SINGLETON
Dean of Pierson College
Yale University

JOHN SHINGLER
Department of Economics and Political Science
McGill University

HAYDEN BOOK COMPANY, INC., NEW YORK

Acknowledgments

Every effort has been made to find the holders of copyright for the various excerpts included in this text, a difficult task when dealing with African literature. We sincerely regret where we have not succeeded. We wish to thank the following proprietors for permission to quote copyrighted works, as follows:

Librairie Gallimard, publisher for Leon Damas
Black Orpheus, publisher for Wole Soyinka and Nicholas Guillen (Guillen translated by Akanji)
Mbari Publications, publisher for Dennis Brutus
Présence Africaine, publisher for David Diop
G. R. Coulthard, translator for Regnor Bernard
Twayne Publishers, for "Outcast" from *Selected Poems of Claude McKay*
Bordas-editeur, publisher of Aimé Cesaire's *Cahier d'un retour au· pays natal*
Editions du Seuil, publisher for Leopold Senghor, and Charles Guenther, translator of Senghor's "Black Woman"

PREFACE

The darkest thing about Africa has always been our ignorance of it.

—GEORGE H. T. KIMBLE

Africa has a place in the modern world, and Africans are claiming it. Africans seek an independent and abundant future that will combine and extend the best of both modern technology and African tradition.

The issues that trouble Africa are those which seem to African leaders to block the way toward the better life they see ahead. The first and greatest desire is for political independence from European colonial rule. Confronted with a choice between independence and prosperity tied to continued foreign influence, most leaders have chosen independence. After independence, a developing and prosperous nation is the goal. Beyond their continent, African leaders seek influence to promote the causes they feel are just, or simply freedom to stay out of other nations' quarrels.

All these aims stress freedom from inferior status, a desire to "break the bonds" or "cut loose" from what Africans consider foreign control of their affairs. But where does this leave African nations once they have in fact "cut loose"? The problems facing a very new, very proud, and very poor nation in today's world are many and difficult. The nationalist enthusiasm that unfurled one more flag must be transformed into long-term effort and plain hard work to overcome illiteracy, poverty, and disease. In these tasks most African leaders are eager to accept aid from other countries.

The individual African, like most other men in the world, thinks in terms of his daily life and daily bread. Changing times and city life have thrown the traditional beliefs of many Africans into confusion. A man educated only to the customs of a cattle-herding tribe does not easily learn to live with automobiles, clocks, telephones, and textbooks. After the personal, unscheduled life of an African village, daily shifts in the mine or factory or office are grinding monotony. A city African feels cut off from the people of his own tribe, surrounded by strangers speaking strange tongues and worshiping strange gods. Dirt, low wages, and a shack of tin and cardboard add to the frustrations of African men and women seeking a new life in the new towns. The story of modern Africa may seem the story of new nations, but it is also the story of a great change in the daily lives of 240 million Africans.

This book is not about Africa, it is about Africans. The introductory chapter describes Africans as they lived before Africa was changed by European influence. From the panorama of hundreds of African peoples five sketches are drawn to illustrate the first point— that African communities differ greatly one from another, ranging from primitive bands to highly sophisticated societies. In fact, the peoples of Africa are more diverse than those of any other continent.

Contrary to popular belief, Africa has a past. Chapter 2 paints a background, highlighting the more colorful moments of Africa's early history. The slave trade demoralized African communities by chaining them to violence, and thwarted their peaceful development. Because the slave trade has poisoned the atmosphere between black men and white from Columbus's day to our own, this dark episode deserves a short chapter. The European scramble in the nineteenth century was the prelude to modern Africa. The lines casually and arbitrarily drawn by Europeans on the map of Africa at the time of partition are the boundaries of today's African nations. The European invasion, and African resistance to it, are covered in the fourth chapter.

Modern Africa begins with the period of European rule known as the colonial era. Part II of this book tries to dispel the myths and prejudices that surround both African and Western thinking about colonial Africa. Civilian officials replaced soldiers as rulers over Africans. A network of railways, roads, and telegraph lines was spread over each colony, preparing for the growth of a modern economy. Schools and hospitals were built, towns and traffic appeared. Peasants left their farms for the towns and the mines.

Africans developed a common identity through the common experience of colonial rule. Increasingly conscious of their poverty and lack of rights, Africans in each of the colonies organized to gain control over their own future. Discontent became the theme of the nationalist campaign for independence.

While most African nations and leaders share the experience of colonial rule and independence, Ethiopia and Liberia are significant and interesting exceptions. A comparison of Congo and Nigeria illustrates another key issue, the question of the internal unity and stability of new African nations. South Africa presents the problem of race and liberty in its most complex and acute form. These important African nations have been singled out for discussion in Part III, which ends with a chapter contrasting the backgrounds and aspirations of four African leaders.

While steps toward cooperation and unity among African nations have occupied the attention of African statesmen, African writers and philosophers have been groping for an idea of "Africanness," or "Negritude," and have searched for meaning in contemporary African life. Part IV sets out these two approaches to unity among Africans.

The last part explores the present and its implications for the future. Are African one-party states democratic? What is African socialism? Will African countries be able to provide a higher standard of living for their people? Can tribal rivalries be contained?

The final chapter describes the problems of African nations in a turbulent world. African leaders are concerned most of all with their own continent. Conflict between black Africans and white-settler Africans threatens to engulf southern Africa in a racial war. Americans are concerned with other matters as well. Will communism be as unsuccessful in Africa in the future as it has been in the past? Are African nations neutral in the cold war between communism and the United States, and are they all neutral in the same way? Why do African leaders often seem hostile to the United States?

This book is written in the hope that its readers will better understand how Africans themselves see their world.

CONTENTS

Africa In Perspective

chapter 1

WHO ARE AFRICANS?

One hand washes another.

—*African proverb*

Africans are usually lumped together as "primitive," and African peoples are called "tribes," putting them all into the same category. Because our standards for measuring advancement are technological (a nation that can put a man in a metal ball and shoot him into orbit around the earth is more advanced than one that cannot), such a view of Africa is a natural one. While many African peoples had highly developed governments, customs, and religions, not one developed a high technology. No African people ever invented a writing for its own language, although Arabic was written by traders, scholars, and holy men of West Africa, and Swahili was the written language of the East African coastal trade. With the exception of the North African Berbers, no African people invented or used the wheel. Cargoes in Negro Africa had to be carried on human backs because of the sleeping sickness that was fatal to horses and oxen.

While Africans never wrote letters or carried their crops in wagons, they did develop food grains from grass and lived in settled farming communities. They mined metals, smelted the ore, and from it cast tools and weapons. They molded bronze statues and carved ivory masks. They prayed and sacrificed to gods. They ruled and were ruled.

The important thing to remember is that African peoples are not alike. While primitive Bushmen lived without seeds or agricultural tools, talking drums of Bantu peoples carried messages vast distances at the speed of sound. Negro African nations like Buganda had farms, armies, and parliaments, and Ethiopia has been a Christian kingdom since the fourth century A.D.

There are ways of comparing people other than by counting their mechanical inventions. Africans can in no way be considered primitive or backward in their dealings with each other. The most important thing to many an African is the welfare of his family and his relatives. African societies have had little need for social security or old-age homes, because people in need have been fed and cared for by their children, or

1

brothers, or cousins. Long before the coming of white men, many African peoples had organized national governments to protect their citizens from foreign invasion and crime. All African communities have had rules to ensure that individuals lived in harmony with one another and that justice was done when conflict broke out. African religions have seen man as part of the universe, and have provided a moral code on which man could rely.

The Continent

Most of Africa is not jungle, but grassland. Veld, sudan, steppe, and savanna are all synonyms for country that looks something like Illinois or Nebraska, but which is dryer and covered with high grass, brush, and spare, flat-topped trees. The Sahara Desert, which is mostly rock, not sand, is the world's dryest area. The tropical rain forest of the

PHYSICAL FEATURES

West African coast and the Congo basin, which is actually not nearly as dense as the jungles of the Amazon or Southeast Asia, is wet for many months of the year.

Africa straddles the equator. All Africa but the Mediterranean coast and part of South Africa has a tropical climate. In the tropics, instead of four seasons there are only two: the wet season when it rains and the dry season when it doesn't.

Africa is essentially a single huge chunk of rock, a vast plateau broken only by the great crack in the earth called the Rift Valley of East Africa. Around the edge of the plateau lies a narrow strip of coastal forest, and from the coast broken hills rise gradually into the interior.

Of the four great rivers of Africa—the Nile, the Niger, the Congo, and the Zambezi—only the Nile can be navigated directly from the sea. All other

CLIMATE AND VEGETATION

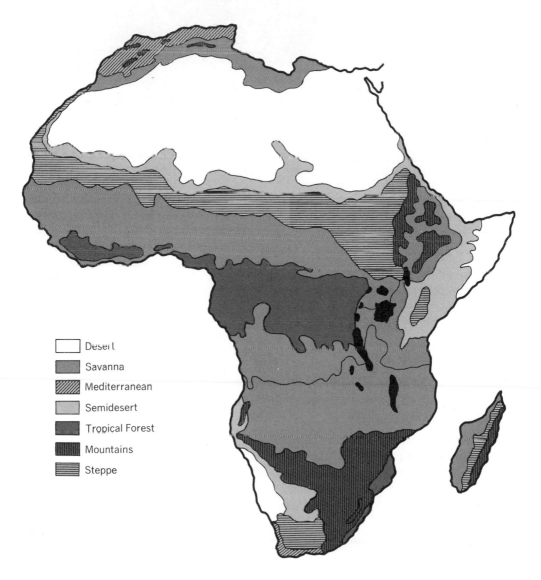

Desert
Savanna
Mediterranean
Semidesert
Tropical Forest
Mountains
Steppe

Zinjanthropus. (National Geographical Society.)

African rivers plunge over falls and rapids from the plateau to the coast. These facts of geography are very important in understanding African history. Africans preferred to remain on the plateau, in the interior, and had no reason to descend to the dense and unhealthy coast lands. On the other hand, the desert to the north and the rapids and coastal forests around the perimeter barred Arabs and Europeans from the interior for thousands of years.

The Origin of Man

The first men probably lived in Africa nearly 2 million years ago. In 1959 anthropologist L. S. B. Leakey found embedded deep in the walls of an East African chasm the skull of an ancient man whom he aptly dubbed Adam's ancestor. This prehistoric creature, called *Zinjanthropus*, after the ancient East African country of Zinj, had only a half-size brain and probably resembled an ape more than a man. In the same

Olduvai gorge where *Zinjanthropus* was found lie the remains of man from his earliest times to our own era. There are pebbles with one side chipped away to form a cutting edge, polished stone axes, bowls of baked clay, and the shell necklaces worn by ancient hunters to their graves.

Traces of another creature, called *Australopithecus*, have been found on the high veld of South Africa. From bones left in the caves where he slept, we guess that *Australopithecus* was a hunter, roaming the veld for game armed with a club made from the broken legbone of an antelope. A big brain and the use of weapons mark *Australopithecus* as a direct ancestor of modern man.

At Tassili, in the Sahara Desert, which was probably a good deal wetter and more habitable many thousands of years ago than it is today, are to be found cave paintings, stone tools, and the funeral paraphernalia of some unknown ancient people. All over the continent archaeologists are now beginning

RACES IN AFRICA

Arabs
Berbers
Arabs

Arabs

Arabs

Cushites
Hamites

Negroes

Bantu

Nilotes

Nilotes

Bantu

CAUCASIAN PEOPLES
Cushites Arabs
Hamites Berbers
European Settlers

NEGROID PEOPLES
Negro Nilotes
Bantu

Pygmies

Bushmen

Bantu

Hottentots

European settlers

IMPORTANT TRIBES

Kabyle Berbers

Rif Berbers

Bedouin Arabs

Tuareg

Mossi   Dinka

Fulani
Mandingo   Malinke   Hausa   Shilluk
Wolof   Ashanti   Tibbu   Nuer
Kru   Fanti   Ewe   Yoruba   Amhara
                    Ibo   Anuak   Galla
                         Sara   Somali
                              Ganda   Wakamba
Fang   Tutsi   Kikuyu
              Mongo   Hutu
         Kongo   Masai
              Luba
              Lunda
                   Rotse   Makua
         Oyambo   Ilova
              Ndebele   Merina
         Bushmen   Sakalana
              Swazi
         Hottentots   Zulu
              Sotho
              Xhosa

to unearth the mysteries of Africa's distant past.

The Races of Africa

Very little is known of the migrations that over thousands of years brought the peoples of Africa to their present homes. All Africa south of the equator was probably once the home of the Bushmen, who with their cousins the Hottentots are a distinct race, not Negroes. The other earliest Africans were probably Caucasians, who at one time occupied all northern and eastern Africa. The ancient Egyptians, the Ethiopians of today, and the North African Berbers are all descended from these early Caucasians. Caucasians migrated south,

replacing the Bushmen of East Africa, but in turn were driven back by Negroes, who are today still expanding at the expense of the other races of Africa.

The home of the Negro was probably somewhere in West Africa, either in the tropical forest of the coast or in the belt of grassland, or *sudan,* that rises slowly from the rain forest until it merges imperceptibly into the Sahara. Statues and fragments of iron and tin show that Negroes used metal in very ancient times. Carthaginian, Roman, and Berber traders brought ivory and gold from Negro Africa before the birth of Christ, while great Negro empires have flourished in the sudan since A.D. 500.

A branch of the Negro race, the Bantu ("bantu" means simply "people"

Bari tribesmen of Eritrea. Peoples of the Horn of Africa, called Hamites, are akin to the Semitic peoples across the Red Sea and to other, more distant Caucasian peoples. (*United Nations.*)

Facsimile of Bushman rock drawing. These drawings were done in bright colors. (*Drawing by Wendy Shingler.*)

in the Bantu languages spoken today in central and southern Africa), broke from the tropical forest of Nigeria into central Africa about A.D. 1000 and spread out quickly over the southern half of the continent. These Bantu farmers struck up a profitable trade with the Arabs of the East African coast who had long exchanged the products of Africa for those of the Orient across the Indian Ocean. Bantu peoples pushed south across the central hills and plains, fighting among themselves for the best land and the glory of their nation, whether Zulu, Luba, Sotho, Shona, or Xhosa, until they were temporarily stopped by the deadly rifles of the white Dutch settlers of South Africa.

Another group of Negro peoples found its way into the swampy region of the lower Nile and into the highlands around the African great lakes: Nyanza, Albert, Victoria, and Tanganyika. These cattle herders, called Nilotes after the river Nile, are very different from the Bantu. Independent, nomadic, and warlike, the Nilotic tribes raided and plundered the Bantu peasants. Unlike the Bantu, Nilotes have disdainfully refused to accept European ways.

The Pygmies are the smallest African race in number and in stature. They live today only in the most inaccessible parts of the Congo rain forest. Pygmies, like Bushmen, live by hunting and by gathering the wild roots and berries of the forest. Pygmies have become part of Bantu communities, serving the chiefs and nobles of the tribe.

Five Sketches

Five African peoples—the Bushmen, the Ganda, the Masai, the Ibo, and the Berbers—illustrate the amazing variety of ways in which men chose to live on the African continent. The sketches that follow show these five peoples as they lived before Europeans transformed African communities. Each of the five is from a different region and a different racial group. Varied as they are, they represent only a random handful of the hundreds of African communities on the continent.

The Bushmen

The high veld and dry plains of southern Africa, from Kenya to the Cape of Good Hope, were once the country of the Bushmen. Scarcely more than 5 feet tall, wearing only skins and leather sandals, Bushmen roamed this great expanse of desert, scrub forest, and grassland as hunters and gatherers before the arrival of the Bantu from the north and the Europeans from the south. They were an integral part of the natural life of the abundant plains.

The Bushmen have no place in the Africa of today or tomorrow—they provide a glimpse of a Stone Age world. Of 250 million Africans, only 10,000 are Bushmen. The Bushmen, whose rock paintings so resemble those of the earliest races, are possibly the direct descendants of those very ancient omen whose stone tools were found at Olduvai. Bushmen bear little resemblance to other Africans. They are not black, but yellow, with wrinkled skins that break into innumerable creases when they laugh, which is often. Slant eyes and high cheekbones give them a slightly Mongol look. Bushmen are divided into several groups, each speaking a different dialect of the Bushman language, which, like the language of the South African Hottentots, uses clicks for consonants. These languages are called Khoisan, pronounced with a click, after the Bushman word for man, *khoi*, and the Hottentot word for man, *san*.

As with other Stone Age peoples, the Bushman economy was a very simple affair. Armed with only wooden bows and stone-tipped arrows daubed with a deadly poison, the men of the band would leave camp soon after sunrise to search for game—the antelopes that wandered in herds over the plains. Stalking their quarry like silent cats, the Bushmen would track the antelope

as far as a hundred miles until it dropped from the poison of an arrow. The women looked for edible roots near the camp. When the hunters returned with fresh meat, the women cut and dried it for future use or pounded it into powder for the toothless old people.

Water was the Bushmen's greatest problem. In the Kalahari Desert, where the last bands of Bushmen survive today, there is no water for several months during the dry season, when even the pools and underground wells known only to the Bushmen are often dry. Bushmen tap underground water by sucking a pipe of hollow reed, preserving the water in hollow ostrich eggs which are carried from camp to camp. For many, the main source of water in the dry season is a melon called *tswana*, found in a camouflage of dry, brittle grass.

As with other natural creatures, the life of the Bushmen was a constant search for food and water. Only rarely would they camp in the same place more than a few days. Their homes were tiny shelters of dried grass bound with leather thongs, almost invisible against the surrounding brush. Bushmen often slept in the open without bed or blanket, holding council or recalling their legends beside a small campfire.

A Bushman band was more like a large family than an organized community. For example, a man, his wife, their small son, and the wife's aging mother might wander alone, only rarely meeting other groups of Bushmen. None of the bands was larger than twenty or thirty. Decisions important to the life of the band—literally the life, for if food and water were not to be found the whole group might die—were made by the agreement of all. Larger Bushman bands moved together from waterhole to waterhole in the rainy season, but broke up into family groups to wander alone during the drought. The survivors met again when the rains came.

Bushman hunters. In the flat, parched country of South-West Africa getting food and water is a full-time job. *(Information Service of South Africa)*

Surprising as it may seem for such wanderers, each Bushman band had its own territory, clearly defined by landmarks such as hills, river beds, and the round depressions called pans that dot the southern African desert. Each band had sole right to all game and water in its territory. The Bushman's struggle for food and water occupied so much of his time that he had little energy left to squabble with his comrades or make war on other bands. The idea of a community organized against other communities simply did not occur to him. Offenders against the band were thrashed or banished, which often meant death alone in the desert. The only judge of right and wrong was the band itself, for no formal laws or rulers were necessary where survival depended on cooperation. Even the idea of property was not strong in the Bushman, for where the only possessions were a few skins, beads, and bows and arrows the distinction of "mine" and "thine" lost its importance.

Like most other African peoples, the Bushmen believed that the animals and plants of their natural world had spirits. The eland, the badger, even the tiny praying mantis were creatures with spiritual purpose in the sweep of natural life of which the Bushman considered himself only a small part. The stars, the clouds, the trees, the birds, and the animals—all were the heroes of Bushman stories and legends.

Bushmen were talented artists and painted their love of Africa's natural life on cliffs and the walls of caves where they once sought shelter. Many Bushman paintings whose brilliance is now faded are thought to be centuries old. Now driven into the desert, the Bushmen have lost the gift of rock painting, and their rich legends are in danger of being lost as well. Bushmen were also musicians. One favorite instrument was a simple bow of stick and string, beaten with another stick. Another was like a lyre, with several strings. Surprisingly, the Bushmen had no drums, and danced to song and chant alone.

Today the Bushman is almost extinct. His story is much like that of the American Indian. Since perhaps the middle of the seventeenth century the Bushman has been attacked on two fronts: from the north by large and well-organized Bantu kingdoms, which swarmed south with cattle, seeds, and armies; and from the south by South African (Boer) pioneers in search of farmland. The Bushmen fought desperately with the Bantu invaders for the land that was their only way of life, but were massacred by Bantu metal spears and axes. No more merciful than the Bantu, and better armed, the white settlers drove the Bushmen from their hunting grounds. When Bushmen retaliated by raiding cattle and homes, they were hunted down and killed by the Boer commandos (scouting parties). This tragic episode ended only when the last remnants of the Bushman bands fled into the wastes of the Kalahari, where they alone could eke a living from the dry scrub, sand, and rocky hollows. Only a few thousand Bushmen remain wild, while their less-fortunate fellows work on white and Bantu farms.

The Ganda

The people of central and southern Africa—from Cameroun in the northwest to Kenya in the east and the Cape Province of South Africa in the south—are members of the same subfamily of the Negro race, the Bantu. Tall and not as dark as the West African Negroes, the Bantu peoples speak similar languages, although a Luba from the Congo cannot understand a Kikuyu of Kenya. Bantu are not hunters or nomads, but settled farmers. Organized under a chief who was often an absolute ruler, Bantu kingdoms also had armies and tax collectors. Many Bantu groups might better be called nations than tribes, for they resemble modern nations more than they do the primitive Bushmen or the Nilotic cattle herders of East Africa. Like the Europeans from medieval times until the present, Bantu nations were constantly at war with one another, trying to expand territory and power at the expense of their neighbors. A series of murderous wars decimated southern Africa during the eighteenth and nineteenth centuries—wars from which many Bantu peoples have scarcely recovered.

The Ganda, the most numerous and most important group in what is now Uganda, formed in the nineteenth century one of the strongest and most stable Bantu states. The British explorer John Hanning Speke, who was the first European to see the Ganda capital, was quite impressed. "The place surprised me," he wrote, "by its extraordinary dimensions and the neatness with which it was kept. The whole brow and sides of a hill were covered with gigantic grass huts thatched as neatly as so many heads dressed by a London barber and fenced around with tall yellow reeds." Near the great grass palace on the hilltop stood the houses of important officials. In front of the palace, where a sacred fire burned night and day, were shrines holding religious objects, including the king's umbilical cord.

The palace of the Kabaka (king) dominated the scene, just as it dominated political affairs. Buganda, as the Kabaka's domain was called, had a system of government appropriate to a well-organized nation, for looking after the million Ganda without any transportation faster than a man could run was a complicated job. Buganda was divided into ten provinces, each ruled by a governor. These provincial officials, like everyone else in the Buganda administration, were appointed by the Kabaka himself. The Kabaka's chief executive and adviser was the Katikiro, or prime minister, who also had the important right to decide who might or might not be allowed to see the Kabaka. There was also a Cabinet, with ministers of taxes, roads, army, and navy, and a parliament that included the governors of the provinces and assorted other officials.

Every day the Kabaka received food, cloth, and beer from his peasant subjects, as well as iron and cattle from the households of officials and wealthy men. Local officials were entitled to a share of the tax, but were responsible for maintaining the remarkable network of good roads (the Ganda had no wheeled vehicles) that connected all parts of Buganda. The great roads leading from the ten provincial towns to the capital were continually traveled by couriers and tax collectors.

As might be expected of a nation ruled by ambitious monarchs, Buganda had a large and efficient army. At the Kabaka's call over 100,000 men quickly assembled at the capital and marched off to fight, commanded by regular military officers. Large war boats patrolled the shores of Lake Victoria and carried troops to conquer the islands.

Some African peoples settled their quarrels by feuding and revenge between families, like the Hatfields and McCoys of the Kentucky hills. In contrast, the Ganda had official courts of justice whose decisions were accepted and enforced. Governors tried the cases, with the people looking on and listening to the arguments brought by the wrongdoer and his victim. Most crimes, such as theft, adultery, or tax evasion, could be atoned for by fines. Verdicts could be appealed to a higher court, until the case reached the Kabaka himself.

Intrigue and backstairs politics made life highly dangerous for ambitious men at the Kabaka's court. The favor of the Kabaka's relatives, particularly his mother and sisters, was crucial. The Kabaka could order an official deposed or executed at any time, and seems to have done so quite often. To be noticed and rewarded by powerful men was the only way to prominence among the Ganda. On the other hand, a slip of the tongue or incompetence on the job could easily cause a politician's death.

The Kabaka, like other African kings and chiefs, was as tightly bound by custom and tradition as the lowliest of his subjects. He could not demand more than the customary tax, or abolish the office of Katikiro, or confiscate the ancestral burial grounds of the Ganda clans. To both the Kabaka and his subjects it was unthinkable that the Ganda way of life could be changed, although personnel, including the Kabaka himself, might be replaced. African rulers had absolute power within the limits prescribed for them by custom, but were likely to be dethroned if they exceeded their traditional privileges.

In most African kingdoms, including Buganda, the choice of a new king was a problem. If the previous king had had twenty or thirty wives, as was usually the case, there were a great many sons available. The wishes of the old king were often ignored while the sons, each aided by his mother and relatives, fought for the throne with political intrigue backed by private armies. When a new ruler emerged from the confusion things went back to normal. The period of anarchy between kings was itself traditional. As far as we know, no Ganda prince tried to enlist popular support by promises of lower taxes or democratic government.

Buganda had neither a class of hereditary nobles, as did medieval Europe, nor slaves or outcasts, as did India, Arabia, and West Africa. While in theory all Ganda were equal, some families were rich and powerful, and kept their position by "pull." Ganda society operated both on unofficially inherited position and on competence and ambition. Promotions depended on the goodwill of the boss. Perhaps this is not too different from American society, although we like to stress competence. The Ganda, in fact, have an Horatio Alger story of their own in which a peasant boy becomes the cattle herder of a chief, is recognized for bravery, and eventually becomes the Kabaka's Katikiro.

The Kabaka, like other Bantu kings, ruled a nation of peasants. The staple crop of the Ganda was the banana, of which more than a hundred varieties were grown. Their diet was bananas roasted, bananas boiled, banana juice, banana beer, and bananas for dessert. Vegetables were also grown, and a peasant family might keep a few goats and a cow or two. Famines were common, because the bananas could not be stored.

Ganda men, like most Africans, aspired to have more than one wife. Many couldn't afford it. Wives not only had to be fed and housed, but were expensive to marry in the first place, because a payment of beer, cloth, and livestock had to be made to the bride's family. Today money can be paid instead of cloth or cattle. Women were expected to plant, hoe, and weed the banana garden, while men cleared the land and made the beer. Some men were ironsmiths who made hoe blades and spear points, while others wove mats, made shields, or built fences. All contributed labor to the roads and the palaces of officials, and served in the army when Buganda went to war.

Peasants did not own their land, but received it on lease from the local village headman. If a peasant wanted to move to another village he simply went to its headman and asked to be "his man" in return for the right to a plot of land. Another taxpayer and road worker was usually welcome. Like the United States, Buganda was a mobile society, for many peasant farmers took advantage of their opportunity to move. A peasant was protected from official tyranny, for if officials and headmen demanded too much of his crop in taxes he could simply pack up and leave.

Ganda religion was gloomy and negative. Each of the many Ganda gods had his shrines and his oracles—men believed capable of interpreting the god's wishes. When a Ganda wanted to consult a god he would go to the local oracle. Usually, however, the oracle demanded a gift so substantial that the peasants took their troubles to a local medicine man instead. Almost anyone could become a sorcerer, with the power to cast magic spells and inflict injury on personal enemies, or the personal enemies of their customers. The sorcerers were feared by everyone. Mistrust and suspicion seem to have been common features of Ganda life.

Some Ganda Gods

Kibuka	god of war
Mukasa	god of children
Musoke	god of rain
Kawumpuli	god of plague
Ndawula	god of smallpox
Kiwanuka	god of lightning
Musisi	god of earthquake
Nagawonyi	god of drought
Dungu	god of hunting

Note how many of the Ganda gods represent disaster and disease.

In the late nineteenth century Christian missionaries and trading company agents followed explorers into Buganda. Religious feuds almost ruined the country. Catholics and Protestants set up rival factions of converts, who vied for control of the Buganda government (an illustration of how everything was channeled into politics). Several times the Catholic and Protestant parties came to blows, and civil war was averted only

A wealthy Indian lady of East Africa. (*David R. Giltrow.*)

by British pressure and uneasy compromise. The missionaries were teachers as well as politicians, however. Officials and poets immediately began to write the Ganda language in the Roman alphabet, and today there is a large literature in Ganda.

Buganda was never very profitable for the trading companies. Ganda peasants, on the other hand, began to grow coffee and cotton for export. Today Buganda is one of the more prosperous farming communities on the continent.

In striking contrast to the rest of Africa, where new leaders discredited and replaced traditional rulers, Buganda government proved adaptable to modern conditions. Religious strife lessened after the British established a protectorate in 1894. Buganda was nourished by the careful rule of Katikiro Apolo Kagwa, who was knighted by the British, and the authority of the Kabaka remained the focus of Ganda loyalty throughout the first half of the twentieth century. After the Second World War Buganda nationalists demanded independence not only from the British but from the other peoples, former enemies of the Ganda, who had been included in the Uganda Protectorate. The young Kabaka was exiled to England in 1953, but returned in 1955 a hero to his people. Many Ganda are still demanding either a separate state or the ruling voice in independent Uganda.

The Masai

The Masai belong to the group of African tribes called Nilotes, who live in the spectacular safari country around the Great Lakes. The Tutsi (Watusi) of Rwanda, the Nuer of the Southern Sudan, and the Masai—all Nilotes—are famous as warriors and keep turning up in tourist magazines and Tarzan movies with their bright feather caps, decorated shields, and long spears.

In one sense, an image of these peoples as "noble savages" is accurate. Nilotic tribes are unmindful of change and dedicated to traditional ways. Nilotes find the "European" way of life far less satisfying and dignified than their own, which provides them with meat, milk, pride in their people, and a feeling that they are any man's equal.

Very tall and slender, with light skin and straight hair, the Nilotes are perhaps part Caucasian. Many Nilotic peoples speak in their legends of invasion from the north and of a marvelous people called the Chwezi, who came to rule with warlike power and great wisdom.

Nilotes have traditionally been cattle people, nomads who moved with their herds and lived solely from the meat, milk, and blood of their animals. Closeness of Masai and beast was essential to Masai life. The ancestry of each animal was known to several generations, and cattle were recognized and appreciated as we recognize and appreciate our friends and relatives. Wealth among Nilotes was measured in terms of cattle alone, and one purpose of war was to carry off cattle from the enemy's herd.

Nilotes have unbounded contempt for farmers in general, including Europeans. Where Nilotic conquerors did not drive off the Bantu farmers, as in Rwanda, Bantu were relegated to the level of an inferior caste and became herders, servants, and serfs for the benefit of their warlike rulers, from whom they were forever separated by race.

The Masai lived in the highlands of Kenya and northern Tanganyika, which provided lush grazing for their cattle. Each band guarded its herds day and night against the lions of the bush. A Masai camp, which could be razed to the ground in a few hours and rebuilt as quickly when the band moved to new grazing grounds, was a circle of mud houses surrounded by a high wall of sharp thorns to give protection against the marauding cats. At night, the herds were brought in from pasture and slept with the Masai in the enclosure.

Masai boys and girls were taught the Spartan virtues of obedience, courage, and endurance—virtues in keeping with the dangers of war and the hunt. Stern justice was meted out by elders to offenders against the Masai code, and even a small boy might be soundly thrashed with herding sticks for disrespect or negligence. Yet discipline was maintained not by the power of nobles or king but by a council of elders which met, held public debate, and voted by show of spears on the question before it.

The Masai illustrate a unique African institution found among Nilotic tribes and among some Bantu and West African peoples as well: the age-set system. An age-set is basically a group of men who are all of the same age and who are promoted together through a series of grades. In each grade the men perform specific duties that are the responsibility of that particular group. An American school class, for example, is an age-set formed at an interval of one year. The difference between a school class and a Masai age-set is that to a Masai the age-set was the most important group in his life, from the time he

was initiated until his death. A Masai would risk his life for an age-set brother, and would never disobey the decision of his comrades.

Masai age-sets were formed about every seven years from the boys of a band. The boys went together to shoot birds and animals to give as gifts to the senior warriors, or guardians, of the band. They were taught Masai lore and Masai virtue by the elders. After initiation, the young men traveled throughout the Masai country meeting other groups of junior warriors and stalking the guardians of the herd as practice for war. By the time of their promotion to the ranks of the guardians they could handle a spear superbly and were a match for any lion.

The Ol Morane, or guardians, were the backbone of the Masai system. Organized in regiments called *sirits*, they protected the cattle, hunted, and fought. The Masai could raise many thousands of men for war, armed with razor-sharp heavy spears and possessing superb knowledge of the terrain, and in the days before the British "pacified" East Africa the *sirits* were feared and unconquerable. When the guardians were promoted to senior status, all married, paying for their wives with cattle. Families were of little importance, however. The age-set, the band, and the duty of a Masai always claimed greater allegiance than relatives. Children, although they lived with their mothers, were raised as children of the whole group.

At irregular intervals the Masai nation met to hold council. From all corners of Masai land the bands assembled and built a huge circle of huts, perhaps a mile in diameter. While the priests offered prayers and sacrificed cattle, the ruling council of elders met under its chairman, the Paramount Chief, to elect new leaders and decide questions before the nation. As in other Masai councils, the elected Paramount Chief had the power of suggestion alone.

Stages of a Masai Life

Approximate Age	Status	Duties
until 14	Ol Ayoni (boys)	When they were twelve or thirteen years old, the boys of a village formed an age-set and prepared for initiation, learning to hunt and tend the herds.
14 to 18	Ol Aibartan (junior warriors)	The newly initiated young men roamed the country, learning to fight and visiting other groups of the Masai.
18 to 32 —18 to 25 —25 to 32	Ol Morano (guardians, or warriors) —Warriors of the Left Hand —Warriors of the Right Hand	The men lived in a barracks, called the *manyatta*. They were organized into regiments, called *sirits*, for war, hunting, and guarding the herds. Senior warriors married.
35 on	Ol Nesher (elders)	The elders held authority over the Masai.
	—Ol Piron (councilmen)	The Ol Piron, which means "firesticks," were the men who sat on the tribal council and governed their Masai band.
	—Ol Aibon (priests)	The Ol Aibon were rainmakers, fortunetellers, and medicine men. The head of the Ol Aibon sanctioned war and blessed the fighters. He supervised the age-sets and their initiation.

When a leader was chosen he was publicly shamed by his people. This custom, practiced in many parts of Africa, reminded a leader that his authority comes from the people, not from himself, and that he must therefore rule in harmony with the wishes of the people and with custom. A newly elected Masai chief was dressed in women's clothes, pelted with mud, and chased to his hut. He emerged the next morning assured of total respect and obedience from his people, but also with a heightened respect for them.

The Masai have been much less eager to copy European ways than their Bantu neighbors, the Kikuyu. Masai called Europeans "the people of the paper." One Masai legend relates that the first men worked with paper, read and made signs, and left their cattle thirsty. The great spirit, En Gai, scolded them, so they burned all their books except one, the Great Book wherein was written all knowledge. The men read the Great Book, and learned, and long disputed the meaning of what was written, and the right and wrong of it. Again the cattle went thirsty. So the priests spoke to the white cow and to En Gai. When the white cow saw no herdsman near she took the Great Book and ate it. To this day the Masai hold the white cow sacred.

The Masai are beginning to feel the pressure of farming and education. Their way of life cannot survive without change in a world of settled farmers, guns, and automobiles. Since the treaty of 1910 with the British, which set up a Masai reserve, the Masai have been free to do as they pleased so long as they kept the peace. In an independent Kenya, dominated by Bantu voters and Bantu politicians, it is less likely that the Masai will be protected. The question that faces the Masai, and other "traditional" African peoples, is this: Can they retain the spirit of their people, its courage, freedom, and pride, while adapting to a modern economy and government? Will the Council of Firesticks encourage schools, new breeds of cattle for export beef, and Masai representatives in government? Or will the elders defy change until the authority of tradition is broken by outsiders?

The Ibo

In West Africa live a great many very different peoples. There are herders, farmers, and traders, Christians, Moslems, and pagans, nobles, peasants, and slaves, great empires and communities no larger than a village. The Hausa, Yoruba, and Ibo, all of Nigeria, speak languages no more like one another than are French, Russian, and English. West Africa alone is diverse enough to prevent generalizations about Africa and Africans.

The land of West Africa is divided into three parallel strips running east-west. A belt of wet forest follows the coast and the river valleys, rising perhaps a hundred miles inland to low hills. To the north the sudan grassland gives way to thorn and heather, until vegetation stops at the southern fringe of the Sahara. Europeans, exploring from the coast, carved West Africa into slices with boundaries running north to south, bisecting many peoples and blocking the natural trade route that ran from Senegal in the west through Nigeria and Chad to the Nile, and from there to Egypt, Mecca, and the Orient.

More will be said in the following chapters about the long history of West African empires, trade, and civilization, and about the darker days of the slave trade. Trade extending far beyond the boundaries of a single state or tribe has always crossed the West African sudan, and there have always been West African cities at the crossroads of this trade. While empires ruled the sudan, the tropical forest became the home of a less attractive side of African life—slavery, headhunting, human sacrifice, and cannibalism. Except for slavery, such practices were, however, neither widespread nor frequent. Nor were African slaves treated as work animals; they were often allowed to have families and become wealthy.

Along with slavery most West African peoples (the Ibo are an exception) were rigidly segregated into social classes or castes. The Wolof of Senegal, for example, had two free classes, nobles and yeomen, an artisan caste, a caste of minstrels, and finally slaves. The minstrels, called *griots*, were expected to sing the praises of the nobleman who supported them. For the nobles, prestige was the important thing, and money was lavished freely and in public on winning friends and influencing people. Today education is sought as a way to gain prestige.

The peoples of West Africa may be divided into two groups, those who live in the sudan and those who live in the coastal forest and the hills beyond. The Ibo are a forest people. About 5 million Ibo live in the hot, damp, swampy delta of the Niger River, and in the neighboring hills. In contrast to most Bantu and the Nilotic peoples, who before the coming of Europeans were thinly spread over large areas, the Ibo have been thickly settled in the delta around large African towns for several hundred years.

Ibo families lived in stick-and-mud houses clustered along the maze of paths that connect their many villages. The family compound, surrounded by a mud wall, included separate houses, with kitchen and storeroom, for each wife, and perhaps the houses of grown sons and cousins as well. Like most Africans, the Ibo took great notice of their relatives, giving or receiving help as fortune dictated. A whole Ibo village was often just a large group of related families.

The staple crop of the Ibo was yams (sweet potatoes), which were planted in March, at the beginning of the wet season, and harvested in September. During the dry season the storage barns were full, but the rainy season before the harvest was often a time of hunger. Ibo women were responsible for most of the farm work, while men cleared the land and gathered the yam harvest. The Niger Delta is palm country. The Ibo gathered palm fruit and made palm oil and palm wine to use and sell.

Ibo villages were grouped around a central market town. In the marketplace women sold pots and baskets, grain and rice. Enterprising traders walked miles to buy cheaply and to sell at a profit. The Ibo not only bartered one product for another but used several kinds of money: small pieces of iron, shells, or brass rods. Most Ibo towns had their blacksmith. Although Ibo metalworkers never matched the artistic achievement of their neighbors of Benin, Ibo wood carving is famous. Ibo carpenters today work throughout Nigeria, many building in European style.

A well-to-do Ibo man quite likely had several wives, each with her own income from trade and farming, and each taking care of her own children. When an Ibo man married he had to pay a substantial sum to the bride's family. (The bride price now varies with her education, showing the high value that the Ibo now place on schooling.) If a wife left her husband, as often happened, he was entitled to a refund on his marriage payment, a refund often hard to collect from the bride's relatives. As might be guessed, Ibo women were not all content to tend their husband's yams. They continually demanded their rights to trade and be educated, and in 1929 gave the Nigerian administration a bad scare by staging a serious riot protesting a tax on women's trade.

More than most Africans, the Ibo relied on the values of individualism and self-advancement. Wealth was open to any man or woman through trade and farming. Men who grew wealthy by their own efforts became the leaders of their communities. Rich people publicized their success by joining the most important title societies, which were men's clubs imposing a substantial entrance fee. Title societies were often a good investment, for if a member lived long enough he would receive more from his share of later entrance fees than he had paid in himself.

The Ibo community supervised all aspects of life, and in so doing made no distinction between public and private behavior. Since everyone in a village was usually related, the committee of elders that ran the village was little more than a meeting of family heads. These family elders arbitrated the very complicated disputes over land use, ruled on questions of morality, and punished offenses against the ancestral spirits. Decisions of the elders had to be submitted to an assembly of all the men for approval or amendment, a procedure much like classical Greek democracy or an American town meeting.

In the spirit of rule by the family, thieves, adulterers, and murderers were punished by their own clan. As with most Africans, government and justice were informal and depended on the people involved rather than on fixed legal rules.

The Ibo never considered themselves one people. Each village, with its own clan and its own title societies, was not only in charge of its own affairs but could also make trouble for its neighbors. Raiding parties for slaves, and for avenging family grudges, were common even after the slave trade had tapered off after its abolition by the British in 1807. Anarchy, violence, and slavery, although accepted as part of the natural order of things, were fortunately not chronic. The treatment of slaves was strictly regulated by custom. Raiding was not constant but sporadic. Feuds between clans were usually settled by mediation, not by blood.

Like most Africans, the Ibo lived in a world of magic and the influence of spirits. Things happened according to the whim of supernatural powers. A good harvest and the health of the children were not the result of proper weeding or a balanced diet but evidence of favorable intervention by long-dead ancestors. The Ibo believed that every man had a soul given by Chuku, the god of creation and father of sun, sky, and rain. The most powerful force was Ale, the earth goddess. Ale, queen of the underworld, owned the souls of men living and dead. Ale judged the morals of men and punished their crimes. If Ale was properly consulted by the priests, and if she was pleased, a good harvest was sure to follow. Ale and other gods had oracles or prophets to interpret their wishes. The oracles were consulted for help and advice. Each clan had its ancestor cult, and the headman of the clan carried a special staff that gave him the magic power to interpret the wishes of the dead to generations living.

Perhaps because Ibo villages formed a sophisticated trading economy and practiced democratic self-government, Ibo have taken to European ways with a vengeance. In Nigerian trade and business Ibo now predominate among the Africans. Ibo have migrated to all regions of the country. African clerks of the civil service are usually Ibo. Education offered by missionaries and by the Nigerian administration has been eagerly absorbed. Many Ibo are now city dwellers or suburbanites who ride bicycles to factories and offices every morning. The first nationalist political party of Nigeria, the National Council of Nigeria and the Cameroons (NCNC), was dominated by Ibo voters and led by an Ibo, Nnamdi Azikiwe. Many have

praised the Ibo for "adopting" the European way of life. The fact seems to be that their traditional way of life teaches the Ibo many values essential to success in modern business and politics.

The Berbers

In the hills of the fertile Mediterranean coast, in the North African mountains, in oases scattered over the rocky Sahara, and in the desolate sun and wind-swept distances of the desert itself live the Berbers. Berbers are descendants of the first Caucasian inhabitants of Africa. Their story, bloody and tragic, can be learned from the accounts left by Phoenician, Carthaginian, Roman, Arab, and French conquerors of the Maghreb. "Maghreb," in Arabic, means "the west," and refers to the habitable part of North Africa between the Sahara and the sea. Hannibal's soldiers, the Almoravid conquerors of medieval Spain, the Barbary (Berber) pirates, and the mountain tribes who fought the French Army through the nineteenth century—all were Berbers.

The outstanding event of North African history was the Arab invasion of the eighth century. North African Berbers, adopting Islam, Arabic speech and writing, and Arab culture, joined the Arabs to build what was at the time (with the exception of China) the world's most advanced civilization. Moslem Spain became the center of learning of the Western world.

In the eleventh century Bedouin Arabs again swept across the Maghreb in a second *jihad,* or holy war, for Islam. According to the fourteenth-century Arab historian Ibn Khaldun, this second wave destroyed the fields and cities in its path "like a plague of locusts." Berbers, who occupied all the Maghreb and shared the Sahara with Negro farmers, were dispersed and driven into the mountains and the desert. Over the centuries even those Berbers who were not completely absorbed by Arab North

Berber village in Algeria's rugged Kabyle region. Figs are the main crop. *(Africa Report.)*

Africa fused Arab culture with their own, adopting Islam and Arabic writing. No Berber language has ever been written, while today only a quarter of the 25 million people of the Maghreb speak Berber dialects.

Although Berbers accepted Islam, they held doggedly to a number of very un-Arabic customs. By strong Berber tradition, a man has only one wife. Berbers also refused to accept the Arab caste system. Only the Sahara tribes lost their independent and democratic political ways. In contrast to the Arabs, most Berbers were not and are not nomads, although the Tuareg and other Berber tribes of the Sahara live like desert Arabs with tent and camel.

Berbers were a settled people who lived on the grain and vegetables grown outside the walls of their fortified towns. Near the fertile Mediterranean coast fig and olive trees competed with wheat and barley for attention, while the date palm sustained the oases. Ber-

bers kept animals for meat and milk, hides, and wool. Unlike Africans south of the Sahara, who depend on their own labor and their iron-tipped hoes to tend the crop, Berbers have used draft animals and the plow since classical times.

Berber towns, whether a small hamlet of 300 or a city of 50,000, were built for war. A high wall with battlements and turrets guarded the narrow streets of the town below, while in the center rose the citadel, last refuge in time of attack and storehouse for the grain. Houses were built of adobe, with walls often 3 feet thick to keep out both heat and cold, for the temperature might change as much as 50 degrees in a single day in the mountains or the desert. Berber houses had two stories, topped with a flat roof that served as terrace and sleeping porch.

Berbers were remarkably jealous of their freedom. They called themselves Imazighen, which means "free men." Although both the Arabs and the Negroes of West Africa, with whom the Berbers had long traded and mixed in the Sahara, segregated themselves into nobles, common folk, despised castes, and slaves, most Berbers would have none of it. The only distinctions among them were those of wealth, and although a rich Berber might pay a poor neighbor to feed his chickens or weed his crops, both were free to become friends, eat together, and cast equal votes at the town assembly.

This democratic outlook carried over from social life to politics. Berber government was of the town meeting variety. Once a week all the men assembled at the mosque or under a tree, and discussed community problems until all agreed on a course of action. Every town sent representatives to a district council, which perhaps included part of a city or several country towns. In time of war, which was often, the district council appointed a military dictator, or *amghar,* to lead the people during the emergency. The *amghar* was jealously watched lest he usurp power, and was cut down to size as soon as possible.

Every Berber community was divided into two opposing factions, called *sofs.* These were not kin groups or welfare societies but political parties, sometimes uniting liberals against conservatives. Although the *sofs* were separated in the town, bloody brawls were common. The desert town of Ghadames was completely partitioned between the two factions, which were separated by a wall. Only the mosque and marketplace were neutral ground.

Like the people of a town, districts were also organized in alliances, called *lefs,* for self-protection. In the mountains of Morocco and Algeria, where Berber life was less drastically changed by the Arab conquest than on the coast, districts of the two *lefs* formed a pattern like the red and black squares of a checkerboard. Allied districts met for

great annual feasts. Yet the real purpose of the system was to lessen the danger of war and dissuade overeager Berbers from plundering their neighbors. When the war alarm sounded, the aggressor district was quickly surrounded and overwhelmed by reinforcements of the opposing *lef.* Although violence was never checked, the *lef* arrangement did give some protection in a war-torn region.

The Maghreb is today a mixture of Arab culture and Berber tradition. Most Libyans, Tunisians, Algerians, and Moroccans count both Arabs and Berbers among their ancestors. The Berber passion for freedom and their willingness to fight for it have, from the African point of view, dominated Maghreb history since the coming of the French. Berbers of the Kabyle region were the leaders of fierce resistance to the French for forty years after the first French landing at Algiers in 1830, and the Berber peasant towns remained the stronghold of the army of guerilla fighters that drove out the French in 1962. The backlands of Algeria are plagued with expanding population and poor land, and are now one of the most depressed areas of Africa.

Tradition and Modern Africa

Few Africans today live in exactly the manner of their forefathers. Yet traditions are not easily eradicated from the fabric of a people's life, even by modern education and technology. Many of the features of African life illustrated in this chapter have survived or been adapted to the new age in Africa.

Africans have always lived in a world where events had a religious meaning and a magical explanation. If a man was eaten by a lion, his death was the will of the gods, or perhaps the lion was influenced by a sorcerer. Africans know very well that lions will kill when hungry, but why that particular man, on

African priest talking things over with the village elders. The gourd in his hand and those in the basket are religious objects. Africa has hundreds of tribal religions. (*White Fathers.*)

that particular day? The power of spirits provides a ready explanation for what Westerners call "fate," "chance," or "accident." African beliefs have been gradually undermined and replaced by the Western faith in science that identifies cause and effect. This is a psychological revolution in Africa. With it comes the conviction that man can control his own future, whether as individual, tribe, or nation.

Custom and tradition have a strong grip on African life. For members of a traditional society, social or technical change is barred, for it would mean breaking "the ways of our ancestors." The traditions are guarded by the priests, the chiefs, the kings, the old men and women, who receive respect bordering on veneration in most African societies. The habit of acceptance continues as long as the traditional way of life is not broken from outside. When

Africans go away in a truck to work in the mines, or talk to the European missionaries and officials, or return from schools with book learning about the facts of human history, then doubts about their own traditional ways of doing things begin.

The extended family of many relatives and the habit of cooperation within traditional communities often help Africans adjust to new ways. Many an African lost in the wilderness of the city has found help and housing with fellow tribesmen or distant relatives. Tribal and clan associations in the city continue the solidarity of the village and provide a link between the old life and the new. Both family and tribal ties are of course less strong in the city and are replaced by ties to other kinds of groups (see Chapter 6). Under the influence of Christianity and European custom the immediate family of man, wife, and children becomes more important. Wanting for himself the things that money can buy, a man rich from trade or wages will try to avoid his relatives.

In many African villages there were few distinctions of wealth or authority. It was often hard to draw the line between law and family discipline, or between public welfare and family help. In Africa today the desire for a government that provides for all the needs of its citizens perhaps owes less to socialist ideas than to the community solidarity and security to which Africans have been accustomed.

In African communities there was little difference between religion, economy, and politics. Spiritual power, wealth, and political leadership went together. This lack of distinction between spiritual and political authority has interesting consequences. If the economy has always been "planned" by a leader of the people, why not so today? Is there really any difference between a chief who inaugurates the planting of crops at a sign from the oracle of the earth goddess and the prime minister of a modern nation who decrees the building of a dam or airport at a sign from parliament, the oracle of the people? Modern African leaders use the religious authority of traditional rulers to gain respect and attention from their people. When Kwame Nkrumah of Ghana called himself Osagyefo, meaning "Glorious and Heroic Leader" or "Redeemer," he had not necessarily fallen victim to conceit, but had inherited the mantle of traditional authority.

Africa has not been a peaceful continent, and few Africans inherit a strong preference for nonviolence from their traditional background. In the past, however, violence had its customary limits. Individual reprisals and feuds between families were kept within bounds, although tribes, nations, and empires made bloody war on one another from one end of the continent to the other.

In traditional Africa all activities were carried on by personal contact. Business, for example, was conducted in full public view in the marketplace, not by checkbook. People of the community kept tabs on one another. Gossip and public opinion were the main restraints on immoral behavior and the violation of custom. Because the duties of a ruler were rigidly set down, the problem was not to choose between different political philosophies but simply to find the most capable man, the one who had been chosen by the gods to rule. Wealth was often distributed among the common people, and rich men were rewarded with respect and positions of leadership for sharing their goods. In African politics and African business personal friendship still means a great deal, and the use of money or other gifts to influence people is not regarded with quite the same disapproval as it is in the United States.

Traditional Africa extends its influence into the present and the future. The rest of this book will show how the many African peoples are changing one another, as modern Africa brings them together.

PROBLEMS

1. Read Vachel Lindsay's poem *The Congo (A Study of the Negro Race)*. Preferably, read it aloud. Is the poem about Africans? Does it capture the spirit of life in Negro Africa? In what way are Americans misinformed about Africa if they accept the ideas of Lindsay's poem and other material like it?

2. Match:

amghar	close ties with all one's relatives
sudan	a regiment of the Masai
Khoisan	a West African minstrel
Nilotes	man's ancestor
age-set	the great desert of southern Africa
Maghreb	a Berber leader
extended family	gifts given in exchange for a wife
Swahili	the click languages of the Bushmen
griot	cattle people of East Africa
bride price	a lifelong group of associates
Katikiro	the language of East African traders
Zinjanthropus	the Prime Minister of the Ganda
Kalahari	West African grassland
sirit	the Arabic name for North Africa

3. Was the fate of the Bushmen inevitable? Compare the story of the Bushmen with the history of the American Indian tribes. Can anything be done to preserve the artistry and naturalist skill of the Bushmen other than by just leaving them alone?

4. Compare the government of the Ganda, the Ibo, the Berbers, and the Masai. Which of these African peoples, considered as a nation, was governed most like the United States? In which group was local government most like that of an American town or city?

5. Would the extended family be likely to speed up or to hold back change in Africa? Would a young African with family obligations be likely to leave his village and try his luck in an unknown city? Is the extended family likely to survive in modern times? Age-sets? Polygamy? The bride price? Why?

6. Which of the peoples studied would have the least trouble adjusting to a modern way of life? The most trouble? What advantages or disadvantages does each people have in the effort to become attuned to changes in their way of life?

7. Without looking at a map, draw an outline of Africa. Show the sudan, the Sahara, the East and Southern African plateau, the Congo basin, and the Kalahari Desert. Add the Niger, Nile, Congo, and Zambezi Rivers, and the Great Lakes of East Africa. If you can do this with reasonable accuracy, you have a good working knowledge of African geography.

READING SUGGESTIONS

Jomo Kenyatta, *Facing Mount Kenya*, Vintage, paper.

Richard Llewellyn, *A Man in a Mirror*, Pocket Books, paper.

Elizabeth Marshall Thomas, *The Harmless People*, Knopf, 1959; Vintage, paper.

Amos Tutuola, *The Palm-Wine Drinkard*, Faber & Faber (London), 1952; Evergreen Books, paper.

Laurens Van Der Post, *The Lost World of the Kalahari*, Morrow, 1959.

part one
AFRICAN HISTORY

Two thousand years of trade, slavery, and conquest mold the Western view of Africa. Westerners have thought of Africa as a "dark" continent, and of Africans as "dark" not only in the color of their skin but in the color of their beliefs and way of life. Until very recently the West knew little of African history or of the societies and cultures which that history reveals.

The folk histories repeated by tribal storytellers from generation to generation tell much about particular peoples. Yet the writings of travelers of the classical world, and of Arabs many centuries later, tell us most of what we know about early Africa. In search of gold, slaves, and spices, the merchants and oarsmen of ancient Mediterranean galleys ventured along the northern and eastern African coasts, recording what they saw and discovered as a guide for future adventurers. An unknown Greek merchant of the first century A.D. wrote a handbook called *The Periplus of the Erythrean Sea*. (The ancient Erythrean Sea is now called the Indian Ocean; Eritrea was a small country of East Africa, now part of Ethiopia.) The Greek wrote:

> East Africa has an abundant supply of ivory and some turtle shell. The inhabitants of the coast, men of huge stature, are given to piracy. They live each in their own districts, their own masters.

North Africa was for centuries the granary of the Roman Empire, and supplied the Coliseum with gladiators, lions, and an occasional giraffe brought from the south. "Ethiopia," "Libya," and "Africa" itself are names that

PART ONE:
African History

come to us from the Greeks and Romans. "Ethiopia," in Greek, means "the country of those who burn their faces black." Ethiopia was to the ancients all the unmapped and unknown southern lands of the Negro peoples.

The Arabs were the first to venture south into Africa. Arabic writings are the best source of information about Africa before the European exploration and conquest. The word "sudan" is Arabic, and, like "Ethiopia" and "Negro," "sudan" means "black." To the Arabs, Africa was "bilad es sudan," the land of the blacks. As Islam spread and Arabs ventured across the Sahara, Arab journalists, scholars, and explorers reported their findings. The cultivated Al Bakri wrote from the Spanish university of Cordoba in 1067 that "the King of Ghana can put two hundred thousand soldiers in the field, more than forty thousand of them being armed with bows and arrows." Three hundred years later Ibn Battuta published *Travels in Asia and Africa (1325–1354)*.

When European seafarers began to skirt the African coasts, direct knowledge of Africa began to reach Europe. Oluadah Equiano, an Ibo freedman living in London, published his memoirs of Africa in 1789. Since then, the West has learned directly from Africans.

The first chapter in this part tells of African empires and civilizations that existed long before Africa was "explored" by European adventurers. It is not a complete history, but only a description of some early African civilizations.

The next chapter describes the first contacts of Europe with Africa, and the slave trade that began in the time of Columbus and ended when the British Navy put down the slavers after the American Revolution. It is important to remember that Europe during most of this era was itself not "modern" and had no industries and few parliaments. Europe had not yet been persuaded that all men were created equal. If white men could be forcibly shipped to America as laborers, why couldn't black men be shipped as slaves?

During the Industrial Revolution of the nineteenth century in Europe and America, Western ideas about Africa and Africans changed. Where Europeans had previously sought slaves they now sought converts to Christianity, raw materials for their new factories, and new markets for their cotton cloth and copperware. European domination of Africa was considered necessary for the safety of missionaries, traders, and prospectors. For 300 years Africans had warred with and raided their neighbors for slaves with European encouragement. The guns and liquor they received increased the violence. Having helped considerably to create such chaos, Europeans then justified the conquest and partition of Africa by the need for "law and order."

Chapter 4 describes the European "scramble for Africa" in the nineteenth century. First came reconnaissance by explorers, missionaries, and traders, followed in the space of a generation by the political partition of Africa into a patchwork of over fifty colonies. Many Africans bitterly resisted the European invasion, but were defenseless under the muzzles of the conquerors' guns.

The aim of these chapters is not to provide a chronicle of events but to develop a background to an understanding of Africa in the twentieth century. A distorted image of Africa—that Africans have always been uncivilized, barbaric, and incapable of self-government —hangs over us today. This section tries to separate popular myth from historical reality.

chapter 2

KINGS AND EMPERORS

Where is the black man's Government?
Where is his King and his Kingdom?
Where is his President, his country, and
his ambassador, his army, his navy, his
men of big affairs? I could not find them.

—MARCUS AURELIUS GARVEY,
*founder of the Universal
Negro Improvement
Association, in 1914*

In the days when Europeans thought ships could sail off the edge of the world, Africa south of the Sahara was the subject of fable and speculation. Herodotus, the famous Greek historian of the fifth century B.C., tells this story:

Some young men from Libya ventured across the Sahara desert, where none of their countrymen had been before. Coming at last to a habitable region, the Libyans stopped to pick fruit from the trees. They were attacked by some little men—of less than middle height—who seized them and carried them off. The speech of these dwarfs was unintelligible, nor could they understand [the Libyans]. They took their captives through a vast tract of marshy country, and beyond it came to a town, all the inhabitants of which were of the same small stature, and all black. A great river with crocodiles in it flowed past the town from west to east.

Since the time of Herodotus Africa has seemed a land of frankincense and myrrh, apes and ivory. It has also seemed a land of bizarre men and strange animals. Tales were believed of men "who do carry their heads beneath their arms," "eat raw dragon's flesh," and "wash their clothes in liquid fire."

The fact is very different from the myth. Early African civilizations, much like early civilizations in other areas of the world, rose and fell in many areas of the continent. Before, after, and between them lived African peoples not civilized at all, though they were not nearly as bizarre as European storytellers made them out to be. The six areas of early African history are:

1. The Nile Valley: Egypt of the Pharoahs, Kush, Meröe, and Axum
2. The Maghreb: ancient trade, Arab conquest, and Islamic civilization
3. The Sudan of West Africa: Ghana, Mali, Songhai
4. The Forest of the Guinea Coast: Benin, Oyo, Dahomey, Ashanti
5. The Central Plateau: Zimbabwe
6. The East Coast: Zanj, Kilwa, Mombasa, Malindi

The Nile Valley

Four thousand years before the birth of Christ the people of the lower Nile (modern Egypt) gave up hunting and began to grow crops for food. Within a thousand years social classes formed, and trade began. Priests and warriors attended their king, the Pharaoh, who was absolute ruler of 2 million people clustered around a few large cities. Egyptians worshiped the Pharaoh as a god on earth. He was responsible for a good crop and the welfare of his kingdom. At death, the god-king was buried in a gigantic tomb, a pyramid, built by slaves at great expense. The great pyramid of Gizeh took 100,000 slaves twenty years to build. It stands almost half as high as the Empire State Building (481 feet) and is built from over 2 million stones weighing 2½ tons each. No Pharaoh went alone to his future life. Surrounded by possessions thought to be of future use—jewels, weapons, pottery, even a royal barge—and attended by servants killed to accompany him,

EARLY AFRICAN KINGDOMS
(Dated Approximately by Century)

An ancient map of the world. According to one ancient theory, the Nile was separated from its sources in the Mountains of the Moon by an "ocean river" cutting Africa in two. Note that the sudan is the land of the "Ethiopines."

the Pharaoh was sealed in his tomb. Divine kings have ruled African empires and kingdoms since the days of ancient Egypt.

Egypt of the Pharaohs was Africa's first great power. The Pharaoh's men sought to extend the Egyptian Empire south into Africa, and Egyptians were Africa's first imperialists. An Egyptian official, Harkuf, ventured south on the Nile as far as modern Ethiopia in 2275 B.C., returning with spices, rare wood, and ivory for the Pharaoh. The booty which pleased the Pharaoh most was a pygmy, and Harkuf received an order from the Pharaoh to inspect his charge ten times a night to make sure the pygmy arrived safely in the capital. Egyptian ventures into Africa have a rather modern ring, considering that Christ lived closer to our day than to Harkuf's.

Harkuf was the forerunner of Egyptians who established colonies along the Nile. In the ninth century B.C., when Egypt was in decline, the former Egyptian colony of Kush became independent. For the next thousand years, until the time of Christ, Kush and its successor kingdom, Meröe, pushed their frontier south into Negro Africa. The conquered black men apparently absorbed their conquerors and became the rulers of Meröe. In Roman times Meröe continued to trade both with the Mediterranean world and with Africa to the south, and African peoples probably learned the skill of metalworking from Meröe. Huge slag heaps visible today near the confluence of the White and Blue Nile show that Meröe was once the Pittsburgh of Africa. Near the slag heaps stand temples, pyramids, and palaces. The ruins of Meröe are among the few existing monuments to black African civilization.

Still farther south, in what is today Ethiopia, the kingdom of Axum emerged as a rival to Meröe. By the fourth century after Christ, missionaries from Egypt and the East were converting many Africans to Christianity. About A.D. 300 Axum became Christian and shortly thereafter defeated Meröe and burned its capital to the ground. The victory of Axum ended the Nile civilization that had endured for 5,000 years, and established the Ethiopian Christian kingdom that still exists today (see Chapter 11).

The temple of Karnak at Luxor. Egyptians built this massive structure in 1360 B.C. (*Arab Information Center.*)

North Africa

The original inhabitants of North Africa were the ancestors of the people we today call Berbers (see Chapter 1). Since the beginning of recorded history, North Africa has been continually invaded and conquered. Phoenician colonies were first founded there about 800 B.C. With the rise of the greatest Phoenician colony, Carthage, North Africa became the southern fringe of the classical Mediterranean world. Greeks, Romans, Vandals, and Goths conquered, plundered, and colonized North Africa in their turn. These European peoples established city-states which became ports and centers of trade. The Berber inhabitants of North Africa became farmers, traders, and soldiers for both their own chieftains and their many conquerors.

In ancient times the Sahara Desert was a bridge linking the Mediterranean world with Negro Africa. Across the bridge to the Mediterranean were carried the trade goods of the ancient world—gold, slaves, and ivory. Negro Africa was one of the main sources of the wealth of the Roman Empire, and probably of greater commercial importance than the lands of the European barbarians to the north. In return for gold and gladiators the Romans sent salt, copper, and cloth to the West African sudan. Berbers were the middlemen who hauled the goods across the desert first by horse and chariot and later on camels, which were imported by the Romans from Arabia after A.D. 300. At the southern fringe of the Sahara, trade was sometimes carried on by silent barter. Without a word being spoken the desert traders would place their goods by a river and retreat to the farther bank. Negroes would emerge from the bush, place gold beside the goods, and then also draw back. If the gold was not enough the traders would wait until the Negroes added to the price. Finally each group in turn would collect its part of the bargain from the riverbank, and the traders would begin the return journey of a thousand miles across the desert.

As time went on Africans organized to take advantage of the trade. By the fifth century A.D. the trading empire of Ghana flourished in the sudan. The source of the gold that maintained Ghana's power was kept a state secret by Ghana's rulers, who knew that their power depended on control of the gold trade.

In the seventh century Europe was cut off from Africa by the Arab conquest of North Africa. The Arab invaders were inspired by the new religion of Mohammed, which spread quickly from its holy city, Mecca, after the death of the prophet in 632. The conquest and occupation of North Africa were swift and thorough. In 639 the armies of Islam swept into Egypt. By the end of the century Arabs ruled at Gibraltar and had driven north into Spain, and even into France, until they were stopped by Charles Martel, King of the Franks, at Poitiers in 732.

Unlike most earlier invaders of North Africa, the Arabs were immigrants and permanent settlers. Overnight the decaying Christian faith of the Romans and the Byzantine Empire was suppressed by the Mohammedan Arabs. City folk and peasants learned Arabic and worshiped Allah. Those who preferred to preserve their Berber ways fled to the hills or to the desert. The thousand-year-old civilization of the Phoenicians, Greeks, and Romans disappeared, leaving traces among a few North African Jews and Egyptian Coptic Christians. North Africans came to consider themselves part of the world of Islam, and do so to this day.

The Arab invasion created an impenetrable wall between Christian Europe and Negro Africa. The religious hatred of Christians and Moslems toward each other was deep and lasting, and reinforced the Arab "iron curtain" over

Africa. Medieval Europeans believed that Christian civilizations had survived in Negro Africa. A legendary African king, Prester John, was thought to rule a fabulously wealthy Christian kingdom south of the Arab lands. The myth of Prester John dominated European "knowledge" of Africa throughout the Middle Ages, but little could be done to reach him.

While European ideas of Africa degenerated into fantasy, the other side of the coin was that Africa lost touch with the progress of medieval Europe. Islam, the Arabic language and alphabet, and Arab ideas and achievements (including mathematics, medicine and architecture) became a part of the way of life in North Africa. Arab knowledge of and influence in the Maghreb and in West Africa was great, while European ignorance remained profound.

West African Empires

Al Bakri, the Arab chronicler of the eleventh century, related the report of a traveler from south of the desert:

When the emperor gives audience to his people to listen to their complaints and set them to rights he sits in a pavilion around which stand his horses caparisoned in cloth of gold. Behind him stand ten pages holding shields and gold mounted swords, and on his right hand are the sons of the princes of his empire, splendidly clad, and with gold plaited into their hair. The governor of the city is seated on the ground in front of the king, and all around him are his ministers in the same position. The gold of the chamber is guarded by dogs of an excellent breed who never leave the king's seat. They wear collars of gold and silver. . . . The beginning of an audience is announced by the beating of a drum, which they call *Daba*, made of a long piece of hollowed wood. When the people approach the king they fall on their knees and sprinkle their heads with dust, for this is their way of showing respect.

From A.D. 300 until the European conquest of the nineteenth century, a

Sudanic warrior in medieval armor.

period of more than fifteen hundred years, great Negro African empires flourished, struggled, and died in the West African sudan.

Ghana

The first of the sudanic empires was known by the name of its king, the Ghana. Ghana lasted from A.D. 300 until it was destroyed 900 years later by Sundiata, the great chief of Mali. As Al Bakri tells us, Ghana was a pagan kingdom, unlike its successors, which were ruled by Moslem Africans. As in Egypt of the Pharaohs, the religion of Ghana was worship of the Ghana himself. Ghana was an empire in the true sense of the word. From the capital city the emperor and his court officials ruled many subject peoples to a distance of four days' ride from the capital.

Ghana's power depended on gold obtained from the mines of Wangara to the south. The Ghana's capital was the southern terminus of the trans-Saharan gold trade, which drew Moslem merchants of the Maghreb south in search of gold for Arab and European markets. The common people of Ghana were Negro peasants who lived poorly in mud huts and benefited little from Ghana's trade, although they were conscripted to fight Ghana's wars. Archaeologists have unearthed in the sudan the remains of an elaborate city a mile square that was home for tens of thousands of people. Mosques and mansions of many rooms, filled with glass, pottery, and ironwork, attest the once-great kingdom. Ghana's other legacy is its name, which the people of Gold Coast have taken for their own country as a symbol of African renaissance.

Mali

Ghana's successor was the empire of Mali. Two small African kingdoms, Kaniaga and Kangaba, were competitors at the time of Ghana's decay. The King of Kaniaga, hoping to eliminate his rivals, murdered eleven brothers of the ruling family of Kangaba, sparing only the crippled child Sundiata. Mercy proved a mistake, for the cripple inherited the throne of Kangaba and began to expand his kingdom. In 1235, Sundiata defeated the armies of Kaniaga and avenged his brothers by killing its king. Within five years Sundiata had conquered Ghana and all surrounding kingdoms, creating one of West Africa's great empires, Mali.

Sundiata and his people were Moslems, and sought to convert their subjects to Islam. The Wangara gold miners, now subjects of Mali, presented a problem. As the miners were converted to Islam, gold production declined. Preferring prosperity to religious zeal, Sundiata allowed the miners to retain their traditional ways.

Another great Mali emperor was Mansa Musa, who was famed throughout Africa, Europe, and Arabia for his fabulous wealth. Mansa Musa's greatest exploit was his pilgrimage to Mecca in 1324. Before the Emperor's horse strode 500 slaves, each with a staff of gold weighing six pounds, while behind walked a troop of camels laden with still more gold. The sumptuous splendor of the Emperor's procession was a topic of conversation in Cairo for years. The generosity with which Mansa Musa distributed his wealth caused a slump in the Cairo gold market, which took years to recover from the wealth of Mali. Mali began to appear on European maps.

The famed Arab geographer Ibn Battuta was quite impressed by Mali on his visit there in 1352:

> The Negroes possess some admirable qualities. They are seldom unjust, and have a greater abhorrence of injustice than any other people. Their emperor shows no mercy to anyone who is guilty of the least act of injustice. There is complete security in the country. No traveller or inhabitant in it has anything to fear from robbers or men of violence. They do not confiscate the property of any white man who dies in their country, even if it be uncounted wealth.

Shortly after Battuta's journey Mali was in full decline.

Songhai

The last of the great medieval empires of the sudan was Songhai. In the fifteenth century, at the time when Portuguese and Spanish mariners were beginning the long period of European exploration and expansion, Emperor Sonni Ali established the Songhai Empire. In 1468 Songhai occupied the university town of Timbuctu, cultural center of all West Africa. Sonni Ali died in 1492, the year of Columbus's discovery, during a campaign to consolidate his now-vast empire. (See map on page 30.) A Moslem general, Askia Mohammed, seized the throne and immediately set out for Mecca with treasure to rival that of Mansa Musa. During Askia's fruitful thirty-one years of rule, the Arabic university at Timbuctu became one of the world's great centers of learning.

Another Arab, named Leo Africanus by Pope Leo X, who ransomed him from Sicilian pirates, traveled as a young man in the sudan. He wrote in his book *The History and Description of Africa*, published in 1550, that "there are numerous judges, doctors, and clerics in

**Courses of the University
of Timbuctu**

Theology
Islamic law
Rhetoric
Grammar
Literature

Timbuctu invited visiting lecturers from the Universities of Cairo (Egypt) and Fez (Morocco).

Notice that Timbuctu was a liberal arts school, teaching only philosophical and literary subjects, and excluding the Arab sciences of astronomy, mathematics, and medicine.

Timbuctu, all receiving good salaries from the King. He pays great respect to men of learning."

Like the Europeans, the Arabs of the Maghreb had long cast envious eyes at the salt mines of the desert and the gold mines of the south. As Portuguese captains tried to penetrate the Guinea rain forest from the sea in search of the source of the sudan gold, Moroccans also launched an invasion across the Sahara bent on seizing sudanese wealth. An army of mercenaries in the pay of the Moroccan King Al Mansur succeeded in crossing the Sahara in 1590. Although his forces were depleted by disease and injuries, Judar Pasha, the expedition's Spanish leader, routed and crushed the armies of Songhai, which fled in panic at the awesome roar of his guns and cannon. Despite their total victory, the Moroccans could not rule in the sudan, for they had neither the men nor the means to hold the Songhai Empire. Chaos and anarchy broke out among the peoples of the sudan. West Africa never fully recovered. A writer of Timbuctu, summing up the effect of the Moroccan invasion, lamented: "From that moment everything changed. Danger took the place of security; poverty of wealth. Peace gave way to distress, disasters, and violence."

Kanem, Bornu, Fulani

As Songhai collapsed after the Moroccan invasion, kingdoms to the east in the central sudan emerged as its successors. Of these kingdoms — Kanem, Bornu, and the Hausa states—little is known. They probably worshiped their early kings before adopting Islam. A King of Bornu, Mai Idris Alooma, imported guns and Turkish military instructors from Cairo in the 1590's. The location of the central sudanic kingdoms gradually shifted south and west into what is now Northern Nigeria. The last of these was the Fulani Empire of Uthman Dan Fodio, who in 1802 led a Moslem *jihad* (holy war) against the Negro forest peoples to the south. In general the central sudanic kingdoms were only pale reflections of the earlier empires to the west.

The Moroccan invasion marked the end of an era of West African history that had lasted more than a thousand years, the era of the empires of the West African sudan which looked north across the Sahara to the Mediterranean and Arab worlds and lived by trade in gold. From the sixteenth century, the attention of West Africa increasingly turned toward the coast and toward Europeans. In the place of gold and ivory, the prize of West African trade and conquest became black gold and black ivory—slaves. African kingdoms whose power rested on the capture and sale of African slaves grew up in the rain forests of the Guinea coast. To the north, the sudan stagnated. Its once profitable trans-Saharan trade withered with the decline of Arab civilization and the rise of Europe.

The Forest Kingdoms

With the decline of the sudanic empires strong Negro kingdoms grew up in the West African forest. Although their origins go back to the thirteenth century they became powerful only after

1500. These kingdoms—Benin, Oyo, Dahomey, and Ashanti—were much alike. Unlike the far-reaching empires of the open sudan, the forest kingdoms were quite small in area and were built around a single town. The forest Negroes were not Moslems and had had no contact with Arab culture, although they did dig gold which eventually found its way to the Mediterranean. The kingdom of Benin, in modern Nigeria, was the most important of the forest states. Benin received its first European ambassador—from Portugal—in 1485, and sent an ambassador to Lisbon in return. The Portuguese introduced Benin to the slave trade, which lasted until the British occupation of Nigeria 400 years later.

Benin and the other forest kingdoms profited greatly from the slave trade. Benin city, like the capitals of Oyo and Dahomey, was far enough inland to be out of range of raiding parties sent by European warships. African middlemen on the coast were eager to buy slaves from the interior. It was better to enslave than be enslaved, and organized kingdoms like Benin, Oyo, and Dahomey

Top: Benin bronze head. Bottom: Soldiers of Benin. (*Bottom, Irving Rosenthal.*) The forest kingdoms of West Africa produced much great art.

became the enslavers. A Dutch geographer reported:

> He is a powerful prince, the King of Benin. He can mobilize twenty thousand soldiers in a day, and raise in a short time an army of eighty to a hundred thousand men. Thus he is the terror of his neighbors, and an object of fear to his own people.

The policy of continued warfare for slaves was self-defeating, for the forest kingdoms surrounded themselves with a wasteland that isolated and strangled them.

The absolute power of the king was an unpleasant side of Benin life. Although one visitor reported that "the inhabitants of Great Benin are generally good-natured, and very civil," others stressed that the people of Benin lived in fear of their king.

> All his subjects, however great they may be, are simply in the position of slaves. They even bear a brand on their bodies as a mark of slavery, which the king stamps upon them during their childhood, when their father or mother brings them into the royal presence.

Rituals of royal power increased the awe of Benin's subjects for their king, who was worshiped as a kind of god. The king was considered the representative of the spirits of the ancestors, and able to talk directly with the gods. He was kept in isolation, and the common folk were allowed to see him only once or twice a year, surrounded by courtiers. In many forest kingdoms the king could not be seen eating, for he was thought to be above such mortal needs.

In the early days of Benin, the funeral of the king provided an occasion for fearful ritual. Here is the account of a Portuguese seaman of about 1550:

> There is in the kingdom of Benin an ancient custom, observed to the present day, that when the king dies the people all assemble in a large field, in the center of which is a very deep well, wider at the bottom than at the mouth. They cast the body of the dead king into this well, and all his friends and servants gather round, and those who are judged to have been most dear to and favored by the king (this includes not a few as all are anxious for the honor) voluntarily go down to keep him company. When they have done this, the people place a great stone over the mouth of the well, and remain by it day and night. On the second day a few deputies remove the stone, and ask those below what they know, and if any of them have already gone to serve the king. . . . It is considered highly praiseworthy to be the first, and he is spoken of with the greatest admiration by all the people.

The forest kingdoms produced beautiful art in brass and bronze, pottery and ironwork. The Benin bronzes are famous, and the ivory masks which survive are among the treasures of world art. The exquisite craftsmanship of the forest kingdoms did not survive their decline during the seventeenth and eighteenth centuries. Their artistic tradition survives today only in the wood carving of the Nigerian descendants of Oyo and Benin.

Central Africa

So far this chapter has described only those peoples in the northern parts of Africa who traded and fought with white men. Because Africans kept no written records, we know about only those African lands reached by Arab and European travelers. A number of Negro civilizations have flourished in central and southern Africa during the past 2,000 years. Our very scanty knowledge of them rests primarily on the remarkable Zimbabwe ruins, in modern Rhodesia. (Following the example of Ghana and Mali, the Africans of Rhodesia have decided to call their country Zimbabwe when they achieve independence.) Zimbabwe meant "royal court" in the lost language of the people who lived there hundreds of years ago. The city was built as a fortress. A wall thirty feet high and twenty feet

The fortresss of Zimbabwe. The builders of Zimbabwe mined copper, gold, and iron on the central African plateau, through Rhodesia, Zambia, and Katanga. *(Damon Kletzian.)*

thick in the shape of an ellipse stands in the center of the city. Inside the wall probably lived the rulers of Zimbabwe and their priests and craftsmen. Clay and stone houses built against the rock spread for miles outside the wall of the citadel.

Throughout the vast dry plateau stretching from Katanga (Congo) in the north to the Transvaal (South Africa) in the south are found mines and the ruins of smaller towns built in the manner of Zimbabwe. This is the region of Africa that holds the mineral wealth of the continent. Zimbabwe was a mining civilization, and, like central and southern Africa today, depended on the mining and export of gold and copper. Sixty to seventy thousand mine workings, shallow diggings in the rock or on the surface of the hard earth, have already been found. At Zimbabwe the gold was smelted and cast into ingots or worked into fine gold ornaments.

Zimbabwe was the home of the Monomotapa kings. The Monomotapa left Zimbabwe sometime during the fifteenth century, perhaps because the salt sup-

ply was running out, and moved north to the Zambezi River, where they were met by Portuguese explorers. The first Portuguese to reach the Monomotapa was a Jesuit missionary, Gonzalo de Silveira. Silveira succeeded in converting the Monomotapa to Christianity, but was promptly murdered and thrown into the river at the instigation of Arab merchants at the court.

Historians believe that the Monomotapa first built Zimbabwe about A.D. 1000, although radiocarbon tests show that the site was settled as early as A.D. 400. The great structures of Zimbabwe —the ellipse and the "acropolis"—were built much later, sometime after 1600. Zimbabwe was finally destroyed in the 1830's by Zulu barbarians invading from the south. When British prospectors arrived in the late nineteenth century, Zimbabwe was a mysterious ruin.

East Africa

From earliest times the Indian Ocean has been a highway of commerce. East Africa was the western fringe of a great trading world which extended from the Mediterranean to Arabia, Persia, India, and even China. East African history, or rather the little we know about it, is the history of city-states involved in this Eastern trade.

Port cities dotted the East African coast from the Red Sea to modern Mozambique and the island of Madagascar. To the ancient Egyptians this was the land of Punt. To Arabs 2,000 years later, it was the land of Zanj. The inhabitants were an exotic mixture of Arabs and Persians from the Levant, Bantu Africans, Indians, and Malays from the Orient. African exports were ivory, gold, and slaves for the luxurious courts of Eastern monarchs.

The tale of the founding of Kilwa shows the difficulty of separating fact from fiction in this intriguing history. In 975 an Arabian sultan named Hassan Ben Ali foresaw the destruction of his kingdom in a vision, and sought refuge across the Arabian Sea in Africa. He came upon an island ruled by an African chief, who agreed to sell it if Hassan would surround the whole island with colored cloth. Hassan in this way bought the island and built the city of Kilwa. Kilwa, on the coast of modern Tanganyika, became one of the greatest of the East African city-states. Three hundred years later the intrepid Arab traveler Ibn Battuta stopped in Kilwa. He noted that "it was a large town on the coast. The majority of its inhabitants are Zanj, jet black in color and with tattoo marks on their faces."

In 1414 the ambassadors of Malindi, another East African coastal city, reached the court of the Ming Dynasty in Peking, taking as an exotic African gift a giraffe, which was duly celebrated by Chinese artists in their paintings.

Into this thriving world burst Portuguese soldiers bent on loot, conquest, and conversion to Christianity. In the era of Columbus the Portuguese sacked and burned many East African towns, and during the next 200 years the once-flourishing city-states were reduced to ruin.

All this is only a glimpse of Africa's early history. There is much that is not known and much that probably will never be learned. What we do know shows that Africans of many regions were kings, soldiers, miners, and traders from earliest times, and that they were in contact with the peoples and civilizations of other continents.

To the early Africa of scattered trade and civilizations came the Portuguese, the vanguard of European expansion at the time of Columbus. Close on their heels followed the other slaving and trading nations of the West. The violence of the slave trade led to centuries of decline and disorder in Africa. The myth of a dark continent inhabited only by savages dates from this later period.

PROBLEMS

1. Match the men with their countries:

Sundiata	Zimbabwe
Hassan Ben Ali	Ancient Egypt
Gonzalo de Silveira	Songhai
The Monomotapa	Fulani Empire
Askia Mohammed	Mali Empire
Uthman dan Fodio	Kilwa
Ibn Battuta	Portugal
Mansa Musa	Arab North Africa
Harkuf	
Sonni Ali	

2. Why do we know so little about African history? Why do Westerners think of Africa as a continent without its own history?

3. Travelers to a foreign land are likely to stress the new, the strange, and the exotic. Was this true of early travelers in Africa? What do the reports leave out? Do we have any way of finding out about the customs and daily life of ordinary people in ancient Africa?

4. Draw a time line showing the main periods and areas of African history. Compare it with a similar outline of European history. Does what we know

about Africa resemble the events of other continents? Until about A.D. 1500 could Europe claim to be clearly more "advanced" than Africa? In what ways?

5. The Arab invasion of the Maghreb was a decisive event in African history. Why? What were its effects? How might African history have been different if Christian Crusaders had conquered and held North Africa?

6. Where are the natural trade routes on the African continent? How did geography both protect and isolate the empires of the sudan? Were the six areas of African history isolated from each other? Draw a map showing possible routes linking early African cities and kingdoms.

READING SUGGESTIONS

E. W. Bovill, *The Golden Trade of the Moors,* Oxford University Press (London), 1958

Basil Davidson, *The Lost Cities of Africa,* Little, Brown, paper.

J. D. Fage, *An Introduction to the History of West Africa,* Cambridge University Press (London), paper.

————, *An Outline Atlas of African History,* St. Martins, 1958.

Roland Oliver, *The Dawn of African History,* Oxford University Press (London), paper.

Jan Vansina, *Kingdoms of the Savanna,* University of Wisconsin Press, 1965.

chapter 3

BLACK GOLD

The merchants daily seize our subjects,
sons of the land and sons of our noblemen
and our relatives. . . . They grab them
and cause them to be sold: and so great,
Sir, is their corruption and licentiousness
that our country is being utterly depopu-
lated. . . . It is our will that in these
Kingdoms there should not be any trade
in slaves or market for slaves.

—AFONSO,
King of Congo, in a letter to
John III, King of Portugal,
about 1525

My children quit their peaceful nakedness,
donning the uniform of iron and bloodshed.

—DAVID DIOP,
modern Senegalese poet

Portuguese Discovery and Conquest

Western contact with Africa dates back more than 500 years. In the early 1400's the European kingdom of Portugal sought a route to the fabled wealth of the Indies and Cathay (China). The rulers of Portugal also wished to find the source of the legendary sudan gold south of the Sahara and the ancient Christian kingdom of Prester John. The Mediterranean road to Africa and the East had for centuries been in the iron grip of the Arabs, and in the fifteenth century it fell to the hated and even more hostile Turks. The only pos-sible remaining route lay around the western coast of Africa, through dan-gerous and unknown waters.

A brilliant and ambitious Prince of Portugal, Henry the Navigator, inspired and led Portuguese expansion in the fifteenth century. While governor of the port of Ceuta, on the northwest coast of Africa, Prince Henry learned from Arab geographers about the flour-ishing trade of the Indian Ocean. His hopes were kindled by rumors that the gold lands of the sudan could be reached

from the African coast and that it was possible to sail around the southern tip of Africa to the Indies. For thirty years Prince Henry single-mindedly prepared for exploration, inventing instruments of navigation, collecting maps, and learning the little that was known in Europe about Africa and the East. Using new sailing techniques—ships having sails with a leading edge that could return home to Portugal against the prevailing northwest winds— Henry's sea captains inched around Africa's Atlantic bulge. In 1445 the Portuguese reached the mouth of the Senegal River beyond the Sahara, find-ing for the first time a green land in-habited by black men. On this very first expedition to Negro Africa, the Portu-guese brought black men back to Europe as slaves.

Portuguese expansion was clearly ex-plosive. In 1482 Diogo Cao crossed the equator and reached the mouth of the Congo. Bartholomeo Diaz rounded the Cape of Good Hope in 1488. In 1499 Vasco da Gama became the first Euro-pean to reach India by sea. By 1550 the Portuguese controlled the rich Indian

Ocean trade and had reached China and Japan. All this was accomplished without maps, in wooden sailing ships smaller than a modern ferryboat.

Portugal became master of the African coast from Senegal to the Red Sea. The Portuguese scoured the Guinea coast, as the Negro land stretching from Senegal to the Congo was called. (The word "Guinea" came originally from the Berber language and meant "land of the black men.") So rich was the gold trade in the first years of exploration that the region was labeled the Gold Coast. The Portuguese built a fort called El Mina, the mine, to protect their African monopoly from other marauding Europeans. El Mina stands today on the coast near Accra, capital of modern Ghana. King John II of Portugal was

COLONIALISM I:

Portuguese Exploration to 1600

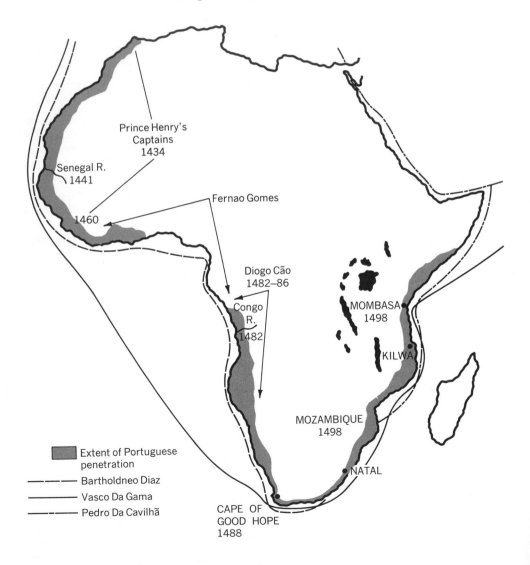

Following their sixteenth-century exploration and conquest, the Portuguese ringed Africa's coast with fortresses at strategic points. Such castles as this one along the Gulf of Guinea became strongholds for slavers of many nations, passing by conquest from one European power to another. (*Wide World Photos.*)

so pleased by his new domain that he added "Lord of Guinea" to his titles in 1482.

In this early period the Portuguese dealt with African kingdoms as diplomatic equals. Seeking trade with Benin (in modern Nigeria), the Portuguese sent missionaries and exchanged ambassadors, and later did the same with Mali and Timbuctu. To the south, a remarkable alliance was established between Portugal and the Kongo kingdom, which had reached the height of its power in the fifteenth century around the mouth of the Congo River, which was called the Zaïre by the Portuguese. (The Kongo people gave their name both to the river and to modern Congo, a country far larger than their original domain.) On his voyage of discovery in 1482, Diogo Cão left four Portuguese-speaking West Africans at the court of the ManiKongo, or Kongo king, and returned to Lisbon with four Kongolese. Relations expanded rapidly, and shortly after 1500 the heir apparent to the Kongo throne was baptized a Christian

with the name of Afonso while on a diplomatic mission to Lisbon.

Afonso might be considered a forerunner of today's African leaders, for until his death in 1543 he tried to introduce Western techniques and learning to his people. Afonso was helped by a group of Jesuit missionaries, who claimed many Christian converts among the Kongo. While missionaries encouraged the spread of Christian civilization on the one hand, Portuguese demands for slaves disillusioned the Kongo rulers and their people on the other. Within fifty years Portuguese aid had stopped, and by 1660 Kongo objections to Portuguese slave raids, which were destroying whole villages throughout the region, brought war against Portugal. The original alliance of equals ended when Africans were forced to defend themselves against the slave trade.

Portuguese destruction of the East African trading cities was part of the Portuguese plan to seize control of the great wealth of all the lands around the Indian Ocean. A Portuguese eyewitness reported the capture of Mombasa in 1508:

> The king of the city refused to obey the commands of the King our lord, and through this arrogance he lost it, and our Portuguese took it from him by force. He fled away, and they slew many of his people and also took captive many, both men and women, in such sort that it was left ruined and plundered and burnt. Of gold and silver great booty was taken here, bangles, bracelets, earrings and gold beads, also great store of copper, with other rich wares in great quantity, and the town was left in ruins.

The Portuguese killed the goose that laid the golden egg, for when they finally ventured inland they could not find the source of these riches. For 200 years the East African coast was the scene of constant bloody battles. The Portuguese built the massive Fort Jesus at Mombasa only to lose it, retake it, and lose it again. By 1700 the Portuguese had withdrawn to their sleepy settlements in Mozambique near the mouth of the Zambezi. Slowly the East African ports revived their trade, but in a new commodity—black slaves for Arabia and the East.

The Atlantic Slave Trade

From 1500 to the middle of the nineteenth century slaves and slavery dominated African history and the lives of Africans. Slavery was nothing new in the world. Greeks, Romans, Arabs, Indians, and Chinese had all owned and used slaves. At the time the African slave trade began Europeans were slaves to North African Arabs, and Africans owned other African slaves. Yet the slave trade across the Atlantic was different in many ways. Men of one race and color, the whites, enslaved men of another, the blacks. Instead of serving their own people in African communities, Africans exported to the Americas were thrown into the totally strange and hostile surroundings of plantation slavery. The slave trade degraded both Africans and Europeans, and has left a legacy of hostility and distrust for later generations.

What was the purpose of exploration and overseas conquest in the days before modern industry? The most obvious prize was gold and ivory, jewels, silks and spices. Except for some gold, Africa had little to offer compared with the wealth of the Orient. Settlers and colonies in temperate lands could supply the mother country with produce and markets. In all Africa known to the Portuguese it was impossible for Europeans to settle. Heat and disease made life difficult and short. Spanish America and later the Thirteen Colonies were better suited to settlement. Furthermore, Africa could not be conquered by Europeans in the fifteenth and sixteenth centuries. Diseases unknown and fatal to Europeans prevented occupation of the interior, and, unlike most Indians in the Americas, African peoples and kingdoms were firmly in control of the land they farmed and were able to resist intrusion.

Need for workers on New World plantations sparked the Atlantic slave trade. The very condition that made Spanish and English conquest easy in the Americas—few native people—made it impossible to start plantations. There was simply no labor force. In the more northern of the American colonies the problem was solved by settlers and small farms. Further south, from Maryland to Brazil, the problem was solved by slaves.

In the very first years after Columbus's discovery it became clear to Spain that the native Indians could not be used as plantation slaves. In 1495, on the Caribbean island of Hispaniola (modern Haiti and the Dominican Republic), Indian slaves revolted against their Spanish masters and were put down with great cruelty, as was the practice of the time. A young Spanish priest, Bartholomé de Las Casas, was so upset by the violence that he sought to protect the Indians. De Las Casas had seen African Negro slaves working in Portugal and Spain. They had seemed to him both hard-working and happy, and he therefore assumed that Africans would fare better than the Indians under the stress of plantation life. De Las Casas petitioned the Spanish Crown to import slaves from Africa, and in 1518, after twenty years of such lobbying, the first Africans arrived in the New World.

Africans were the most reluctant of all New World immigrants. The slave trade which carried them from Africa lasted more than three hundred and fifty years. The last shipload of Africans arrived in Cuba in the 1890's, thirty years after the Civil War was fought on the issue of slavery and eighty-five years after the last legal slave ship docked in the United States. During this

ATLANTIC SLAVE ROUTES:
The Triangular Trade and the Middle Passage

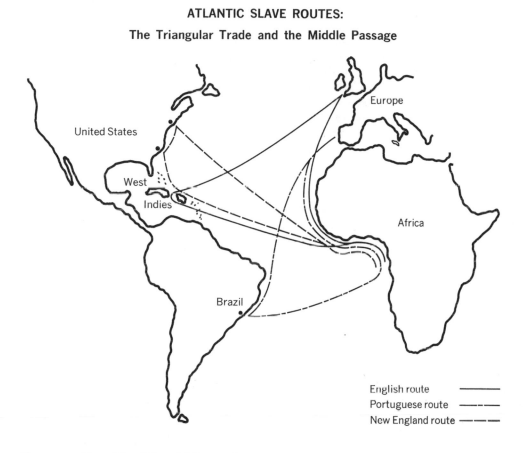

English route	———————
Portuguese route	— — — —
New England route	—— —— ——

time more than 35 million Africans died in order that 15 million men, women, and children might be taken as slaves to the New World. Many more Africans died in the slave trade than lived to see New World plantations. Some died in the holds of slave ships, others in the dungeons of the prison forts along the Guinea coast, but most died fighting to resist capture by black African slave raiders in their home country.

All the Western nations, including the United States, were heavily involved in the slave trade. The list of names reads like the roll of a European diplomatic conference: Spain, Sweden, Denmark, Brandenburg, Holland, France, Britain, the United States, Portugal. The motive of the trade was simple—money. The "triangular trade," as the slave trade was called, was immensely

profitable, often yielding in a single voyage a return of $5 for every $1 spent. One Yankee skipper from Rhode Island, a hard and thrifty Puritan, expressed his attitude very clearly: "Money? I'd plow the ocean to porridge for money." And plow the ocean they did, year after year. On the first leg of the triangle, from New England or Europe to the West African coast, the slave ships carried rum and guns, cloth and iron. For six or eight months after reaching Africa, the slavers edged along the Guinea coast, exchanging their goods with African traders for a slave here, two or three more there, until the ship was jammed like a sardine tin with black men, women, and children. The shortest leg of the triangle was the notorious "middle passage" from West Africa to Brazil, the West Indies, or the

American South. After discharging his cargo at slave markets in the Americas, the skipper picked up molasses, cotton, or other plantation products for his final trip home to New England or Europe.

The horrors of the slave trade were well described by an English sea captain, John Newton. Newton himself commanded slave ships while a young man, but in later life became a preacher and worked to abolish the slave trade. In 1788 he wrote a pamphlet called *Thoughts upon the African Slave Trade* as abolitionist propaganda describing the conditions of the slave ships he knew in the 1750's.

Captain Newton on the Slave Trade

Captain Newton, a patriotic Englishman, thought first of the effects of slaving upon his fellow countrymen:

> There is a second evil which either is, or ought to be, deemed of importance, considered in a political light: I mean the dreadful effects of this trade upon the minds of those who engage in it.

There are doubtless exceptions and I would willingly except myself. But in general, I know of no method of getting money, not even that of robbing for it upon the highway, which has so direct a tendency to efface the moral sense, to rob the heart of every gentle and humane disposition and to harden it, like steel, against all impressions of sensibility.

The inhumanity of the trade, and its effect on white slave traders, were revealed by numerous incidents:

> A mate of a ship in a long-boat purchased a young woman with a fine child of about a year old in her arms. In the night the child cried much, and disturbed his sleep. He rose up in great anger and swore that if the child did not cease making such a noise he would presently silence it. The child continued to cry. At length he rose up a second time, tore the child from the mother, and threw it into the sea. The child was soon silenced indeed, but it was not so easy to pacify the woman: she was too valuable to be thrown overboard, and he was obliged to bear the sound of her lamentations until he could put her on board his ship.

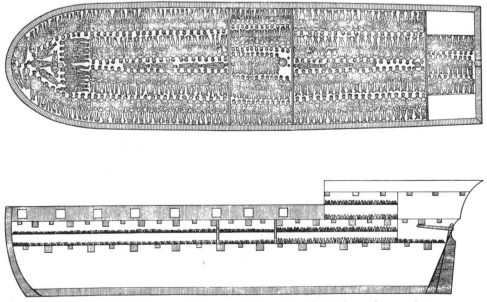

The slave ship *Brookes* of Liverpool. This plan shows how the maximum number of slaves was crammed below decks, chained and unable to stand upright.

Conditions during the middle passage to America were hard indeed:

> With our ships, the great object is to be full. When the ship is there, it is thought desirable that she should take as many as possible. The cargo of a vessel of a hundred tons, or a little more, is calculated to purchase from two hundred and twenty to two hundred and fifty slaves. Their lodging rooms below the deck, which are three (for the men, the boys, and the women), besides a place for the sick, are sometimes more than five feet high, and sometimes less; and this height is divided towards the middle, for the slaves to lie in two rows, one above the other, on each side of the ship, close to each other like books on a shelf. I have known them so close that the shelf would not easily contain one more. And I have known a white man sent down among the men to lay them in these rows to the greatest advantage, so that as little space as possible might be lost.
>
> Let it be observed that the poor creatures, thus cramped for want of room, are likewise in irons, for the most part both hands and feet, and two together, which makes it difficult for them to turn or move, to attempt either to rise or to lie down without hurting themselves or each other. . . . The heat and smell of these rooms, when the weather will not admit of the slaves being brought on deck, and of having their rooms cleaned every day, would be almost insupportable to a person not accustomed to them. If the slaves and their rooms are constantly aired, and they are not too long detained on board, perhaps not many die; but the contrary is often their lot. They are kept down by the weather, to breathe a hot and corrupted air, sometimes for a week; this, added to the galling of their irons, and the despondency which seizes their spirits when thus confined, soon becomes fatal, and every morning, perhaps, more instances than one are found of the living and the dead, like the captives of Menzentius, fastened together.

Revolt was the greatest danger, for the Africans were not easily reconciled to the loss of their freedom:

> One unguarded hour or minute is sufficient to give the slaves the opportunity they are always waiting for. An attempt to rise upon the ship's company, brings on instantaneous and horrid war; for, when they are once in motion, they are desperate; and where they do not conquer, they are seldom quelled without much mischief and bloodshed on both sides.

What awaited the slaves at the end of their voyage? Africans in the New World were regarded as animals, commodities of work and profit. Newton relates:

> [A West Indies plantation owner] said that calculations had been made, with all possible exactness, to determine which was the preferable, that is, the more saving method of managing slaves; "Whether to appoint them to moderate work, plenty of provision, and such treatment as might enable them to protract their lives to old age?" or, "by rigorously straining their strength to the utmost, with little relaxation, hard fare, and hard usage to wear them out before they became useless and unable to do service; and then to buy new ones to fill up their places?"
>
> He further said that these skillful calculations had determined in favor of the latter mode, as much the cheaper; and that he could mention several estates, on the island of Antigua, on which it was seldom known that a slave had lived above nine years.

African Slavers

The slave captains of the middle passage had their African equivalents, although we have few details about the horrors of slaving at its African source. African slaves were bought by the white slave traders at the coast from black men who made fortunes capturing and selling fellow Africans. Americans often wrongly think that white men themselves raided African villages for captives. The truth is that African chiefs and even entire communities such as Benin and Dahomey (see Chapter 2) raided neighboring villages or peoples, captured men, women, and children, chained them together, and marched them to the coast, where they were kept in prisons for sale to passing slave ships. All parts of the Guinea coast from Angola to Senegal suffered, and many regions fell into a state of continual war. Whole populations were wiped out in the attacks and counterattacks that provided America's "black ivory."

The Arab Slave Trade

Arabia in the East was just as eager for slaves as were the Americas. The great plateau of East and Central Africa was the hunting ground for Arab slavers. After the Portuguese were driven out of East Africa (except Mozambique) slaves became the most important commodity of Arab trade. Unlike Europeans, Arabs themselves raided far inland, terrorizing communities from Lake Chad to Lake Nyasa and from Zanzibar to the Congo, with guns and bands of African mercenaries. The Arab slave trade reached its height in the nineteenth century, during the decline of the Atlantic trade, and was not stopped until after the partition of Africa in the 1890's.

Reform

The slave trade was suppressed and slavery abolished in the West for both moral and economic reasons. In England and the American colonies, the Quakers protested as early as 1700. The cry for reform was taken up by English-speaking preachers, lawyers, politicians, and

European buyers examining slaves. Note the African slave trader at right.

freed slaves, such as the Ibo Olaudah Equiano. Under Article I, Section IX, of the Constitution of the United States, Congress, in 1808, prohibited the slave trade. After years of pressure by abolitionists like Captain Newton, the British Navy was allowed by international treaty to suppress slavery by force. British men-of-war patrolled the Guinea coast, capturing slave ships and freeing their cargo. A few slave ships bound for Brazil, the Caribbean, and the United States continued to run the blockade until slavery itself was abolished in the Americas after 1860.

In working against the slave trade, Christian reformers found an ally in the new industries of Europe. With the coming of the Industrial Revolution, businessmen found they needed African goods, such as palm oil for soap. Trade in people, causing warfare and violence, made trade in goods impossible. It was in the interest of the new industrialists of England, France, and the Northern United States to suppress the slave trade.

The Effect on Africa

The slave trade did more than kill and deport individual men, women, and children from Africa. African societies were disrupted, and African peoples were set at war against one another more viciously and more frequently than before. African kings were encouraged to become absolute and despotic rulers because they needed strong armies for slave raiding and defense. As might be expected, Africans became fearful of and hostile toward foreigners, whether white men or Africans from beyond their own country.

Before the Europeans reached Africa by sea, the center of African wealth, trade, and civilization had been the inland plateau beyond the hills and forests of the coast. The early empires of the sudan had expanded from the plains toward the sea. Now all was reversed.

This engraving showing the horrors of the East African slave trade was made in 1875 from sketches of the missionary David Livingstone. Abolitionist pressure forced the ending of the West African (European) slave trade around 1800; the East African (Arab) trade was not put down until the late nineteenth century.

The kingdoms of the forest and the peoples of the coast, profiting from the slave trade, became the center of African enterprise and activity. Beginning with the slave trade and continuing into our own time, the Africans of the coast have carried into the hinterland the new Western ideas and techniques that are remaking contemporary Africa.

PROBLEMS

1. Draw an outline map of Africa and show the areas of both the Atlantic and the Arab slave trade. Compare this map with the population density map in Chapter 1. Were most African communities south of the Sahara affected in some way by the slave trade?

2. The Portuguese of today look back to the era of Henry the Navigator as their great age. Do you agree with the statements of Portuguese leaders that because the Portuguese were the first in Africa, and have been there 500 years, they have a right to rule in Africa today and forever?

3. In the nineteenth century European missionaries and explorers reported that Africans were constantly fighting with one another, and that they were ruled by despotic kings who terrorized their people. Was this impression justified in Nigeria in 1800? Would the situation have been different in West Africa 500 years earlier? How did the effects of the slave trade distort Western ideas about African civilization?

4. Was the slave trade a racial matter of white against black? Did the motives of African, Arab, and European slave traders differ? Why, do you think, did Europeans trade rum, guns, and iron, rather than cloth or matches, for slaves?

5. What is the original meaning of the following words: Guinea, Niger, Ethiopia, sudan?

READING SUGGESTIONS

Basil Davidson, *Black Mother,* Little, Brown, paper.

Daniel P. Mannix, *Black Cargoes,* Viking, paper.

chapter 4

THE SCRAMBLE FOR AFRICA

The Power which shall henceforth take possession of a territory, or of any part of the coasts of Africa, situated outside their actual possessions, or who shall assume control of the same, shall accompany the said act with a notification, addressed simultaneously to the other Powers represented at the present conference, in order that they may be enabled either to recognize or to make good their claims.

—*The Berlin Act, 1885*

In the last two decades of the nineteenth century, the map of Africa was cut up like a jigsaw puzzle by Europeans. When World War I began in 1914 the puzzle had over fifty pieces. All but two—Liberia and Ethiopia— were ruled from European capitals. While the boundaries on the map and its patchwork of colors were the result of hasty diplomacy in London, Paris, and Berlin, the whole scramble had been unwittingly prepared by an earlier generation of missionaries, explorers, trading company agents, and prospectors.

African rulers reacted to the European invasion in different ways. Some welcomed the white men as allies against their African enemies. Others fought a vigorous but hopeless war, and found that spears are not the answer to guns, nor drums the reply to books.

Exploring Africa

The curiosity of British scientists and scholars, ministers and merchants had been aroused by Europe's blank map of Africa. On one long-forgotten but important day near the end of the eighteenth century some English gentlemen remained at their club, after its regular meeting had been adjourned, to discuss the matter of the exploration of Africa. At this adjourned meeting of the Saturday's Club at the St. Alban's Tavern, on the 9th of June, 1788, it was

RESOLVED: That as no species of information is more ardently desired, or more generally useful, than that which improves the science of geography; and as the vast continent of Africa, notwithstanding the efforts of the Ancients, and the wishes of the Moderns, is still in a great measure unexplored, the members of this club do form themselves into an Association for Promoting the Discovery of the Inland Parts of that Quarter of the World.

Western Sudan

The African Association, as it came to be known, sent the first and most daring of the great explorers, Mungo Park, into the African continent. At this time the main interest of geographers was to find the source and direction of Africa's great rivers. They hoped that

51

African rivers would be open highways to exploration and trade, as the Missouri and Columbia Rivers would prove to be several years later when Lewis and Clark crossed the American continent by following them to the Pacific. Europeans knew so little about Africa that they confused the river Niger with the river Nile (see map on page 2) and suspected that the Nile flowed from the Atlantic coast to Ethiopia before turning north toward Egypt.

Mungo Park was sent to trace the course of the Niger from its known source in the hills near the Atlantic coast. He set out from Gambia in 1795, equipped in a way which today's Boy Scouts would consider laughable, accompanied by a freed slave named Johnson, as interpreter, and a Negro servant boy named Domba. Park wrote:

> I was furnished with a horse for myself (a small but hardy and spirited beast, which cost me to the value of £7.10s) and two asses for my interpreter and servant. My baggage was light, consisting chiefly of provisions for two days; a small assortment of beads, amber, and tobacco for the purchase of a fresh supply as I proceeded; a few changes of linen, and other necessary apparel, an umbrella, a pocket sextant, a magnetic compass, and a thermometer; together with two fowling pieces, two pairs of pistols, and some other small articles.

Park was gone three years. He explored the western sudan, found the source of the Niger, and discovered that it flowed from west to east. On his wanderings Park encountered friendly Negroes and hostile Moors—wild desert Moslems descended from Negroes, Berbers, and Arabs. Deserted by his interpreter and robbed of his goods, Park was stranded in an unknown country, and his return was a miracle of perseverance. He related his adventures with dignity:

> February 29, 1796
> The Moors are here in greater proportion to the Negroes than at Jarra.

They assembled round the hut of the Negro where I lodged, and treated me with the greatest insolence: they hissed, shouted, and abused me. They even spit in my face with a view to irritate me and afford them a pretext for seizing my baggage. But finding such insults had not the desired effect they had recourse to the final and decisive argument, that I was a Christian, and of course that my property was lawful plunder to the followers of Mahomet. They accordingly opened my bundles and robbed me of everything they fancied.

After being captured by the Moors, Park was given a hut, but was not permitted to rest in peace and quiet, for his captors were fascinated by the Englishman's strange garments.

> March 12, 1796
> . . . I was obliged to take off one of my stockings and show them my foot, and even to take off my jacket and waistcoat to show them how my clothes were put on and off. They were much delighted with the curious contrivance of buttons. All this was to be repeated to every succeeding visitor for such as had already seen these wonders insisted on their friends seeing the same, and in this manner I was employed, dressing and undressing, buttoning and unbuttoning, from noon to night.

Ali, the leader of this band of robbers, asked a weary Park to explain the mysterious workings of his pocket compass:

> March 18, 1796
> Ali was very desirous to be informed why that small piece of iron, the needle, always pointed to the great desert; and I found myself somewhat puzzled to answer the question. To have pleaded my ignorance would have created a suspicion that I wished to conceal the real truth from him; I therefore told him that my mother resided far beyond the sands of Sahara, and that while she was alive the piece of iron would always point that way, and serve as a guide to conduct me to her, and that if she was dead it would point to her grave.

Ali, frightened by the magical powers of the compass, gave it back.

In 1805 Park dared a second journey into West Africa. This time he was sponsored by the British government, and his expedition included thirty-nine other white men and their baggage. Again the plan was to reach the Niger, and there build a boat to sail to the river's mouth. By the time the party had cut through the coastal forest to reach the Niger, twenty-nine men had died of fever; by the time a small canoe had been built, only four survived. Park and his four companions pushed off and were never seen again. The story is known from the journal brought back to the coast by a courageous African guide.

After Park's disaster another Englishman, Captain Hugh Clapperton, was sent out in 1822. Instead of hacking through the coastal forest, Clapperton traveled across the Sahara to West Africa. He finally established that the Niger flowed south into the Gulf of Guinea. The explorer sojourned at the court of the Sardauna of Sokoto, ruler of the great Fulani Empire which covered what is today Northern Nigeria. The Sardauna requested a physician and an ambassador from the British King, beginning the friendship that endures to this day between the British and the ruling house of the Fulani. When the Sardauna had been humored by gifts and gadgets, Clapperton tactfully raised the question of the slave trade. This exchange followed, according to Clapperton:

Sardauna: Everything is wonderful; but you are the greatest curiosity of all! What can I give that is most acceptable to the King of England?

Clapperton: The most acceptable service you can render the King of England is to cooperate with His Majesty in putting a stop to the slave trade on the coast; as the King of England sends every year large ships to cruise there, for the sole purpose of seizing all vessels engaged in this trade, whose crews are thrown into prison; and of liberating the unfortunate slaves, on whom lands and houses are conferred at one of our settlements in Africa [Freetown, in today's Sierra Leone].

Sardauna: What! Have you no slaves in England?

Clapperton: No. When ever a slave sets his foot in England, he is from that moment free.

Sardauna: What do you then do for servants?

Clapperton: We hire them for a stated period, and give them regular wages, nor is any person in England allowed to strike another, and the very soldiers are fed, clothed, and paid by the government.

Sardauna: God is great! You are a beautiful people.

Presents of Clapperton to the Sardauna of Sokoto

2 new blunderbusses, highly ornamented with silver
2 double-barreled pistols, pocket compass, and embroidered jacket of the late Dr. Oudney
3 cases of gunpowder, with shot and balls
3 razors
3 clasp knives
3 looking glasses
6 snuff boxes, 3 of paper and 3 of tin
1 spy glass
a large English tea tray
a scarlet bornouse trimmed with silver, a pair of scarlet breeches, 30 yards of red silk, 2 white, 2 red, and 2 Egyptian turban shawls, the latter trimmed with gold
4 pounds each of cloves and cinnamon

Clapperton's presents include items of royal luxury and useful industrial curiosities like penknives and razors.

An incredible young Frenchman, René Caillé, who had been fascinated by tales of West Africa since childhood, saved 2,000 francs from his meager pay and in 1827 set out alone across the Sahara. Caillé was the first European to reach Timbuctu, then in decline after its former glory and menaced by Saharan bandits. Caillé's achievement is one of the greatest in the history of African exploration. He persevered in spite of scurvy, harassment by bands of robbers, and Moslem hostility. Caillé's disguise as an Arab and his knowledge of Arabic saved him many times from death or slavery. After a year wandering in the sudan Caillé returned across the Sahara with an Arab caravan to find safety with the French consul in Tangier.

For the next thirty years Europeans continued to probe West Africa. The last of the great explorers was Dr. Heinrich Barth, a German working for the British. Barth traveled back and forth across the sudan for six years, methodically recording the details of African life and politics. By the time of the American Civil War the map of West Africa was relatively clear to Europeans. Interest began to shift to the unknown center of the continent and the eastern coast.

East Africa

In the early nineteenth century East Africa was under the waxing influence of Arab traders in slaves and goods. The bases of the Arabs were the trading ports of the East African coast from Somalia to Mozambique. These towns had grown from small colonies founded by Arabs from Oman, a kingdom at the southern tip of Arabia. A young prince, Seyyid Said, became the Imam of Oman in 1806 by murdering his father. Seyyid Said shifted his capital from Arabia to the East African island of Zanzibar, introduced cloves from the Indies (Zanzibar today produces nine-tenths of the world's supply of cloves), and established his rule over Arab traders in all East and Central Africa. His power rested on exports of slaves and ivory from the region of the East African lakes. Zanzibar's proud boast was that "when they play the pipes in Zanzibar the people on the shores of the Great Lakes dance."

While Zanzibar's web of trade expanded from the east, another power, Egypt, pushed into Africa from the north. Egypt in the nineteenth century was a part of the crumbling Turkish Empire. It was easy for Mohammed Ali, a Moslem Albanian serving with the

David Livingstone.

Turkish Army in Egypt, to seize power. In 1820 Mohammed Ali invaded the upper Nile in search of Negro recruits for his growing army. By the time that Seyyid Said had consolidated his influence in Zanzibar, Mohammed Ali's soldiers had penetrated to within a few miles of Buganda, north of Lake Victoria.

After Mohammed Ali died in 1849, slave raiding from both east and north became a commercial enterprise for independent Arab traders. To the south, a chain of Portuguese slave forts stretched almost across Africa from Angola and Mozambique into the interior. By the time the first European explorers reached the lake region, slave trading had laid waste to the country.

From the beginning of the nineteenth century British agents had tried with little success to cut off the Arab slave trade at its root in Zanzibar. Interest was not confined to the British. In 1847 two German explorers, Krupf and Rebmann, became the first Europeans to see the extraordinary snow-covered peaks of Kilimanjaro and Mount Kenya. The great mystery of African geography was solved when in 1862 the English-man Speke found the source of the Nile in the heart of Africa at Lake Victoria.

Livingstone

The most famous of all African ex-plorers was the Scot David Livingstone (1813–1873). For twenty years this ex-traordinary man tramped back and forth across Central Africa, accom-panied only by his porters and his jour-nal. So famous was Livingstone's writ-ing that Europeans and Americans waited eagerly for his next report from "darkest Africa." By his Christian mis-sionary zeal, human concern, and un-flagging determination Livingstone in-flamed the conscience of Europe against Portuguese and Arab slave trading and publicized the poverty, ignorance, and disease which were the scourge of Africa.

Livingstone was a self-made man who believed in the ideals of the age of Queen Victoria: Christian conduct, hard work, and the civilizing effect of trade. He was born the son of a poor tea mer-chant, and grew up in the grinding poverty of a nineteenth-century factory town. With characteristic modesty Liv-ingstone described his struggle for education:

> At the age of ten I was put into the factory as a "piecer," to aid by my earnings in lessening my mother's anxiety. With a part of my first week's wages I purchased Rudiman's *"Rudi-ments of Latin,"* and pursued the study of that language for many years after-ward, with unabated ardor, at an eve-ning school, which met between the hours of eight and ten. The dictionary part of my labors was followed up till twelve o'clock or later if my mother did not interfere by jumping up and snatch-ing the books out of my hands. I had to be back in the factory by six in the morning, and continue my work with intervals for breakfast and dinner, till eight o'clock at night.

With his own savings Livingstone worked his way through the University of Glasgow, becoming a medical doctor. He wanted to go to China as a medical missionary, but instead joined the Lon-don Missionary Society and was per-suaded to go to Africa.

Livingstone served for more than ten years in South Africa before embark-ing in 1853 on the first of his great journeys of exploration. Walking north from South Africa, he reached the Por-tuguese settlement at Luanda on the Atlantic coast, stayed four months to recoup his strength, and set off again eastward. Following the Zambezi River, he became the first white man to see the majestic falls, twice as high as Niagara, which were called by local Africans "the smoke which thunders." Livingstone re-named them Victoria Falls in honor of his Queen, before pressing on to the mouth of the Zambezi in Mozambique. Livingstone was the first European to cross the continent. The publication of his journal made him famous overnight.

Three years later the Scotsman em-barked up the Zambezi on his second journey, which lasted five years (1859–1864). In village after village he was met by astonished Africans who feared the color of his skin. Livingstone wrote:

> There must be something in the ap-pearance of white men, frightfully re-pulsive to the unsophisticated natives of Africa; for on entering villages previ-ously unvisited by Europeans, if we met a child coming quietly and unsuspect-ingly towards us, he raised his eyes and saw the men in "bags," he would take to his heels in an agony of terror, such as we might feel if we met a live Egyptian mummy at the door of the British Mu-seum. Alarmed by the child's wild out-cries, the mother rushes out of her hut, but darts back again at the first glimpse of the same fearful apparition. Dogs turn tail, and scour off in dismay; and hens abandon their chickens and fly screaming to the tops of houses. The so lately peaceful village becomes a scene of confusion and hubbub, until calmed by the laughing assurance of our men, that white people do not eat black folks, a joke having oftentimes greater influ-ence in Africa than solemn assertions.

Livingstone was in general impressed with the human warmth of African life. He stressed that Africans worked, played, and worshiped like all other men, despite their strange customs and simple way of life. In Livingstone's journal there are many passages like the following:

> The Maganja are an industrious race; and in addition to working in iron, cotton, and basket-making, they cultivate the soil extensively. All the people of the village turn out to labor in the fields. It is no uncommon thing to see men, women, and children hard at work with the baby lying close by beneath the shady bush. When a new piece of woodland is to be cleared, they proceed exactly as farmers do in America. The trees are cut down with their little axes of soft native iron; trunks and branches are piled up and burnt and the ashes spread on the soil.

By describing the havoc wrought by slave raiders hunting men as they would hunt game, Livingstone brought home to Europeans the horrors of the slave trade:

> The dry grass in Africa looks more like ripe English wheat late in the autumn than anything else we can compare it to. Let us imagine an English village standing in a field of this sort, bounded only by the horizon, and enemies setting fire to a line of a mile or two, by running along with bunches of burning straw in their hands, touching here and there the inflammable material—the wind blowing toward the doomed village—the inhabitants with only one or two old muskets, but ten to one no powder—the long line of flames, leaping thirty feet into the air, with dense masses of black smoke—and pieces of charred grass falling down in showers. Would not the stoutest English villager, armed only with the bow and arrow against the enemy's musket, quail at the idea of breaking through that wall of fire. When, at a distance we once saw a scene like this, and had the charred grass, literally as thick as flakes of black snow, falling around us, there was no difficulty in understanding the secret of the slave trader's power.

In 1867 Livingstone set out for the third and last time. He was absent for so long in the still-unknown continent that the public became alarmed. Sensing one of the great scoops of the century, the editor of the *New York Herald* sent a young reporter, Henry Morton Stanley, to find the missing Livingstone.

Stanley was an impatient man of great ambition. Escaping the cruel discipline of an orphanage in Wales, he had stowed away on a steamer to New Orleans, where he was taken in by a kind man named Stanley, whose name he adopted. Consumed by need for adventure and success, Stanley had roamed the battlefields of the Civil War, sought his fortune in the American West, and made a reputation as a foreign correspondent among the Kurdish tribesmen of Turkey.

The American journalist started from Zanzibar in 1871 with five caravans and a total of 162 porters, servants, and soldiers—a force that had cost more to hire and equip than all previous African expeditions put together. On his way across Africa Stanley shot game and loaned his porters to Arab slavers who were fighting a bloody war against an African chief. Ten months later, in November 1871, Stanley was led to the village of Ujiji, on the eastern shore of Lake Tanganyika, by the reports of Livingstone's presence that had spread widely among Africans. The meeting of the flamboyant reporter and the dedicated missionary has become a legend. Stanley gathered his porters and gave the command, "Unfurl the flags and load your guns." The volley brought out crowds of villagers shouting welcome. Preceded by a large American flag Stanley marched into Ujiji to find a weary man with a gray beard and gray tweed trousers.

True to his mission, Livingstone stayed on at Ujiji to convert the heathen and tend the sick. Two years later he died of fever. So close was the

Stanley's journey to the mouth of the Congo. First to follow the river, Stanley crossed Africa from east to west. The men of his expedition were recruited in Zanzibar.

bond between Livingstone and his African friends that they carried his body wrapped in bark and sailcloth 600 miles to the coast.

Missionaries

As Europeans became more aware of Africa, the Christian churches of Europe became concerned about the spiritual condition of Africans. The missionaries wished to atone for the degradation of the slave trade. They wished to enlighten the minds of Africans through education and heal their bodies with newly discovered medicines.

In 1792, two years after the African Association had been formed by geographers and interested citizens, English Baptists founded the London Missionary Society. Within a few years other Protestant denominations in England, Scotland, Switzerland, and Germany began similar missionary enterprises. When Frenchmen grew interested in

black Africa shortly after, Catholic missions as well were sent to Africa.

Christian missions were concentrated in a few separated pockets—Buganda and Lake Nyasa, most of Southern Africa, the disease-ridden west coast, the jungle around the mouth of the Congo River. Protestant and Catholic missionaries tended to cluster in separate areas, with the exception of Buganda, where hostility between converted Ganda Protestants and converted Ganda Catholics almost caused a civil war. The religious division hardened when Africa was partitioned between Protestant and Catholic European powers. Protestants clustered in British Africa and were discouraged by the colonial governments of the Belgian Congo and the Portuguese colonies.

Throughout the nineteenth century wave after wave of missionaries poured into Africa. Two problems plagued these early arrivals. Continual tribal war in many areas threatened the lives and meager possessions of the missionaries. Far more serious was the unbending hostility of African chiefs and priests, who knew they would lose their authority if their people ceased to believe in the gods of the tribe and became Christians. Mutesa, Kabaka of Buganda until 1884, persecuted Christians with unrestrained ferocity. A missionary recounted the narrow escape of Apolo Kagwe, a young Ganda convert destined to become Buganda's Katikiro (prime minister):

> The same day Apolo Kagwe was called into the king's presence with another youth; a stormy scene ensued. The king, acting on an impulse of uncontrollable fury, attacked the other lad with a spear, gashing him frightfully, and he was hurried away and murdered by the executioners. Then the king turned to Apolo; "Are you a reader" he cried, trembling with passion. "I read, my Lord" was the brave reply. "Then I'll teach you to read" shouted the angry king, and gashed him too with his spear, and then took the wooden handle and broke it over his back. At last, breathless with exertion, his anger having apparently spent itself, he told him to be gone.

Kagwe's life was saved.

In this incident Kagwe was accused of being a "reader" by the Kabaka. From the time of their arrival missionaries combined education and Christianity, so that to Africans, learning to read and write became synonymous with becoming a Christian.

When the missionaries were blocked in their task by war and persecution they naturally sought the protection of their governments in Europe. The publication of the journals of Livingstone and others raised public outcry against slavery and violence in Africa. Missionary societies became a powerful lobby in European capitals, seeking protection for their men in the field. Many argued for direct intervention in Africa by European governments to guarantee law and order.

Traders and Prospectors

With the decline of the Atlantic slave trade, the representatives of Europe's new factories began to trade in Africa. Throughout the continent they sold products new to Africa—knives, guns, axes, iron pots, cloth and clothes, glass, mirrors, and beads. African products began to trickle into Europe: palm oil to make soap for the dirty hands of Manchester and Liverpool; gold and diamonds to sparkle in the salons of Paris and Berlin; mahogany and ivory for fine furniture.

Like the missionaries, traders were often prevented from selling their wares by warring African chiefs. Like the missionaries, trading companies appealed to their governments for protection.

Protected by the British Crown and bolstered by the investments of rich Englishmen, great British trading companies sought to develop modern commerce in three areas of Africa. The Imperial British East Africa Company built a railroad across the scrublands of East Africa from Buganda to the sea. The land around the railroad became Kenya colony. In the west the Royal Niger Company sent European and African agents beyond the swamps of the Niger Delta. The agents extended the lines of trade from the West African coast into the sudan. They signed treaties with African chiefs, and the area they entered became modern Nigeria. The British South African Company of Cecil Rhodes was the most successful, for it tapped and took to Europe the gold and diamonds that lay buried beneath the South African veld.

Settlements

Besides the inland gropings of explorers, missionaries, and traders, a few tiny European settlements had hugged the fringes of the continent for centuries. These early settlements, haphazardly scattered along the 18,000 miles of African coast, determined later colonial boundaries (see map on page 65). When the race for Africa began in earnest the European nations used their little coastal towns as a base from which to extend their territory inland.

South Africa

Bantu, Boer, and Briton

In the seventeenth century a young and dynamic seafaring nation of Protestant Europe Holland challenged Portugal for control of the rich Indian Ocean trade. The Dutch needed a port near the tip of Africa to provision their ships on the long sea road to the Indies. Jan van Riebeeck was sent by the Duth East India Company to establish such a base. On the 6th of April 1652 three East Indiamen dropped anchor under the protective shadow of Table Mountain at the Cape of Good Hope.

Although it had no intention of founding a permanent colony, the Dutch East India Company began farms to grow the vegetables and fruits needed to prevent the ships' crews from getting scurvy. As in America, independent and hardy settlers pushed inland in search of fertile soil. The Dutch pioneers were reinforced by German immigrants and by Huguenots fleeing persecution in France. In the 1790's, inspired by the successful fight of the American colonists and by the French Revolution, those pioneers established tiny independent republics in South Africa. The settlers were called Boers ("boer" means "farmer" in Dutch), and their communities were Boer republics.

When Napoleon conquered Europe, France fell heir to the empire of the Dutch. Britain, mortal enemy of Napoleon and his ambitions, determined to seize the Cape, a strategic point on the route to the East. By 1815, when Napoleon was defeated at Waterloo, the British held the Cape and were extending their rule into the interior.

During the rest of the nineteenth century the Boers, a little people, fought to preserve their independence from the remorseless encroachment of the world's strongest state, the British Empire. Britain found moral justification for action against the Boers in the protests of English missionaries against cruel treatment of the native Hottentots (a light-skinned people related to the Bushmen) on Boer farms. When in 1833 the British colonial government in Cape Town tried to enforce the abolition of slavery, tension snapped. The Boers packed their women, children, and possessions into covered ox-wagons and began the Great Trek north into the unknown plains. A leader of the Great Trek was Piet Retief, who proclaimed the Boer ideal:

> We quit this colony under the full assurance that the British government ... will allow us to govern ourselves.... We are resolved that we will uphold the just principles of liberty; but whilst we will take care that no one shall be held in a state of slavery, it is our determination to maintain such regulations as may suppress crime and preserve proper relations between master and servant.

Deeply religious, the Boers saw themselves as the Chosen People. Drawing strength from the stern doctrines of the Old Testament, they firmly opposed "un-Godly equality" between white man and black, ex-master and ex-slave.

Over the next seventy years the Boers time and again tried to establish independent republics, which the British time and again annexed as colonies of their empire. The most important of the Boer republics were Natal, the Orange Free State, and the South African Republic, which today are the three northern provinces of the Republic of South Africa. The basic doctrine of the republics was the famous clause of the original Transvaal constitution: "No equality in Church or State."

Unlike the American pioneers whom the trekkers greatly resembled in many

SOUTHERN AFRICA IN 1899

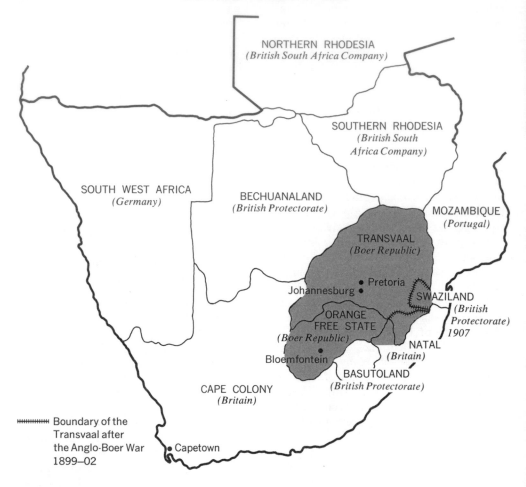

other ways, the Boers fought a continual and bitter war with native peoples who were numerous and settled. Bantu Negroes had been in southern Africa for centuries and as part of the great Bantu expansion were pushing south toward the Cape. As early as 1750 Boer commandos clashed with the Bantu vanguard, the famous Xhosa people (pronounced k-osa with a click). For the next 150 years both Boers and British settlers fought the Bantu in the east and the north. So fiercely did the African farmers and warriors resist that only in the twentieth century, in 1906, was the last African resistance put down.

Black Napoleon

At the beginning of this century of violence a brilliant general seized power over the fierce and proud Zulu people. Chaka, cruel tyrant and dictator of the Zulu, has become an African legend. Chaka took the Zulu throne in 1818 and in a short time became master of Zululand and of the surrounding Bantu peoples. Two new military tactics made these conquests possible. While African warriors generally hurled their spears from ambush at the enemy, Chaka trained his soldiers to hold on to their short spears, called *assegais,* and to use them to stab the enemy in hand-to-hand combat. The second tactic was a pincer movement to outflank, surround, and crush the enemy. Both ends of the long line of Zulu regiments would sweep around like a whip, enclosing the unfortunate enemy in a deadly circle of merciless spears.

Chaka imposed iron discipline and extracted a fierce loyalty from his men. His army was organized into regiments, called *impis*, and he could muster 100,000 soldiers for a battle. An incredible story illustrates Chaka's ruthlessness and his power. According to the story Chaka ordered an *impi* to march toward the edge of a cliff. Without hesitation the entire regiment, to the last man, marched over the edge and plunged to death below.

In the ten years of his rule Chaka devastated the lands for hundreds of miles around. Surrounding tribes fled to the north, to the west, and to the south. Only the vultures prospered.

A Bug in the Queen's Blanket

A different kind of man was Moshesh, founder of the Sotho (Basuto) nation. In the 1820's Moshesh and a band of followers sought refuge from the surrounding war and destruction in the rocky fortress of the Drakensberg mountains. Over the next thirty years the kingdom of Moshesh grew in size and influence. Moshesh, pondering how to save his people from the expanding Boers, the pursuing British, and the warring Africans, found the answer in diplomacy. To defend his independence he played the Boers against one another and the British against all. Finally seeking the protection of the British Crown, Moshesh sent a letter to the Governor of the Cape Colony appealing to British pride and sense of fair play. "I am nothing but a little bug seeking the protection of Her Majesty's [Queen Victoria's] blanket," wrote Moshesh. The protectorate was established, and today his country remains an independent island surrounded by hostile South

Cecil Rhodes.

African territory, a monument to one man's statesmanship.

Cecil Rhodes

The various and complex strands of conflict in South Africa all seem to lead to the fabulous figure of Cecil John Rhodes. An imperialist with a vision, Rhodes dreamed of an African map colored the traditional British red and of a railroad which stretched from Cape to Cairo. When asked how long he thought his name would endure, he is said to have replied, "About four thousand years."

The son of a poor English clergyman, Rhodes was sent in 1870 at the age of seventeen to South Africa so its dry climate could cure his weak lungs. Starting with next to nothing Rhodes gradually bought up diamond diggings and soon became a millionaire many times over. So forceful was his personality that by the time he was twenty-nine, men twice his age called him "the old man." Ruthless in disposing of all opposition to his growing financial empire, Rhodes eventually came face to face with the one man who could rival him, Barney Barnato. Barnato was a Jewish Londoner who had arrived in Cape Town years before with two boxes of cigars—which he sold at a large profit—and his clothes. Like Rhodes, Barnato became a millionaire. Indeed, he owned almost everything that Rhodes didn't, and stood between Rhodes and a world diamond monopoly. After years of rivalry the affair culminated in 1887 in a long night of cajoling, bluster, and argument. Rhodes, impatient and ruthless, bludgeoned and wheedled, inventing new arguments and repeating old ones. Barnato stalled through the wee hours, only to capitulate at dawn when Rhodes played his trump—membership for Barnato at the anti-Semitic Kimberley Club.

The career of Rhodes was meteoric and, like a meteor, burned itself out. Before he was forty, Rhodes's money and force of personality had made him Prime Minister of the British Cape Colony. At the same time, in the independent South African Republic (today the Transvaal), gold was discovered. Financiers and prospectors began to suspect the existence of those vast deposits which have made South Africa the richest country on the continent. In the 1880's Johannesburg became a boom town, as Americans, Poles, Germans, Russians, Swiss, Britons—men from every corner of the world—poured in to stake their claims. Faced with the onrush of despised foreigners, Paul Kruger, President of the South African Republic (Transvaal), did not budge an inch. "Uitlanders" could neither vote nor hold office. Their earnings were heavily taxed by the Boer government. Official red tape strangled their enterprise. To the south lay the Orange Free State, another Boer republic, an agricultural buffer between Rhodes and the South African Republic (Transvaal).

During the gold rush Rhodes had expanded both his domain and that of the British Crown. Other European powers, who had until the 1880's hesitated on the brink of Africa, now prepared to take the plunge. North of the Cape Colony German agents landed in South-West Africa and pressed into the interior in search of minerals and land. Portuguese soldiers from Angola and

Paul Kruger, leader of the Boer republic of the Transvaal. This photograph was taken in 1900, just as the Boer War began. (*Information Service of South Africa.*)

Mozambique were trying to join forces across the continent, thereby blocking the British road to Cairo. His imperial dreams in danger, Rhodes struck to the north. First he signed a treaty with the chief of the Tswana, and in 1885 obtained a protectorate over the huge tract of barren scrub later called Bechuanaland. At a blow he barred the Germans from Central Africa and, more important, blocked Paul Kruger on the Transvaal's eastern flank (see map on page 60).

Gold had been found in Matabeleland beyond the Limpopo River. For Rhodes financial gain was again coupled with imperial design. Lobenguela, vain King of the Matabele, fell easy victim to flattery and persuasion. Rights to all minerals in his territory were bought in 1888 for 1,000 guns, 100,000 rounds of ammunition, a yearly allowance of 1,200 pounds (about $6,000 at that time) and a steamboat on the Limpopo River. In 1889 the British government handed over the right to govern this area to the British

South Africa Company, a private corporation controlled by Rhodes. The boy with the "weak lungs" had ensured British domination of Central Africa.

A piece of the puzzle remained out of place: the rich gold fields of the Transvaal. The granite-like Paul Kruger was not to be softened by arguments either for reform or for federation with the Cape Colony. Rhodes, a sick man, feared the imperial dream of a South Africa united under the British flag would slip from his grasp. In desperation, he supported a plan for revolution within the Transvaal. Dr. Leander Starr Jameson, British South Africa Company agent and Rhodes's right-hand man, was poised in Bechuanaland on the Transvaal border with 500 men, awaiting orders to ride on Johannesburg. At the last moment the Transvaal mining magnates who had conspired to organize the revolution postponed their plan with the agreement of Rhodes. Rhodes's frantic cable to Jameson never reached him, for the telegraph line had been cut. Following Rhodes's ruthless advice to "take what you can get and ask me afterwards," Jameson crossed the border. The tiny expedition was a farce, and within forty-eight hours Jameson and his men were captured by the Boers. Kruger prudently overrode his more hotheaded followers, who wanted a firing squad, and to the great embarrassment of Rhodes and the British handed the rebels back to them for discipline.

Rhodes was ruined. He resigned as Prime Minister of the Cape Colony and as chairman of the British South Africa Company. He died a broken man in 1903, leaving his vast fortune to educate men of Anglo-Saxon descent—the Rhodes Scholarships.

The career of Rhodes illustrates the combination of energetic and forceful men, private financial interest, and government support that partitioned Africa. The same story was repeated on a less-grand scale in many other areas of the continent.

The Boer War

The hardy and stubborn Boers were not to be spared. The passing of Rhodes did not mean the end of his imperial dreams, for they were advanced by a force far greater than Rhodes himself. Three years after the Jameson raid the Boer Republics were pitted against the might of the British Empire. The Anglo-Boer War (1899–1902) laid waste the farms and the veld of the Transvaal and its sister republic the Orange Free State. In *Commando*, Denys Reitz, son of the President of the Orange Free State and a Boer guerilla fighter, has described how this lonely people went to the defense of their country against an unending supply of men and money, guns and cannons:

> As far as the eye could see the plain was alive with horsemen, guns, and cattle, all steadily going forward to the frontier. The scene was a stirring one, and I shall never forget riding to war with that great host.
>
> It has all ended in disaster, and I am writing this in a strange country, but the memory of those first days will ever remain.

Within months after the war began in 1899 British troops occupied Pretoria and Bloemfontein, the Boer capitals, but the Boers did not surrender. Leaving farms and families behind, the Boer commandos retreated to the hills to raid and harass the army of occupation. The British reply was swift and to the point. They placed the Boer women and children in concentration camps, burned the farms, and killed the livestock. After four years of guerilla war the Boers were forced to give up the hopeless fight. The Boers had lost a battle, but within a generation they had gained a leading position in the long struggle for dominance in South Africa (see Chapter 12).

North Africa

The Barbary Pirates

At the beginning of the nineteenth century the North African, or Barbary (from Berber), coast from Tripoli to Tangier harbored dens of pirates. The Barbary pirates plundered merchantmen of all nations and held their wealthy prisoners to ransom. The pirates were protected and even encouraged by local rulers, of whom the most notorious was the Dey of Algiers. Governments of trading nations were blackmailed into paying protection money to the Barbary rulers, and in 1798 the United States was forced to send twenty-six barrels of gold dollars to the Dey.

Bouyant with newly won independence, American leaders determined to put an end to this international shakedown racket. An American in Tripoli asked, "Shall America, now that she has acquired manhood, resources, and experience, bring her humiliation to the basest dog kennel of Barbary?" In 1801 the Pasha of Tripoli cut down the flagstaff of the American consulate. The United States Navy was sent to avenge the insult, giving the Marines a line for their battle hymn. For fifteen years American warships bombarded Barbary strongholds to subdue the pirates. By 1815 the pirates were thoroughly whipped, with the aid of treaties to placate the Barbary rulers.

France and Algeria

In the years after Napoleon's defeat, France longed to regain national glory. A diplomatic incident of 1830 afforded an excuse. The French consul at the court of the Dey of Algiers was struck twice in the face with a fly-whisk by the Dey himself in the course of an argument. Some months later a fleet of battleships sailed into the harbor of Algiers, bombarded the city, and landed 37,000 men to subdue the Dey, who surrendered within a month. The French were surprised to find that the expedition paid for itself. In all, 15,500 pounds of gold and 220,000 pounds of silver were taken from the Casbah treasury, leaving the French a handsome profit of 7 million francs.

The French government had a problem: What was to be done with conquered Algiers? Seven plans were drawn up, ranging from complete withdrawal to occupying Algiers and the country around. The latter was chosen. For the next fifty-four years the French Army fought campaigns against Arabs and Berbers. A growing sense of Algerian patriotism rallied Arabs and Berbers under the banner of a national hero, Abdel Kader. A French historian of the time described the suppression of a Berber revolt in 1851:

> More than three hundred villages were burnt. War was waged also on plantations and on trees. In the basin of the Sahel several thousand olive trees were destroyed. . . . Friendly tribes had their throats cut as if they had been enemies. . . . The consequence of these useless atrocities was that the Kabyle people were the more obstinate in their resistance, and that the cause of Bu Baghla, the leader, became a national one.

The Algerians were finally conquered but never reconciled themselves to French occupation, and took up their guns again in 1954.

The French decided to colonize Algeria. By as early as 1846, 100,000 settlers had arrived to occupy the land previously farmed by Algerian peasants. By the end of the nineteenth century Algeria was French. The Algerian majority had no voice in the government and worked for low wages in the vineyards and on the farms of settlers.

The Suez Canal

The idea of a canal from the Mediterranean to the Red Sea is an old one. The first canal was dug by the Persian Emperor Darius about 500 B.C., and the job was repeated by the first Ptolemy (about 300 B.C.) and by the Arab conquerors of Egypt in the seventh century. The idea was revived in Europe in the nineteenth century by Ferdinand de Lesseps, a brilliant French engineer.

Egypt's weak ruler, Khedive Said, was cajoled by De Lesseps not only into footing most of the bill but also, by a secret agreement, into providing, at no cost, labor to dig the canal. The French government threw its weight behind the project. Earth began to move in 1865, and four years later the canal was opened with pomp and circumstance by Empress Eugénie of France.

The Suez Canal afforded a short sea route to India and the East. Because of its strategic importance Suez quickly became a bone of contention among the European powers. British Prime Minister Benjamin Disraeli quietly borrowed a huge sum from private bankers and bought shares in the Suez Canal Company. In 1875 he announced to his own startled Cabinet that Britain controlled

COLONIALISM II:

Partition 1885

the Canal Company and had secured its sea route to India. The other powers, particularly the French, who had built the canal and who had competed with the British in Egypt ever since Napolon was driven from Egypt by the British in 1801, were enraged.

The unfolding of the Suez story shows nineteenth-century European imperialism at its most arrogant and selfish. Khedive Ismail, who had succeeded Said in 1863, was forced to pay an indemnity of some $8 million for trying to prevent the use of Egyptian forced labor to build the canal. Ismail was unfortunately a spendthrift who borrowed large sums at high interest rates from European bankers. Egypt's peasant economy was bled to its limit to pay for Ismail's extravagances and for his overambitious program of railway and telegraph lines, irrigation, and export crops. Egypt went bankrupt in 1878. The British and French creditors took over, deposing Ismail and setting up a puppet government whose obvious purpose was to make sure that over half of Egypt's annual revenue went into European banks.

Egyptians reacted. In 1882 an army colonel, Ahmed Arabi, came to power and proceeded to ignore the "advice" of the British and French official controllers. Predictably, British and French warships steamed into Alexandria harbor and on July 11, 1882, British shells set the town afire. The canal was seized, and on September 13 British troops slaughtered Arabi's peasant army at Tel-al-Kebir. Egypt—and the Suez Canal—passed under British control.

Partition

Throughout the nineteenth century European interest in Africa had been steadily increasing. Missionaries, traders, and a few great imperial companies were urging reluctant governments to occupy those parts of Africa in which they were interested. Influential men held out the hope that African trade and

minerals would enrich their countries. Yet, except for the French in Algeria and the British at the Cape, European governments had by 1880 established no significant colonies in Africa.

What worried European statesmen most was that other nations might outstrip their own in competition for national power and international influence. For this reason the diplomats had long kept a wary eye on one another's ambitions in Africa. Like runners in a race, the European nations increased their pace to match their fellows, anticipating the final sprint. The British occupation of Egypt in 1882 barked like the starter's gun on European ears. Yet all the powers were agreed that it was better to carve up Africa in peace than blow up Europe in war. All abided by the rules, and over the next thirty years the colonial map of Africa was drawn without war between the powers.

Leopold and the Congo

Leopold, King of the Belgians, had personal ambitions in Africa. Leopold's curiosity had been aroused by Stanley, the American adventurer, who in 1877 came to Europe to describe the hitherto-unknown region of the Congo. Stanley had followed the Congo River from its source to its mouth and was convinced of the wealth and possibilities awaiting an interested power. Leopold seized his opportunity. In 1879 Stanley returned to the Congo as Leopold's agent, empowered to take the first steps toward establishing a personal empire for Leopold along the great river. By 1884 Stanley had achieved such success in signing treaties with African chiefs and planting trading posts along the river that Leopold felt he could present his Congo domain to Europe as an established fact. He called a meeting of the European powers.

The Berlin Conference

From December 1884 to February 1885 representatives of fourteen nations, including the countries of Europe, Russia, Turkey, and the United States, met in Berlin. In the terms of the Berlin Act they agreed to suppress the slave trade, now practiced mainly by Arabs in East Africa, and they agreed that any power which took possession of African territory should thereby acquire it. In other words, Africa was for the taking.

The staking of claims by King Leopold and by Germany precipitated the scramble. The Congo Free State of King Leopold had been recognized before the conference by France, Germany, and the United States, in a maneuver clearly designed to forestall the British. The other powers had to follow suit in accepting Leopold's flag, two gold stars on a blue background. Up to this point Africa had been an open continent, in which explorers, traders, and missionaries had been free to travel and settle as they pleased. Now Europe was confronted with the presence of a large area at the heart of Africa ruled by officials of a single flag.

Germany

The other country that began the scramble was Germany. German Chancellor Otto von Bismarck sent agents to four separate parts of Africa, and in eighteen swift months from 1883 to 1885 Germany laid claim almost without notice to four separate territories—South West Africa, German East Africa (now Tanganyika), Togoland, and Cameroun. Bismarck in person announced to the startled delegates at Berlin that Germany laid claim to East Africa. The sprint was on.

France

The strategy of the French was clear —to drive to the east from their coastal base in Senegal, blocking British expansion north from Freetown (Sierra Leone), Accra (Gold Coast), and Lagos (Nigeria). At the same time the French

explorer Savorgnan de Brazza led expeditions to the north from the Congo River town which now bears his name—Brazzaville. The pincers met on the desolate shores of Lake Chad, effectively containing both the British and the Germans. A further attempt to create a band of French territory from east to west 5,000 miles across the African continent was stopped when a French force was turned back by the British officer Horatio Kitchener at Fashoda in the southern sudan. In North Africa, the progressive Dey of Tunis was forced to accept a French protectorate in 1881. French forces joined across the Sahara, and in their campaigns to subdue the restless nomads of the desert created the famous French Foreign Legion.

Britain

Britain, with by far the best headstart, simply pushed inland from the settlements it held. From the Cape Colony, Cecil Rhodes and his British South Africa Company pushed as far north as Nyasaland, where they encountered the settlements of Scottish missionaries. In East Africa, a protectorate was established over all the land from Buganda and its neighbors to the sea. Later the unwieldy protectorate was split into two, Uganda and Kenya. To join Egypt with the British territories to the south, Egyptian soldiers under British officers conquered Arab nomads of the desert and primitive Negro tribesmen of the upper Nile swamplands. This inflammable mixture was thrown together as the Condominium of the Anglo-Egyptian Sudan. In West Africa Captain Frederick Dealtry, later Lord Lugard, one of Britain's most famous colonial adventurers, achieved his greatest triumph in laying the groundwork for contemporary Nigeria. Lugard brought together the Moslem Hausa and Fulani peoples of the sudan and the pagan and Christian Yoruba and Ibo peoples of the forest. For years the British had been blocked from expanding their small colony on the Gold Coast by the powerful Ashanti confederacy.

Portugal

The Portguese, who had been in Africa the longest, added least to their African empire. Only in Angola did a small group of able and energetic men stretch Portuguese boundaries into the hinterland.

Italy

Italy was the last to join the imperial game. Only the Horn of Africa and parts of the Mediterranean coast remained for the latecomer. After establishing bases on the coast in Somalia and Eritrea, Italian forces invaded the ancient Christian kingdom of Ethiopia in 1896. Armed with French rifles, the Ethiopians stood their ground at Adowa, and the routed Italian Army stumbled back down the mountains to the coast. To sop their wounded pride the Italians occupied the Libyan coast in 1911.

The Atlantic Enclaves

Some small colonial territories on the Atlantic bulge of Africa completed the imperial pattern. Spain held a few crumbling forts on the Saharan coast and claimed a large piece of desert behind. Britain extended the coastal settlements of Gambia and Sierra Leone. Portugal held a small piece of the Guinea coast.

With the exception of Liberia and Ethiopia, the homeland of every African people lay under the shadow of a foreign flag.

African Resistance

African reaction was mixed. Some rulers loaded their muskets, sharpened their axes, and prepared to do battle. Others were reconciled to European rule. Still others welcomed the foreigners as allies against traditional African enemies. In territory after territory European officers commanding a force of African mercenaries marched from village to village, informing the baffled local chiefs that henceforth they were to obey some remote white ruler. Opposition was easily quelled with a few scattered gunshots.

For many Africans colonial rule was at first only an irritation. African peasants knew nothing of the world beyond their own village, and the division of the continent at first meant little to them. Only with the appearance of the colonial district officer and the tax collector did partition begin to affect the lives of ordinary Africans.

In those parts of Africa where a nation or great leader commanded the loyalty of a large number of people, African resistance stopped the European advance, if only for a time. European imperialists called the defeat of African resistance "pacification." In several areas "pacification" took as long as twenty years.

Algeria and South Africa

Where European colonists tried to settle on occupied land, resistance was fierce and continual. Abdel Kader led Algerian armies against the French from 1832 to 1847. In South Africa, the other country where there were permanent settlers, strong Bantu peoples such as the Zulu and the Xhosa fought both Boer and English armies for more than one hundred years.

Morocco

Morocco was partitioned between France and Spain in 1912. In 1921 Abdel Krim, a Berber from the wild Rif Mountains of northern Morocco, gathered scattered Berber tribes around him and welded a guerilla army which routed Spanish forces and confined them to the coast. For four years Krim was master of the mountain strongholds. Beneath the mountains, the French were uneasy. In 1924 French fears were confirmed when Krim swept on to Fez with his wild horsemen. The French governor in Morocco was Marshal Louis Lyautey, a brilliant man who foresaw Moroccan independence and the need for education in French Africa. Lyautey saw the danger from Krim but fell back because his Paris superiors had refused to send the reinforcements he had requested. The proud and independent mountain Berbers were attacked and defeated a year later.

The Mahdi

"Mahdi," in Arabic, means "messenger of salvation" or "prophet." Throughout the history of Islam men have appeared who called themselves "Mahdi." Many of these prophets were fundamentalist religious reformers and led *jihads,* or holy wars, against those who had become lax in the worship of Allah.

To the south of Egypt, the people of Sudan had become impatient with the harsh rule of Egyptian officials, who extorted heavy taxes and shipped slaves to the armies and harems of the Middle East. In 1850 a young holy man, Mohammed Achmed, withdrew to a cave on an island in the Nile to meditate. He stayed there more than twenty years. Believing himself to be descended from the Prophet Mohammed, Achmed took the title of Mahdi. From village to village he preached salvation through puritanical devotion to Islam, and rallied the people against the wicked and degenerate Egyptians.

In 1881 the Mahdi organized his followers and proclaimed a *jihad* against Egyptian rule. His army of dervishes, as the Mahdi's fanatical followers were called, annihilated a British-led Egyptian force of 10,000 men and besieged Egyptian garrisons along the Nile. The Mahdi was hailed as "the invincible one." Clearly, Egyptian—and British—rule was about to disappear in the Sudan.

In February 1884 General Charles Gordon of the British Army led a force to the relief of Khartoum, Sudan's capital, only to find himself surrounded and besieged by the Mahdi's men. For 316 days Gordon's artillery held off the dervishes. On the 317th day the dervishes burst into the town, killing Gordon and some ten thousand others. A British expedition sent to Gordon's relief arrived sixty hours later. But the Sudan could not be held.

The Mahdi died the following year. His successor, the Khalifa Abd Allahi, could not command the moral power and religious authority of his former leader, and instead ruled by the sword. The Khalifa carried war against the enemies of the Mahdi to the pagan southern sudan, to Christian Ethiopia, and to Egypt itself. Tribes and towns were massacred and plundered until a great famine swept the land in 1889, adding the death toll of starvation to that of war.

By the 1880's, the government of Sir Evelyn Baring (Lord Cromer) had put Egypt back on its feet. With Egypt's administration in order, its treasury solvent, and its army retrained and reorganized, the British and Egyptians were ready to recapture Sudan from the Mahdists. In 1896 General Horatio Kitchener began to move down the Nile, building a railroad as he went to carry men and supplies. On September 1, 1898, Kitchener's army faced 52,000 dervishes at Omdurman (Khartoum) and slaughtered them with modern weapons.

The Sudan remained under joint British and Egyptian rule—the Condominium—until 1955.

Samory Touré

In the West African sudan, near the heart of the ancient Mali Empire, a latter-day hero, Samory Touré, created and extended an empire of his own. Unfortunately for Samory, his own ambitions conflicted with those of the French. For sixteen years, from 1882 until 1898, Samory Touré held the French at bay. Only after he was betrayed by one of his own men could the French occupy Samory's territory.

Samory Touré has become a legend. The territory he ruled is now divided between Guinea, Mali, Upper Volta, and Ivory Coast, and his name is a byword in French-speaking Africa. The President of Guinea, Sékou Touré, claims descent from the famous Samory.

The Ashanti Wars

The Ashanti, who live in modern Ghana, were persistent opponents of British colonial expansion. Ashanti was one of the West African forest kingdoms. The king of the Ashanti, called the Asantahene, possessed a Golden Stool as a symbol of his office and of the strength and unity of the Ashanti people. Ashanti profited immensely from the slave trade and was for many years at war with the peoples of the coast. The British, who for centuries had held the forts along the Gold Coast, were the allies of the coastal tribes. The feud between the Ashanti in the hinterland and the British along the coast dated from the turn of the nineteenth century. In 1863 Ashanti armies tried to drive the British into the sea. They failed. In 1873 and 1894 they tried again and failed again. In 1900, hoping to settle the conflict once and for all, the British Governor decided to undermine Ashanti morale by obtaining the Golden Stool. The Governor, Sir Frederic Hodgson, spoke to the assembled people of Kumasi, the capital of Ashanti:

Where is the Golden Stool? Why am I not sitting on the Golden Stool at this moment? I am the representative of the paramount power; why have you relegated me to this chair?

The Ashanti were stunned and outraged. Three days later they attacked the British again. This time they were crushed.

Imperialism

In the short space of a hundred years, roughly from 1800 to 1900, Africa was explored, partitioned, and conquered by the nations of Western Europe. The motives for partition were many, and the explanation of European "imperialism" is not simple. Missionaries felt a moral duty to uplift Africans by teaching them Christianity. Traders wished to pursue profit in peace. Public opinion, particularly in Britain, demanded that the slave trade be put down by force. Finally, both the peoples and the governments of European nations were concerned lest their European rivals get the better of them in the European competition for national power and glorious empire. The result, both by design and by accident, was the scramble for Africa.

It remained for the imperialists to rule where they had conquered.

PROBLEMS

1. The history of South Africa before 1900 is similar to American history in many ways. What experiences and attitudes were shared by early Americans and the South African Boers? Draw a time line listing important events in South African history, and match them with similar ones in America. What was the main difference between the situation faced by the Boers as they pushed into Africa and that of the American pioneers?

2. David Livingstone and Cecil Rhodes illustrate the different aims of Europe in Africa in the nineteenth century. What were the aims of Livingstone?

Of Rhodes? What qualities of character did they have in common? Both wanted British government intervention in Africa. How would government intervention advance the aims of both?

3. Why was Africa partitioned among the European powers? Was economic gain the most important consideration to the men who met at Berlin in 1884? What was the importance of Suez to Britain? Were the diplomats more concerned about Africa than about Europe or Asia?

4. Look at the list of Clapperton's gifts to the Sardauna of Sokoto. Why do you think the Sardauna was pleased? Do these gifts give us a clue as to why a few European soldiers could conquer all Africa in twenty years at the end of the nineteenth century? What is the connection between technical progress (inventions and industries) and imperial conquest?

5. Find an account of African explorers (this chapter mentions only a few) and draw a map showing their travels. How long did it take to explore Africa? Did the nations most active in exploration get the biggest chunks of Africa at partition?

READING SUGGESTIONS

C. Howard, *West African Explorers,* Oxford University Press (London), 1951.

David Livingstone, *Missionary Travels and Researches in South Africa,* Harper & Row, 1858.

Sarah Gertrude Millin, *Cecil Rhodes,* Harper & Row, 1933.

Thomas Mofolo, *Chaka,* Oxford University Press (London), 1931.

Alan Moorehead, *The White Nile,* Dell, paper.

Jack Simmons, *Livingstone and Africa,* English Universities Press (London), 1955; Collier, paper.

Henry Morton Stanley, *How I Found Livingstone,* Scribner, 1872.

Donald L. Wiedner, *A History of Africa,* Random House, 1962; Vintage, paper.

part two
COLONIES AND NATIONALISTS

Under colonial rule one idea was emphasized above all others: the superiority of the European and the inferiority of the African. The superiority was quite real in technology and organization, but was assumed by the white man in culture, religion, and moral values as well. The colonial era in Africa was a period of great change. Africa was introduced to a modern economy and came to depend on export trade. A transportation and communications network was built, although Africa still had few industries. Education opened African minds to modern ideas and began to erode traditional African beliefs. Modern medicine gave better health and longer life. Yet it was always the African who was forced to adapt *his* beliefs, *his* economy, and *his* government to that of the European rulers.

Beginning in small ways, such as a tribal association in a new European town, Africans began to reorganize to meet the new challenge. Those who were educated and those who had learned the white man's skills soon began to question the utility and the morality of colonial rule. The campaign for independence was both a condemnation of colonialism and evidence that Africans had learned and accepted enough to challenge Europeans at their own game.

In response to the solid barrier of European supremacy, African protest was channeled into a single crusade for political independence. Political parties and nationalist organizers led the revolt. The transition to independence was relatively painless in most countries, but violence was used wherever necessary to achieve African control. In 1966 Africa was a continent of forty independent nations. Fifty years after the advent of colonial rule, Africa had been flung headlong into the modern world.

PART TWO:
Colonies
and Nationalists

chapter 5

WHO CARRIED THE WHITE MAN'S BURDEN?

Take up the White Man's burden—
Send forth the best ye breed—
Go bind your sons to exile
To serve your captives' need;
To wait in heavy harness,
On fluttered folk and wild—
Your new-caught, sullen peoples,
Half-devil and half-child.

—RUDYARD KIPLING,
1899

When the white man came, he had the
Bible and we had the land; now we have
the Bible and he has the land.

—African proverb

The colonial policies of the European powers differed as much as did those powers themselves. All colonial policies, however, were based on the belief that Africans were inferior. It was assumed that Africans had little respect for human life or the property of others. Africans were thought to be intellectually inferior, incapable of understanding modern science and technology, and lacking the ability to invent machines, build bridges, or create fine art. Some Europeans argued that Africans were biologically inferior and therefore permanently so. Others believed that over a long period of time Africans might attain the level of European civilization. The argument might have been stated somewhat as follows: "Two thousand years ago our ancestors, the Angles, Saxons, and Jutes, dyed themselves blue and ran naked through the forests of Germany. It will therefore take 2,000 years for the natives of Africa to become civilized like ourselves."

Some Europeans were a little more enlightened, even if still wrapped up in the myth of European superiority, and argued that while African culture was inferior, individual Africans could acquire European ways. In a few scattered areas to this day, diehard white settlers may be found who will argue that "Africans are just down from the trees." Fortunately these are a small and disappearing minority. By and large nowadays the argument about the superiority and inferiority of races is recognized for the sterile debate that it is—except of course in South Africa, where this dangerous obsession is undermining a country.

Colonial Policies

Among the various colonial philosophies and practices there were two main trends. The one, British, tried to protect native rulers and encourage native arts, languages, and customs. The other, French and Portuguese, emphasized the superiority of the colonizer's culture, pressed Africans to adopt the European language and religion, and undermined

COLONIALISM III:

Colonial Africa, 1920

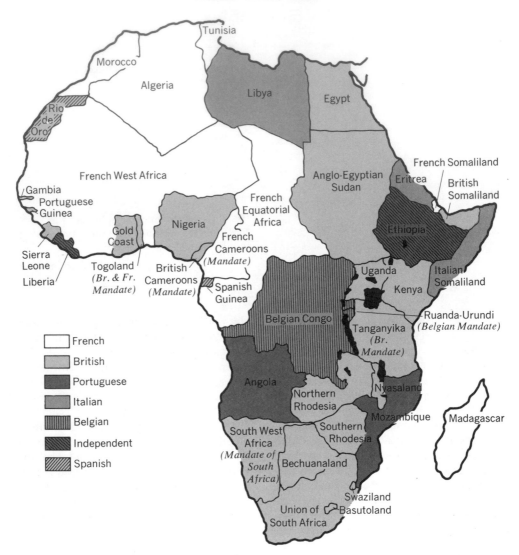

the authority of the traditional African rulers. Somewhere between these two tendencies lay Belgian policy.

Britain

To the British, colonial rule was "the white man's burden." Europeans had a duty to educate and civilize the natives. Civilization meant, in particular, the impartial administration of justice and adherence to rules of fair play. Civilization in this form could be introduced only by educated African officials who were outside politics. In fact, however, policy differed from colony to colony. The settlers of Kenya, the Rhodesias, and South Africa were, despite African protests, left to run their own and African affairs, with little heed being paid by the British to the fate of

Africans there. On the other hand, in West African colonies, African interests were considered much more favorably.

One of the most important features of British colonialism was the policy of "indirect rule." The idea behind indirect rule was that it was neither right nor possible to tamper with African traditional societies or to break the bonds of loyalty between African peoples and their chiefs.

Indirect rule was first proposed by Captain Frederick Dealtry, later Lord Lugard. Lugard had great respect for African tradition—he also had only a handful of soldiers. When he faced such rulers as the Kabaka of Buganda and his army of 100,000 men, or the Fulani Emirs of Northern Nigeria, Lugard's policy of incorporating these rulers as part of the British administration was the only practical one. In some places, such as the Ibo region of Nigeria, British officials went looking for chiefs where they didn't exist and so had to create them to fit the scheme. Naturally, "chiefs" such as these were considered stooges of the foreigners.

The chief was expected to act as a British official. He had to collect taxes, abolish local customs that the British opposed, such as cruel punishments and slavery, and build roads and bridges with the labor of his people. The result was the very opposite of what the British expected, for the chiefs were identified with the conquerors, and rapidly lost the respect and support of their people.

As with all the other colonial powers there was a strong strain of paternalism in British policy. Paternalism is the attitude that a stern but well-meaning father takes toward his children. Like all fathers, the British realized that their charges would someday become independent, but they were in no hurry to hasten the parting. In the early days of colonial rule the Governor's authority was complete. He made the laws and saw to it that they were carried out. The British did not expect this arrangement to last forever. They just had to start somewhere.

At first the Governor appointed an Advisory Council of British officials, to which in time were added local "leaders," such as European and African lawyers, doctors, and businessmen. Later some of these advisers came to be elected—not simply appointed. However, only men of property or education were able to vote. The Advisory Councils eventually became Legislative Councils, with power to pass laws, rather than merely advise. Ultimately the Legislative Council became the African government. In British eyes their task had been accomplished: Their wards had become men capable of self-government.

France

In her book *The Colonial Reckoning*, Margery Perham gives a graphic illustration of the difference between English and French rule. Miss Perham, traveling in West Africa before World War II, visited the opulent palace of a Nigerian Emir, who received her with the pomp and circumstance and dignity befitting his elevated position as a traditional ruler backed by the British administration. Crossing the border into the French colony of Niger she drove with a French official to visit another Emir of the same traditional status. The French official stopped the car by the roadside and honked the horn. From the doorway of a nearby hut hurried, to Miss Perham's horror, the deferential figure of the Emir.

There was nothing indirect about French rule in black Africa. Village headmen were responsible to the local French commandant, who held absolute power in his district. The Governor in each colony was in charge of the commandants, who, depending on the number of districts, might number up to ten or twenty in a colony. The Governor was under the direct authority of the French Governor-General (for West

Africa in Dakar, for Equatorial Africa in Brazzaville), in turn remotely controlled from the desk of an official in Paris.

Just as the chain of command over Africans had its anchor in Paris, so the French language and French culture were expected to spread over Africa. The French believed that their culture was superior to all others and that France had a *mission civilisatrice* (civilizing mission) to perform. At first the policy was called *assimilation,* and the goal was, literally, to make Africans into Frenchmen. France and French Africa would become one nation, peopled by French citizens living under the same laws and enjoying the same rights. *Assimilation* was a pipe dream. Could less than a hundred thousand colonial officials transform more than fifty million Africans into their own likeness? And would the peasants, workers, and shopkeepers of France accept Africans as equals?

French doctrine was modified, and *association* emerged as the new goal. Africans were now to enjoy the fruits of French culture under the shade of their own trees. Those Africans who had proved themselves capable of becoming French by learning the French language and passing stiff examinations became an assimilated elite. The remainder, who were the vast majority, were in a much less favorable position. A set of laws, called the *Indigenat,* or Native Code, brought most Africans under a harsh and demanding regime. A few assimilated Africans and the French officials, missionaries, and traders enjoyed the privileges of French citizens.

The French, who took their *mission civilisatrice* seriously, were never quite reconciled to African independence.

Belgium

Belgian policy carried the idea of paternalism to an extreme. In the Belgian Congo society looked like a two-tiered pyramid, white on top and black on the bottom. Africans were considered to be like children, incapable of voting, of absorbing a high school education, or of assuming responsibility for their own welfare or their own behavior. Trained as factory workers and miners by the great Belgian companies, Africans were expected to do their job and keep in their place. The Belgian administration was a benevolent parent. Most Congolese workers had decent housing, adequate pay, and pensions in their old age. Medical care was the best in Africa. Like an unwise father the Belgians forgot that children grow up (see Chapter 10).

Portugal

Portuguese colonial philosophy has not changed in 500 years and reflects the unbending virtues and harsh methods of the days of Henry the Navigator, who pioneered Portuguese expansion in the 1400's (see Chapter 3). Cornerstones of Portuguese policy are the duty of the Portuguese to spread Christianity and the duty of the Africans to become "civilized" through work. The fact is that few enjoy the benefits of Christian civilization, but all work—for the Portuguese. Portugal is itself a poor and underveloped country by European standards and has not been able to develop a modern economy or raise the standard of living in its African colonies. The forced labor of Africans has built the roads and picked the coffee of Portuguese planters.

The Portuguese claim that they do not discriminate against black men. They point to the many instances of intermarriage and the integration of schools and cities. They stress that any African who meets the test of being a civilized Christian may apply for equal status as an *assimilado,* or assimilated African. In fact, the obstacles to assimilation are almost insuperable. The African candidate must somehow find the education to pass an examination that most Portuguese would fail; he must be personally acceptable to the local Portuguese official; and he must have a spotless record of support for Portuguese colonial rule. Only a very few of the 10 million Africans in Portuguese colonies are *assimilados*, the remainder being denied all political rights.

Settlers

Wherever European settlers have come to Africa, colonial policy toward Africans has been harsh. In every case the white settlers have taken land for themselves and sought political control over the Africans. The greater the number of settlers the more difficult the

GERMAN AND ITALIAN COLONIES

situation has been. Settler communities have ignored and opposed any and all pleas for African education, promotion of Africans to responsible jobs, or the exercise of political rights such as the freedom to express opinions or form organizations. Only in South Africa, where the logic of settler dominance has been carried to its extreme in the racist doctrine of *apartheid,* do the settlers still have the upper hand. In the other white-settler countries—Algeria, Kenya, the Rhodesias, Angola, and Mozambique —the settlers are either hard pressed to maintain their position or have already lost it to African majority rule.

The first settlers in the era of European colonial expansion were the Dutch and the British at the Cape. Since 1652 colonists from Holland, Germany, France, and Britain have come in a small but steady flow to the southern tip of Africa, where they have worked and fought to establish independent South Africa. In 1840, in the equally charitable Mediterranean climate of Algeria, at the opposite end of the continent, several thousand Frenchmen and other Europeans began to settle. By 1900 more than half a million had arrived, each new wave occupying more of the narrow belt of fertile land along the coast.

In the rest of Africa settlers came later and in smaller numbers. Until the late nineteenth century the hinterland of the two major Portuguese colonies, Angola and Mozambique, was ruled by adventurers who held huge tracts of land against all comers. Only after the development companies and soldiers of Portugal had subdued the Africans of the backlands did settlement begin in earnest. The other areas of settlement were the Rhodesias and East Africa. In Southern Rhodesia the Bantu Africans were pushed off the land into "Native reserves," following the pattern which had emerged in South Africa a generation earlier. These Native reserves are like United States Indian reservations.

Many of the displaced Africans became sharecroppers and servants for Afrikaner or British farmers, or sought work on the mines in order to eke out a living and to pay the tax imposed by the colonial authorities. In Kenya, the "White Highlands" were in fact unoccupied by Africans when Britons began to settle there at the beginning of the century. Yet, according to Kenya Africans, the Kikuyu people had only temporarily left the area because of an epidemic. The highlands are today gradually returning to African ownership.

The most numerous immigrants in East Africa and in the Natal province of South Africa are not Europeans but Indians. Starting either as indentured laborers on the Uganda railroad and the sugar plantations of Natal or as trading agents for the East India Company, enterprising Indians gained control over local commerce in the areas to which they had been brought. They have come to dominate the export trade of East Africa.

The Debate over Colonial Development

Africa, we are continually being told, is underdeveloped. It lacks industries, roads, and educated men. Most Africans eat what they grow in the plot beside their hut and very little else. A critical African might point to the years of colonial rule in Africa and ask, "If we are underdeveloped, who underdeveloped us? Why did the Europeans build African economies that depended on European industries for manufactures and on European markets for the sale of Africa's raw materials? Why did they give so little attention to education? Why were Africans forced to work deep in the mines and on the farms? For whose gain have Africa's copper, gold, and diamonds been shipped across the sea, just as Africans themselves were shipped for centuries?"

EUROPEAN AND ASIAN SETTLERS

To this indictment, a European colonial administrator might reply by pointing to the changes taking place in Africa: "Before the coming of the European, Africa had not one factory. Wheeled travel, let alone trucks, railroads, and airplanes, was unknown in many regions. All of Africa south of the Sahara had not a single school, and most Africans were dead of disease or killed in war before they could grow gray hair. Nowadays Africans are beginning to appreciate the benefits of civilization, its radios, airlines, and frozen foods, and criticisms of colonialism by men educated at Oxford or the Sorbonne are mere carping and sour grapes."

This, then, is the crux of the debate: Was the colonial period in Africa a time when modern industry, communications, education, and health were brought to Africa as a modernizing force for the benefit of all, or were technology and social services merely the backwash of a greedy colonial system that drained Africa of its wealth and exploited African labor for the profit of the colonialists alone? In many ways this is a sterile debate. The important question is to what extent and in what ways Africa and Africans did develop and change under colonial rule.

Colonial Monopolies

How did European businessmen find, collect, and transport the raw materials of Africa to their overseas destinations? Just as colonial administration held a monopoly of political power, so colonial companies were economic monopolies, usually closely tied to government. Colonial economies had little in common with the competitive free enterprise system. The usual practice in the colonies was to grant a company exclusive rights in a certain area, both to trade and to mine all the minerals found there. Cecil Rhodes's British South Africa Company occupied and ruled Rhodesia until the British government took over responsibility after World War I. In resource-poor French Africa development schemes were often planned directly by Paris bureaucrats. In the Congo only five companies, controlled in part by the Belgian government, accounted for 70 percent of the country's trade in 1950. The greatest of these companies was Union Minière du Haut Katanga, which had the rich Katanga province to exploit. The Portuguese were too poor to finance the development of their colonies and had, reluctantly, to allow British, Belgian, and German companies to do it for them. One example of the pure form of colonial exploitation is Diamang, the Diamond Company of Angola. Diamang had exclusive rights to all diamonds found in Angola, and the Portu-

Shaft-sinking at a Rand gold mine. (*Information Service of South Africa.*)

guese administration granted Diamang the use of all labor in the Lunda area.

Minerals

One of the burning hopes of all the European colonial adventurers in Africa has been to find the yellow stuff of wealth and power, gold. In South Africa the prospectors, and those who flocked after them, have been most fortunate. South Africa has been the West's main producer of gold and diamonds for nearly a century. It is not the only rich country on the continent. In the first decade of the twentieth century the world's largest copper deposit was found straddling the border between Congo and Northern Rhodesia. The area has become famous as the Rhodesian Copperbelt and Katanga. Iron ore is hidden in the hills of Guinea, Liberia, and Sierra Leone, while huge reserves have recently been found in the Sahara, in Mauretania, and in South Africa. As the railroad and the steel mill have given way to the airplane and the nuclear reactor, prospectors for American and European companies have started to look for oil, aluminum, and uranium. Oil has been found in Libya, the Algerian Sahara, Angola, and Eastern Nigeria; prospecting continues there and in other countries. Bauxite (for aluminum) is mined and exported from Guinea and Ghana, tin from Nigeria. The United States used Congolese uranium to build the first atomic bomb and today imports from Congo two rare but essential minerals, tantalum and titanium, used for electronic instruments and metal alloys for spaceships.

Cash Crops

Cash crops, not minerals, are the chief source of wealth and main commodity of the export trade in Africa. Only in Zambia (former Northern Rhodesia), Congo, and the Republic of South Africa does the value of mineral exceed that of agricultural exports. Elsewhere crops grown for export—and not for local consumption—are the basis of the growing money economy in Africa. Cocoa, used in the making of chocolate, cakes, and beverages, is one of the main exports of Ghana, Western Nigeria, and Ivory Coast. The dryer parts of West Africa, particularly Senegal and Northern Nigeria, produce peanuts (often called groundnuts in Africa), which are exported to Western Europe where they are converted to peanut butter and cooking oil. The Ganda of Uganda now grow cotton and coffee for export, and Sudan (the former Anglo-Egyptian Sudan) also depends largely on cotton in its export trade. Plantations in Tanganyika grow sisal, a plant from Florida introduced into East Africa by an American, which provides fiber for bags and ropes. Valuable hardwood is hauled with difficulty from the wet and roadless tropical forest of Ivory Coast and Gabon. Until iron ore was discovered in the Bomi Hills, Liberia depended on rubber exported by the Firestone Company.

Talk of cash crops can be misleading. Unlike American farmers, most African peasants do not sell their crop and buy goods with the money received. On the contrary, most are subsistence farmers who grow just enough food for their families and themselves. This is as true

African farmers in Ruanda-Urundi being paid for their cotton crop. A white man, probably a colonial official, weighs the crop and gives out the money. (*White Fathers.*)

in the Maghreb as it is in tropical Africa and the countries to the south.

Effects of the Export Economy

African colonial economies were totally dependent on export trade—the exchange of African raw materials for manufactured goods from the colonial power. In most countries African peasants carried on as they had for centuries, untouched by the demand for raw materials and without cash to purchase goods from Europe. The only real exception to this situation, even at present, is South Africa, whose growth has made it the only country with an economy solidly based on industry, manufacturing for home markets, and modern agriculture. The colonial powers were never concerned with trade between African colonies. African economies were not based on the most suitable regions, commodities, mineral wealth, or lines of communication. Instead they grew out of a patchwork quilt which had been formed in deference to political—not economic—interests. African countries have unfortunately never cooperated economically because these separate patches were tied to different European states.

Colonial rulers encouraged the production of only a few materials in each colony, at the expense of stimulating the growth of diverse industries and crops needed to sustain an independent country. Since each colony was a part of an entire empire, why, from the colonial point of view, should each colony be self-sufficient? If Senegal was the best peanut producer in French Africa, or if cotton from Sudan was the most useful export as far as the British were concerned, then Senegal would grow peanuts and Sudan cotton. The result of pushing the best crop at the expense of all the rest was to make each colony heavily dependent on the world price of its single export. If the world supply of copper were to double because of new deposits discovered in Brazil, the boom in Katanga and Zambia would swiftly come to an end. The prosperity or poverty of Ghanaian farmers depends directly on the price of cocoa in the world market. While this may not matter to empire builders, it matters a great deal to Africans and African governments, who can live in only one country at a time. In the African view, one-crop export economies were an extra burden imposed on Africa by colonialists who developed Africa with little regard for the welfare of Africans.

Industries were not developed in the African colonies; instead, the colonial country processed the raw material in its own factories. If Liberian rubber were made into tires in Liberia, or Uganda cotton into cloth in Uganda itself, American and English workers might be out of work. Raw materials were bought from the African colonies at low prices by the European ruler. At the same time the European colonizers imposed high tariffs (import taxes) in the colonies to keep out all goods which were not manufactured in the ruling European country.

In Africa, materials were usually processed just enough to render them suitable for export. Peanuts went unshelled, logs were often shipped with the bark still on them. Until the late 1950's the only industries, outside South Africa, were some light industry in Algeria, a few textile plants in Sudan and East Africa, palm oil mills in Nigeria, and a single steel plant in (Southern) Rhodesia. Factories in Africa were a spoke in the wheel of export and did not serve African needs or markets.

Obstacles to Industry: Markets, Labor, Transport

The slow development of industry in Africa was due to more than the selfishness of colonialists. In the first place, a market for industrial goods was lacking. Why should anyone manufacture wire or chemicals in Africa if Africans used no

Building the Kenya-Uganda railway. In Africa, labor is cheap by American standards, and far more plentiful than machinery. (*World Bank*.)

electricity and bought no house paint? This problem, at first almost insurmountable, is now disappearing. Jobs in the new towns have put cash in African pockets, which are themselves a new development. While in the early days Africans spent most of their cash on basic goods—food and clothes—they soon began to buy more expensive and sophisticated wares such as radios and sewing machines.

Lack of labor, particularly skilled labor, was another obstacle to establishing industry in Africa. When an African first went to work for wages, he often intended to earn only a sum decided on beforehand, sufficient to buy a bicycle, for instance. In the first years of colonial rule, therefore, the higher the wages the sooner the workers were likely to quit. This situation has of course changed as Africans have settled in the towns and have developed a steady demand for all manner of new goods, not just a single article. The problem for businessmen trying to set up industry in Africa was, and is, that steady labor is scarce and often has to be recruited

from a great distance. Skilled labor is even scarcer.

The greatest obstacle to the development of African industry continues to be the lack of what the French call *infrastructure*: transport, communications, electric power. Without cheap and plentiful power, industry is helpless. Although Africa has abundant water-power resources (more than North America and Europe together), the only projects undertaken in colonial days were dams in the Belgian Congo and the Kariba Dam across the Zambezi River in Southern Rhodesia. When Africa was partitioned, men with dreams of empire, like Cecil Rhodes and Leopold, King of the Belgians, pushed railways into the interior from the coast. Today railways are still few and far between, and they were built to carry materials to the sea for export, not to serve or help create a complex modern economy. In Africa, railroads are hard to build and expensive to operate because tropical rains wash out the roadbed and bridges. On the French-built Ethiopian railway it cost more to ship a ton of hides 500 miles from Addis Ababa to the port of Djibouti than across 5,000 miles of ocean from Djibouti to New York.

Trucks are today becoming the most popular method of transportation in Africa, although the continent does not have a network of roads in the American or European sense. In fact most African roads are just dirt, impassable in the wet season and in need of large-scale repairs after the rains. The life of

a truck on African roads is about two years, and an automobile often needs to be tuned up after a single day's drive. For travel across the continent today airplanes are used, although travelers often must fly via London or Paris to get from one African capital to the next.

Agriculture

Colonial regimes encouraged cash crops and exploited minerals, laid the foundations of a transportation system,

AGRICULTURAL AND MINERAL PRODUCTS

Fe: Iron
P: Phosphates
Cr: Chromite
Cu: Copper
Mn: Manganese
Pt: Platinum
U: Uranium

Diamonds   Nuts
Bananas   Grain
Cattle   Sugar Cane
Coarse Fibers   Lumber
Oil   Peanuts
Coffee   Cocoa
Corn   Fruit
Rubber   Palm Oil
Cotton

and in the process taught a good many Africans how to operate a wrench, a pneumatic drill, or a palm oil press. On the other hand, colonial regimes neglected Africa's food supply. While medicine spurred population growth, little was done to increase the productivity of African farmers. In the most fertile regions Africans were prodded to grow cash crops for export, while other farmland was worked harder than its weak tropical soil could bear. Erosion, usually the result of intensive cultivation, heavy rain, and the lack of effective contour plowing, was rarely noticed and stopped. Europeans found that their ignorance of African disease, soil, and climate often made European farming techniques useless. Livestock was wiped out by sleeping sickness, and land went acid despite the efforts of colonial experts. The experts began to appreciate

POPULATION DENSITY

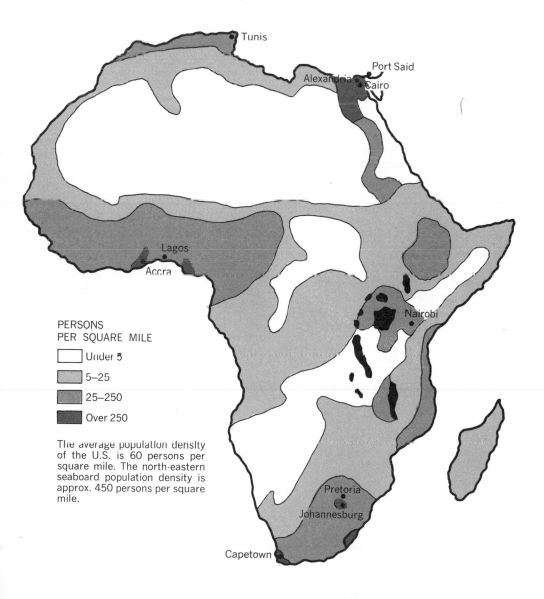

PERSONS
PER SQUARE MILE

☐ Under 5

▨ 5–25

▨ 25–250

■ Over 250

The average population density of the U.S. is 60 persons per square mile. The north-eastern seaboard population density is approx. 450 persons per square mile.

traditional African agricultural methods, by which land is burned over after only a year or two of use and then is left fallow for as long as seven years before being used again.

Africa as a whole is sparsely populated. People live in clusters separated by belts of arid, unusable land. Many of these islands of population do not now produce enough to feed themselves and have to import food from elsewhere in Africa, or even from outside the continent. Mines and cities draw men from the land, undermining the traditional economy. The women who remain can hardly produce enough food for themselves, let alone a surplus for the men in the towns. The only way out of the vicious circle of more people, fewer men, less food is to raise more food from the same amount of land with fewer farmers, as Americans have learned to do.

Two ambitious agricultural schemes, one a success, the other a failure, illustrate the difficulties and the spotty record of colonial agricultural development. In Sudan where the Blue Nile from the Ethiopian mountains meets the White Nile flowing north from Lake Victoria lies a plain called Gezira, which means "island." Fifty years ago only a few goats and cattle browsed the parched land. Today Gezira cotton is the mainstay of Sudan's economy. Cotton growing began in Gezira after 1926, when the British built a dam across the Blue Nile together with 3,000 miles of irrigation canals.

Land in Gezira is owned by the farmers who grow the cotton. Since no one can own more than 40 acres, or divide his land among tenants, the Gezira has avoided the blight of absentee landlords and impoverished tenants that plagues Southeast Asia and Latin America today. Every farmer's cotton crop is divided into three shares: 40 percent to the farmer; 40 percent to the Sudan government, which provides the water;

The Gezira. This Sudan farmer adjusts the gate that regulates the flow of water to the neighboring fields. (*United Nations.*)

20 percent to the Gezira managing board, which gins the cotton, markets it, and keeps the locusts away. Other crops that the farmer grows are his own.

After World War II the British became enthusiastic about the peanut. With a great deal of fanfare and little careful consideration, the great groundnut scheme was born. The advice of several agronomists was brushed aside, a site in Tanganyika was chosen more or less at random, and rusting American bulldozers were imported from the Philippines. Tanganyika's stony soil and tough roots proved too much for the secondhand bulldozers; the irregular rainfall permitted no more than an occasional crop. The great groundnut scheme suffered an ignominious death, at a cost of several million dollars to British taxpayers.

African Labor

The *"native policy"* of colonial regimes was almost always a *labor* policy. The Portuguese have always been the most blunt about their intention to use the African as a worker. Within months of the abolition of slavery in the Portuguese colonies at the end of the nineteenth century a system of indentured labor appeared. In 1943 a Portuguese Colonial Minister wrote that "if we are to civilize the native we must make him adopt as an elementary moral precept the notion that he has no right to live without working." Work for Europeans, presumably, serves humanity and civilizes the African in a way that work on his own land for his own family does not! A system of enforced contract labor has operated in Angola and Mozambique all through the present century. Africans could be taken from their village at any time to work on roads or other public projects, or made to work on mines or plantations. In 1961 the beginning of the Angolan war and mounting international disapproval led to a change in the law. But actual labor practices seem to have changed very little.

In the neighboring country of Congo, the Belgian administration provided a happy contrast to Portuguese labor practice. Congolese workers of Union Minière and other companies were given houses, education, sick pay, pensions, technical training, and sound medical care by their employers. However, this relatively high standard of living was not accompanied by opportunities for promotion or by freedom to organize. The Congo crisis which started in 1960 (see Chapter 10) revealed the weakness of this one-sided approach in the Belgian Congo.

French labor policy, like that of the Portuguese, was forced, although not as harshly. Africans were required to work for the government for a certain number of days every year as a kind of tax. Although this forced labor was legal for public works only, many private concerns, such as the lumber plantations in Ivory Coast, were "helped" by the government. The Maghreb was different. With all the good coastal lands in the

hands of the settlers, there were few jobs for Algerians. Every year half a million went to France as unskilled workers in search of jobs, while their wives and brothers remained unemployed at home. The army of destitute Algerian peasants, landless and out of work, became in time the guerilla army that defeated the French.

British labor policy was a good deal more subtle than Portuguese, Belgian, or French. Wherever workers were needed a money tax was imposed on every hut or every cow that a man owned. Of course, most Africans had no cash to pay the tax, and the only way they could earn it was by working for Europeans on farms, factories, or mines. In Uganda, Nigeria, and Gold Coast trade and cash-crop farming soon made money available to all; but not in South Africa and Rhodesia, where men came to the cities to earn the money that would pay their poll tax.

Health

Most Africans are sick. They are sick from birth to the day of their early death. Many African languages do not have a word meaning "healthy," because the condition is not known. The list of African diseases is long and unpleasant. Some diseases, like malaria, attack the smallest baby, weakening the victim for the rest of his life. Others, like smallpox, strike and kill swiftly. It is the diseases that malinger that sap the vitality of Africans. Chief among these is malnutrition, which makes those who suffer from it less resistant to other diseases as well. With the exception of a few cattle-herding peoples, all Africans lack protein and hence suffer from malnutrition from weaning until death.

One of man's greatest enemies in Africa is the tsetse fly. This small creature carries a protozoan called *trypanosoma*, which when transferred by the fly's bite to man or beast causes the dreaded sleeping sickness. Almost all of Africa is infested with this scourge; where the fly rules, man and beast cannot be sure of life. In 1900, in one small area of Uganda, two out of every three people died in a sleeping sickness epidemic which swept the country. The tsetse fly, by making it impossible for horses and most breeds of cattle to survive, denied most Africans the use of draft animals. It is for this reason that human backs were the only source of power and transportation in many parts of Africa.

Colonial governments attacked the health problem from the beginning of

AFRICAN DISEASES

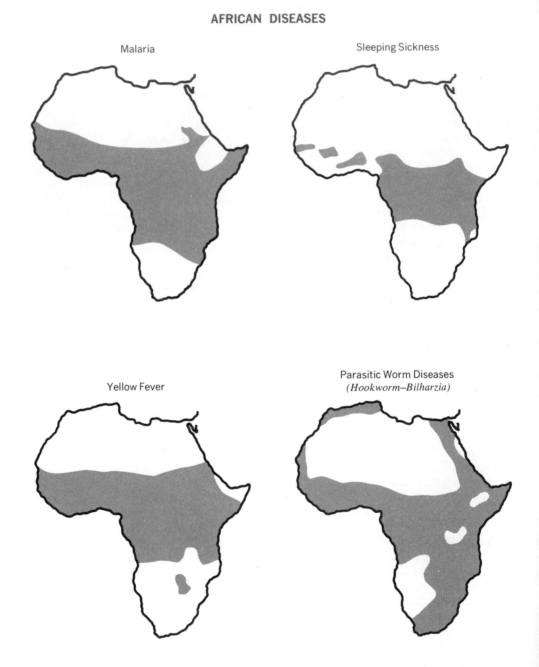

Malaria

Sleeping Sickness

Yellow Fever

Parasitic Worm Diseases
(Hookworm–Bilharzia)

their rule. Dr. Albert Schweitzer was only one of the many dedicated medical men who have helped check, if not eliminate, disease in Africa. As usual, the greatest obstacles to a successful campaign against sickness are ignorance and poverty, themselves partly a result of disease. Africans, who had thought (many still do) of medicine as a potion to ward off spirits, rather than as a direct physical protection, had to be persuaded to trust the strange and outlandish remedies of European doctors. The Belgian Congo, by training Africans to persuade their relatives in the villages to accept vaccination and medicine, took the lead in controlling disease. Today the force of African medical technicians who carry the war against disease into the bush by bicycle and dispensary truck is steadily increasing. The World Health Organization of the United Nations and UNICEF have, in recent years, been of key importance in this work, especially in filling the gap left by the departing colonial rulers. Ignorance may soon cease to be a problem as the younger generation sees the effect of medical care on parents living longer and stronger lives. Poverty, however, remains.

African diseases can be treated and cured. On the other hand, people can be prevented from contracting these illnesses only if swamps are sprayed and Africans regularly inoculated. This is a very expensive undertaking and has not been done either by the colonial or the new African governments. Although African doctors are being trained and hospitals built, the main problems of preventive medicine—lack of sanitation and bad diet—remain.

Education

At the early mission stations the first bold Africans came and learned the skills of the white man. The fabric of their beliefs was torn by Christianity, yet they were armed with an understanding of the mystery of the written word, a new power which excited others and inspired them to seek education for themselves. European education was soon recognized as the key to, literally, a new world. Today African children crowd the schoolhouses hoping for a seat in the class and compete fiercely for the few places in the high schools and universities.

The role of the Christian missions, both Protestant and Catholic, in African education has long been a subject of controversy. In the great expanse of Moslem Africa, including the Maghreb, the Sahara, and the West African sudan, Christian schools had little success. Elsewhere Christian ethics—equality, the brotherhood of man, peace, charity, humility—found a ready reception among Africans who had been ravaged by war in the past and were distressed by white domination in the present. The practices of Christianity were another matter. Men resisted attempts to make them abandon their extra wives. Often women, who believed that they were economically protected by this system of marriage, were more strongly opposed than men to change. With time this resistance faded, however, and monogamy came to be practiced by African Christians. But tribal initiation ceremonies, which missionaries opposed, lingered on and still exist today. Yet the missions did succeed in teaching the three R's to thousands. Missionaries put hundreds of African languages into writing, using the Roman alphabet of English and French. The Bible was translated into scores of tongues, and African stories, poems, and folk tales were put into print for the first time.

Pressure to educate more Africans came from two directions at once. Colonial enterprises and colonial administrations needed literate labor and clerical help, and Africans wanted to master the skills of their rulers. In the 1940's colonial governments incorporated the mission schools into public education

AFRICAN RELIGIONS

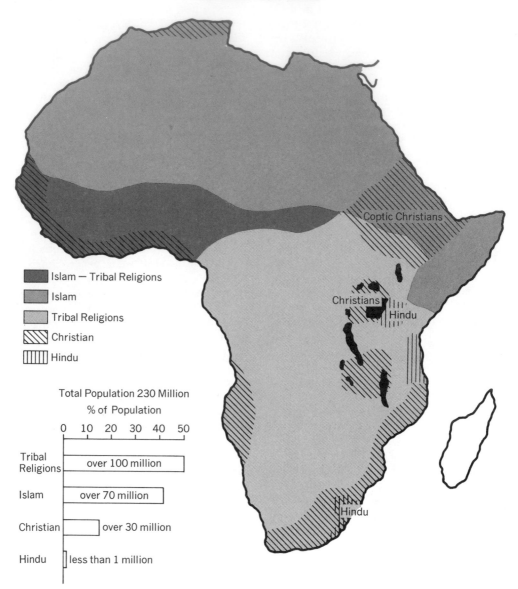

Islam — Tribal Religions
Islam
Tribal Religions
Christian
Hindu

Total Population 230 Million
% of Population

0   10   20   30   40   50

Tribal Religions | over 100 million
Islam | over 70 million
Christian | over 30 million
Hindu | less than 1 million

programs. The education policies of colonial governments followed their colonial philosophies closely. On the one hand the British and Belgian view was that Africans should not be transformed into Europeans but should retain their own way of life. On the other hand the French and the Portuguese believed that the most worthwhile product of education was an African who was in-

distinguishable in culture and behavior from his European counterpart.

British policy is clearly summed up in the report of a colonial commission of 1925:

Education should be adapted to the mentality, aptitudes, occupations, and traditions of the various peoples, conserving as far as possible all sound and healthy elements in the fabric of their social life; adapting them where necessary to changed circumstances and progressive ideas, as an agent of growth and evolution.

Missionaries were helped to continue their educational work, often teaching in African languages. In Gold Coast (now Ghana) the British came close to providing free universal education at the primary level, followed by a university education in one of the new university colleges in West or East Africa, or, for the more talented and fortunate, in Britain. In those East and Central African colonies where white settlers had strong influence over the government, few African children received an education.

The Belgians left education mainly to the Catholic Church, which worked closely with the administration and the mining companies. The aim of the educational system was to produce skilled workers, not leaders or planners. Few Congolese were ever taught "academic" subjects. As a result Congo now has thousands of well-trained technicians and very few leaders or administrators.

French schools, including those of the Maghreb, trained an elite of African Frenchmen. The subjects taught in the schools of Tunis and Dakar were exactly like those taught in schools in Bordeaux or Lyon. Only French was spoken in the classrooms, and pupils in both France and Africa read history textbooks which opened with the words, "Our ancestors the Gauls . . ." Until after World War II only a few Africans received this excellent French education, and those few were often the sons of chiefs. In the 1950's the French began a program of technical education and tripled the number (still small) of children in primary school.

The Portuguese stress Catholic Christianity above all else. There are two separate school systems in Portuguese Africa: "native" schools to teach Africans Catholicism and the value of work, and Portuguese schools attended by the children of settlers and a handful of Africans. The illiteracy rate in Angola and Mozambique is about 99 percent.

In general, with some outstanding exceptions, the spread of education and literacy in Africa has been remarkable. Especially in the last few years many high schools and universities have been built. Africans appreciate the progress that was made in education under colonial rule, and few independent African governments have changed the school systems they inherited from their predecessors.

Summing Up Colonialism

What did colonial rule do to Africa?

After fifty years of colonial rule millions of Africans had received some education—mostly from Christian missionaries at mission schools. This education prepared the way for African development and self-government along modern lines, although only the British intended such a result.

Many Africans were, and are, healthier because of the services of European and African doctors and nurses. Today African babies have a better than even chance of living to be adults. Yet better health has meant more babies and more people. In less than twenty years the population of many African countries will double; such a population explosion will mean greater poverty for many Africans.

Administrative order, trade, and the need for labor changed the face of Africa. Men in search of work, trade, or education could travel without fear of violence over the network of African bushpaths—still the most extensive transportation system on the continent —which linked the villages to the harbors, roads, railroads, and airports built for colonial trade. Slowly, as the colonial economy pulled more and more African communities together like threads in a pattern, Africans became cash-crop

farmers, traders, clerk, lawyers, and laborers. They began to learn about and
cooperate with one another. African national loyalties, transcending tribe and
region, began to form.

Europeans gained much from colonial
economic development. Where minerals
were discovered, mining companies
made large profits, and where trade
flourished, colonial export companies
skimmed the cream. In the Maghreb,
Kenya, and South Africa, Europeans
took the best land and incurred fierce
hostility from the dispossessed Africans. Even local trade went to foreigners. West African petty traders competed with immigrant Syrians and
Lebanese from the Middle East. Indians
monopolized local trade in East and
Southern Africa, and *petits blancs* (poor
whites, literally "little whites") controlled trade in the Maghreb. All this
caused African resentment, from one
end of the continent to the other.

Forced labor in Portugese Africa until 1961, and in French Africa until
1946, did little to endear colonial regimes to Africans. Work in the gold
mines of South Africa or on the Copperbelt of Congo and Rhodesia might have
"civilized" the African migrant worker, but often the routine of monotonous
work for long hours underground, harsh
treatment by white overseers, and the
unpleasantness of "compounds" where
men lived for months at a time without
their families made such work resemble forced labor endured to pay the
taxes imposed by an alien master.

Most unpleasant of all to Africans
who accepted European values was the
obvious contrast between European and
African standards of living. Europeans,
even the unskilled and ill-educated,
lived far better in Africa than they did
in Europe. Colonial governments and
companies encouraged Europeans to
come to Africa by offering such entice-
ments as cars, houses, servants, high
pay, and long holidays. Often enough

Would you expect to see a Sudan soldier
playing the bagpipes! In all areas of activity, European customs have affected
African life. (*Arab Information Service.*)

the wealthy corporations were able to
outbid the colonial administrations.
White South Africans enjoy a standard
of living as high as that of the United
States—with fewer dishwashers but
more servants—while in the Belgian
Congo the average income of the Europeans was fifty times that of the African Congolese. To many Africans these
differences of wealth and pay seemed
excessive and unjustified, especially
when they worked side by side with
Europeans doing the same job. The contrast was of course most obvious in the
settler countries. In Kenya, Algeria,
and South Africa, African resentment
grew with European prosperity.

Who Benefited?

Defenders of colonial Africa claim that
the material benefits of colonialism were
not only great but could not have been
achieved in any other way. They ask,
"Who but colonial governments would
have paid for African education and

medical care? Who but companies interested in trade and minerals would have opened the mines and encouraged the cash crops?" They argue that colonial governments built not only schools and hospitals but roads and railways and ports and airfields—the foundations of a modern economy. They maintain that Africans in great numbers are enjoying the material goods of civilization bought with money earned working for Europeans; that Africans have been taught a whole new way of life, better beyond measure than the savagery and superstition they knew before; that they have been taught the value of work and the need for self-improvement.

Africans, and many others, dispute these claims. Embittered by the assumption of European superiority and hurt by the fact of white supremacy and racial discrimination, they accuse colonial governments of economic exploitation and of neglect of African welfare. They argue that the African was treated as a commodity and herded into mine shafts and plantations for the profit of greedy Europeans. Fragile export economies were imposed on Africa, they say, tying colonies to a world market controlled by European capitalists to the disadvantage of African economic needs. Settlers robbed Africans of their land. The wealth torn from African soil went straight into European pockets instead of being used for the development of industry in Africa itself. The education and development efforts of recent years, they conclude, were too small and came too late, the products of a guilty conscience.

PROBLEMS

1. Organize a debate on the topic: "Resolved: That colonial rule in Africa was both necessary and beneficial to Africans."

2. What kind of prejudices would Europeans in Africa be likely to acquire by employing African workers who knew nothing of modern technology and who had to be taught to use a ladder or a wheelbarrow? Would these prejudices be likely to disappear as fast as Africans learned how to repair a car or take a photograph?

3. If Africa had been declared an open continent to traders of all nations, rather than being divided up among competing powers, do you think Africa today would have better transportation, more industry, and be less dependent on export trade?

4. Did America ever have an export economy? To what extent was the American Revolution a reaction to a colonial economy like those of twentieth-century Africa?

5. The Belgians claimed that taking good physical care of African workers while educating them very little was the best way to make them happy. Do you agree? Would a British official in Nigeria have agreed? How does the answer change as Africans in other countries become educated and begin to think about running their own affairs?

6. Suppose you are a settler who paid the Kenya government for a farm in the White Highlands, built a house there, and worked hard for twenty years to make the farm efficient and prosperous. How would you react to the

demands of African politicians that you sell the farm to Africans because you are rich and the African peasants are poor and without land? Is there a "right" and a "wrong" side to this settler problem?

7. Suppose you were a Kikuyu farmer with little land, and you could not buy more, but could only raise money by working long hours at low wages for harsh masters. How would you look upon white usurpers?

READING SUGGESTIONS

Joyce Cary, *Mister Johnson*, Harper & Row, 1948.

Robert Delavignette, *Freedom and Authority in French West Africa*, Oxford University Press (London), 1950.

Elspeth Huxley, *On the Edge of the Rift*, Morrow, 1962.

George T. H. Kimble, *Tropical Africa*, 2 volumes, Anchor, paper.

Margery Perham, *The Colonial Reckoning*, Knopf, 1962.

chapter 6

THE CITY COMES TO AFRICA

My father called me "lazy"!
But with what has he paid the tax?
With the earnings of my work.
If he insults me again, I will go to Ketao.
There I will find a truck for Kumasi,
And I will earn money for myself!

—*Song of the young men*
of a town in Dahomey

For the last fifty years one of Africa's most common sights has been a man trudging along a dusty road, stick in hand, followed single file by his wife with a battered suitcase on her head and a baby on her back. Another family is moving to the town.

Since the glory days of Athens, Rome, and Byzantium, the city has been a mighty engine of civilization. The towns of colonial Africa were no different, for like the towns of ancient China or medieval Europe they drew men in search of opportunity, adventure, and wealth. Migration offered a chance to escape the restricting customs of the village and the demands of hosts of relatives.

Most Americans think of these migrant Africans as "emerging" from tribal village darkness into the light of the modern age. To an African peasant, the situation was just the reverse. He was leaving a familiar and well-ordered community to enter a strange and confusing new world.

The problems of an African migrant to the city were much like the problems of an Italian or Polish immigrant in Boston or Detroit in the year 1900. Where can a man find a job if he does not speak the language, can't read or write, and has no useful industrial skills? Where can he find a place to live? Whom should he approach for help in learning the meaning of street signs or the whereabouts of the cheapest local market? In Africa, the answers to these questions were much the same as they had been for the American immigrants. Africans found work as unskilled laborers: miners working deep underground with pick and shovel, construction workers hauling bricks and mortar, longshoremen, delivery boys, domestic servants. If a man was fortunate enough to know how to read and write or drive a car, he might be hired as an office boy or cab driver.

As at all other times when men have flocked to the towns, living conditions for the immigrants were worse than bad. The old story of immigrant slums was repeated in Africa. A newcomer was lucky to get a single room for himself

99

Shantytown. The shacks are built of corrugated iron strips fastened together, and have no plumbing, water, or electricity. (*Information Service of South Africa.*)

and his family, even at an exorbitant rent. In the open spaces around the commercial center of the city grew huddles of shacks and tenements—flimsy shelters of castoff metal sheets, crates, cardboard, and burlap. These African slums were called shantytowns, or, in French, *bidonvilles*. They had no electricity, no running water, no plumbing. Often thousands of people shared a single water tap. As in other slums past and present, liquor, gambling, disease, and crime were part of daily life.

African Towns

There are basically two kinds of towns in Africa: mining towns and commercial towns. Many commercial cities grew from European trading posts along the coast. All the African ports, with the exception of the age-old Mediterranean ports of North Africa, are new cities

This woman and her daughter, cooking a meal of coarse flour beside a mud wall, are poor by any standards. Yet, modern times are breaking out—the woman cooks with evaporated milk in a metal pot and both wear factory-made cloth and rubber sandals from Japan. (*David R. Giltrow.*)

East Africa is a melting pot of European, Indian, Arab, and African elements. This shop, owned by an Indian, sells Christian religious pictures as well as hardware. The sign is in English but the writing under the Pepsi-Cola poster is in an Indian language. The poster at the top, in Swahili, proclaims Tanganyika's independence on December 9, 1961.

built by Europeans. These export centers are dominated by the wharves, railroad sidings, and gray warehouses of the colonial trading companies.

From the ports the railroads wind their way inland toward the sources of minerals and cash crops and toward the colonial administrative capitals. Some of the inland cities, such as Kumasi and Kampala, were the capitals of African nations. (Kumasi was the capital of Ashanti and Kampala of Buganda.) Most are European creations which bear European names—Leopoldville and Stanleyville after King Leopold of Belgium and his American explorer-agent Stanley, Johannesburg after a Boer trek leader, Salisbury after a British Prime Minister.

Most southern African cities grew up around the mines. They are gray towns of smog and slag heaps, with workers' barracks nestled under the mine shafts.

The cities of Moslem Africa—Khartoum, Cairo, Tunis, Algiers, Casablanca —were medieval Arab towns of narrow, twisting streets and overhanging eaves or mud brick houses. Today the old Arab quarter, or casbah, is dominated by high-rise apartments, government offices, and banks.

Port Towns

City	Country
Dakar	Senegal
Conakry	Guinea
Abidjan	Ivory Coast
Accra	Ghana
Lagos	Nigeria
Freetown	Sierra Leone
Monrovia	Liberia
Matadi	Congo
Cape Town	South Africa
Durban	South Africa
Luanda	Angola
Lourenço Marques	Mozambique
Dar es Salaam	Tanganyika
Mombasa	Kenya
Zanzibar	Zanzibar
Cairo	Egypt
Tripoli	Libya
Tunis	Tunisia
Algiers	Algeria
Oran	Algeria
Casablanca	Morocco

Dar es Salaam, one of the world's finest natural harbors. The East African coast is low, flat, and dry. (*White Fathers.*)

Mining Towns

City	Country
Johannesburg	South Africa
Lusaka and others	Zambia
Elisabethville	Congo

Inland Commercial Towns

City	Country
Kampala	Uganda
Nairobi	Kenya
Salisbury	Rhodesia
Stanleyville	Congo
Leopoldville	Congo
Brazzaville	Congo Republic
Khartoum	Sudan
Kumasi	Ghana
Ibadan	Nigeria

The Migrants

African migration to the city was usually both a short-distance and a short-term affair. A young man might leave his village to seek adventure and to earn the bride payment demanded by his sweetheart's parents. A few months later he would return on a bicycle with the cash in his pockets and spend the next few weeks making his rivals green with envy at his tales of city life. Like as not, others would follow.

When a man arrived in town, his first impulse was to seek out his kinsmen. By African tradition a man was expected to support all his relatives when necessary, and families established in the city were often deluged by country cousins at loose ends. A man making good wages as a bicycle repairman or shoemaker might be supporting five or six relatives in addition to his own family. The advantage was that no one starved. On the other hand, the breadwinner began to wonder about a tradition which robbed him of his earnings, particularly when there seemed to be an endless supply of relatives. Yet family solidarity served as the means by which new arrivals were introduced to the strange city.

Migrants to the city were cut loose from the repetitive pattern and fatalistic beliefs of their traditional background. No longer would the young men accept the word of their village elders that crops should be planted or houses built a certain way "because that is the way it has always been done." No longer would the women think only of caring for their husbands and tending the fields. The example of change and the ideas of change spread slowly but thoroughly from the towns to the country.

Africans were not, and are not, divided into two groups, city "detribalized" Africans and rural "traditional" Africans. Almost every village has its returned adventurer, while the towns constantly digest new migrants from the villages.

For Whites Only

Cities in black Africa were, and to some extent still are, segregated by race. The Europeans (in Africa all white men are "Europeans") had a section to themselves, with their own stores, churches, and schools. Apart from the white man's quarter clustered the African shantytowns that housed the city's workers and servants. The African sections were sometimes sprawled around the warehouses and government offices that were the center of town life, or were arranged by the Europeans in blocks separated by belts of trees. In the mining towns of southern Africa the African workers were confined to a compound and were permitted outside only if they carried an approved pass. This pattern survives today in Johannesburg, a city of a million people.

The effect of the color bar, and of the obvious difference between living conditions for white and black, was to make race prejudice obvious and hateful to Africans. In villages visited only by an occasional white trader or colonial agricultural officer discrimination by race was not important. In the city, with its

An African entrepreneur. The clothes he makes will be sold on the spot. Migrants to the towns find ways to do business with only a few dollars of capital. Along with the bicycle and the radio, the sewing machine has profoundly changed African life. (*White Fathers.*)

buses and cabs, restaurants and movie theatres, the color bar was everywhere.

The extent of segregation varied. South Africa, both the most urban and the most race-conscious country, represents the extreme of total segregation of the races. The French always insisted that they never discriminated by race, but only according to education and cultural level, and this was usually true. In every country, however, black Africans were made acutely aware of European dominance and the myth of African inferiority that went with it.

Africans Organize

The forerunners of the political parties and nationalist movements of the 1950's were the organizations formed by migrant Africans in the new towns. Few realized that from the small, unnoticed

Bazaar in Benghazi, Libya. Merchants selling similar wares cluster together, keeping an eye on the competition. *(Arab Information Center.)*

gatherings of fellow tribesmen, sports lovers, women, clerks, or classmates would develop an organized mass campaign demanding the end of European rule in Africa.

The most natural kind of group for a newly arrived migrant to join was an association of others from his own tribe or region. When a young man arrived in town he sought out the local head of his "nation." The sound of a familiar language and the chance to relax with friends at Sunday evening *tam-tams* (parties) was solace to an African beset with the rigors of job hunting or learning to read.

These tribal associations, while keeping ties between town and country, could not maintain the strict control of parents, chiefs, and elders over their members' lives and behavior. If a man wanted to forget his wife or make friends with members of a rival tribe, that was now his own business. Young, educated, eager men took over the tribal associations in the towns and through them brought radical ideas of change to the country. By keeping open the paths (literally paths, traveled by foot and by bicycle) of communication between town and country the tribal associations laid the foundation for cooperation between the city folk and the village African. One example was the Egbe Omo Oduduwa, an organization of the rich (from cocoa growing) and numerous Yoruba people of Nigeria. Led by Chief Obafemi Awolowo, Egbe Omo Oduduwa became in 1951 the Action Group, the important Yoruba political party of Western Nigeria. The importance of tribal associations, however, cut both ways. While tribal loyalties afforded an easy way to spread the ideas of change, politics based on tribal loyalties threatened to split the many African nations with several strong tribes and peoples within their borders.

The tribal associations kept African culture and African art alive amid the weariness and honky-tonk of shantytown. In reciting the tales of his people, and dancing the dances of his village, an African depressed and doubtful in his new surroundings and shaken in his beliefs found much that was good and much that was fun in his African background. In this way the tribal associations were not relics of the past but promises of a future renaissance of African culture.

Other kinds of associations, representing practically every side of town life, contributed to the return of African self-confidence. Football (soccer) clubs were formed in every town and mine compound. A match between, for example, the Mighty Poisons and the Great Titanics brought together Africans from many parts of town and country to meet one another and perhaps talk politics.

Welfare associations were the most direct way to raise the large amounts of money that every African sometimes needed. Every Saturday the members of the welfare society would contribute a tiny sum from their week's earnings, and each member would receive the collection in turn. The expense of a funeral, traditionally an important event to many African peoples, might take half a year's salary, or the life's savings of a widow. Burial societies helped meet the expense. Welfare clubs and Friendly Societies provided money for weddings and new suits, so that their members could escape the 30 percent monthly interest rates charged by African usurers. The welfare cooperatives provided more than just money in time of need. Like the other associations, they were debating societies for Africans dissatisfied with the colonial regime.

African Labor Unions

The Africans were, in the white man's economy, laborers. African workers, like workers anywhere, wanted higher wages, better working conditions, and protection against harsh bosses. Coming to the towns and the mines from varied tribes and distant places, Africans met one another and began to organize for common purposes. From small, informal discussions labor unions grew, demanding the right to speak for African workers.

In most African colonies European business and the colonial government worked together. The mines, warehouses, and plantations were operated with government encouragement and under government regulation. African labor disputes with European plantation owners, mining companies, or factory foremen often involved the colonial government. Until after the Second World War, to strike for better wages or working conditions was illegal, and strike leaders were sent to prison. For these reasons, labor unions were soon involved in politics. In towns where many workers belonged to the union, the union became a kind of unofficial government representing African interests. Unions in many countries provided both leaders and followers for the political parties that demanded independence in the 1950's. Two of Africa's most colorful leaders, Sékou Touré, now President of Guinea, and Tom Mboya of the Kenya African National Union, rose to power directly through the labor movement.

There are two important things to remember about African workers in general and African labor unions in particular. First, the workers and the unions represent only a small minority of Africans. Perhaps only one out of five African men earns regular wages. Of the wage earners, probably only a quarter belonged to unions in the days of colonial rule. Most African workers were and are migrants who left their village to work for a few months at a time in the town or in the mines. A man shuttling back and forth from country to city is an excellent bearer of news and ideas, but he does not make a good union member, for an effective union requires that its members stay on the job, attend meetings, vote, and pay dues from a steady income.

The second and more important fact is that those few Africans with steady wage-earning jobs were the ones essential to the economy of the colony. Without clerks, teachers, skilled miners, railway workers, and longshoremen the economy would collapse. The men in such jobs were likely to form unions, and were fully capable of building an effective organization and using it to put pressure on the colonial government.

The policy of the various colonial governments toward unions was generally the same as their attitude toward African demands and aspirations in general. Where and when unions were permitted, they were organized, as in French and British Africa, after 1945. Where unions grew, as in Nigeria, French West Africa, and Kenya, they provided a training ground for African leaders and a chance for Africans to learn how to organize themselves and run their own affairs. Where unions were suppressed, as in the Belgian Congo and South Africa, another grievance was added to African resentment of colonial rule.

Africans trying to organize their fellow workers had their hands full. Even where unions were legal, colonial employers regarded union organizers as agitators with sinister motives. The usual response to a strike was to fire everyone concerned and hire new workers from the many unemployed and migrant Africans (as did many American employers during the emergence of U.S. labor unions in the 1920's and 1930's). African workers who wanted the higher pay and opportunities for promotion that the unions demanded often just did not understand why they had to pay a few shillings or francs every month to the union treasurer. Distrust of the leaders often arose among the rank and file, for the union leaders were usually clerks separated from their followers by higher pay and the ability to read and write. Leaders were accused of working for personal advantage and influence, of stealing union funds, and of being "company stooges." Workers deserted unions in large numbers when negotiations or a strike failed. It took time to create among the workers the loyalty, discipline, and perseverance needed to bargain successfully and to strike without resorting to violence.

Through unions African leaders gained political experience, and their followers learned the skills of democracy, party discipline, and protest without violence. Many Africans voted for the first time in union elections, and many leaders made their first speech to a crowd of workers gathered in a slum square or behind the company office. Union committees sat down with their bosses to negotiate. In time, African union leaders learned to display their power. On the Rhodesian Copperbelt it is said that a confident union leader once walked into the manager's office, took the best chair, put his feet on the desk, and lit a cigarette, before suggesting to the by-now-intimidated executive that unless he wanted 5,000 men out on strike the next morning he had better approve a pay raise. Where they were strong, the unions produced African leaders who were capable of dealing on equal terms with European managers and officials.

The first grievances of Africans were as workers, for their place in the colonial regime was that of a worker. Yet union battles were in the end fought not with the colonial companies but with the colonial government. British government commissions mediated strikes. When Congo workers wanted a raise, they had to get official approval. In French West Africa a third of all African wage earners were paid directly by the government, and the principle of equal pay to white man and black for equal work was debated and passed by the French parliament in Paris. It was soon obvious to Africans, leaders and followers alike, that economic goals—higher wages and opportunities to be promoted to responsible jobs—would have to be won in a political campaign against the whole colonial system.

Youth

The resurgence of Africa is the result of change in the opportunities and aspirations of young Africans. Young African men and women, particularly those with some education and experience of city life, held and still hold a very important position in African society. In America parents, businessmen, and political leaders can understand both the position of youth and the needs of the nation. In Africa this was not so. The older generation knew only traditional ways. Few could read a newspaper, let alone understand the needs of the new African society in the European town. Most of the elders thought only in terms of their tribe and scarcely knew of the thing called "Nigeria," or "South Africa," or "Senegal." A new community had come into being, the national community within colonial boundaries, and within this new community the younger generation would work and live. In Africa the energy and pressure for change common to young people everywhere was not guided by the experience of older men, because the elders had no knowledge of the problems their children faced. The impulse for change not only came from youth but had to be led and carried out as well by the younger generation.

A New Confidence

The great social change—the coming of the city and the modern way of life— was not a pleasant experience for the Africans who were and are caught up in it. The new men of the towns and the mines lived in a world of bitter poverty and great personal frustration. The harsh discipline of a regular job and the loneliness of being a stranger made an African envy the familiar life of his less-enterprising brothers at home in the village. On every side the African in the town was confronted and brushed aside by the vastly greater wealth, education, and skills of his European rulers, from whom he was separated by a social gulf as great as the difference between his tiny shack and their comfortable houses with many servants. And whether it was called color bar or culture bar, the African's pride and self-confidence were hurt by European prejudice.

Amid the poverty and ignorance of the shantytowns, Africans began to grope for unity and control over their own fate in the strange "European" world. It began with groups of tattered black longshoremen meeting under a naked bulb in a tin hut to discuss how to find a job for a newly arrived villager. It took heart from the example of an African lawyer with a black um-brella on his arm, fit to talk and argue in the white man's court. It grew with the stirrings of a crowd listening to a wild-eyed prophet preaching black salvation, and with the quiet thoughts of Algerian schoolboys told of the Liberty, Equality, and Fraternity that was the heritage of their French rulers. It learned from the procession of illiterate miners walking slowly past a ballot box to drop in slips of paper on which the symbol of the leader of their choice had been marked by an "X."·

PROBLEMS

1. Think of the city you know best. Is any one group a relatively recent arrival there? Do they live together? In what part of town? Are they richer or poorer than those who have lived there longer? What do you expect will happen to this newly arrived group as they get used to the city, meet other kinds of people, and get better jobs?

2. A frontier is a place of adventure and opportunity where an independent man can work to make life better for himself and his children. Were African cities a frontier in this sense? Why? Would you call Africans who migrated to the city "pioneers"?

3. One of the strong demands of many African labor unions was that individual Africans be promoted to responsible jobs as foremen and managers if they were qualified. Why was this demand resisted by white employers? How does it cut to the heart of the myth of white superiority? Would you expect opposition to promotion of Africans to be greater in Senegal or in South Africa? Why?

4. Why were the associations of the new towns so important for the future of Africa?

READING SUGGESTIONS

Cyprian Ekwensi, *People of the City*, Heinemann (London), paper.

Peter Gould, *Africa: Continent of Change*, Wadsworth, paper.

Thomas Hodgkin, *Nationalism in Colonial Africa*, New York University Press, paper.

chapter 7

THE NEW MEN OF COLOR

The problem of the twentieth century is the problem of the color line—the relation of the darker to the lighter races of men in Asia and Africa, in America and the islands of the sea.

—W. E. B. DU BOIS,
London, 1900

I am only the forerunner of an awakened Africa that shall never go back to sleep.

—MARCUS AURELIUS GARVEY

New World Reactions

The scramble for Africa in the last years of the nineteenth century proceeded under the watchful gaze of men of color who had only recently been released from slavery in the New World. And in the first decades of the twentieth century, Negro Americans were leaders of movements which tried to prevent the abuse of colonial power over Africans.

William Edward Burghardt DuBois (1868–1963)

The outstanding early champion of the African cause and the father of the movement today called Pan-Africanism was W. E. B. DuBois. DuBois was born and raised in Massachusetts, studied at Fisk College, at Harvard, and finally in Berlin. He was undoubtedly the best-educated and most brilliant American Negro of his time.

In 1900 DuBois went to London to attend the first Pan-African Congress. This congress was organized by a West Indian lawyer with the rather un-African name of Henry Sylvester-Williams,

who was living in London at the time. The thirty delegates who attended came from England, the United States, and the West Indies—none was from Africa. It was at this meeting that DuBois spoke the prophetic lines quoted above, which have become a byword among African intellectuals. DuBois was inspired to embark upon a lifetime odyssey in search of Negro African unity, Negro African renaissance, Negro African revival—in a word, Pan-Africa.

The purpose of this first Pan-African Congress was to protest the colonial partition of Africa. The delegates wished to show that black men outside Africa were concerned about the fate of a continent whose people could not yet speak for themselves. The British government promised the congress that it would not "overlook the interests of the native races." However, with the death of Henry Sylvester-Williams shortly after the congress, the moving spirit of that time was lost. DuBois had in the meantime returned to the United States, there to urge full equality for American Negroes. In 1910 he helped organize the

National Association for the Advancement of Colored People.

After World War I the victorious Allies met at Versailles to draw up terms
of peace with Germany. DuBois decided
to take advantage of the Versailles Conference and use it to focus interest on
Africa. He hoped to persuade the Allies,
including the colonial powers, Britain,
France, and Belgium, to adopt a Charter
of Human Rights for Africans. One
hundred and forty-three years after the
American Declaration of Independence,
the idea of human rights for Africans
was a new idea for many white men! In
spite of strong opposition from the
United States government, DuBois was
able to bring fifty-seven delegates to
Paris, including for the first time a
number of Africans. The *New York
Evening Globe* described the meeting as

> ... the first assembly of its kind in his-
> tory, [which] has for its object the
> drafting of an appeal to the Peace Con-
> ference [of Versailles] to give the
> Negro race of Africa a chance to de-
> velop unhindered by other races. Seated
> at long green tables in the council room
> today were Negroes in the trim uni-
> form of American Army officers, other
> American colored men in frock coats or
> business suits, polished French Negroes
> who hold public offices, Senegalese who
> sit in the French Chamber of Depu-
> ties ...

The delegates, in moderate tones, requested the establishment of a code of
law for the "protection of the natives of
Africa." The resolution passed at the
meeting urged the complete abolition of
slavery, the right of Africans to own
land, the right of Africans to participate in colonial government, and the
right of all Africans to an education in
their own language. The immediate
achievement of this congress was small,
but it was important because it brought
together Negro American leaders and
Africans, and because it set an idea before the new leaders and students of the
colonial countries.

Two years later, in 1921, the Second
Pan-African Congress was held. This
time the majority of the delegates were
Africans. DuBois was still the leading
figure and formulated a "Declaration to
the World" in which he proclaimed that
"the absolute equality of races, physical, political, and social, is the founding
stone of human advancement." DuBois
continued his work until the Great Depression cut off his source of funds
(largely wealthy American Negroes)
and broke the back of his movement. Before the Fifth Pan-African Congress in
1945 the world was transformed by
events which changed the campaign for
African advancement and independence
from the dreams of pioneers like DuBois
to the strenuous activities of energetic
African politicians.

Marcus Aurelius Garvey (1887–1940)

DuBois and his colleagues were a frail
crust of intellectuals on the fringes of
Negro discontent. Another man, of another type, was to capture and to hold
the imagination and the emotions of the
masses. The first modern Negro mass
movement was the personal creation of
a Jamaican, Marcus Aurelius Garvey,
who in the 1920's operated from Harlem
in New York City. The poor son of a
poor man, Garvey had little education
and few opportunities, yet by the time
he was thirty-three years old his name
was a household word among both
American Negroes and Africans.

As a young man Garvey traveled
through the Caribbean and Central
America. Everywhere he went he saw
black men living in poverty and subjec-
tion, and was "sickened with fever and
sick at heart over appeals from his people for help on their behalf." In 1912
Garvey went to London where he min-
gled with Egyptian nationalists lobbying for independence. Garvey learned
an important lesson: Men could organize a campaign against poverty and oppression. He returned to Jamaica

transformed by a vision which he expressed with characteristic flamboyance:

> My brain was afire [with the idea of] uniting all the Negro peoples of the world into one great body to establish a country and government absolutely their own.

Garvey saw

> ... a new world of black men, not peons, serfs, dogs, and slaves, but a nation of sturdy men making their impress upon civilisation and causing a new light to dawn upon the human race.

Burning with fervor and fury, Garvey founded the Universal Negro Improvement and Conservation Association and African Communities League in August 1914. The day of the beginning of World War I—the war which spelled the end of European domination of the world— also marked the beginning of the first modern militant Negro movement. Jamaica was too small for Garvey. In 1916 he came to New York and in Harlem established the headquarters of his movement.

In the years that followed, Garvey preached his message to all who would hear him, and even to those who wouldn't: "Africa must be redeemed, and all of us pledge our manhood, our wealth, and our blood to this sacred cause. . . . If Europe is for the Europeans, then Africa shall be for the black peoples of the world." Garvey's words inspired today's slogan: "Africa for the Africans."

Garvey was a racist as well as a nationalist. As far as he was concerned, the blacker the man the better. He believed in segregation and used the same arguments as white racists to oppose intermarriage or social mixing of black and white. For Garvey the solution to the problem of segregation in the Americas and colonialism in Africa was the rule by black men of a single country—Africa.

In order to realize his dreams, Garvey in 1920 called an International Convention which drew black men from Africa and all other parts of the world. The public highlight of the convention was a huge parade through the streets of an astonished and applauding Harlem. At the head strode the African Legion, in uniforms of dark blue with narrow red trouser stripes, followed by the Black Cross Nurses, dressed in white. The convention elected Garvey Provisional President of Africa. The mayor of Monrovia, Liberia, who was at the conference, became Secretary of State, while a Negro actress was dubbed Lady Commander of the Sublime Order of the Nile. Garvey addressed 25,000 cheering Negroes at Madison Square Garden, telling them: "We are the descendants of a suffering people, we are the descendants of a people determined to suffer no longer."

Garvey was obsessed with color. To build up a Negro financial empire and to transport Negroes back to Africa, Garvey founded the Black Star Line, a steamship company owned by Negroes whose ships were captained by Negroes. (Today the steamship line of Ghana is called the Black Star Line in living testimony to the pioneer of black nationalism.) The *Negro World*, Garvey's newspaper, refused to accept advertisements for skin bleach and hair straighteners. Instead it advertised black dolls and carried pronouncements issued by the African Orthodox Church, which worshiped a black God, a black Christ, and a black Virgin Mary.

Three years after his triumph at the International Convention Garvey was found guilty of mail fraud. The facts of the case are confused and confusing. Three things are clear. First, Garvey was not trying to obtain money for personal gain. Second, he had surrounded himself with incompetents who miserably mismanaged the Black Star Line and other undertakings of the Universal Negro Improvement Association. Third, the money of Negro investors was irresponsibly solicited and spent. Garvey refused the help of a lawyer. After four years in prison he was deported from the United States to Jamaica. Without the great personal magnetism of its founder, the whole Garvey movement, badly organized as it was, swiftly collapsed.

Garvey's tempestuous career, the bitterness with which he clashed with his foes, the gaudy uniforms and elaborate orders and titles of his movement all appear somewhat ridiculous today. In his own time, however, Garvey was revolutionary and startling. Nearly all the ideas of African leaders today were espoused by Garvey more than forty years ago. Two West Africans who later led their countries to independence, Nnamdi Azikiwe of Nigeria and Kwame Nkrumah of Ghana, acknowledged their passionate interest in Garvey and his followers when they studied in the United States in the 1930's. They, together with many other present-day African leaders, read and were inspired by *The Philosophy and Opinions of Marcus Aurelius Garvey.*

Garvey saw that Africans needed the encouragement and the self-respect that would go with their own country, capital, statesmen, writers, artists, stock exchanges, and armies. Among Africans Garvey became, and has remained, a symbol of black revival.

Stirrings in Africa

The first stirrings of Africans under colonial rule took place at the very time DuBois was addressing conferences in London and Paris and Garvey was haranguing crowds in Harlem. Protest took two forms. On the one hand the lawyers, doctors, teachers, and clerks of the tiny African upper class organized small political groups. On the other hand the workers and peasants looked for a leader who would relieve them of the burdens of colonial rule—taxes, slums, and foreign masters.

African Churches and Prophets

Many Africans sought and found an outlet for their frustrations in fervent religious revivals. Africans raised in the religious atmosphere of tribal societies were ready to follow African preachers and prophets who had changed Protestant Christianity into a fundamentalist African faith. Converts to Christianity broke away from Protestant mission churches to found separate African denominations. New black prophets claimed divine powers. Like traditional African priests, they claimed the ability to heal the sick and to intercede with God. These prophets preached a heaven of black men, guarded by black angels and governed by a black Christ. It took little urging to persuade Africans that they were the lost children of Israel, oppressed by white task masters. Prophets became the leaders of thousands, promising to show their fanatic followers the way to the promised land.

African separatist sects were called "Ethiopian" churches and their members "Ethiopians." Of course they were not Ethiopian at all, but took the name because Ethiopia represented fifteen hundred years of African civilization, Christianity, and independence. The Ethiopian churches and black prophets flourished in the settler countries where advancement was blocked, becoming a safety valve for the frustrations of Africans. South Africa has the longest and the liveliest record, with Congo and the Rhodesias close behind.

John Chilembwe

In 1892 an eccentric Englishman, John Booth, came to Africa as a missionary. In the tradition of English religious dissent, he bitterly opposed British colonial rule in Africa. Searching for support in his efforts to restore African independence, Booth, with a young African colleague, John Chilembwe, journeyed to the United States. In America the two parted, Chilembwe remaining to study at Negro colleges in the South. In the early 1900's Chilembwe returned to Africa imbued with a belief in African freedom and a Negro revival, learned from his American Negro friends. With the aid of American Negro missionaries and American funds, Chilembwe founded the Providence Industrial Mission in Nyasaland.

Chilembwe's preaching attracted many followers. After the outbreak of World War I he denounced British plans to draft Nyasaland Africans to fight German soldiers in neighboring Tanganyika. "We understand," wrote Chilembwe, "that we have been invited to shed our innocent blood in this World War . . . In time of peace everything for Europeans only. And instead of honour we suffer humiliation with names contemptible. But in time of war it is found that we are needed to share hardships and shed our blood in equality." His pleas were ignored. In 1915 Chilembwe led a revolt against the British. It failed, and Chilembwe was slain in the fighting.

Simon Kibangu, and Others

The suddenness, force, and fervor of the prophet revivals is shown in the story of Simon Kibangu and his followers. In 1921 an obscure carpenter, Kibangu, a Congo Christian, claimed to have received a vision calling upon him to go forth and heal the sick. Followers soon gathered around him and thousands upon thousands of Congolese came to be healed and to wonder at the divinely appointed Simon. The European missionary churches of Congo were deserted as converts flocked to Kibanguist meetings in the towns and villages.

Like other Christian revivals, the Kibangu movement was both puritanical and militant. African religious symbols were torn from African huts and replaced by the cross. Surplus wives were discarded as chiefs and their people were baptized as Christians. As the Ki-

bangu movement took on a political tinge, the Belgian colonial government became alarmed. Kibangu and his disciples, conscious of their righteousness, compared their work to the fight of David against Goliath. Workers deserted plantations as the radical idea of equality began to spread. "Onward, Christian Soldiers" became a fervent revolutionary song. Planters and European merchants panicked and pressed the colonial government to act.

The Belgians sought to arrest Kibangu. In a village near Leopoldville soldiers of the Congo's Force Publique started a riot by firing on the crowd around the prophet, and then proceeded to loot the village. In the confusion Kibangu escaped. When martial law was declared by an uncertain government, Kibangu gave himself up. At the village of Kambo hundreds of Africans chanted around a huge bonfire as Kibangu and his disciples were led away to prison.

At his trial Simon was accused of inciting blacks to hate whites, of gathering rebellious crowds by posing as God's prophet, and of preaching the subversive doctrine of a God more powerful than the State. The court admitted that Kibangu had never in any way organized a rebellion or translated hostility into action. Yet for his preaching Kibangu was sentenced to death. While European traders bayed for the full penalty, Protestant missionaries pleaded for clemency. Kibangu was jailed for life. He died in a Congo prison in 1950.

There were many others. Elijah Shembe, founder of the Nazarite (Ethiopian) Church of South Africa, expected that all white men would be turned away from the Gate of Heaven "because they, as rich men, have already received their good things." The Watchtower movement, started by fundamentalist Jehovah's Witnesses from the United States, spread rapidly through Nyasaland and the Rhodesias. Under the name of Kitawala the same doctrines were introduced into the Belgian Congo by a prophet who called himself Mwana Lesa, "the Son of God." Africans stirred restlessly throughout Central Africa, and the colonial governments acted swiftly to protect their rule. Mwana Lesa was hanged in Northern Rhodesia in 1926, one of many who were martyrs to their cause.

Although the prophet movements were an expression of African discontent, they nevertheless opposed colonial government improvements in education and medicine. The followers of Simon Kibangu refused to take medicine because Kibangu himself had received divine powers to heal the sick. Followers of a prophet often refused to pay taxes and regarded secular governments with contempt. Obedience to the prophet's teachings, ensuring salvation, was more important than improvement on earth. The fanatic emotional state of the followers of these movements clearly rendered them dangerous to colonial regimes, and they were accordingly suppressed.

More recently African governments have had trouble with the sects. In Northern Rhodesia the Lumpa sect led by Alice Lenshina, a prophetess, grew and flourished among the Bemba people. Lenshina instructed her devoted followers to organize cooperatives and work for self-improvement, but to take no part in politics. This did not sit very well with the fervent young organizers of Kenneth Kaunda's United National Independence Party (UNIP), who were trying to mobilize everyone behind the Kaunda government, newly in power just before independence. In July 1964, violence flared between UNIP youths and the Lumpas. Police were dispatched, riots began, and finally Kaunda ordered the army to put down the disorders. To defuse the situation, Lenshina was imprisoned, the militant UNIP youth group was restrained, and its local leaders were sent to other parts of the country.

The New African Elite

After World War I an increasing number of Africans acquired European and American university educations and embarked upon professional careers in Africa, becoming lawyers, doctors, teachers, and government civil servants. The professional men, together with a growing number of those who had become rich in trade and farming, formed a new upper class, an elite. Some of these men were the sons of traditional African rulers educated to rule in their fathers' place. Others were the talented sons of Christians who had lost their place in tribal society and who were encouraged by their missionary teachers to seek an education abroad.

The African business and professional men were city people to the core. Aspiring to live like the Europeans from whom they had learned so much, they ate roast beef and potatoes, drank imported French wine, wore stiff white collars and ties to work under the hot African sun, carried umbrellas, and mixed drinks on their verandas. Volumes of Shakespeare and Baudelaire replaced the village elder telling stories of the past; the Bible and modern science took the place of tribal religions and beliefs.

The efforts of these few Africans to gain entry into European colonial society met with varied receptions. In Africa under French rule, "civilized" Africans were accepted as equals by the French. In Dakar, the capital of French West Africa, the fashionable quarters were open to both black and white, provided that the African could show that he was sufficiently French. The reverse was true in the settler areas where racial segregation was rigidly imposed, regardless of a man's personal qualities or qualifications. In the other British colonies Africans were encouraged to become educated and qualify as lawyers, doctors, and teachers, but they were never accepted as social equals.

Educated Africans were suspended between colonial society, from which they were barred, and traditional Africa, to which they did not want to return. As the educated African tried to gain acceptance by the Europeans from whom he had learned his new ways, he lost touch with the mass of uneducated Africans. Clerks at the Rhodesian mines were regarded by the pit miners as "company stooges." On the other hand an African lawyer who pleaded for the right of African workers to strike was considered by Europeans to be an agitator who didn't appreciate the education and status he had been granted. In politics, as in culture, the "assimilated" African was caught across an unbridgeable gap.

Early African Political Groups

While prophets and priests were leading religious parades through the streets and preaching salvation around village bonfires, lawyers and doctors, clerks and teachers were founding small political groups. These organizations did not represent the mass of the people at all, but they achieved some important goals. They persuaded colonial governments in Africa to allow black men to become members of advisory bodies and even sometimes of legislative councils. They established the idea that Africans could and should participate in government and, most important of all, that a new generation of men, who were not chiefs and who were cast in a different mold, could speak on behalf of fellow Africans.

In the French colonies political organizations for educated Africans were prohibited before World War II. Throughout French Africa alumni associations served as camouflage for political parties. Some students from the Fouta Djallon of Guinea requested permission of the authorities to form a club called The Voice of the Highlanders, on the grounds that it would "help them to overcome their shyness."

Touched by this humble and seemingly innocent request, French officials allowed the group to organize. It later became the Socialist Party of Guinea.

The first attempt to form a national political party in an African country took place in 1912 in South Africa. Pixley Seme, a brilliant South African who had been educated at Columbia University in New York, succeeded in bringing together men of all groups (Xhosa, Zulu, Sotho, and many others) to form a single organization. Seme's South African Native National Congress had an Upper House (Senate) for African chiefs and a Lower House of lawyers and merchants, who ran the organization. Until World War II the Congress spoke with a voice of moderation, requesting such reforms as the right to vote and the right to buy land. An earlier group, the Native United Political Association of the Transvaal, had petitioned King Edward VII of England for the repeal of a law prohibiting "aboriginal natives" from using the sidewalks. This early period was a low point in African confidence. Albert Luthuli, former President of the banned African National Congress, remembers singing this song just after the passage of the 1913 Land Act, which prohibited Africans from purchasing land outside the small African reserves:

Where are we Africans?
We seem to be nowhere,
We shall wander, and wander, and
   wander.
How far shall we go?
Behold, people of Africa, what a burden
   we bear!
We shall wander, and wander, and
   wander.
The Englishman this side, the
   Afrikaner this side,
The German this side, the German this
   side,
We shall wander, and wander, and
   wander.
How far shall we go?
Behold, people of Africa, what a burden
   we bear!

Over the years African movements became more militant. In the 1920's the famous Clements Kadalie led hundreds of thousands of black South Africans in his Industrial and Commercial Union. Like Garvey's Universal Negro Improvement Association it too hinged on one man and collapsed under the combined pressure of government hostility, incompetence, and quarreling among the leaders.

West Africa, like South Africa, had a long tradition of European influence and missionary education. In both regions the professional men had developed political skills—committee organization, fund raising, public relations and publicity, controlling meetings, and speaking to crowds. As early as 1897 rich Gold Coast chiefs and lawyers had founded the Aborigines Rights' Protection Society to bar the sale of their land to Europeans. In 1920 the West African National Congress was formed, with headquarters in Accra, Gold Coast, and branches in Nigeria, Sierra Leone, and Gambia. The founder was J. Casely-Hayford, a lawyer from the Gold Coast. A similar organization, the Nigerian National Democratic Party, was set up in Lagos by another black man, Herbert Macaulay.

Two Generations

The names of today's black African leaders—Nnamdi Azikiwe, Kwame Nkrumah, Sékou Touré, Jomo Kenyatta, Tafawa Balewa—are African, not European. This is no coincidence, for while these leaders are proudly African, the leaders of the first generation under colonial rule tried proudly to be European. Today many Africans question whether this first generation of lawyers, teachers, and clerks ever really wanted African independence. They have tagged it "moderate" and willing to compromise with what they regard as the absolute evil of colonialism.

The first colonial generation did perform a valuable service. While during the 1920's and 1930's the mass frustrations of Africans erupted in strikes, religious revivals, and sporadic violence, the voices of chiefs and lawyers kept open the channels of communication and the hope of compromise. Their organizations nominated the first Africans to run for political office, taking the first small step toward self-government. They bargained with European colonial officials, who for the first time met Africans who spoke to them on their own terms in their own language. Africans and Europeans had begun to negotiate as equals.

However, conditions in Africa were changing rapidly, and new men were needed for new times. By the late 1930's young men such as Nnamdi Azikiwe, Kwame Nkrumah, and Jomo Kenyatta were openly dissatisfied with both colonial rule and the timid opposition to it led by lawyers with European names. The chance of the Young Turks was soon to come. While these students huddled with Negro intellectuals in Harlem or Jamaican socialists in London, the Ethiopian churches and wild-eyed prophets led the first mass protests in Africa and the professional men laid the foundations for African self-government by discussing municipal budgets in Accra. Where the prophets and the preachers failed, the returning student-politicians succeeded. These new men combined the mass following of Kibangu and the political skill of Casely-Hayford with the passion of Garvey and the ideals of DuBois. All the earlier movements flowed together like streams into a river to produce the torrent of African nationalism of our own day.

PROBLEMS

1. Why did *American* Negroes speak for the African during the early years of colonial rule in Africa? Were W. E. B. DuBois and his fellow intellectuals inconsistent in affirming that there should be no distinction between the races and then becoming concerned about Africans because they were black men like themselves?

2. Do you think Marcus Garvey was really interested in Africa? What did Africa represent to American Negroes? Did they have a clear idea of what was happening in Africa in 1920? Did other Americans?

3. The Bantu prophets were the first messengers of the African revival in Central and Southern Africa. Why did men of religion, rather than men of business or men of politics, first arouse Africans? Were the doctrines preached by Kibangu, Mwana Lesa, and the others the kind of beliefs that would help Africans find a place in the modern world of towns and machines?

4. Suppose it is the year 1924 and you are Governor-General of the Belgian Congo. In the towns Congolese in large and growing numbers are not coming to work, while village peasants refuse to pay their tax, saying, "It will make no difference when I am saved." An unknown man named Kibangu is going from village to village preaching black divinity. All the Belgian government workers, traders, and missionaries are on the verge of panic. What would you do?

5. Collect newspaper clippings of the statements made by American Negro leaders today and compare them with the statements of Marcus Garvey. Is the tone different? Do American Negroes today consider Africa their homeland? Have there been any "back-to-Africa" movements since Garvey?

READING SUGGESTIONS

Edmund D. Cronin, *Black Moses,* University of Wisconsin Press, paper.

W. E. B. DuBois, *Souls of Black Folk,* McClure, 1903; Crest, paper.

Edward Roux, *Time Longer than Rope,* Gollancz (London), 1948.

chapter 8

THE POLITICAL KINGDOM

Seek ye first the political kingdom.

—KWAME NKRUMAH

A middle-class elite, without the battering-ram of the illiterate masses, can never hope to smash the forces of colonialism. Such a thing can be achieved only by a united people organized in a disciplined political party and led by that party.

—KWAME NKRUMAH

The young leaders of postwar Africa believed passionately that political action was the key to their success. By striking directly at the colonial government of the Europeans, Africans could with a single sweep win back their place in the sun. Reforms were no longer enough. National independence for each colony meant, in the minds of the African leaders, the restoration of rights and dignity. Independence seemed the answer to economic and social discrimination, and a simple refutation of the white superiority preached for so long by colonialists and particularly by white settlers.

The battering ram of African nationalism was the mass political party. In almost every colony discontent and the demand for independence were to be embodied in a *single* national party. For the first time, large numbers of Africans were enlisted to oppose European rule in an organized way. African political parties were mass parties. However, the African parties were more than casual associations of people with similar interests. The African parties which organized and led the campaign for independence were fervently and devotedly regarded, by leaders and followers alike, as the hope of African resurrection.

The mass party came to represent the idea of the nation and of national unity in each colony. The feeling of national unity had to be built from scratch in African countries composed of many different peoples arbitrarily pulled together. Common opposition to European rule rallied illiterate Africans from different tribal groups. Trade unions, student groups, tribal associations, and many other African organizations became affiliated with the political party, uniting all African groups in a single campaign for independence. Inevitably, the single political party and its leaders remained to rule after independence.

What Is African Nationalism?

Nationalism in Africa is the desire of an African people to have an independent government in order to control its own affairs. In Africa the primary aim of nationalists was to drive European rulers out of African countries. The campaign against European rule was and is called "anticolonialism."

In Africa, nationalism also means the effort to create a nation by uniting the peoples within a country's boundaries. The peoples within an African country, unlike Frenchmen, Russians, Chinese, or Americans, do not share a common culture or history. Many African peoples were divided by colonial boundaries. For example, the Ewe are divided between Ghana and Togo, the Somali between Somalia, Kenya, and Ethiopia, and the Lunda between (former Belgian) Congo, Angola, and Zambia (former Northern Rhodesia). The number of tribal groups in an African country is seldom less than ten and sometimes more than one hundred. If African nationalists were to claim the support of "the people," they had to unite the different groups behind them. "Unity" took its place beside "independence" as a nationalist aim.

Nationalism was a deeply felt emotion for many Africans. Leaders took the passion and fervor of Marcus Garvey and Simon Kibangu, and transmitted it to the crowds. Nationalism gained the force of a religion.

The Young Men Take Over

The first expressions of African nationalism had come during the 1920's and 1930's from intellectuals, mainly lawyers, who were far removed from their fellow Africans in the villages. These early nationalists were in fact more like Europeans than like Africans. They advocated moderation and praised the benefits of a colonial rule that "raised Africans from their benighted condition." They argued that the people had to be educated before they could claim the privileges of citizenship in a modern nation and that this would certainly take a long time. Meanwhile the

This young man on his way to work carries the flag of new Tanzania. His clean white shirt and the newspaper in his pocket mark him as one of the educated elite. (*David R. Giltrow.*)

few educated Africans tried to persuade Europeans that someday Africans would claim equality with them. These moderates spoke on behalf of the peasant and the city worker, but never spoke with him. They were out of touch with the people they wanted to represent.

In the 1940's young people, and particularly those few who had studied in England, France, and America, reacted strongly against this moderate approach. The new leaders directed their attention to the Africans of town and village, not to the European officials. They were no longer content to accept the tone of persuasion and gradual reform, but were set on direct action toward the goal of independence. The new atmosphere was summed up in the tone of the slogan of Gold Coast (Ghana) nationalists: "Self-government NOW!"

Just after the end of World War II in 1945, Africans gathered in Manchester, England, to spell out a strategy for the winning of African independence. The Atlantic Charter of Franklin Roosevelt and Winston Churchill, affirming "the right of all peoples to choose the form of government under which they may live," and the founding of the United Nations encouraged Africans to organize their campaign. Two hundred black delegates poured into Manchester from all over the English-speaking world. Unlike earlier Pan-African Congresses this one included young politicians, labor leaders, heads of farmers' organizations, and students who were in touch with the African "grass roots." The leaders at Manchester are now famous men—George Padmore from the West Indies, Jomo Kenyatta of Kenya, Peter Abrahams of South Africa, Nnamdi Azikiwe, the radical Nigerian editor of the *West African Pilot,* and a young man named Kwame Nkrumah. W. E. B. DuBois, vigorous at seventy-three, was flown across the Atlantic to Manchester to be the grand old man of the meeting.

The Manchester Congress marked the beginning of militant African nationalism. Many leaders who had felt isolated were encouraged by the efforts of those in other countries. The tone of African leaders changed from pleading and compromise to impatience and demand. The congress passed innumerable resolutions spelling out colonial misdeeds and a positive program of reform, such as freedom of the press (most colonies had official press censorship) and universal free education.

The Manchester Congress was not all talk, for the young politicians were

A village political meeting in Tanganyika. Only by going to the people could city politicians build up the support needed to win independence. (*Damon Kletzian.*)

determined to organize in Africa. Within months they had hastened back to the shantytowns and port cities to begin the long job of building organized and powerful nationalist parties.

These new leaders were professional politicians who devoted all their time and energy to the nationalist cause. Their very livelihood depended on the support of the people, for without the contributions of African sympathizers —a bed for the night, a meal, vegetables, or a few pennies in dues to the new party—the politicians were just unemployed Africans and their cause was lost. The leaders had to make publicity for themselves, and they had to produce results.

The men of this second, postwar generation of African nationalists today rule Africa. They were the first to voice rigid opposition to colonialism, and to insist on independence. They built the political party machines and led the guerilla wars. Starting as local politicians and city bosses, many of them became national heroes, and later statesmen.

The Decline of the Chiefs

Colonial rule in Africa had not destroyed the position of the chiefs, although migration to the cities and the spread of education and ideas had eroded their traditional influence. Attempting to preserve their authority, the chiefs became agents of the colonial administration and supported the moderate demands of the intellectuals. Because the chiefs were allies of the administration and the moderates, they were political enemies of the new nationalists.

The stakes in the political battle between the chiefs and the nationalist city politicians were high—nothing less than the loyalty of the mass of Africans, particularly the great majority who were village peasants. If village Africans remained loyal to their chiefs, the nationalists could be dismissed by colonial officials as nothing more than a disgruntled city minority out of touch with the people.

The cards were in fact stacked against the chiefs. The colonial regimes tried to keep Africans loyal to their traditional rulers, while at the same time developing a modern export economy and educating Africans. This contradictory policy did not work and ended in the destruction of the political power of the chiefs. An African clerk, mine laborer, or war veteran could not be expected to pay attention to his tribal chief while working in a city far from home. He certainly was not going to pay part of his hard-won earnings to the chief's treasury. Men schooled by missionaries who were dedicated to freeing their charges from "heathen superstition" were not likely to accept the claim of a chief to have divine powers or an "in" with the tribal gods, and thus could not accept the chief's religious claim to political authority.

"One man, one vote" was a revolutionary slogan of the new politicians. In this plebiscite in Cameroun, the writing on the ballot box poses in Hausa, Fulani, and Kanuri the question, "Are you in favor of deciding the future of Northern Cameroon at a later date?" The majority voted "yes." (*United Nations.*)

The Mass Party

The new nationalist politicians were faced with the task of organizing parties strong enough to win independence. In Kwame Nkrumah's powerful language, quoted at the head of this chapter, the politician had to build "the battering ram of the illiterate masses" to "smash the forces of colonialism." Most of the nationalist leaders were spectacularly successful.

The nationalists realized that they needed discipline, for violence and terrorism would only bring out the colonial police. Africans in the villages and the shantytowns had to be taught about the party—its purposes and its plans for reform. Party meetings, a party newspaper (for those who could read or be read to), rallies, slogans, and flags made the party known and drew men to its banner. Party members had to be organized and convinced of the need for

strikes, demonstrations, and voting. This took time and money, and a core of trained and dedicated party workers. Most of all, the party needed a leader. Inevitably there arose in many colonies a single leader who became the focus of mass hopes, a man to be both the Great Emancipator and the Father of His Country.

All this would work only where the colonial government allowed Africans to organize, to demonstrate, and to speak their minds in print and in public. In the Belgian Congo and the Portuguese colonies Africans had no political rights. In settler Africa—Algeria, South Africa, Southern Rhodesia, and Kenya before 1958—settlers pressured the colonial government to oppose African independence and suppress nationalist activity. As a result, these countries have been plagued with violence and revolt (see Chapter 9). The two independent African states, Ethiopia and Liberia, have had no nationalist parties either (see Chapter 10). African nationalism and the mass party were in great measure results of the changes brought about by colonial governments.

Party Organization

The matter of party organization may not seem very important or exciting. Yet the stuff of political power—"who really runs the party"—is a matter of organization. Most African nations are now controlled by a single party. Whether these states are responsive to the will of their people or not depends on the character of the party itself.

Most African parties organized their followers through a tightly knit network of committees. The Democratic Party of Guinea (PDG) is the best example. In every village and city block party members formed a branch, or cell. Party members attended meetings to listen to the opinions and instructions presented by their leaders. The main job of the cells was to enlist more supporters from among their friends and neighbors, to collect dues, and to get out the vote if the colonial administration offered an election. The Democratic Party of Guinea, and others like it, became very successful political machines.

Full-time party workers, called *militants* in French, were responsible for seeing that the decisions of party leaders were somehow translated into action. The *militants* were the real bread-and-butter men of the party. If they did their job well, party plans became strikes, demonstrations, and election victories. If they failed, the party's leaders were left without mass support. Often the party relied on local bigwigs of traditional importance, such as tribal chiefs, *marabouts* (Moslem religious leaders in West Africa), or local headmen, all of whom could produce cash or a large block of votes if properly flattered and rewarded.

African parties were and are run by a central committee, which meets frequently. At such meetings the party leader discusses party policy with his most trusted advisers and decides the program and strategy of the party. African countries had no public opinion polls to tell party planners what the people wanted. Most African newspapers were propaganda, reflecting only the views of the political party that published them. Party leaders had to rely on intuition, "feel," and the reports of party workers in making decisions, often not knowing what public reaction would be to a new policy. The successful African politicians were those with a sensitive "feel" for the wishes of the black man in the street.

After independence, when the party is running the country, it is more difficult to make sure that the party is responsive to the wishes of the people (see Chapter 17).

The "Total" Party

African nationalist parties were not and are not totalitarian, for they do not try to control the beliefs and the activities of their members to the same extent as Communist or Fascist parties. Yet they are "total" parties.

Being a party member in the days before independence was a much more significant commitment for an African than for an American Republican or Democrat. Day in and day out the "struggle against colonialism" was kept before his mind, as the party tried to increase the "consciousness" of its rank and file. Party songs, party uniforms, and party cards constantly reminded an African of his role as a party member and of his new identity as an African nationalist. The party perhaps ran the local beer hall, interceded with the white boss for a longer vacation, organized Sunday picnics, and generally took up much of a member's daily life.

In addition to trying to monopolize the attention of their members, the

African nationalist parties were "total" because they tried to bring all other African organizations under the wing of the party. Imagine the AFL-CIO, the Chamber of Commerce, the American Legion, the Boy Scouts, and the women's clubs all part of a single political party and working for a single political end. This gives some idea of the situation in countries such as Guinea, Tunisia, or Tanganyika where the nationalists were well-organized.

Most Africans were still loyal to their fellow tribesmen and to their tribal elders. The political parties tried to use local tribal associations by making them part of the nationalist movement. In the city of Abidjan, in Ivory Coast, local branches of the dominant Democratic Party of Ivory Coast (PDCI) were really associations of fellow tribesmen who happened to live in the same neighborhood, just as Americans of Italian or Irish or German descent tend to live together in the United States. Although tribal loyalties often divide Africans within a country, they were also harnessed to the cause of the nationalist party.

Labor unions were part and parcel of the nationalist parties. It is not correct to say that the unions were taken over by the nationalist politicians, because often the reverse was true and union men became political leaders. Labor unions were a critical part of the nationalist movement because they included those African workers with key jobs. Mass parties such as the Convention People's Party of Gold Coast (Ghana), the Democratic Party of Guinea, and Neo-Destour of Tunisia worked with the unions to organize strikes designed to cripple the colonial economy. Sékou Touré of Guinea and Tom Mboya of Kenya began their careers as labor union leaders and took their followers with them into the nationalist parties.

The mass parties developed a whole arsenal of party organizations to recruit different kinds of members. Almost all of them had a women's group, particularly important in West Africa where women were traditionally active in commerce and politics. All had a youth organization, which acted as a strong-arm squad to pressure recalcitrant party members to vote, to carry out boycotts, and to stay away from work when a strike had been called. Many parties had student groups, which were expected to provide the brains of the party in the future.

Why did the mass parties try to include and control all other organizations? During the campaign for independence African leaders had to prove that their demands for self-government were more than demands for personal power. The burden of proof was on African nationalists to show the colonial government that they represented all groups, not just a tiny educated minority. They had to show that the peoples of their country were united in their demands. Colonialists had assumed that African countries were a jumble of tribes held together by European administrators—not nations capable of self-government—and that the end of colonial rule would mean local squabbles and tribal warfare. This view was probably quite correct when the Europeans first partitioned Africa, but it failed to note the unifying effect of those very changes in communication, economy, and education brought about by colonial rule itself. Nationalist leaders had to mold unity, or at least cooperation, among the various peoples of their country. Some, like Nkrumah and the Nigerian leaders, succeeded, at least temporarily. Others, like Kasavubu and Lumumba in Congo, failed.

The final reason for the total nature of African nationalist parties was the total nature of the colonial regime they opposed. In Africa, export and mining companies worked very closely with the officials, as did the churches and even the schools, which were staffed by

An African street orator in Leopoldville.
Most of the leaders of the independence
movement were young men. (*United
Nations.*)

missionaries from the "mother country."
The colonial "Establishment" of officials, businessmen, missionaries, and
(in some countries) settlers seemed to
ordinary Africans to be a single machine. If a man wanted to sell his land,
he had to get the approval of the District Commissioner. If he wanted a
raise, his union leaders had to negotiate
with officials as well as employer. His
son's missionary teacher was paid by
the government. To deal with what appeared to be, and usually was, the united
front of the Europeans, a single united
organization of all Africans—the mass
party—was needed.

Party Action

The African in the street had to be
persuaded to follow and obey new nationalist leaders and local party acti-
vists, rather than tribal chiefs and
colonial officials. He had to be taught
not to think in terms of his tribe.
Finally, he had to be persuaded that
"colonialism" was the enemy and that

national independence would further
his desires for higher wages, lower
taxes and the good things of life. The
easiest way to do this was not by cir-
culating newspapers, pamphlets, and
books, because many Africans could not
read them; it was by holding meetings,
rallies, meetings, picnics, and more
meetings.

The mass party carried out the first
essential task of any government: It
organized the nation. Party workers
took the city-bred gospel of nationalism
and spread it to the villages of the bush,
by truck, by bicycle, and on foot. Picture a huge baobab tree in a village
clearing, surrounded by the round
thatch houses of the village. From the
top branch hangs a party flag, and the
villagers are gathered underneath to
take advantage of the scanty shade.
Drummers beat messages in the wait
before the speakers arrive, while village
women trot through a dance to keep up
the festive spirit. Perhaps an hour after
the meeting has been scheduled to begin, the party speakers drive up in a
broken-down truck which raises a pall
of dust along the dirt road. The village
headman, who is perhaps the party's
local agent as well, introduces the
speakers from the city with glowing
praise. After a party song the speeches
begin, and the villagers are addressed
in their new role of party members,
African nationalists, and citizens.

In contrast to the small village meetings designed to bring national politics
to the African peasants, massive open-
air rallies were held in the city stadiums
to publicize party campaigns. The rallies, often held at night, drew multi-
tudes to show the extent and the inten-
sity of support for the nationalist party.
Speakers whipped the crowd into a mood
to boycott the stores, or to strike, or
to refuse to obey the police.

These party campaigns were called
"positive action," a phrase used by
Kwame Nkrumah for his general strike
of 1949 in the Gold Coast. "Positive ac-

tion" meant any kind of nationalist campaign short of open violence or terrorism and was in fact the African version of Mahatma Gandhi's strategy of nonviolent resistance which proved so successful in gaining independence for India. The most powerful weapon of "positive action" was the general strike, which left trains without crews, restaurants without waiters, and docks without longshoremen. In a matter of hours, if the strike had been well organized by the party and the labor unions, the whole economy of the colony would grind to a halt. The colonial officials had either to call out the police to force the strikers back to work, or to come to terms with the African leaders.

Nationalist leaders had to keep their followers aroused — angry followers were a potent weapon in negotiations with the colonial government. Yet the nationalists also had to bargain in a reasonable way for reforms and independence. The trick, as Tom Mboya has demonstrated, was to sound like a black dragon ready to swallow colonialists on sight, and at the same time to negotiate discreetly, using the unspoken threat of violence by passionately aroused African followers to twist the arms of the officials. This proved a successful strategy for nationalists everywhere except in South Africa, Algeria, and the Portuguese colonies. The fiery oratory confused many Americans, who couldn't decide whether African leaders were irresponsible demagogues or responsible national leaders.

The Mass Party Becomes African Government

Long before they became the legal ruling party of independent nations, African mass parties were governments in fact. The party looked after its workers —even politicians must eat. In every campaign of "positive action" a few died and many were jailed, and the party supported the widows and the families of prisoners. As the party grew

in strength and its treasury with it, all those who in the eyes of the party had suffered injustice were eligible for help —a loan, a party job, a back room in which to live.

Africans in every country felt that the colonial administration, with its police, its whitewashed offices in big new buildings, and its stuffy officials, was something alien to them and directed against them. In city and village Africans turned to the local leaders of the mass party, and not to colonial officials, when they needed a house or a job, or were involved in a land dispute or a lawsuit. To the party offices, which were usually only a few back rooms in a warehouse or an old house in the African shantytown, came requests for loans and inquiries after lost relatives. One branch of the Democratic Party of Ivory Coast (PDCI) in Abidjan even ran a marriage bureau. Almost all parties had employment agencies to guide new townsmen to jobs, and legal aid offices to help Africans through the frightening experience of appearing in a white man's court. In many cities Africans would obey party orders where they would not obey the regulations of the officials. Such strong parties as Ghana's Convention People's Party, the Somali Youth League, and the Kenya African National Union organized their own police forces to preserve order in the shantytowns. Maintaining order is the basic function of any government, and the mass party had become in many respects the government of the African towns before independence.

The Mass Party and African Dignity

The mass parties, like the tribal associations and the labor unions, showed Africans that they could influence their own future. Campaigns of "positive action" against the colonial regime brought home to many Africans what they had perhaps long suspected: that men, not the gods, determine what happens in the world. By marching with

African National Congress office in Lusaka, Zambia. A butcher shop shares the small and modest building. (*Damon Kletzian.*)

banners through the streets and refusing to go to work Africans could force their white rulers to grant higher wages or the right to vote. If an ignorant peasant waving a placard with crude letters saying "Self-government NOW" could help force the Europeans to "go home," then that poor, illiterate African must be in some small way important. The influence of magic, the gods, and fate began to be replaced in African beliefs by the influence of living men and their actions. In this way the mass parties and their campaigns greatly speeded the psychological revolution which still continues in Africa.

The Mass Party and Independence

Those colonial governments that gave African nationalist parties a chance to organize and campaign allowed Africans to *prepare themselves* for independence. In all but the settler countries of French and British Africa the colonial government acted like a boxer who, by sparring with a less-skillful but very determined opponent, taught the novice the tricks of the trade. Through years of sparring African nationalist leaders learned the skills of negotiation and the frustrations of raising money. They

learned how to organize and how to restrain their followers. The mass parties gained experience by carrying out many tasks of government before independence. The ideas of nation and citizen began to take root in the minds of African tribesmen.

Where African nationalists were suppressed, disaster was the usual result. Congo leaders were given neither the freedom nor the time to organize and to learn the skills of government. The upshot was chaos when independence was finally and hastily thrust into African hands. Countries where the suppression continued, such as Algeria and Angola, were faced with revolution and guerilla war.

The mass nationalist parties and the young and radical men who led them determined the future of Africa in the eventful years after World War II. Because national independence was the hope of all African groups from tribal elders to factory workers, and because only the mass parties could obtain and hold independence, the party was recognized as the voice of the African nation-to-be. From opposition against colonial rule to self-government was the next short, but difficult, step.

PROBLEMS

1. You are an African nationalist leader about to address a crowd in Nigeria in 1950. Compose a five- or ten-minute speech in which you try to persuade the audience of African peasants recently moved to the city to join your political party. What will you promise them as benefits of independence? What sacrifices must they make? Will your argument be "reasonable" or "emotional"?

2. Draw a diagram (called an organization chart) showing how an African mass party is organized. Show what each level in the party does and what kind of people hold jobs at each level. Where are the decisions made?

3. Why was there usually one, and only one, mass nationalist party in most African countries? Would competition between African leaders have given the colonial government an opportunity to stay? Why did African leaders try to enlist village peasants in the party? Why did they try to bring in all other African organizations?

4. African nationalists claimed that they were only demanding for themselves the freedom which Frenchmen, Englishmen, and Americans had demanded and won many years before. Do the African slogans "Self-government NOW," "Africa for the Africans," and "One man, one vote" express ideas important to Americans? Were Africans right in saying that if France and Britain did not grant independence they would be following a double standard—democracy at home and oppression abroad? Is democracy the same thing as national independence?

READING SUGGESTIONS

Mary Benson, *The African Patriots*, Praeger, paper.

William Conton, *The African*, Heinemann (London), paper.

Alfred Hutchinson, *Road to Ghana*, Gollancz (London), 1960.

Kenneth Kaunda, *Zambia Shall Be Free*, Heinemann (London), 1962.

Gamal Abdel Nassar, *Egypt's Liberation: The Philosophy of the Revolution*, Public Affairs Press, paper.

Kwame Nkrumah, *Ghana: The Autobiography of Kwame Nkrumah*, Nelson, 1957.

Anthony Sampson, *The Treason Cage*, Heinemann (London), 1958.

chapter 9
"UHURU"

Europeans, scram out of Africa!

—TOM MBOYA,
Kenya nationalist leader

Their very discontent is a measure of
their progress.

—LORD LUGARD,
*former British Governor
of Nigeria*

Africa, which had been changing for half a century, suddenly "took off" in the years after World War II. Both colonial governments and Africans realized that the old pattern of colonial dominance was slowly but irrevocably passing away. The attitudes of Europeans and Africans toward one another were changing. Where there had been chiefs, medicine men, and peasants, now there were lawyers and ministers, students and laborers. Cities, schools, and factories brought new ideas and habits to many Africans. In the face of these changes, the independence of African countries was only a matter of time.

The Africans' demand has been constant and unyielding: full self-government for the African majority with no strings attached. Most Africans harbor little resentment for their former colonial master, and economic and cultural ties continue after independence. The African political movement was directed at colonial rule, not at Europeans as such. Only in settler areas where racial superiority was stressed and violence used by whites have Africans replied in kind.

The course of events that brought independence to almost all African countries by 1966 was not identical throughout the continent. In a few countries— Sudan, Ghana, Tunisia, Morocco—independence came rapidly after an early start. In Nigeria, Uganda, Tanganyika, and French black Africa (twelve countries) independence came a little later. In none of these countries, however, did the British or the French suppress the nationalist movement or hold out inflexibly against independence. Mass parties were allowed to organize and campaign for independence, and the transition from colony to nation was not violent, though it was often turbulent and unruly. In the Belgian Congo and the Portuguese colonies of Angola and Mozambique colonial regimes prohibited and suppressed nationalists, rigidly opposing political change, let alone African self-government.

The real diehards were and are the white settlers in Africa. In Algeria a million people died as a result of the seven years' war for independence fought against both settlers and the French Army. In Kenya 60,000 settlers stubbornly refused African demands until frustration and embitterment boiled up into the terrible Mau Mau rebellion of 1952–1954. British Central Africa—the Rhodesias and Nyasaland —was united in 1953 into a federation that gave white settlers of Southern Rhodesia even more of a ruling voice. This federation took African nationalists ten years to break. South of the Limpopo, Africa's earliest nationalists, the white Afrikaners, crushed black nationalists and imposed the racist dogma of *apartheid.*

Americans are likely to think that the colonial era in Africa lasted centuries. This is not the case. European rule in Africa was barely established by the time of World War I. Only a generation later, reeling from the destruction of World War II, Europe began the retreat from Africa. Beginning with the independence of a few isolated countries the nationalist trickle became a torrent.

The Effect of the War

Throughout these chapters the words "after World War II" keep appearing when changes in Africa are mentioned. This is neither a coincidence nor just an easy way to keep track of time. The turmoil of the war acted like a bucket of ice water on the stirring body of colonial Africa. Many Africans were drafted to fight for the British and the French. They were taken from the cities and the villages, issued clean uniforms and strong boots, and taught how to fire a gun, tend a radio receiver, or fix a truck or airplane motor. The African who reached the front saw white men bleed, die, and run away like any other living creature. The black African fired on the white enemy and found himself treated as an equal by his target.

Through wartime experiences many Africans from different colonies and traditional backgrounds came to reject, once and for all, the myth of white superiority.

Throughout the war the hopes of African leaders, soldiers, and workers for a complete change in colonial policy increased with each pronouncement of the Allied leaders. Under pressure from President Franklin Roosevelt, both Winston Churchill of Britain and General Charles de Gaulle of the Free French endorsed equality and self-determination of peoples as aims in the war against the Nazis. With the coming of peace in 1945, these hopes and pronouncements spilled over into African demands and demonstrations. Colonial administrators, often far more opposed to change than their superiors at home, reacted sharply, fearful that the new African spirit spelled the end of their rule.

The Madagascar Rebellion

Although it was not noticed, and is little known to this day, the most serious uprising in Africa just after the war was the Madagascar rebellion of 1947. Madagascar had long been governed by the French as the private estate of a few large plantation companies. While during the war many French colonial officials had worked with De Gaulle's Free French government in London, others had followed the pro-Nazi Pétain regime in occupied France. Madagascar officials had given their wholehearted support to Pétain. After the war they refused to carry out the reforms laid down in Paris, such as the abolition of forced labor and the *Indigenat* (special code of laws for natives). Despite the diehard attitude of the colonial officials, Madagascar was ready for reform. Many Malagasy (as the people of Madagascar call themselves) were literate. The island had an established university. Local political

INDEPENDENCE I: 1945

parties represented every shade of opinion—nationalist, pro-French, and even Communist.

Official obstinacy and petty tyranny mocked both African hopes and demands from Paris for reform. On March 29, 1947, French garrisons all over the island were ambushed and surrounded. Frenchmen sought protection in the city of Tananarive as the countryside passed into rebel control. Within a few weeks the French had checked the revolt and began to hunt down the African guerillas in the countryside. At least fifty thousand Malagasy were killed in the repression.

The French have tried to blame the revolt on Communists. In fact, the Communists were not nearly strong enough to have organized it. Blaming African disturbances on Communists has been a favorite tactic of colonial regimes and settlers reluctant to face the reality of African nationalism. Kenya authorities originally blamed Communists for Mau Mau. Today nationalist rebels in Angola have been labeled Communists by dictator Salazar of Portugal. The Afrikaner government of South Africa, in its Suppression of Communism Act of 1950, implicitly equates black nationalism or any challenge to white supremacy with communism. As the case of Madagascar shows, African nationalism has been, is, and will be a far more potent force than Communist propaganda.

Morocco and Tunisia

Unlike Algeria and the countries of French black Africa, which were administered from Paris as part of the French Republic, Morocco and Tunisia were considered "associated territories," almost equal in status to France. In Tunisia, nationalist movements, influenced by the Arab nationalist revival in Egypt and Syria, were strong even before 1900. Successive generations of nationalists, each one more vigorous than the last, agitated in Paris and Tunis for French withdrawal. In 1920 the Destour (Liberal-Constitutional) Party was formed by middle-class lawyers and doctors, a group much like the early leaders in Ghana and Nigeria. In the 1930's a young lawyer named Habib Bourguiba became dissatisfied with the old leadership and split to form his own party, the Neo-Destour. Like Azikiwe in Nigeria and Nkrumah in Ghana, Bourguiba published a nationalist newspaper, organized a mass party, and was thrown into jail for his activities.

Invasion by German, British, and American soldiers during the North African campaign of World War II, and the total loss of control by the French between 1942 and 1945, confirmed the belief of Tunisian nationalists that they were as capable as anybody else of running their affairs. By 1950 Tunisians no longer looked to Paris for reform. Guerilla bands began to gather. Bourguiba was again imprisoned for nationalist agitation, and other leaders of the Neo-Destour fled into exile. Fighting broke out in 1952, and for two years Tunisian terrorists harassed the French

Army. The situation soon became hopeless for the French. Unlike Algeria, Tunisia had no large group of French settlers to provide diehard opposition to a French withdrawal, and independence was granted in 1956 without a major war.

Morocco had been the last African country to fall under European control. Although a protectorate had been declared by France in 1912, the guerilla forces of Abdel Krim were not defeated until 1924. The nationalist movement in Morocco began in earnest with the formation of the Istiqlal (Independence) Party in 1944. Istiqlal succeeded in rallying both the middle class and the peasants to support its campaign for independence. The Sultan of Morocco, Mohammed V, at first refused to back Istiqlal because he feared that constitutional government would destroy his monarchy. In 1953 the French exiled the Sultan to Madagascar, making him a national hero. Istiqlal also was banned by the French, who relied on local landowners and nobles to keep Morocco in line. As in Tunisia, the men of Istiqlal, now supported in their aims by the Sultan, took to the mountains. After two years of fighting the French agreed to restore the Sultan. With Tunisia, Morocco became independent in 1956.

The Algerian War

On May 8, 1945, green-and-white Algerian flags and nationalist banners waved in a demonstration in the city of Setif. When police fired on the crowd, the demonstration became a riot, and riots soon spread to other Algerian cities. The French put down Algerian nationalism with artillery and bombs.

By 1950, after 100 years of French rule, a million Europeans were living in Algeria. While Frenchmen, and particularly the Algerian settlers, called *colons* or *pied-noirs* (black feet), thought of France and Algeria as "one and indivisible," the 9 million Algerian

Moslems thought otherwise. The best land, the factories, the schools, the government jobs—all were held by the *colons* for the benefit of the *colons* and France. The wealth of the *colons* was in alarming contrast to the poverty and misery of Moslem Algerians. France ruled through the French Army and the French Foreign Legion, and showed no sign of withdrawing peacefully.

On November 1, 1954, a young French sergeant in the town of Bathaq received a phone call telling him that the French Army barracks had been attacked and the arsenal raided for guns and ammunition. Radio Cairo, the voice of Arab nationalism, announced: "At one o'clock this morning Algeria began to live a worthy and honorable life." The Algerian war against the French, which was to last eight years and take a million lives, had begun.

The Algerian guerillas were the army of the National Liberation Front (FLN). The soldiers of the FLN were called simply *fellagha*, or peasants. They were recruited from the hundreds of thousands of young Algerians who had no land, no jobs, and no future.

Eight years of terror and counterterror, reprisal and counterreprisal ended with the desperate attempts of the *colons* to defy Paris and seize Algeria for themselves. In 1962 the Secret Army Organization (OAS) blew up hospitals, schools, and libraries in a final attempt to set up a settler military dictatorship free of control from Paris. But General de Gaulle, now the French President, was prepared to negotiate with the leaders of the FLN. In July 1962 Algeria became an independent republic.

French Black Africa Becomes Twelve Nations

In 1944 Charles de Gaulle, leader of the Free French, called a conference to formulate a postwar policy for French Africa. Administrators from all the

Recruits of the Algerian FLN (National Liberation Front) prepare to fight the French. North Africa's rugged hills and mountains hid the guerillas during their successful seven years' war. *(Associated Press Photo.)*

French territories met in Brazzaville, in the French Congo. Two principles were laid down. Reforms were necessary and would be carried out. Independence could not be considered. The conference declared:

> The finishing of the work of civilization accomplished by France in the colonies precludes any idea of autonomy, any possibility of evolution outside the French structure of the Empire. Eventual establishment of independent governments in the colonies, even in the long run, is out of the question.

France's African subjects had other ideas. African leaders in Paris met to address a manifesto to the French people. Within weeks thousands of Africans had assembled in Bamako, the capital of the French Soudan (now Mali), to form an African mass party. The name of the new party was the Rassemble-ment Democratique Africaine (African Democratic Union), or RDA. Its leaders and organizers came from territories of French West and Equatorial Africa. The President of the new party, Félix Houphouet-Boigny (today President of Ivory Coast), set an aggressive note, demanding "the liberation of Africa from an odious tutelage—imperialism."

The only French party which was willing to support the RDA and its demands for independence was the French Communist Party. Until 1949 the RDA and the Communists worked hand in glove despite increasing opposition from the French government. The colonial administration in French West Africa set about breaking up the RDA with a vengeance. Meetings were raided and leaders jailed, especially in Ivory Coast. Against the advice of many of his associates and over the bitter opposition of the French Communists,

INDEPENDENCE II: 1959

Houphouet-Boigny decided to break with the Communist movement. The conflict between factions left the RDA weak and silenced the nationalists in French black Africa until the middle 1950's.

In the six years after the French Constitution of 1946 most French black Africans were given the right to vote. First only those who spoke French—the assimilated Africans — were eligible. Then those who owned property or had a driver's license. Finally all heads of families and mothers of two or more sons "living or dead for France" were permitted to vote. At the polls voters picked up a card with the symbol of their party—an elephant (the RDA), a giraffe—and dropped it into the ballot box.

In 1956 instability in France and unrest in the colonies impelled the French to pass the famous *Loi-Cadre* (fundamental law). Under the *Loi-Cadre* each territory in the Federations of West and Equatorial Africa elected its own legislative assembly. Effective government in the territories passed into local African hands. The territories were becoming separate nations.

In 1958 General de Gaulle, who had recently come to power in France, decided to settle the status of French black Africa. A referendum was held in each of the twelve territories. A "no" vote meant that the territory would become totally independent. A "yes" vote meant that the territory would become part of the new French Community. Nations within the Community would run their own internal affairs, but would leave foreign policy and military matters to France. De Gaulle stumped French black Africa trying to persuade African leaders to join the Community. In Conakry, the capital of Guinea, sitting on a platform next to Sékou Touré, leader of the Democratic Party of Guinea, De Gaulle heard Touré demand nothing less than full independence for Africans:

> We have a grave and pressing need: our dignity. But there is no dignity without freedom. For any subjection, any coercion, dishonors the man who submits, deprives him of part of his humanity and arbitrarily turns him into an inferior being. We prefer poverty in freedom to riches in slavery.

Touré and his party associates worked to get everyone to the polls on referendum day. The party machine did its job well. As in the heyday of Tammany Hall, everyone knew how to vote. The result was 97 percent for Touré and Guinean independence.

The party machines were just as effective elsewhere. Houphouet-Boigny's Democratic Party of Ivory Coast (PDCI) brought in 99 percent of the votes in favor of Houphouet and the Community. It is clear that the people of Guinea and Ivory Coast voted as their leaders told them to vote.

The final tally for French black Africa was eleven new countries in the French Community, and Guinea independent and on its own. The French had taken twenty years to get into Guinea, but they took only two weeks to get out, taking with them all that could be moved—telephones, legal records, electric light switches. The success of Guinea in managing to survive as an independent country set an example which nationalist leaders elsewhere hastened to follow. In 1959 and 1960, as one country after another declared its independence, the French Community fell apart.

Egypt

Although according to the geographers' maps Egypt is in the northeast corner of Africa, it stands apart from all the other countries of the continent. Egypt is one of the oldest countries of the world and it has traditionally looked to the Middle East and Europe more than to Africa.

Until 1952, Egypt was ruled by incompetent kings and corrupt politicians. British influence had been dominant there since the 1880's. Egypt's nationalist party, the Wafd, and the liberal party, the Saadi, were as bumbling and ineffective as the monarch himself. Both were parties of a few rich men, who did nothing about either the increasing poverty of the city masses or the misery of the *fellaheen* (peasants). The price of food went up, people were without jobs, wages fell, and the population grew. The defeat of the Egyptian Army by Israel in 1948 was the straw that broke the camel's back. In 1952 a group of army officers including Colonel Gamal Abdel Nasser seized power. King Farouk, the last monarch and the direct descendant of the Albanian adventurer Mohamed Ali, who had seized control 150 years before, was banished.

Nasser and the army officers ruled directly. Parliamentary government, they argued, would give power back to the wealthy landlords and corrupt politicians who opposed social progress. All political parties, including both the Communists and the fundamentalist Moslem Brotherhood, were prohibited. Since 1952, Nasser has attempted to overhaul his country. Land reforms have broken the power of the landlords and have given the peasants a stake in the country. Illiteracy is a crime in Egypt for young people. Factories, mainly textile mills, have been built, although it will take a long time to develop the industrial economy that Nasser wants. The high dam at Aswân, now under construction, will control the water of the Nile on which Egypt depends and will provide hydroelectric power for industry. Irrigation and better farming techniques are improving the lot of the *fellaheen*. Egypt under Nasser has had no political freedom, but a start has been made in the long and difficult task of economic development.

The Suez Crisis

The Suez Canal is a very valuable piece of real estate. More than 19,000 ships use it every year, and pay a king's ransom in tolls. To Europeans, Suez is a bottleneck through which flows oil from the Persian Gulf vital to Europe's economy. To Egyptians, Suez is part of Egypt and a symbol of past humiliation and domination by foreigners (see Chapter 4). When the revolutionary military government took power in Egypt in 1952, conflict over control of the canal was inevitable. In 1954 the British agreed to evacuate their military base at Suez, but the canal itself remained the property of the European-owned Suez Canal Company.

Tension mounted over Egypt for other reasons as well. Israel, regarded as enemy number one by all the Arab states, had been trading border raids and violent propaganda with Egypt across the Gaza Strip, and both sides appeared to be spoiling for a fight. Eager to show his independence of the West, President Nasser accepted in 1955

Sunken ships bar the entrance to the Suez Canal at Port Said after the British-French-Israeli attack on Egypt in 1956. British divers clear the canal after the troops have gone home. (*Wide World Photos.*)

both guns and economic aid from Russia. In reaction, the United States in July 1956 withdrew its offer to build the Aswân Dam, the key project in Egypt's economic development plan. On July 24 Nasser denounced the United States and said Russia would build the dam. Two days later, a wildly cheering crowd at Alexandria heard Nasser announce that Egypt was taking over the Suez Canal.

Britain and France, feeling that protection of their vital oil supply required control of the canal and grossly underestimating the vigor of Egyptian nationalism and the temper of the times, prepared to retake Suez by force if necessary. Israel was a willing collaborator in trying to bring down Nasser's hostile regime. On October 29 Israeli troops invaded Egypt, routing the Egyptian Army in Sinai and driving westward to the canal. On October 30 the British and French governments ordered Egypt to withdraw from the canal. Carrier planes bombed Port Said, and two days later British and French paratroops occupied Suez.

Nasser remained defiant. Egyptians sank several ships at Port Said, blocking the canal (and Europe's oil supply), and prepared to fight the invaders in the streets of Cairo. Unlike the British and the French, Nasser realized that in the twentieth century small states had powerful allies against aggression. India and other Asian countries created a furor at the United Nations. The United States, far from backing its Western allies, told them in no uncertain terms to get out of Egypt and Suez. Faced with such hostility, the invaders withdrew. A United Nations Emergency Force saw them out and cleared the canal.

The Suez crisis was a decisive event for African nationalism and independence, for it proved that old-fashioned high-handed imperialism was a dead letter in the mid-twentieth century. America and Russia, not the older European powers, called the tune. If Egypt could nationalize the canal—an Egyptian resource on Egyptian soil—and make it stick against a European invasion, then Africans elsewhere could also triumph.

Sudan

In 1953 Sudan, which had been under the joint rule of Britain and Egypt since 1899, became the first British possession in Africa to gain independence. Sudanese leaders tried to set up parliamentary government along British lines, but were overthrown by a military *coup d'etat* in 1958. The new ruler was General Ibrahim Abboud, who had been educated at Sandhurst, the British military academy. In 1964 Abboud was himself overthrown by labor unionists, students, and the moderate political parties that now rule the country.

Ghana and Nigeria

Ghana and Nigeria led the surge for independence in black Africa. Kwame Nkrumah of Ghana and Nnamdi Azikiwe of Nigeria (see Chapters 10, 13, and 17 for the later destinies of these men and their countries) had for many years been the most active nationalist leaders on the continent. Nationalist parties in Ghana and Nigeria were in the field before World War II, and recent nationalist triumphs were the culmination of a great deal of previous effort and activity. The first black mass parties— the Convention People's Party of Gold Coast and the National Council of Nigeria and the Cameroons (later the National Council of Nigerian Citizens)— were an inspiration for nationalists in all other British African colonies. Ghana became Africa's first independent black nation in 1957, followed three years later by Nigeria, the most populous country in Africa.

In West Africa the transfer of power from British to African hands was smooth and relatively painless. The gradual transition to independence in Ghana and Nigeria showed that reasonable colonial administrators and militant African nationalists could come to terms without large-scale violence. After World War II the Colonial Office in London accepted the distasteful idea that Gold Coast and Nigeria would be independent within a generation. Once this mental hurdle had been overcome, with an assist from demonstrations, strikes, boycotts, and mass rallies in West African cities, the British set about laying the foundations needed to sustain an independent nation. The leaders of mass parties in Gold Coast and Nigeria were quickly discovering how to topple a government. They had yet to run one—a different and a far more difficult task.

British reforms were many and effective. Gold Coasters and Nigerians were promoted to responsible positions within the government, where they studied the methods of budgeting and taxation in the Treasury and learned to cope with the difficulties of managing a school system in the Ministry of Education.

Reforms were just as sweeping outside government. Universities were established at Accra, Ibadan, and Zaria. Thousands of recently imported radios in Gold Coast and Nigeria began to receive programs locally broadcast by Gold Coast and Nigerian networks modeled on the British Broadcasting Corporation (no commercials). African labor leaders visited factories and trade union schools in Britain.

British (and French) policy in black Africa, unlike Belgian, Portuguese, and settler rule, extended political rights to the African common man and his leaders. As in French black Africa, more and more Gold Coasters and Nigerians were given the right to vote. Nationalist politicians competed for election to the colony's legislative council and eventually formed cabinets led by African prime ministers. This meant that before independence the leaders of mass parties became responsible for carrying on the day-to-day business of government.

In 1951 Kwame Nkrumah, then a prisoner serving a sentence for sedition in an Accra jail, received a message from the British Governor of Gold Coast requesting him to lead the government (see Chapter 13). The British Governor of Nigeria once suggested to Abubakar Tafawa Balewa, until recently Prime Minister, that he go out on the streets and condemn "our British colonial masters" more strongly, lest he lose the support of the rank and file to someone less reasonable. These were subtle British politicians trying to avoid the kind of head-on clash that cost the French so much blood and money in Algeria. "If you can't lick them, join them" was a strategy which worked, once the decision to accept African independence in the near future had been made.

March 6, 1957, was a glorious date in African history. The British flag came down, and the new flag of Ghana was proudly hoisted. A colony had become a black African nation. All over the continent black men rejoiced at the news, and other nationalist leaders knew the time of their own independence and power had drawn closer.

East Africa

The countries of Eastern Africa contradict many of our notions about Africa. East Africa has no jungle, but lies on a high grassy plateau. The people of East Africa include not only Bantu farmers and cattle-herding Nilotes but also Arabs, Indians, and European settlers. In spite of this racial infusion, East Africa is economically underdeveloped. Nairobi, Kampala, and Dar es Salaam cannot match the mining towns and industries of the south or the large and bustling commercial cities of the west. The three countries of East Africa—Uganda, Kenya, and Tanzania —differ greatly, yet between 1961 and 1963 all became independent.

Uganda

Uganda is an unusual country. The Ganda people, who hold most of the country's wealth, are only about 40 percent of its population. Unlike almost every other traditional African state, Buganda (see Chapter 1) has managed to hold the loyalty and attention of the Ganda people to the present day. Ganda are villagers who raise coffee and cotton for export; many read newspapers and most are Christians. Many of the other African peoples within Uganda's boundaries are quite the opposite of the sophisticated Ganda—cattle herders or backward peasants who work as hired migrant laborers on Ganda farms. When nationalism revived among the Ganda in the early 1950's the British deported their Kabaka. This blunder aroused the Ganda as nothing else could, and within two years agitation forced the British

Mau Mau guerillas surrender to a British soldier. The secret society's brutal practices turned most Kenya Africans against the Mau Mau, and made it possible for British and African troops to put down the rebellion. (*Wide World Photos.*)

to restore Mutesa II to his throne. "Kabaka Yekka" ("the Kabaka alone") was the slogan of the day.

The political issue in Uganda in recent years has been a power struggle between the Ganda minority and their neighbors, not between nationalists and the British. Two of five Ugandans are Ganda; not surprisingly all attempts to found a nationalist mass party embracing all Ugandans have failed.

The British had long been prepared to leave as soon as the conflict between the Ganda and the others was reasonably settled. After years of political wrangling between Buganda nationalists (the Kabaka Yekka) and other parties, a coalition was formed led by the Uganda People's Congress of Milton Obote. The British left in 1962, but the Ugandans are still an uneasy nation balanced on a knife edge of tribal compromise. In 1966 the Kabaka was driven into exile and President Obote took full powers of government.

Kenya and Mau Mau

The episode of the Mau Mau revolt has been exaggerated out of all proportion in the United States. Books like Robert Ruark's *Something of Value* see Mau Mau as the expression of a dark and brutal spirit incarnate in all Africans. To this day white settlers in Southern Rhodesia and South Africa regard all African nationalist demands as threats of revolt and justify their resistance to demands for reform by pointing to Mau Mau. The point is not that Mau Mau was not bloody and brutal. It was. The point is that Mau Mau was not typical: Nowhere else on the African continent have anticolonial movements resorted to such awful means. And Mau Mau failed, while the militant yet nonviolent mass nationalist parties that opposed and yet cooperated with colonial governments succeeded.

Mau Mau, like all Kenya politics, centered on the Kikuyu, a large tribe of Bantu farmers in central Kenya. The Kikuyu resented the fact that land they had once occupied was now owned by white settlers. These 30,000 settlers of the White Highlands, who had staked their fortunes and years of their lives in Kenya farming, quite naturally refused to return their farms to the Kikuyu. As Kikuyu population grew (Kenya now has almost 10 million Africans) the size of Kikuyu farms shrank, until they provided only a meager subsistence of grain and vegetables. Resentment against the white settlers increased.

Kikuyu leaders emphasized traditional tribal practices at the expense of learning the new European skills and attitudes which were changing the rest of Africa. They rejected the help of missionaries and set up separate Kikuyu schools and churches. Crude and painful initiation practices were extolled because they were a part of traditional Kikuyu life. Kikuyu nationalists isolated themselves not only from white settlers and Indian immigrants but also from the other African tribes of Kenya. The self-preoccupation of the Kikuyu and their unreasonable emphasis on tribal ritual and the tribal past ended in the tragedy of Mau Mau.

The leader and the hero of the Kikuyu revival was Jomo Kenyatta, "the Burning Spear." Kenyatta went to London in 1931 and stayed there for fifteen years. At one time he shared an apartment with Paul Robeson, the American Negro singer, and Peter Abrahams, the colored South African novelist. He also visited the Soviet Union, staying several months in Moscow. In 1938 Kenyatta published *Facing Mount Kenya,* an account of Kikuyu tribal life which is regarded as one of the finest works ever written about an African people. Kenyatta worked with Kwame Nkrumah to organize the 1945 Pan-African Congress (see Chapter 8), and shortly thereafter returned to lead Kenya's nationalists.

In the late 1940's a secret society called Mau Mau spread among the Kikuyu. No one knows just how and when it began, or how it got its name. The words "Mau Mau," as far as is known, have no meaning in Kikuyu or any other language. Kikuyu were drawn into Mau Mau by being forced to take the most solemn tribal oath that any Kikuyu could swear, an oath so sacred that most Kikuyu would rather die than break it. The oath was taken in the forest, at night, in an atmosphere of mortal terror. The aim of Mau Mau's peasant leaders was to draw the whole Kikuyu people into a web of commitment. The purpose of Mau Mau was clear and direct: to return the "lost lands" to the Kikuyu by ridding Kenya of the white man.

The Kenya government declared a state of emergency in 1952, as Mau Mau bands began to terrorize the homesteads of white farmers. At its height Mau Mau terrorism spread from the country to the towns. Mau Mau was not a war of black against white but a civil war

among the Kikuyu. In all only forty-three white civilians were killed, and about one hundred white troops. Thousands of Africans were hanged by the British government for carrying firearms and *pangas* (machetes), and thousands more were killed in clashes between government forces and Mau Mau terrorists. In a campaign that lasted several years, government troops and the Kikuyu Home Guard hunted down the guerillas with aircraft and police dogs until, in 1956, Mau Mau was broken.

Over the opposition of the settlers, British officials permitted Africans to resume political activity after 1956. As in Gold Coast and Nigeria, reforms allowed Africans to vote and sit on the legislative council. Land in the White Highlands was bought by the government and resold to landless African peasants. Jomo Kenyatta and other leaders of the Kenya African Union were tried and imprisoned for allegedly organizing Mau Mau. Kenyatta has denied the charge to this day, and the leading witness against him has in fact been convicted of perjury. While Kenyatta was in prison, a young labor unionist, Tom Mboya, organized Kenya nationalists. In the seven years between 1956 and 1963 the nationalists, like their West African counterparts, held meetings in remote villages, led workers out on strike, and wrote anticolonial editorials in the party press. *"Uhuru,"* which means "freedom" in Swahili, was the slogan of the snowballing campaign.

Kenya settlers slowly came to accept the inevitability of African rule, although some diehards clung to the hope that "Britain will not desert us." Some settlers even espoused the nationalist cause. Wing Commander Bruce MacKenzie, sporting a handlebar mustache and carrying a black umbrella, strode across the pavement of London airport shouting *"Uhuru"* on the way to a meeting with the British government, accompanied by none other than Kenyatta,

Mboya, and Oginga Odinga. In 1963 Jomo Kenyatta became first Prime Minister of independent Kenya.

A Central African Federation

The three British territories of Central Africa—Northern and Southern Rhodesia, and Nyasaland—were quiet until the late 1940's. But the settlers of Southern Rhodesia had long looked with an envious eye on the mineral wealth of the Northern Rhodesian Copperbelt, and the thousands of unemployed Nyasalanders completed a classic picture of economic interdependence. By 1949 support for a federation of the three countries was widespread among the settlers, who took their case to London. The British government was at first cool to the suggestion, but finally gave in, and in 1953 the Federation of Rhodesia and Nyasaland was formed.

The Federation was born amid a chorus of African protest. African leaders were convinced that the Federation was a scheme designed to extend settler supremacy from Southern Rhodesia into the two northern territories. They feared that African political rights, advancement in jobs in the Copperbelt, and education for Africans would be blocked by the extension of the color bar throughout the Federation.

The first Prime Minister of the Federation was a settler, Sir Godfrey Huggins. Huggins's attitude is perhaps best summed up in his statement that "all Africans are liars," a remark made as Lord Malvern (which he later became) while explaining the settler point of view to the British House of Lords. Huggins was succeeded by Roy Welensky. Son of a Lithuanian immigrant, Welensky began as a fireman stoking coal in Rhodesian locomotives and furthered his fortunes as a boxer. He rose through the white labor unions, where he warned of the threat of African labor to the supremacy of white workers. In

1955, at the age of forty-eight, Welensky became Prime Minister of the Federation, which he dominated until it collapsed in 1963.

African leaders worked to break up the Federation and to bring self-government to each of the three territories. During the economic boom of the 1950's, nationalism became vocal and organized in the Copperbelt. Hastings Banda, an American-educated medical doctor, was called back to Nyasaland to lead what became the Malawi Congress Party. In Northern Rhodesia Kenneth Kaunda used the nonviolent methods of Mahatma Gandhi to coax independence from the British government. Kaunda has often resisted demands for violent action made by his followers. A Spartan politician, Kaunda neither smokes nor drinks, and has tried to impose his strict standards on the turbulent membership of his United National Independence Party (UNIP).

After ten years of demonstrations, constitutional wrangling in London, strikes, violence, and intrigue, the Federation finally collapsed. Banda became Prime Minister of Nyasaland, and Kaunda of Northern Rhodesia. Following the growing precedent of choosing African names to erase the colonial origin of the nation, Nyasaland became Malawi, and Northern Rhodesia, Zambia.

The fate of Southern Rhodesia, now called Rhodesia, is not determined. Rhodesia has been the home of 220,000 British settlers, who have managed the Federation's commerce, grown tobacco for export, and since 1923 run the country's government. Four million Africans outnumber the settlers 19 to 1. African nationalists who wish to rule the country as Zimbabwe under black majority government have met diehard resistance, and white Rhodesians have grown steadily more committed to permanent white supremacy along South African lines (see Chapter 12). In recent years nationalist leaders Joshua Nkomo

African Independence

Country	Date	Colonial Ruler	Settlers
Ethiopia		None	None
Liberia	1847	None	80,000 Americo-Liberians
Union of South Africa	1910	Britain	3 million Afrikaners, British, Indians
Egypt	1922	Britain	None
Libya	1951	Italy	None
Sudan	1955	Britain	None
Morocco	1956	France	None
Tunisia	1956	France	None
Ghana	1957	Britain	None
Guinea	1958	France	None
Cameroun	1960	France	None
Central African Republic	1960	France	None
Chad	1960	France	None
Congo Republic (Kinshasa)	1960	Belgium	A few Belgians
Republic of the Congo (Brazzaville)	1960	France	None
Dahomey	1960	France	None
Gabon	1960	France	None
Ivory Coast	1960	France	None
Malagasy Republic	1960	France	None
Mali	1960	France	None
Mauretania	1960	France	None
Niger	1960	France	None
Nigeria	1960	Britain	None
Senegal	1960	France	None
Somalia	1960	Italy, Britain	None
Togo	1960	France, Britain	None
Upper Volta	1960	France	None
Tanganyika	1961	Britain	A few Indians
Algeria	1962	France	1 million French, Italians, others
Burundi	1962	Belgium	None
Rwanda	1962	Belgium	None
Uganda	1962	Britain	A few Indians
Kenya	1963	Britain	60,000 British, Indians
Zanzibar	1963	Britain	None
Malawi (Nyasaland)	1964	Britain	A few British, Indians
Zambia (Northern Rhodesia)	1964	Britain	80,000 British, Afrikaners
Gambia	1965	Britain	None
Botswana (Bechuanaland)	1966	Britain	None
Lesotho (Basutoland)	1966	Britain	None

Colonial Dependencies		Ruler	Settlers
Angola		Portugal	200,000 Portuguese
Portuguese Guinea		Portugal	A few Portuguese
Mozambique		Portugal	50,000 Portuguese
Spanish Sahara and other small dependencies		Spain	None
Rhodesia (Southern Rhodesia)*		Britain	200,000 Afrikaners, British
Swaziland		Britain	None
South-West Africa		Republic of South Africa	70,000 Germans, Afrikaners

---

* In November 1965, the settler-dominated government of Rhodesia unilaterally —that is, without British consent—declared Rhodesia independent (see below).

INDEPENDENCE III: 1966

(Zimbabwe African People's Union) and Ndabaningi Sithole (Zimbabwe African National Union) were restricted and jailed, and the government began to talk of declaring Rhodesia independent of Britain in order to perpetuate the dominance and privileges of the settler minority. In November 1965 Prime Minister Ian Smith and his extremist backers—called the "cowboys"—in the Rhodesian Cabinet took the plunge into a unilateral declaration of independence (UDI). Faced with British economic sanctions, total hostility from independent African countries (except, of course, South Africa), and 4 million restive Africans within Rhodesia's own borders, the success of "independence" for a handful of settlers remains in doubt.

The Belgian Congo

According to the Belgian philosophy of paternalism, the people of Congo were to be brought gradually, like children, into the modern world. The "father knows best" attitude of the Belgian officials kept Africans from studying abroad, from forming political parties or labor unions, and from gaining any experience in government. For many years, it looked as if Belgian policies were working smoothly. Colonial officials in other countries were plagued with young men who, freshly returned from England, America, and France with notions of African independence, set about forming mass parties, criticizing the colonial government in the press, and leading workers out on strike. To these embattled officials the Congo seemed a calm and sensible place where colonial development proceeded in an orderly manner.

Had Congo been on the moon, the Belgians might have succeeded in their policy of "gradualism." In 1955 the Belgians estimated that at *their* present pace it would be at least twenty-five and probably one hundred years before Congo was "ready" for independence. They failed to notice the breakneck pace of the nationalist campaign elsewhere in Africa and its effects on Congo. A few Congolese leaders went to the All-African Peoples' Conference at Accra, Ghana, in 1958 (see Chapter 14). One of these was Patrice Lumumba, who was to be the first Premier of Congo. Lumumba, who had neither higher education nor political experience, came home to agitate for independence. Political parties were hastily formed, most of them representing a single tribe, for tribal loyalties—Luba, Lunda, Kongo, Mongo, and others—were the only loyalties that Congolese knew.

In January 1959, riots broke out in Leopoldville. The Belgians panicked. They did not make the long-overdue effort to give the future leaders of Congo a college education (at independence there were fewer than twenty college graduates among the 13 million Congolese!). They did not encourage

Congolese to hold government jobs under Belgian supervision. Most important, Congolese leaders were given no time to organize national rather than tribal political parties or to teach Congolese peasants what being a citizen was all about. Instead, the Belgians simply set a date for independence and, on July 1, 1960, turned over the government to the Congolese. But Congo was a nation on paper only. Independence brought tribal warfare, anarchy, and the complete breakdown of the central government at Léopoldville. The Congo crisis (see Chapter 10) brought occupation by foreign troops under the flag of the United Nations and war to prevent the rich Katanga province from becoming a separate state. Today Congo remains unstable, plagued by rebellion, tribal violence, and rootless political factions, a source of anxiety to African leaders.

Portuguese Africa

Portuguese colonialists announce firmly that they are in Africa to stay, and that they will never accept even in principle the idea of African independence. Portuguese Africa is governed as part of Portugal, and the Portuguese treat African nationalists as traitors, just as they would treat rebels at home. The attitude of dictator Salazar and his officials is much like that of the Afrikaners in South Africa: Africans are inferior in their culture and way of life, their duty is to work for "civilized" Europeans, and no freedom or responsibility can be granted them. In recent years Portuguese peasants have been brought to Angola and Mozambique in an effort to bolster Portuguese rule. With the settlers has come a new (for the Portuguese) emphasis on the *racial* superiority of the white man.

Angola and Mozambique are still undeveloped. Perhaps only one of every hundred Africans can read and write. Little money has been spent to build

Rifles, masks, and machetes captured by the Portuguese from rebels in northern Angola. The weapons bear the initials of Holden Roberto's Union of the Peoples of Angola, now recognized by other African states as Angola's African government in exile, and the name of Patrice Lumumba. (*Wide World Photos.*)

roads, develop industries, or improve peasant farming. The reforms of 1961 have done little to change the system of forced labor that takes Africans from their homes and villages.

In 1961 nationalists began a guerilla war against the Portuguese in Angola. Portuguese troops have retaliated by burning African villages, and more than 100,000 refugees have fled to neighboring Congo. The rebel leader is Holden Roberto, who directs the revolt from a house in the African quarter of Leopoldville. Judging from the French defeat in Algeria, it seems unlikely that so poor a nation as Portugal can fight a long and expensive war against Angolan guerillas, particularly now that the rebels can move soldiers and supplies freely across the Angola-Congo border. In 1963 guerilla warfare began in Mozambique, and also in the tiny colony of Portguese Guinea, where the rebels are helped and supplied by Sékou Touré's Guinea government. This has put a triple strain on Portugal's meager resources. So far, however, the Portuguese have resisted with considerable success.

The United Nations Trust Territories

The German colonies of Tanganyika, South-West Africa, Togo, Cameroun, and Ruanda-Urundi became mandates of the League of Nations after the German defeat in World War I. After World War II these countries, plus the former Italian colonies of Libya and Somalia, became Trust Territories of the United Nations. In the Trusteeship Council of the United Nations pressure to grant independence was brought by India and other anticolonial countries. Yearly reports from British officials in Tanganyika, French officials in Togo and Cameroun, Belgians in Ruanda-Urundi, and Italians in Somalia gave United Nations members a chance to criticize colonial policies in Africa.

In 1951 Libya became independent. Shortly thereafter King Idris I abolished political parties and reestablished an absolute monarchy. Oil has recently made the monarch rich, but little has been done to improve the living conditions of the desert people or to revive the once-fertile coastal plain near Tripoli. The United States has an air base and 3,000 troops in Libya, while Britain buys most of Libya's oil. The other former Italian colony, Somalia, became independent in 1960, in accordance with the United Nations timetable. The Somalis are a Moslem people, most of whom still herd cattle and sheep over the wide reaches of their barren desert country.

Togo and Cameroun also became independent in 1960. Part of Togo, which had been ruled by Britain, voted to become part of Ghana. In 1963 Togo's widely respected President, Sylvanus Olympio, was assassinated, and Togo is now governed by a coalition of politicians and generals. Cameroun's history has been even more stormy. Cameroun's mass party, the Union of the Peoples of Cameroun (UPC), banned by French officials in 1955, subsequently mounted an off-and-on guerilla war in the Cameroun hills and forests. The UPC leader, Felix Moumié, was murdered in Geneva in 1960, after he accused the French of rigging the 1960 election, which made moderate leader Ahmadou Ahidjo President. Cameroun struggles along under the Ahidjo government, which has been able to compromise with the UPC to end the fighting.

Tanganyika followed the pattern of other British-ruled countries to independence. Under the leadership of Julius Nyerere (see Chapter 13) the Tanganyika African National Union (TANU) united Tanganyikan peoples in support of independence and constructive effort. Nyerere's slogan is not simply *"Uhuru"* but *"Uhuru na kazi"*—"Freedom *and work"* and later *"Uhuru na moja"*—"Freedom and unity." Tanganyika is a very poor country—hot, dry, flat, with few resources and little opportunity for the development of modern industry—and much work will be needed to raise the standard of living of Tanganyikans beyond grass huts and corn. Nyerere and his party became the new government of Tanganyika in 1961 and federated with Zanzibar in 1964 to become Tanzania.

Ruanda-Urundi is not one country but two, Rwanda and Burundi. Although both are smaller than the state of Connecticut, both have been self-governing nations since 1962. In both countries a class of cattle-herding warriors, the Tutsi (who are much like the Masai described in Chapter 1), ruled the far more numerous Hutu, Bantu peasants. In Rwanda, but not in Burundi, democracy brought about a Hutu revolt at the polls. The seven-foot-tall Tutsi, accustomed for centuries to ruling by the power of their spears, were soundly beaten by the power of the ballot. When the Hutu politicians took over, tribal war broke out. Many Tutsi fled Rwanda for Congo and neighboring Burundi, ruled by a Tutsi Mwami, or king. In Rwanda Tutsi land was redistributed among their former Hutu serfs.

South-West Africa is legally a Trust Territory of the United Nations. In fact, South-West Africa is ruled by South Africa without regard to United Nations demands for reform or independence. Much of South-West Africa is desert, the Kalahari Desert of the Bushmen, and only half a million people live in the country. In recent years African nationalist parties have sprung up in spite of government opposition. The nationalists are either in jail or in exile, trying to gather support for their cause.

Islands in Settler Africa

Three former British protectorates—Swaziland, Bechuanaland, and Basutoland—are surrounded by the white-settler countries of Southern Africa. Bechuanaland became independent as Botswana in 1966. Basutoland, as Lesotho, also became independent in 1966. The Sotho descendants of wise King Moshesh, who made his country a protectorate in the nineteenth century to stave off land-hungry settlers, are now faced with the problem of getting along with South Africa on an international basis. Tiny Lesotho could become a center of controversy and intrigue, for black South Africans may use the country as a base of operations against South Africa's white government. Swaziland, also self-governing, is under the rulership of the traditional monarchy. All three small countries are tied to the economy of South Africa, their giant and potentially hostile neighbor.

White Nationalism in South Africa

While black nationalism has swept tropical Africa from Senegal to Malagasy and from Chad to Malawi, another nationalism, more fanatical and equally powerful, has gripped the southern tip of the continent. In 1948 the Nationalist Party of the Afrikaner (Boer) settlers won a democratic election, ending the uneasy coalition between British and Afrikaner politicians that had governed South Africa since 1910. The

Afrikaner nationalists were much like black nationalists in other African countries. They relied on the votes of poor Afrikaner farmers—men much like the "poor whites" of the American South—who were moving to the towns and the mines in search of city jobs and cash. The Nationalist Party was anticolonial, which in South African terms meant that the Afrikaners, and not the British, should rule. The Afrikaans language, the Dutch Reformed Church, and the long-held conviction that the Afrikaners were God's Chosen People combined to give Afrikaner nationalism the same passionate fervor and sense of mission felt by black nationalists throughout the continent.

The Afrikaner government drew up the *apartheid* (separation) laws which today impose the world's most rigid racial segregation on South Africa. Black Africans find no place in white society, and least of all in government. Black African political parties have been suppressed, and in fact any antigovernment action or criticism by black men is severely penalized. The leaders of the African National Congress of Chief Albert Luthuli, who won a Nobel Peace Prize for his efforts to press black rights without violence, were tried for treason in a trial which lasted from 1956 to 1961, and were finally acquitted. As far as the black African is concerned, South Africa has become a totalitarian state dedicated to white supremacy at any cost.

Summing Up: Colonial Rule and Nationalism

The short period of colonial rule, which lasted from the turn of the twentieth century until about 1960, was an era of great change that transformed the Africa of traditional tribal societies into the Africa of independent and modernizing nations. In many scattered areas colonial governments laid roads and railroads, supported mission schools, provided medicine, and built homes and water pipes for Africans who had moved to the mine and the town.

Yet in Africa colonial rule meant that white men were rich and black men were poor, and that black men, for the first time, knew it. The African was regarded as uncivilized and inferior by colonial officials and particularly by white settlers. This applied equally to Moslem Algerians of Arab and Berber ancestry and to Bantu Negroes in Congo or South Africa. To poverty and discrimination was added the frustration of learning to cope with modern life, the ways of the city. The city was the center of colonial development. At the same time its slums and wharves, mine shafts and markets were the incubator of the African reaction to colonial rule: nationalism.

Beginning with the declarations of W. E. B. DuBois and the visions of Marcus Garvey in the *Negro World*, the campaign for African independence took root in the passionate convictions of African students in France, England, and America. These were young men in a hurry, and in the climate of expectation that followed the Allied victory in World War II they returned to Africa to weld the many peoples of their countries into nations seeking independence. Working closely with African labor unions, nationalist political parties brought Africans of all groups and regions into a single organization. By providing services that met new needs, such as finding jobs or providing insurance, the mass parties won loyalty away from the chiefs and the tribe. By blaming all African grievances—slums, low wages, lack of political rights, discrimination—on "colonialism," the new politicians generated an enthusiasm for independence that proved irresistible.

The result of the African campaign for independence depended on two conditions. The first was the degree of economic progress and education. The second was the amount of freedom permitted politicians by the colonial government. Where there were both progress and freedom, as, for example, in Nigeria, Senegal, Tunisia, or Uganda, Africans achieved independence without violence, and in the process usually learned how to govern their new nation. Where officials or settlers opposed freedom while encouraging development, disaster resulted. Algeria was almost ruined by seven years of war. Congo fell into chaos when given independence without preparation. The turn of South Africa, which has both the greatest economic development and the greatest political repression, is yet to come. Finally, there are those few countries which have not felt the pulse of change, which remain lands of poor village peasants and few educated men. Such are Ethiopia and Liberia, the two countries that escaped the scramble for Africa.

Colonial rule set Africa on a path of change which led Africans to seek independence from their colonial rulers. As Lord Lugard, a famous colonial ruler, said of Britain's African subjects, "Their very discontent is a measure of their progress."

PROBLEMS

1. Match the country with the fact:

Algeria	the first Negro nation to become independent
Kenya	under military rule since 1952
Ghana	scene of a rebellion against Portugal
Zambia	the only French colony to reject the French Community
Angola	scene of Mau Mau
South Africa	a country divided by tribal politics
Egypt	formerly Northern Rhodesia
Guinea	a country ruled by white nationalists
Uganda	scene of a seven years' guerilla war

2. Make a time line of the independence movement in Africa since World War II. Do you think that the independence of Ghana in 1957 had a snowball effect on nationalism in other Negro African countries? Why, in your opinion, were the non-Negro countries of the Maghreb and the Nile Valley the first to become independent?

3. Do you agree with Lord Lugard's opinion that in Africa discontent was a sign of progress? Were the most discontented countries, and those most eager for independence, the most advanced in economic development, the growth of cities, the number of educated people, and the organization of political parties? Would an African who had never seen a car (as many had not) be upset about the fact that white men had cars while he did not?

4. Was Mau Mau a nationalist party? Would nationalist leaders like Kenya's Tom Mboya have supported Mau Mau? As literacy and education increase, and as cities grow, will Africans be more or less likely to turn to movements like Mau Mau? Why?

5. Did the resistance of Algerian settlers to the independence movement make any difference in the final outcome? What could the settlers have done to avoid the loss of hundreds of thousands of lives, the waste of billions of

dollars, and the flight from Algeria of almost all the settlers themselves that were the actual results of the Algerian war? What reforms might the Portuguese adopt in Angola? Will it be possible to work out a permanent compromise short of independence?

READING SUGGESTIONS

John Gunther, *Inside Africa*, Harper & Row, 1953.

John Hatch, *Africa Today—and Tomorrow*, Praeger, paper.

Josiah Mwangi Kariuki, *"Mau Mau" Detainee*, Penguin African Library, paper.

Joseph Kraft, *The Struggle for Algeria*, Doubleday, 1961.

L. S. B. Leakey, *Mau Mau and the Kikuyu*, Methuen (London), 1953.

Jacques Servan-Schreiber, *Lieutenant in Algeria*, Knopf, 1957.

part three

AFRICAN CONTRASTS

The African continent is home to many dissimilar peoples, and now to many different nations. While almost all were colonies that produced African nationalists who used the education and techniques learned from colonialists to unseat their rulers, the African nations that have emerged are necessarily varied in tradition both African and colonial, in economy and geography, and in the policies of their leaders and governments.

So it is time to look more closely at some specific countries. The five countries in this part have been chosen for their importance and for the special conditions and problems which they illustrate. All but Liberia—the one African nation with a strong historical tie to the United States—are large countries in size, population, and resources, countries whose policies, successes, and failures mean a great deal for Africa's future.

Congo has been Africa's rogue elephant, the horrible case of independence run amok. Nigeria, on the other hand, has been held up until recently as a model of African peace and progress under moderate democratic leadership. Yet both countries are faced with the staggering problem of welding diverse and often hostile African peoples into a single nation. What accounts for the difference, and what is the outlook for the future?

Liberia and Ethiopia are the two African countries that escaped being gobbled up by Europeans. Never having been colonial perhaps has its drawbacks. Both the regime of the Americo-Liberians and Ethiopia's completely

PART THREE:
African Contrasts

different tradition of Christianity and empire are in striking contrast to the ways of most ex-colonial nations.

Finally, South Africa, where the face-off between black men and white looks more and more like the famous metaphor of two scorpions in a bottle. What makes the South African tangle of racial hostility, black nationalism and white, great wealth and little freedom such a vicious impasse?

The last chapter in this part is devoted to African nationalist leaders— the men of power who by their individual personalities and talents are shaping African history.

chapter 10
CONGO AND NIGERIA

Together, my brothers, we are going to begin a new struggle, a sublime struggle which is going to lead our country to peace, prosperity and grandeur.

We are not going to let a peace of guns and bayonets prevail, but rather a peace of courage and good will.

I ask all of you to forget the hazardous tribal quarrels which exhaust our strength and make us contemptible to the foreigner.

We are going to show the world what the black man can do when he works in freedom. . . .

—PATRICE LUMUMBA,
Excerpts from Independence Day speech, June 30, 1964

Congo and Nigeria are large nations in population, in territory, and in resources. Events in these two countries will influence decisively the future of Africa.

Like most other African countries, Congo and Nigeria include within their borders distinct and often rival African peoples who had in common no language, culture, history, or religion before they fell under the rule of a single colonial power. Imagine yourself part of a "nation" that included Americans, Mexicans, Russians, and a large number of Eskimos, with its boundaries drawn by foreign rulers. How is such a "nation" to be governed? Who shall rule? How can anarchy and civil war be prevented, and the nation kept together? How can the different peoples be persuaded to work together for the betterment of all? These are the problems of such African countries as Congo and Nigeria.

Congo

Heart of Darkness

One thousand miles from east to west, one thousand more from north to south, Congo is the very center of black Africa. Nine other African countries touch its borders. The great river for which the country is named flows more than two thousand miles from the heart of Africa in a great arc, its tributaries rising in the hills and highlands of eastern Congo to merge into the broad and swift river that flows through dense tropical forest to the sea.

Congo was the last part of the African continent to be explored by Europeans. In 1874 the American journalist and explorer Stanley reached the river from the highlands around Lake Tanganyika and followed it westward to its mouth. From Stanley's sensational and widely read reports came the impression of Congo still uppermost in many minds —a land of vast possibilities, full of crocodiles and cannibals, a land of brooding and sinister savagery.

The great novelist Joseph Conrad christened Congo by the title of his magnificent tale, "Heart of Darkness." Conrad reached the Congo River in 1890 and traveled upstream in a small steamer. His description is awesome:

> The reach was narrow, straight, with high sides like a railway cutting. The dusk came gliding into it long before the sun had set. The current ran smooth and swift, but a dumb immobility sat on the banks. The living trees, lashed together by the creepers and every living bush of the undergrowth, might have been changed to stone, even to the slenderest twig, to the lightest leaf.
> It was not sleep—it seemed unnatural, like a state of trance. Not the faintest sound of any kind could be heard. You looked on amazed, and began to suspect yourself of being deaf—then the night came suddenly, and struck you blind as well . . .
> We had a glimpse of a towering multitude of trees, of the immense, matted jungle, with the blazing ball of sun hanging over it—all perfectly still . . .

King Leopold's Ghost

On his return to Europe Stanley found Leopold, King of the Belgians, eager to listen to his tales. The ambitious Leopold wanted fame and fortune, and Congo seemed to be his great opportunity. Leopold sent traders deep into Congo to rule and profit in his name, while Stanley and others mounted a well-planned public relations campaign in Europe and America. In 1884 Leopold presented his creation, the Congo Free State, to the other European powers.

Congo was a land laid waste by slavery. By the 1880's eastern Congo had become a favored hunting ground for Arabs from Zanzibar such as Tippoo Tip, notorious king of the Arab slavers, who held forth on a huge scale. Famine had forced tribesmen to become cannibals, and once-flourishing regions were empty, the villages burned and the people enslaved or fled.

Once he was handed this huge piece of real estate, the responsibility—and the profits—were Leopold's alone. He was ruthless in the pursuit of money. With a stroke of the pen he "annexed" huge tracts of land and sold them to companies hunting minerals. Traders at posts along the rivers were required to turn in a certain amount of rubber and ivory each month, with no questions asked about the means used to get it. After forced trade came forced labor. Any resistance was rebellion, and was put down by killing and torture.

Bit by bit, tales from Congo reached the outside world. Faced with a mounting outcry for reform, the Belgian government took over Congo from Leopold in 1908. Leopold was by now one of the richest men in Europe. According to the reformers, a million Africans had died on his personal estate in tropical Africa.

Twenty-five years of concentrated exploitation had taught Congolese to suspect, avoid, and hate the white man.

The Showcase Colony

The motto of the Belgian colonial government was *"Dominer pour servir"* —"Rule in order to serve." Pierre Ryckmans, Congo's most famous Governor-General, wrote that "this is the sole excuse for conquest. It is also its complete justification." Belgian officials considered Africans children, and called their colonial policy "paternalism." In official eyes, the African was a creature who with full belly and empty mind would joyfully obey and work for a benevolent white master.

Congo turned out to be rich. For the past fifty years prospectors have been finding minerals in the southeast corner of Congo, called Katanga. In 1955 Katanga produced almost 10 percent of the world's copper, 60 percent of the West's uranium, 75 percent of the world's cobalt, and 80 percent of the world's industrial diamonds. In other re-

Union Minière. (*Africa Report.*)

gions, plantations grew coffee, cotton, palm oil, rubber, and cocoa. These products came by railroad and riverboat to Matadi, Congo's Atlantic port, to be shipped abroad to Europe and America.

The 1940's and 1950's brought an economic boom to the Belgian Congo. Mining output tripled. Dams were built across tributaries of the great river, and Congo's own electricity powered the railroads and the mines. Factories began to make shoes, cloth, and packaged food. Houses were built of Congo cement. Profits poured into the coffers of the mining companies and the Belgian government. The boom naturally changed the lives of many Africans. One of every three Congolese worked for wages. Two of every five lived in a city, the highest proportion of city dwellers in Africa. One of every ten owned a bicycle. Slums in the cities were rare, as the Belgians built "model" townships for their "wards."

The great mining companies, of which by far the biggest was the Union Minière of Katanga, were states within a state. Union Minière gave houses to workers and their families, provided the best medical care in Africa, and paid pensions to retired Africans. The Belgians let Union Minière run Katanga as its private estate, on condition that Congolese employees were well paid and cared for, and on condition that Union Minière paid its taxes. In fact, Union Minière provided half the Congo government's income.

Defenders of the Belgian Congo point out that three-quarters of Congo's children were in school in 1958. Yet only a few thousand were in high schools, and *less than twenty had college degrees.* Education was the responsibility of Catholic mission schools that worked closely with the officials and mining companies in running the country. In 1958—two years before independence— Belgian officials estimated that Congolese would be trained in universities for responsible jobs only after another thirty years.

Under Belgian rule, white men gave the orders, black men did the work. In the civil service Congolese could become clerks, but never officials. In the companies they could become skilled workers, but never executives. Many were trained as medical assistants, none as doctors. Half the money earned in the Belgian Congo went to the whites— and there were 135 Africans for every white man.

Because higher education was denied Congolese, the "culture bar" and the "color bar" were the same. Black and white did not mix, and never learned to understand each other. Congo's city folk had been thoroughly exposed to the white man's big houses, cars, and liquor, and wanted the same for themselves. Yet few, even of those with well-paying jobs, had the education or experience to understand the difficulties of running the country or its economy. The result was a modern country managed by Belgians—but a country in which the

Congolese had no say or stake. The Belgian Congo was in no way *their* country.

Throughout the 1950's the Belgian Congo with its booming economy, African welfare, and efficient administration was considered a model colony. Paternal rule, it seemed, worked very well indeed. British and French officials elsewhere, continually faced with strikes, demonstrations, and manifestoes, envied Congo's tranquillity. The shoe was soon to be on the other foot.

A House Divided

While Congo was one country under Belgian rule, the Africans within its borders were by no means one people (see map on page 5). The Kongo people around the mouth of the river (from whom river and country take their name) had fallen into decay after a great past. Many had moved to the capital city of Leopoldville. In the south and west, Luba men were moving to the cities, taking good jobs as clerks and foremen in Katanga and at the diamond mines of Kasai province. Their traditional enemies, the Lunda, watched Luba progress with envy and dismay. Central Congo was home to many small tribes called Mongo. In the northeastern Oriental province lived wild Nilotic tribes, and in the north the Ngombe.

Tribal conflicts continued to smolder under Belgian rule, both in the city and in the country. Congolese were never allowed to form political parties or to organize in any independent way, either to oppose Belgian rule or to support it. Where in other colonies such as Nigeria the new political parties tried to unite all Africans for the independence campaign, this never happened in the Belgian Congo. Political parties were the cement that held African countries together; deprived of this unifying force, tribal differences and rivalries were bound to darken Congo's future.

The Belgians thought of their Congo as a world apart, isolated from the rest of Africa. If it had been so, the Belgian

Patrice Lumumba. (*Africa Report.*)

policy of slowly educating and enriching the Congolese might have worked. As the Belgians — and others — have since discovered, Congo was very much a part of Africa. Ideas are hard to stop, and in the 1950's the ideas of African independence and the equality of black man and white seeped slowly into Congo.

Unrest began in the tribal associations and small groups of high school graduates in the early 1950's. In 1955 Belgian Professor A. A. J. Van Bilsen proposed a thirty-year plan of reforms leading to independence. But independence, not reform, was in the air. In 1956 Joseph Kasavubu, leader of the Kongo people in Leopoldville (the ABAKO Party), declared that thirty years was too long. In 1958 Patrice Lumumba organized the National Congolese Movement (MNC). Other leaders, drawing support from fellow tribesmen in separate regions, began to gather their followers. Lumumba went to the 1958 Pan-African meeting in Accra (see Chapter 14) and returned in December to demand complete independence before a cheering crowd. Kasavubu, who had been prevented from making the trip to Accra at the last moment at Leopoldville airport by Belgian officials, was equally radical. Six days later 30,000 unemployed workers marched through the streets of Leopoldville. Riots broke out, and demonstrators were shot down by the Force Publique. Villagers refused to pay taxes or obey officials. The King of the Belgians announced immediate reforms.

Colin Legum, in his *Congo Disaster,* has summed up the events of the following eighteen months leading to Congo independence on June 30, 1960. He writes:

> No colonial power in history was destroyed more quickly, and by such a rabble: there was not even a coherent nationalist movement which could command nation-wide support. But there was rebellion; a rebellion of the mind that rejected paternalism and all it stood for. The children were children no longer.

Congo Disaster

Legum's words were prophetic. A creature of, by, and for the Belgians, Congo simply fell apart after independence. Six years later Congo has as yet no "coherent nationalist movement" capable of commanding loyalty and no government capable of keeping order. The fires of rebellion continue to burn, seemingly without end.

The Congo pattern of violence and chaos was established in the very first weeks of independence.

June 30: At independence ceremonies new Congo Premier Patrice Lumumba spoke curtly of Belgian rule as "the humiliating bondage imposed on us by force."

July 5: The Force Publique, Congo's army, mutinied against its Belgian officers. Lumumba called for order and promised a pay raise, but the soldiers refused to put down their arms.

July 6–8: Soldiers ran amok. Tribal fighting broke out between Luba and Lulua in Kasai, and between Kongo and others in Leopoldville. Belgian civilians fled the country in panic, mobbing the airports and jamming the ferry from Leopoldville to Brazzaville.

July 11: Belgian paratroops landed in Leopoldville and Elisabethville to restore order and protect European civilians. Moise Tshombe, in Elisabethville, announced the secession of Katanga from Congo.

July 13: Lumumba and Kasavubu denounced Belgian "aggression," asked the United Nations to send troops.

July 14: The Security Council, for once with both Russian and American approval, agreed to send United Nations troops to see the Belgians out, and to provide technical assistance. Within forty-eight hours the first troops—from Ghana—had arrived in Leopoldville.

The Martyr

The next chapter of the Congo story belongs to the remarkable Patrice Lumumba. Lumumba was one of those men who had the qualities of a madman and a saint. He burned with a feverish devotion to Congolese independence. He inspired men and crowds to follow him, but lacked the hard-bitten realism and practical judgment of the politician or the statesman. Lumumba failed to save either himself or his country in the hour of need, and became a martyr to African independence.

Lumumba became Congo's first Premier when he was only thirty-five years old. He had been in jail for embezzling funds from a village post office. He had been a public relations man for a brewery. He had been a politician for a scant two years before independence and *had never held public office.*

Lumumba stood firmly on two principles: (1) that Congo was a single country and could be held together only by a strong central government; and

(2) that independence meant just that —continued Belgian rule from behind the scenes was not to be tolerated.

When Belgian paratroops landed and Katanga seceded, Lumumba saw red. He lashed out at United Nations Secretary General Dag Hammarskjöld for refusing to order UN troops to fight their way into Katanga, and wildly threatened to call in Russian troops to fight Katanga and the Belgians. He ordered the bloody repression of Kasai, where Luba leader "King" Albert Kalonji had proclaimed a separate "Diamond State." He berated his advisers, gave contradictory orders, drank, used narcotics, and slept hardly at all. Lumumba was driven to distraction, frustrated and enraged by problems which overwhelmed him.

President Kasavubu fired Lumumba as Premier on September 6, barely two months after independence. Scarcely a week later, the government was taken over by Army Colonel Joseph Mobutu, who put Lumumba under house arrest. Three months later Lumumba walked past his UN guards and drove off toward Stanleyville. He was seized by troops of the Force Publique, put on a plane for Katanga, and placed at the tender mercies of his archenemies, Katanga leader Tshombe and Tshombe's Interior Minister, Godefroid Munongo. Lumumba and his two companions were never seen again—almost certainly killed while the prisoners of Tshombe.

The death of Lumumba numbed Africa and the world. For all his failings, Lumumba had stood for unity and independence—the twin African ideals. An Indonesian poet wrote:

> The news came early in the morning
> Lumumba is dead
> Lumumba is dead
> Anger split the whole world asunder

Civil War

Congo had splintered into fragments. "King" Kalonji's Diamond State held southern Kasai against the central government. Lumumba's deputy Antoine Gizenga, armed and recognized by several African countries and the Soviet Union, ruled northeast Congo from Stanleyville. Katanga, led by Tshombe and controlled by white mercenary soldiers in the pay of the giant Union Minière, held out against both Leopoldville and the United Nations. In a rage at Lumumba's death, Congo factions killed all the rival leaders they could lay their hands on. While the cities lay quiet under UN protection, terror spread to the villages.

President Kasavubu remained cool. He appointed Cyril Adoula Premier of a newly formed government, which was the legal heir to Lumumba's government and was accepted by all but Tshombe. Gizenga continued to receive supplies and encouragement from the Communist bloc. But his own soldiers and politicians deserted him for Adoula's Leopoldville government, and the northeast returned to Congo. Katanga remained apart.

Katanga soldiers move out against Luba guerillas loyal to the Leopoldville government during the Katanga secession. Many of these same troops fought under the flag of Tshombe's Leopoldville government against the Congo rebels in 1964-1965. In all phases of the Congo crisis tribal conflicts fueled the violence. (*Wide World Photos.*)

As in other wars, civilians get the worst of it. This village and mission station in Katanga was razed by invading tribesmen from Kasai. (*Wide World Photos.*)

The Katanga Secession

Katanga had seceded from Congo eleven days after independence. The reasons are not hard to see. The 35,000 Belgian settlers of Katanga had long clamored for secession. Moise Tshombe, supported by the chiefs of the Lunda and Bayeke tribes, wanted to be President—of Katanga if not of Congo. Most important, however, independent Katanga was the creation of Union Minière, the mining company that controls nearly half of Congo's wealth and owns practically everything in Katanga. How could Union Minière better avoid the turmoil and complications of Congo independence than by creating a state of its own, dependent upon company funds and subordinate to Belgian "advisers." Union Minière supplied guns, money, and Belgian army officers. Britain, which had a big financial stake in Union Minière, put its weight behind independent Katanga. A well-oiled propaganda machine stirred support in Europe and the United States for "Katanga Freedom Fighters," portraying Moise Tshombe as an upright and moderate man fighting the twin evils of communism and savage anarchy and disorder.

The "Katanga Freedom Fighters" were in fact white mercenary soldiers paid by Union Minière. Many were Belgians—settlers and workers. Some were South Africans who believed in fighting for white rule in Africa. Some were Frenchmen from Algeria, driven from that country after the Algerian war. They called themselves *les affreux*, "the frightful ones," and were specialists in terrorism.

No Congolese leader could accept the secession of Congo's economic heartland. Lumumba, Kasavubu, and Adoula all had urged in the strongest terms that the UN put down the secession by force. The Africans of Katanga were not united and never showed that they favored secession or even supported Tshombe. North Katanga was in fact the scene of a savage war between the white mercenaries and Tshombe's Lunda followers on one hand and the Luba people on the other. The terror spread by gangs of young men of the anti-Tshombe Balubakat was matched by the bombing and burning of Luba villages by Tshombe's forces. More than 100,000 Luba refugees sought UN protection in Elisabethville.

Tshombe, although dependent on Union Minière money, was no fool. He slid in and out of compromises with the slipperiness of an eel. Elisabethville was peaceful and orderly, and things were run just as before independence. Nineteen sixty-one was financially one of Union Minière's best years!

The UN Security Council finally decided that the mercenaries had to go and ordered UN troops to expel them from Katanga. Katanga whites cleaned their guns and barricaded their homes. Fighting broke out between UN troops and the mercenaries, who fought from houses, schools, churches, and trucks marked with Red Cross insignia. The last holdouts were Union Minière buildings which had been used as a camp and ammunition depot. Only in December 1962, 2½ years after the Congo operation began, was Katanga restored to the Leopoldville government.

The UN Contribution

Three-quarters of the Belgian doctors, engineers, and skilled workers left Congo during the disorders that followed independence. The United Nations men began to put Congo back on its feet. Harbors clogged with silt were dredged, railways repaired, and people and goods began to move again. The airports were opened and the telephones fixed. United States planes flew food and medicine to areas hard hit by tribal fighting. This UN relief and technical aid kept Congo alive through two years of chaos and civil war.

The United Nations mission left Congo in June 1964. The effort to put Congo together again had emptied the UN treasury and an indefinite UN stay in Congo was out of the question. Unfortunately for Africa, Congo was not

A young rebel in Congo. Most rebel soldiers were teenagers, and many fought armed only with spears. They were called *simbas*, which means "lions" in Swahili. (*Wide World Photos.*)

yet ready to stand on its own feet, and the UN departure signaled a new chapter of bloodshed and confusion.

Civil War Again

In the spring of 1964 tribal terrorists ravaged Kwilu, in southern Congo. The Adoula government fell, and President Kasavubu, looking for a man with the ability to lead, appointed as the new Premier none other than Moise Tshombe! From Kwilu and Maniema in the east rebellion spread like brushfire until almost half the Congo was out of government control.

Like the previous installments of chaos, anarchy, and tribal warfare which followed independence, the Congo civil war of 1964–1965 was brutal, savage, and primitive. The rebel soldiers, most of them boys under sixteen, were called *simbas* ("simba" means lion in Swahili, the language of eastern Congo). These youths massacred educated Africans, local officials, and often white teachers and missionaries—anyone who had connections with what had been under Belgian rule the white man's world and way of life. Stiffened and led by white mercenary soldiers hired by Tshombe, government columns retook the towns of eastern Congo, capturing Stanleyville, the rebel "capital," in November 1964. Shops and towns were looted, and rebel soldiers or sympathizers who fell into the hands of the Congolese Army were shot. Civilians had the worst of it from both sides. Many were killed, and hundreds of thousands fled their homes.

The 1964 rebellion posed a serious dilemma for other African leaders: to accept a leader they despised or to interfere in the internal affairs of another African country. Many African leaders had never forgiven Tshombe for leading the Belgian-backed Katanga secession or for the murder of Patrice Lumumba, and Tshombe again recruited white mercenaries — including South Africans — to fight Congolese. Yet Tshombe was the head of Congo's central government, the very government that African leaders and the UN worked so hard to preserve after independence. President Nasser of Egypt, who considers Tshombe a personal enemy, and others flew guns to the rebels and threatened to recognize the rebel government-in-exile of Christopher Gbenye. This precedent of interference is not a happy one, for interference could lead to chaos and violence in many other parts of Africa.

Tshombe, as the legal head of Congo's government, asked for and received Belgian and American aid. In November 1964, with Tshombe's permission, Belgian paratroops dropped from American planes evacuated hundreds of European and American civilians from Stanleyville, where they had been held as hostages by the rebels. Africans denounced the operation, which most Americans considered a humanitarian rescue mission, as imperialism against Africa and became even more firmly convinced that Tshombe was an "imperialist stooge." Russian guns from Egypt and Russian and Chinese propaganda aided and encouraged the rebellion, raising the danger of bringing the cold war to Africa.

The Congo rebellion collapsed in the spring of 1965 as mercenary-led units of the National Congolese Army closed the Congo-Sudan border and cleaned out rebel towns and pockets—Bunia, Paulis, Fizi—one by one. The cause of the rebellion's failure, however, was disorganization, the feuding of rebel leaders Christopher Gbenye, Pierre Mulele, and Gaston Soumialot, and the lack of any positive program. Most Congolese peasants and tribesmen who were rebels lashed out from a growing feeling of grievance and frustration; their goals, if any, were local and tribal. Though the rebellion is now over, unrest still simmers under Congo's surface.

Hope for Congo?

While the end of Congo's time of troubles may not yet be in sight, several conclusions may still be drawn. Congo is not a nation and does not command the loyalty of Africans within its borders. Without a sense of common purpose and willingness to cooperate among Congolese leaders, Congo will be torn by political factions, secessions, and rebellion, whether the leader's name be Lumumba, Kasavubu, Mobutu, Adoula, Gizenga, Gbenye, or Tshombe. Reconstruction of Congo—if Congo is to survive at all—will take a long time. An army to maintain law and order must be trained and disciplined. Many young Congolese must be educated to lead and manage and administer. A strong national government, with hard-driving leaders, must set about these tasks. Eventually, national pride and cooperation must take the place of tribal rivalry and rootless dissatisfaction and rebellion among Congo Africans.

Kano. Northern Nigeria reflects the Islamic heritage and history of the west African Sudan. A few signs of the twentieth century are swallowed up by the old city. (*Africa Report.*)

Nigeria

Forest and Sudan

One of every six Africans is a Nigerian.

Like Congo, Nigeria is a big country carved out of Africa by colonialists, including within its borders many different peoples. In the 1880's British traders pushed inland from their West African coastal bases at Lagos and Port Harcourt, and British soldiers followed the pattern of the traders' paths. In the open sudan hundreds of miles to the north, British adventurers met French —and another line was drawn on the map.

Nigeria dominates West Africa from its position at the inner corner of the West African bulge. Like other West African nations created by colonists pushing inland from the coast, Nigeria includes two regions which had nothing to do with each other until the partition of Africa: the coastal forest and the sudan. The coast is swampy, hot, dense, and wet six months of the year. The

jungles of the coast become rising hills covered with brush forest—the West African "bush." To the north, hills level to the hot, dry sudan.

Nigeria's coast for a long time had a name, like Gold Coast or Ivory Coast. It was Slave Coast. The Ibo of today's Eastern Nigeria were frequently raided for slaves, and in the West the powerful forest kingdoms of Ife, Oyo, and Benin (see Chapter 2) sold their neighbors to slavers for hundreds of years. Dialects of the Yoruba language of Western Nigeria can be heard today in the hills of Brazil.

The Moslem North was a world apart. On the great east-west trade route, Hausa merchants in their skullcaps and flowing, bright-colored robes roamed the length and breadth of the open sudan from Senegal to the Nile. The rulers of the Nigerian sudan were not Hausa but Fulani. In 1802 the Fulani Emperor, Uthman Dan Fodio, led a *jihad* against his enemies and conquered all of what is now Northern

Nigeria. Uthman Dan Fodio's crusading warriors, like the soldiers of Mali and Songhai before them, were stopped as they rode south by the forest wall and by the tsetse fly, which killed their horses. The Fulani still rule in Northern Nigeria. Fulani nobles, called *emirs*, wield both political power and the religious authority of Islam, often meting out justice according to rigid and harsh codes of medieval Islamic law. Fulani aristocrats were regularly elected by the Hausa peasants and traders to local and national parliaments. The Sardauna of Sokoto, traditional leader of the Fulani in time of war, was Premier of Nigeria's Northern Region from 1960 to 1966.

About half of Nigeria's 50 million people live today in the northern section of the country. The 10 million Hausa are the largest "tribe" in all Africa. Moslem Hausa and Fulani, copper-skinned heirs of sudan civilization, look down upon the many small tribes in what is called the "Middle Belt," separating Northern from Southern Nigeria. Many of the black Middle Belt pagans were slave-raiders and cannibals before the British put an end to tribal feuding.

The 5 million Ibo are the majority in the eastern part of Nigeria. (The Ibo are described in Chapter 1.) The Ibo were never united, and only within modern Nigeria have they come to think of themselves as one people. In the mangrove swamps and twisting channels of the Niger River Delta (something like Louisiana bayou country) live African communities which have made their living on trade with Europeans since the eighteenth century.

Western Nigeria is the home of the Yoruba, a proud nation with a long history and a tradition of strong kingdoms. While Lagos, Nigeria's modern capital, was originally a trading post for European ships, Ibadan, Nigeria's second city, has been a Yoruba town for hundreds of years. Loyalty to the chiefs, called *obas*, is still strong among the Yoruba. Most *obas* are now educated leaders.

The Creation of Nigeria

During the nineteenth century the old slave-hunting country around the delta of the Niger River became Britain's main source of palm oil, an important commodity used to make lubricants for British machines and soap for British workmen. Britain staked its claim along that part of the West African coast, and finally, in 1914, the three regions of Lagos, Southern Nigeria, and Northern Nigeria were thrown together by the Colonial Office in London to form a single country. The first Governor-General was the remarkable Lord Lugard, whose wife Flora had first proposed the name "Nigeria" for the colony in 1897.

When British soldiers and traders moved north from the coast in the late nineteenth century, many of the coastal people went with them as government clerks or trading agents. Many of the black-skinned Southerners were Christians, pupils of the Protestant mission schools that had sprung up along the coast with the abolition of the slave trade. They were total strangers to the historic sudan (see Chapter 2.) In this way, unification began.

The British developed Nigeria slowly. Compared with Congo, Nigeria was a poor country, and Britain did not seek great profits. Under Lord Lugard's theory of indirect rule, *emirs* and *obas* were left to rule as in the past. Roads and a railroad were built from the coast to the north, tying forest to sudan, and Yoruba coffee planters and Ibo palm oil traders began to prosper in the new export economy. In the South, the cities of Lagos, Ibadan, and Enugu grew steadily, as migration from overcrowded Iboland to the cities and to the North continued. In contrast to the Belgian Congo, Africans were allowed and encouraged to move around, to get an education, and to go into business for themselves. Nigerians became teachers, lawyers, businessmen (and business-women!), and engineers. A growing number left the mission schools for universities in Britain and America.

While the South grew, the sudan remained a poor land of dust, heat, and cattle, where Hausa peasants scraped a living from barren ground. Joyce Cary's novel *Mister Johnson,* about the adventures of a Southern Nigerian government clerk in the North, described an outpost of the world's greatest empire in the 1930's:

> Fada station has been on a temporary site for twenty years, because nobody has had time or interest to move it. It stands in the thin scrub which covers two thirds of the emirate; that is, all but the river valleys and swamps, where high jungle and tsetse fly are still more discouraging to progress of any kind.
>
> It is as if some giant had tossed down a few scraps of old rotten hay on a mangy lion skin, tufted with moth-eaten fragments of the hair and scarred with long, white seams. These are the marks of temporary water-courses or drains.
>
> The fort, on a slight hill which represents the flattened head-skin of the lion, is a square of earth rampart which has been levelled by time almost to the ground, so that the guard-room inside it, a mud hut with a porch of corrugated iron, stands up like a miniature cracker hat, a kepi, stuck there, on one side of the lion's battered head, in derision. The tin porch is slightly crooked over the gaping door, like a broken peak pulled down over a black, vacant eye. The gateway of the fort is merely a gap in which dogs like to sleep.

Mangy as these district stations may have been, they did bring slow change to the Nigerian sudan. British district officers worked hard to set up schools, build roads between isolated towns, and encourage trade.

In Kano, Kaduna, and other Northern cities, Southerners who had come north as clerks, traders, and teachers lived in a separate town walled off from the ancient Moslem city of the Hausa and Fulani. The strangers were resented be-

The great mosque at Kano. (*Irving Rosenthal.*)

cause they were Christians, because they held the best jobs, and because they challenged the rule of the *emirs.* As the events of January 1966 (see below), and their aftermath, show, the long political battle for the North between traditional *emirs* and modernizing "strangers" from the South continues.

Long Road to Independence

Nigerian nationalism followed the pattern described in Chapters 6, 7, and 8. Nigerians were early given the freedom to publish newspapers and form political groups. In the 1920's African lawyers, many of them *obas* from Western Nigeria, began to organize under the leadership of Herbert Macaulay. In 1937 a young Ibo, Nnamdi Azikiwe, returned to Nigeria from his studies in the United States to publish the *West African Pilot* in Lagos. "Zik" and his newspaper opened a new, radical era in West Africa. In his editorials blasting British colonial policy, "Zik" broke with the older generation of lawyer-politicians. He also broke with their organization to set up the National Council of Nigeria and the Cameroons (NCNC) in 1944.

NCNC tried to become the nationalist party for all Nigeria, but failed. Nigeria was, and is, just not a one-party country. Young Yoruba Chief Obafemi Awolowo formed a rival party, the Action Group, which won the support of many Yorubas. The *emirs*, under their traditional leader, the Sardauna of Sokoto Sir Ahmadu Bello, served notice that they wanted no part of radical nationalism and lined up Northern votes behind their own conservative Northern People's Congress. Within Azikiwe's own party young radicals started the "Zikist" movement, to drive the British out by violence. "Zik" himself would have none of it and managed to stall the hotheads.

There was no question about eventual independence. British reforms drew Nigerians into government. Local councils were elected shortly after World War II. Regional parliaments met a few years later, and by 1957 the Eastern, Western, and Northern Regions each had their own premier — naturally enough Azikiwe, Awolowo, and the Sardauna of Sokoto, respectively. The parties and leaders argued and quarreled over whether Nigeria should have a centralized or a federal form of government. They squabbled over regional boundaries. They fought one another more than they fought the British.

The Federation

Nigeria became independent in 1960 as a federation of three regions, East, West, and North. In each region a single political party ruled with the support of the region's dominant African group: Azikiwe's NCNC (renamed the National Council of Nigerian Citizens) in the Ibo East; Awolowo's Action Group in the Yoruba West; and the Northern People's Congress of the *emirs*. The Federal Parliament in Lagos included representatives of all regions. Sir Abubakar Tafawa Balewa, a Northerner, was Prime Minister from the time of independence.

For five years after independence, the Nigerian Federation was upheld as evidence that democracy could work in Africa. The Federal Parliament saw many compromises between the regional parties and leaders, who somehow managed to settle their quarrels through laws and elections and not with guns and spears. Yet the compromise remained an uneasy and precarious one. In 1963 Chief Awolowo was accused of trying to split the Western Region from the Federation. Azikiwe and the Northerners used their influence to convict him, and Awolowo was jailed until 1966, when the government of Yakubu Gowon released him. A new Mid-West Region, in the area of the old forest kingdom of Benin (see Chapter 2), was carved from the Western Region. And many Southerners continued to suspect that the Northern *emirs*, who in fact controlled the Federal Parliament, had no interest in building a modern, educated, industrial Nigeria and were just using the Federation to hold back progress.

The Collapse

In January 1966 Nigeria's rickety federal system collapsed. The trouble began the previous October, when Akintola, the Premier of the Western Region, rigged an election to prevent his being voted out of office. Akintola's support came from the Northern Region Premier, Sardauna of Sokoto Sir Ahmadu Bello, and he was opposed by Southern "progressives," including both the Action Group and its old nationalist rival, the NCNC. Stuffed ballot boxes in a clear test of North against South led many Southerners to believe that the top *emir* and his allies were determined to sit on Nigerian progress forever and by any means. Nigeria seemed to be in for a long period of conservative rule, with a group of entrenched politicians growing fat through patronage and a weak central government bullied by the regions.

Violence followed the balloting in the West, as Action Groupers took their frustration into the streets. Over a hundred died in riots and beatings. A dusk-to-dawn curfew was clamped down over the Western Region. In Lagos, the federal capital, editors of the *Daily Telegraph* and *West African Pilot* were jailed for "sedition" when they continued to report that the election had been rigged.

A group of young army officers, all Ibos, decided to take matters into their own hands. The plan was direct and brutal. On the night of January 15, 1966, the plotters shot Ahmadu Bello at his palace in Kano. Akintola was also murdered. Three days later the body of Prime Minister Tafawa Balewa was found by a roadside far from the capital.

It seems that only afterwards did the top generals of Nigeria's army find out about the plot. In the confusion General J. T. U. Aguiyi-Ironsi proclaimed army rule "to restore order." Such was the inglorious end, for the time being at least, of Nigerian democracy.

The army government may do more than just "restore order." It has shown signs of tackling Nigeria's political problems, with the backing of practically everyone who counts, from bureaucrats to market women. In fact the Nigerian "establishment"—except, of course, the *emirs*—jumped on the army bandwagon. The honeymoon is not likely to last too long, though, particularly if the generals make a real effort toward national unity (an end to regional privileges and independence) and faster economic development. In such a large country with so many different and competing political factions, tribal groups, and economic interests, any active policy will step on someone's toes.

Nigerians seem to think that democracy was abused by Nigerian leaders, and that a "progressive" military government is better than an inefficient and somewhat corrupt parliamentary one. Yet while the Federation foundered on regional conflict, there is no evidence that Nigerian citizens rejected the idea of government "by the people." Eventually, a new way must be found to give the many active and interested Nigerians a say in national policy.

Groping Progress

As under the British, Nigerian economic development is going slowly and has been marked by fumblings and failings. The very ambitious plan for economic development from 1962 to 1968—

Nigerian Political Questions

Problem	Proposed Solution	Action
Domination of the country by the Northern Region and its leaders through the Northern majority in Parliament.	Splinter Nigeria into many small units.	Under consideration by the army government.
Conflict between regions and competition for funds.	Strengthen the power of the federal government.	Military governors directed from Lagos now rule. Regions abolished.
Excessive politicking and, in some instances, corruption. Growth of a "political class" with special privileges.	Strong government, by a single party or the army. Crackdown on waste and corruption. Stress on competence.	All politicians now have lost their jobs, servants, and limousines— and their access to the public treasury.
Lack of dynamic and purposeful leadership.	More "progressive" leaders in power.	Remains to be seen.

an achievement in itself—depends on foreign aid (see chart on page 281). The United States agreed to back the plan in an effort to show that progress is possible in Africa under a free enterprise economy. A huge dam will provide power for cities and factories, the first bridge across the Niger River will soon be in use, and an oil refinery is being built at Port Harcourt in the East. Modern education, long eagerly sought in the South, is spreading to the Moslem North at last. Oil, recently discovered in the Niger Delta, will help pay for development. Yet the obstacles to progress are great. Nigeria is not rich in minerals, Iboland is already overcrowded, and little can be done with the dry plains of the North. For years to come most Nigerians will continue to scrape a bare living from the soil.

Yet while progress is slow it has been steady. In contrast to Congo, there *are* Nigerian planners, budget makers, census takers, and economists to chart the course of the economy—men trained under British rule. Small businesses, run by Nigerian men and women, sprang up during the British regime, and many have prospered since independence, continuing a long Nigerian tradition of commerce begun in the days when sailing ships of many European powers traded along the Nigerian coast. Again unlike Congo, the foreign companies in Nigeria such as the giant Unilever trained Nigerians for responsible posts, and Nigerians are managing foreign trade, banking, and finance. While the January 1966 army takeover was a political change of great importance, Nigeria's economy was not damaged and may even be helped under a more austere and development-conscious regime.

Whose Responsibility?

It is easy enough to say, as many have done, that the relative success of such an improbable country as Nigeria

was due to a wise British policy of preparation, while Congo's brutal anarchy and economic ruin resulted from Belgium's failure to educate Congolese and its subsequent hasty grant of independence to a jumble of tribes held together only by Belgian officials and industries. Praise or blame for colonialists, however, is not enough, for in Africa it is the future, not the past, which counts.

Nigerian leaders, whether civilian or military, must grapple continually with the problem of unity. Southerners, divided among themselves, protest what they consider the dead hand of the tradition-bound Islamic North on progress and modernization. While oil revenues and aid from the outside world may ease the strain on development funds, bringing schools and literacy, factories and jobs to over 50 million people is a staggering task under even the best of circumstances. The battle for orderly development has only begun.

Congo's problems boggle the imagination. Katanga's riches could finance development if profits are diverted to Congo's government—and then wisely used. Plantation agriculture, too, could produce food and fibers for Congolese to eat and wear, rather than export. The fine social and medical services begun by the Belgians could be revived and expanded. The hundreds of thousands of unemployed men in the streets of Congo's cities want work and pay, and their children would rather join schools than streetcorner gangs. But all this takes men, and points to the glaring absence of Congolese willing and able to plan, lead, and administer in the slums and in the "bush."

After years of tribal warfare, Humpty Dumpty must be put back together again. When is a man Congolese, and not Ngombe, Luba, or Mongo? For better or worse, Congo has its independence, and the burden now lies squarely on Congolese leaders to stop bickering for personal power, feuding, seceding, rebelling, and calling on outsiders, and to get on with the job of nation build-ing. The new military regime of General Mobutu claims that it will try.

Ironically, both Nigeria's seemingly steady course and Congo's violence and disorder ended in military takeovers. Perhaps, in spite of all other differences, any nation so large and so torn by tribal and regional loyalties needs a strong hand at the helm. Another moral, judg-ing from the criticism of both Congolese and Nigerian leaders as corrupt, power-seeking politicians, is that national leaders must demonstrate that they put the people's welfare before their own. Whatever the praise or blame due colonialists, the responsibility, once claimed by Africans, is theirs.

PROBLEMS

1. Although today's African leaders say little about it, the theories and doctrines of the colonial powers (see Chapter 4) had a great influence on the progress of their colonies, both before and after independence. How is this shown in the cases of Nigeria and Congo?

2. Names of people and places multiply through this chapter. Match:

Ibadan	the most powerful *emir* in Nigeria
Kasai	Congo's seaport
Leopold II	NCNC boss
Obafemi Awolowo	owner of the Congo Free State
Antoine Gizenga	diamond region of southern Congo
Matadi	Nigeria's capital and port
Sardauna of Sokoto	people of Katanga and Zambia (Northern Rhodesia)
Yoruba	Yoruba leader
Nnamdi Azikiwe	Western Nigerians, or most of them
Lunda	headquarters of Union Minière
Lagos	Lumumba's lieutenant
Elisabethville	old African city of Western Nigeria

3. What does the question "Are Africans capable of governing themselves?" really mean? Draw up a list of conditions necessary for self-government by the people of *any* large country.

4. In what circumstances would you favor outside intervention in an African country? Outsiders capable of intervening include the United States, the Soviet Union, the former colonial ruler, other African states, and the United Nations. How many of these did in fact intervene in Congo? Which kind of intervention sets a good or a bad precedent for order and stable progress?

5. One solution to the problem of unity within African countries is a federal government like that of the United States, or of Nigeria until 1966. Could Congo have been held together as a federation? What does federal government require of politicians and regional leaders? Has American federalism ever broken down? Why?

6. Draw up a plan for reconstruction of Congo, dealing with these problems:
    a. Tribal versus national loyalty among Congolese Africans
    b. Foreign control of all mining and industry
    c. Lack of trained men for local administration, the army, and economic planning

d. Absence of any strong nationwide political parties or other African organizations

What kind of government would be required to carry out your plan? Have the Nigerians solved these problems?

READING SUGGESTIONS

Nigeria

Chinua Achebe, *No Longer at Ease,* Obolensky, 1961.

———, *Things Fall Apart,* Obolensky, 1959.

Obafemi Awolowo, *Awo: The Writings of Obafemi Awolowo,* Cambridge University Press (London), paper.

Nnamdi Azikiwe, *Zik: The Writings of Nnamdi Azikiwe,* Cambridge University Press (London), paper.

Joyce Cary, *Mister Johnson,* Harper & Row, 1948.

Chief H. O. Davies, *Nigeria: The Prospects for Democracy,* Weidenfeld (London), 1961.

Cyprian Ekwensi, *People of the City,* Dakers (London), 1954.

F. D. Lugard, *The Dual Mandate in British Tropical Africa,* Blackwood (London), 1922.

Lois Mitchison, *Nigeria: Newest Nation,* Praeger, paper.

Congo

Georges Brausch, *Belgian Administration in the Congo,* Oxford University Press (London), paper.

Joseph Conrad, *Heart of Darkness,* New American Library, paper.

King Gordon, *The UN in the Congo,* Carnegie, 1962.

Smith Hempstone, *Rebels, Mercenaries, and Dividends,* Praeger, 1962.

Richard G. Lawson, *Strange Soldiering,* Hodder and Stoughton (London), 1963.

Colin Legum, *Congo Disaster,* Penguin, paper.

Alan Merriam, *Congo: Background of Conflict,* Northwestern University Press, 1961.

Conor Cruise O'Brien, *To Katanga and Back,* Simon and Schuster, 1963.

Ruth Slade, *The Belgian Congo,* Oxford University Press (London), paper.

chapter 11
ETHIOPIA AND LIBERIA

This country can no longer afford the luxury of able-bodied men loafing from one center to another and living off their brothers who are gainfully employed. We shall strictly enforce the proposition that he who is able to work and can find work but will not work, should not eat.

—WILLIAM V. S. TUBMAN
President of Liberia,
Fourth Inaugural Address, Jan. 4, 1960

Sawan mamman ba-kantu naw. [It is futile to trust in man.]

—*Amharic proverb woven into wool rugs*

Liberia and Ethiopia are the only countries in all of Africa that remained independent after its partition. Today they are among the continent's least-developed countries, and their backwardness points by reverse example to the benefits of colonial education and economic development elsewhere. Both countries are governed by minorities who wish to preserve the privileges of the past: Ethiopia by an emperor, princes, and noblemen; Liberia by the True Whig Party of the Americo-Liberian ruling class. In neither country are the mass of the people pressing for change. This is not surprising, for outside the ruling groups almost no one can read or write, and almost all are subsistence farmers growing their food in a plot beside their hut as their fathers have done for the past thousand years.

The United States has been concerned with Liberia since its origin in the 1820's as a home for American Negroes freed from slavery. Recently Ethiopia has received much American aid, and Emperor Haile Selassie has long been popular with Americans. Both Haile Selassie and President William Tubman of Liberia are skillful diplomats who take an active part in African affairs. But here the similarities end. Both Ethiopia and Liberia are unusual countries—even for Africa. The Liberian upper class, descended from American slaves, has brought the culture of the Old South to Africa. Ethiopians, on the other hand, have been Christians since the fourth century, and Ethiopia is a nation older than the nations of Europe. Liberia's dense and humid tropics are the African geographic extreme from Ethiopia's cool highlands.

Both countries are now being thoroughly explored and prospected for the first time. The only certainty is that change is just around the corner.

Liberia

Liberia lies on the southeast corner of the West African bulge, only 5 degrees north of the equator. It is one of the smaller African countries, about the size of Pennsylvania. The Liberian coastal plain, extending 20 to 40 miles inland from the coast, gets more than 200 inches of rainfall every wet season, between April and October. Temperatures and humidity remain in the nineties. Behind the coastal strip the land rises gradually to the inland plateau. The low hills are covered by forest, the West African "bush."

No one knows how many Liberians there are. Estimates range from less than a million to four million. About 80,000 people live in Monrovia, the capital.

The Founding of Liberia

In the early years of the nineteenth century influential Americans, concerned with the growing number of free slaves in Northern and Southern cities, sought to repatriate them to Africa. The American Colonization Society, founded in 1816, was sponsored by such Americans as Henry Clay, John Marshall, and President James Monroe, for whom Monrovia was named. The United States Congress appropriated $100,000 to help the settlers with teachers, farm tools, and the construction of homes.

In 1822 the Colonization Society landed its first settlers near the present site of Monrovia. The colony was named Liberia—"the Free Land." From the first, the settlers, now called Americo-Liberians, clashed with the local tribesmen, and more than once called on the United States Navy to protect the coastal settlements. In 1847 the Americo-Liberians declared Liberia independent. Although Britain immediately recognized the new nation, the United States did not do so until 1862—mainly because recognition would have meant accepting a Negro ambassador in Washington.

Black Colonialism

Like whites elsewhere in Africa, the Negro colonists were strangers to the native tribes of Liberia. The policy followed by the Americo-Liberians from 1847 to 1944 was colonialism of the cruder variety, more like Portuguese than British or French policy.

The Americo-Liberians started by "buying" a strip of land 130 miles long and 40 miles wide from the local Dei and Mamba chiefs. As usual, no one bothered to question whether the chief had any right to sell the land of his people. Skirmishes between Liberian troops armed with guns and tribesmen armed with bow and spear occurred often. Treaties of friendship and protection (which as far as the Africans were concerned represented the kind of "protection" given by racketeers to businessmen) extended the rule of the coastal settlers. The Grebo, Kru, and Mandingo peoples put up a stiff resistance which did not end until the 1930's. For most of Liberia's history, the hinterland has been ruled by military occupation.

The supremacy of the Americo-Liberian minority was enforced in other ways. Native Africans were forced to work on the farms of Americo-Liberians for little or no pay. Forced labor ended only in the 1930's after a League of Nations accusation that Liberia permitted and even encouraged slavery. Hut taxes and other special taxes were levied at will by local officials. Tribal leaders who resisted were deported from their home areas. Tribesmen were not allowed to move to Monrovia or other Americo-Liberian towns without permission. In fact, the Americo-Liberians were separated from the native peoples by laws which greatly resembled the *apartheid* policy of South Africa today.

President Tubman and Unification

In 1943 William V. S. Tubman became President of a country that had been shaken repeatedly by scandals of slavery and of corruption in high places. The new President was young and energetic, and he understood that reform was necessary. President Tubman's unification policy sought to integrate the tribal peoples with the Americo-Liberians in a single nation and to begin the modernization of Liberia.

Over the past twenty years, Tubman's efforts have in part achieved their aim. Roads and bridges have been built to bring the nation under a single network of communications. Doctors, teachers, and agricultural experts have been sent to bring literacy, longer life, and more food to the people of the hinterland. The iron mines and plantations operated by American companies under Tubman's "open door" policy have brought jobs and regular wages to many tribesmen. Irreversible economic revolution is bringing all of Liberia slowly into the modern age.

Tubman has done much to lessen the division between the Americo-Liberians and the "other element," as the natives are called. He regularly tours the back country dispensing personal justice and listening to complaints against local Americo-Liberian officials. All Liberians who pay taxes can vote. A few Liberians from the interior have been appointed to high government positions. To break down social discrimination, Tubman has appeared in tribal dress, has adopted tribal titles, and has encouraged traditional arts and dances. His policy of moderate reform has made him popular both in Monrovia and in the hinterland.

The Americo-Liberians

The Americo-Liberian elite are known as "honorables." The honorables are descended from the 15,000 freed slaves who came to Liberia from the New World. The Americo-Liberians live in Monrovia and in adjoining Maryland and Montserrado Counties along the coast.

The Americo-Liberian community is in many ways a caricature of nineteenth-century America, and in particular of the Old South, which was the home of the slave ancestors of the Americo-Liberians. Tail coats and top hats are worn to social functions in 90-degree heat. Stately homes of leading Monrovia families resemble the plantation houses of Carolina or Mississippi. The wealthy Liberian is a gentleman farmer who lives in gracious style and goes to a Protestant church on Sundays. His name might be Sherman or Barclay, he is a member of the True Whig Party, and, of course, he speaks only English.

The Oligarchy

Within the Americo-Liberian community perhaps fifteen very wealthy families rule the country. This is a true oligarchy—rule by the wealthy few. The oligarchy rules by personal influence and by patronage within the True Whig Party. By way of illustration, in 1960 President Tubman's brother-in-law was Ambassador to the United States. His wife's cousin was Secretary of State. Two of Tubman's own cousins were Ambassador to the United Nations and Inspector of Counties (an important internal administrative post). Two brothers of Vice-President Tolbert were Secretary of Commerce and Senator from Montserrado County. These two families are related by marriage to almost everyone in the Liberian government. To complete the circle, President Tubman's son William Jr., head of the General Confederation of Labor, recently married the daughter of Vice-President Tolbert.

Even the strongest constitution could not survive such a web of personal entanglements. The Liberian Constitution is almost a carbon copy of the American, and was in fact written by a Harvard professor in 1847. All the senators, representatives, and judges, with the exception of six representatives from the interior, are of course Americo-Liberian honorables. Most are related to the handful of ruling families.

The True Whig Party, whose name brings echoes of Henry Clay and Daniel

Webster, has dominated Liberia for eighty years and is supported by the whole Americo-Liberian community. In 1959 President Tubman, running on the True Whig ticket, polled 530,472 votes to 55 for his opponent. The real opposition to the True Whig oligarchy is the African native majority, which has no effective political voice.

Patronage benefits the ruling group. Sons of honorables are sent by the hundreds to study in the United States on Liberian government scholarships. To create plush diplomatic jobs for Americo-Liberians, Liberia maintains embassies in most important world capitals and in almost all independent African countries as well. At home, a swollen bureaucracy well greased with "dash" (petty bribes) is rewarded with houses, cars, and trips abroad.

Economic Change

If by chance you lost your way near Mount Nimba in northwestern Liberia, your compass would be of little use. Mount Nimba is a huge chunk of high-grade iron ore, which can be mined simply by carting away the mountainside. The iron ore at Nimba and at the Bomi Hills in central Liberia has become the main prop of the modern sector of the Liberian economy. Deposits of manganese, lead, and bauxite (from which aluminum is made) have not yet been touched. Two railroads carry the ore to the coast, and four artificial harbors have been built in the last twenty years to handle Liberia's export trade.

Until the late 1940's exports of natural rubber supported Liberia. The Firestone Rubber Company began operations in 1924. Firestone plantations today account for 87 percent of Liberia's rubber exports and employ 22,000 workers, most of them tribal people from the interior. The Liberian government has on occasion prevented Firestone from raising the wage of its workers, because this would force Americo-Liberian plantation owners to do the same.

Tapping a rubber tree on the Firestone plantations in Liberia. The plastic basin will catch latex dripping from the cut in the bark. (*Africa Report.*)

Since 1944, when President Tubman proclaimed the "open door" policy, Liberia has encouraged foreign investment. Four hundred million dollars, mostly from the United States, has been invested by twenty-five companies. Through contracts, legal fees, and taxes these American investments maintain the wealth and position of the Americo-Liberians, who have traditionally shunned trade and industry, preferring politics to business. In 1950 fully 90 percent of Liberia's exports went to the United States. In 1959, following the postwar recovery of Western Europe and Japan, the United States took only 60 percent. By 1960 Liberia had received $88 million in direct aid from the United States. In addition, Americans train and equip the Liberian Army.

In spite of these changes, the great majority of Liberians are still subsistence farmers or fishermen in a tribal economy. Liberian peasants have just begun to feel the pull of industrial jobs.

The Future

Liberia is still a colonial country which has not yet experienced the storm of modern African nationalism. Liberia spends almost nothing on education for the "other element." The benefits of foreign investment continue to go mainly to the Americo-Liberians, while workers on Americo-Liberian plantations earn less than 50 cents a day. As the economy grows the gap between rich and poor increases. The government has done little to develop the interior, and Liberian officials outside the capital are still mainly tax collectors. Liberians of tribal background suffer severe social discrimination and must learn the English language and Americo-Liberian customs before they are allowed to mix with honorables.

To add to this serious situation, the Americo-Liberians themselves have forfeited a useful place in their country's development. Sons sent away to school study liberal arts and law, and are not trained as the doctors, teachers, engineers, and businessmen which Liberia needs. Foreigners, not Liberians, run and profit from Liberia's export economy. On the other hand, the number of African Liberian students educated at Protestant mission schools and at the Episcopalian Cuttington College is growing rapidly. In time, these students

Ethiopian journeys can end like this. Much of the country can be reached only by air in the wet season. (*World Bank*.)

and the iron miners and rubber plantation workers may become the leaders of a Liberian nationalism of the "other element," demanding a greater share of wealth, education, and privileges, and posing a direct challenge to the Americo-Liberian ruling class.

Ethiopia

Ethiopia is *in* Africa, but it is not *of* Africa. Over more than fifteen hundred years Ethiopia has evolved its own unique tradition of Christianity and empire atop its rugged and almost inaccessible highlands. For thirty-five years Haile Selassie, Emperor of Ethiopia, Lion of Judah, and Negus Negusi, King of Kings, has been nudging his country toward modernity. Today he is trying to link Ethiopia to modern Africa after a millenium of isolation from the rest of the continent.

Ethiopia became to both Westerners and Africans a symbol of African civilization. The Greeks named the lands to the south of the Sahara "Ethiopia"— "the lands of those who burn their faces black." To the Christian Europeans and Crusaders of the Middle Ages, Ethiopia was the land of Prester John, a fabulous Christian empire beyond the enemy Moslem lands.

Modern Ethiopia cannot be understood apart from its long history, which could easily fill a volume of its own. That history, and its continuation in the present, has been shaped by geography and by religion. Ethiopia has been called the Christian Highlands, and that phrase is the key to Ethiopia past and present.

Geography

Ethiopia is the size of Texas, New Mexico, and Arizona, and is in the jagged northeast corner of the great East African plateau. Like walls protecting the highland, sheer red cliffs rise several thousand feet from both the sudan lowlands on the west and the strip of desert along the Red Sea coast to the north. The Christian heart of the empire has always been the north-central region, where mountain ridges rise to over 13,000 feet. To the southeast, the plateau falls away to the low desert grazing lands of the Galla, Sidamo, and Somali peoples. The plateau is cut by deep canyons that are almost impossible to cross. The gorge of the Blue Nile, which begins at 6,000-foot-high Lake Tana, is at places the size of Arizona's Grand Canyon. While the heights above are cool and rocky, the bottom of the valley is a thick tropical jungle that has never been thoroughly explored.

Modern visitors, like other invaders and travelers over the past 2,000 years, are blocked by the formidable terrain. The few dirt tracks that pass for roads (one cannot drive directly from Gondar to Addis Ababa) are quagmires during the June-to-October season of the Big Rains, and not even foot bridges have been built over many of the mountain rivers.

The highland plateau is dotted by the high, flat-topped cores of extinct volcanoes. They are called *ambas* and are something like the mesas of the American West. The tops of the *ambas* can be farmed or used as pasture. In the past, Ethiopian feudal barons and their followers fortified *ambas* against all comers. On Wehni, the Mountain of the Princes, near the ancient capital of Gondar, were confined all those many sons and relatives of the emperor who might challenge his claim to the throne.

Religion

In the fourth century A.D. the Ethiopian kingdom of Axum adopted Christianity. According to the story, this fateful event was the result of a romantic accident. Two small Greek Christian boys and their tutor were traveling on board a ship bound for East African ports. The ship was captured by pirates, and all were put to death except the two boys. These orphans were found by the

Castle at Gondar.

local king and raised as princes. One of them converted the king to Christianity. He then traveled to Alexandria, in Egypt, was made a bishop by the Egyptian Patriarch (this was 300 years before the birth of the prophet Mohammed), and returned to convert the kingdom of Axum. He is called Saint Frumentius, founder of the Ethiopian Church.

Ethiopian Christianity is of the Egyptian, or Coptic, variety. This African branch of Christianity broke with both the Church of Rome and the Greek Orthodox Church in A.D. 451 in a doctrinal controversy.

The Ethiopian Church flourished during the Middle Ages. Churches with elaborate stone carvings and pillars were hewn from the solid rock of the mountainsides and decorated with paintings celebrating the deeds of saints, kings, and martyrs. As in medieval Europe, monasteries flourished, and monks were the scribes who recorded the deeds of emperors. The medieval Ethiopian chronicle, called the *Kebra Negast*, or Book of Kings, was written by monks in Gheez, the ancient language of the Ethiopian Church.

Ethiopian Christanity is strange to the West, although it is a more direct descendant of the early Church than are Western Protestant sects. An English traveler once asked his guide, "What is that strange howling noise which I hear among the trees? I have heard it several times when the rustling of the wind has died away for a moment. It sounds something like a chant or a dismal moaning song; only it is different in cadence from anything that I have heard before." The guide answered that the strange sound was the chant of the bearded Ethiopian monks.

History

Ethiopia was for 1,200 years a Christian nation holding its mountain stronghold against the encirclement of Islam. In the last 100 years, the arrival of the modern West in Africa has put Ethiopia on a new course. It is adapting its tradition to a less religious but much more technological age.

The first Ethiopian state was the kingdom of Axum, which lasted from the third to the seventh century A.D. The kings of Axum raided the Nile Val-

ley, where they destroyed the iron-making city of Meröe (see Chapter 2), and even ventured across the Red Sea to Arabia. In 570 the Prophet Mohammed was born at Mecca; in that same year the armies of King Kaleb of Axum almost captured the city.

The first great wave of Islamic expansion, which carried Moslem armies to Central Asia in the east and across North Africa and Spain to France in the west, bypassed Ethiopia. During the seventh century Arabs captured the Red Sea coast, and the Christian Highlands were cut off from the outside world. The next 500 years were the Ethiopian Dark Ages, marked by hundreds of local wars and hundreds of crusades against the Moslem states on the coast. Christian Europe, fighting one of history's longest and fiercest wars against Islam, once almost broke through the Moslem barrier to reach the Christians to the south. In 1182 an expedition led by a French Crusader set sail on the Red Sea for the "Empire of Prester John." The Crusaders were overtaken by an Arab squadron and annihilated.

In the fifteenth century Portuguese sea captains found the African sea route around the Moslem barrier (see Chapter 3). In 1520 a Portuguese force headed by the Jesuit missionary Francisco Alvarez reached Ethiopia. Father Alvarez's detailed *Narrative of the Portuguese Embassy to Abyssinia, 1520–27*, finally enlightened Europe about the legendary empire of Prester John. The truth was strange enough. The empire had no capital, and the emperor traveled constantly with his thousands of retainers from place to place to surprise any prince or chieftain who might be planning to rebel. Reported Father Alvarez:

Ancient obelisk at Axum.

> The Prester John rarely travels straight, nor does anyone know where he is going. This multitude of people travels along the road until they find a white tent pitched, and there they settle down each in his own place . . .

The altar stone or stones of all the churches are treated with much reverence on the way, and are carried only by mass priests, and always four priests go with each stone, and four others to take turns with them; they carry these stones as if on a stretcher raised on their shoulders, and covered with rich cloths of brocade and silk. In front of each altar or stone, for all go together, walk two deacons, with thurible [incense burner] and cross, and another with a bell ringing it. . . .

Also whenever the Prester travels with his court, four lions always go before him; these too travel by the straight road, and they go bound with strong chains. . . .

The Moslem powers feared an anti-Islamic alliance between Ethiopia and Portugal. As soon as Father Alvarez and his mission left in 1527, a strong Moslem army under Mohammed Granj, the left-handed, invaded and overran the highlands. Churches with their paintings and manuscripts were burned and monks murdered, and the emperor fled to a fortified *amba*. Seeing Ethiopia about to go down under the Moslem attack, Portugal sent a relief expedition in 1541. After defeat, hardship, and the death of their captain, the Portuguese gathered an Ethiopian army, attacked the Moslem camp at dawn, and drove off the invaders.

Unfortunately for the Portuguese, Jesuit missionaries sent to convert Ethiopia to the Church of Rome offended their hosts. The Jesuits were expelled by Emperor Facilidas in 1632, and Ethiopian isolation and hostility to foreigners continued for another 250 years.

Gondar became the permanent capital of the King of Kings. The empire, however, became a fiction as robber barons and their private armies plunged Ethiopia into a bloody feudalism. Serfdom was the lot of every peasant, and slave-raiding a major occupation of the war lords.

Finally a robber baron named Kassa became Emperor in 1855 and took the name of Theodore. Ethiopians learned of the progress of the Western world, and Theodore imported Swiss, German, and English engineers to bring technology to Ethiopia. Prey to a growing madness, Theodore later imprisoned the Europeans. In 1868 British General Robert Napier led an army to Ethiopia to free the captives. British Prime Minister Disraeli, with a true imperial flair, exclaimed, "We have hoisted the standard of St. George on the Mountains of Rasselas." The British left carrying the sacred *Kebra Negast* and Theodore's crown.

Menelik II, who became Emperor in 1889, finally united Ethiopia under strong rule. Menelik conquered what is today southern and eastern Ethiopia from the local Galla and Somali rulers and established his capital at Addis Ababa. He introduced the first telephones, electric lights, and public schools. Thus the first modernizer was not a European but an Ethiopian emperor.

Britain, France, Germany, and Belgium had carved up Africa—only the horn of the continent was left. The Italians, eager for some spoils, invaded Ethiopia in 1896 from their coastal colony of Eritrea. Menelik was well-prepared. At Adowa Ethiopian soldiers routed the Italians in a major battle. This was the first and only lasting victory of an African country against European imperialism.

In 1930, young Ras (Prince) Tafari became Emperor. He claimed unbroken descent from Solomon and was crowned Emperor Haile Selassie, which means "power of the Trinity." Yet for all this stress on holy tradition the young Emperor has been gently modernizing his country ever since.

In 1935 the Italians were back, this time with aircraft, bombs, and poison gas. Haile Selassie was forced into exile while patriot guerillas continued to harass the Italians. In 1941 British and Ethiopian troops restored the Emperor.

The People

The rulers of Ethiopia are the Amhara people of the north and central highlands. Amharic is the official language of Ethiopia. The Amhara are peasant farmers, formerly serfs of Amhara feudal lords and *ras* (princes). They are copper-colored and are descended from the original African Caucasians (often called Hamites). Amhara always considered themselves "white," in contrast with African Negroes. When Europeans arrived in the sixteenth century they were naturally called "pink," and are so called to this day.

Ethiopia is a true empire, for within its borders the Christian Amhara rule a number of other peoples wih distinctively different cultures and ways of life (see map on page 5).

Along the western fringe of Ethiopia, where the highland plateau drops to the lowlands, live primitive Negro tribes. The Amhara regard these *shingalla* (Negroes) with disdain, and ignored them for centuries, using western Ethiopia as a slave-raiding preserve.

Since the sixteenth century another group, the Galla, have been migrating westward from the horn of Africa into Ethiopia. The Galla, like the Amhara, are a Hamitic people, but, unlike the Amhara, they are horsemen and nomads. Some Galla adopted Christianity and intermarried with the Amharas. Others have become Moslems. Most keep their Galla religion and culture.

In the desert eastern provinces, Haud and Ogaden, live Moslem Somalis. The Somalis are camel nomads who wander between Ethiopia and Somalia, ignoring the international boundary. Somalia claims these eastern provinces conquered by Ethiopia. The intermittent border war between Somalia and Ethiopia flared up again in 1963. Like most other African countries, Ethiopia has the problem of many peoples within a single country. Yet unlike most others, it has a long tradition of empire and a strong ruling group.

With modern methods and machinery, carefully applied, Ethiopia could feed perhaps 100 million people. This tractor plows land to be planted with cotton. (*United Nations.*)

Modernization

Ethiopia is at present one of Africa's more backward countries. No one knows how many Ethiopians there are. The government estimates about twenty million, others estimate less. All but a tiny educated group living in Addis Ababa, the capital, are peasants or nomads living in their traditional way and happy to continue as before. There is as yet no popular mandate for change.

What change has come has been pressed from the Emperor down upon sometimes balky subjects. Haile Selassie is his own Minister of Education, symbolizing the importance he attaches to having his people learn modern skills. Yet perhaps no more than two or three of every hundred Ethiopians can read. The University College of Addis Ababa was dedicated by the Emperor in 1950, and today has about 500 students.

Ethiopia, unlike most African countries, was not forced into dependence on world trade by the colonial development of an export economy. Coffee is grown for export by Amhara peasants on the fertile highlands, and hides come

Africa Hall in Addis Ababa, headquarters of the Organization of African Unity (see Chapter 14) and the United Nations Economic Commission for Africa. *(United Nations.)*

from the southern ranges. These products are shipped over the single-track railroad from Addis Ababa to the port of Djibouti in French Somaliland. Ethiopia probably has vast mineral resources. The World Bank is at present assisting in finding them.

Ethiopia is still an absolute monarchy —one of the last left on earth. Parliament meets, but its members are local chieftains who take orders from the Emperor and accept the laws he submits. There are no political parties. In 1960 a group of dissatisfied Addis Ababa intellectuals tried to overthrow Haile Selassie while he was away in Brazil. The rebellion failed, because it had no support among the peasants outside the capital.

Haile Selassie continues to modernize his country slowly, in the manner of a true conservative. He wants technical progress, but he also wants to preserve Ethiopia's tradition of Christianity and empire.

Ethiopia Comes to Africa

In 1935 Haile Selassie became a world-famous statesman when he denounced Italian aggression against Ethiopia before the League of Nations at Geneva. In the 1960's, Haile Selassie is using the Ethiopian heritage of independence and his own renown to become one of Africa's elder statesmen. Ethiopia is no longer isolated from Africa.

The 1963 Pan-African meeting (see Chapter 14) was held in Addis Ababa. African nationalists such as Kwame Nkrumah and Sékou Touré toasted their host, Haile Selassie, in the palace of the Lion of Judah, though a more striking contrast could scarcely be found than that between the Emperor claiming descent from Solomon and the peasant boys made good whose only title for many years was "P.G."—prison gradu- ate. Africa Hall in Addis Ababa is now headquarters for both the Organization of African Unity and the United Nations Economic Commission for Africa (ECA).

What Price Modernization?

In colonial Africa—all Africa except Ethiopia and Liberia—white men from across the sea brought the tools and ideas of modern times to African communities. Cities, mines and plantations, money and taxes, roads and railroads, the beginnings of mass education, bureaucracy and paper work—all were imposed by the colonial outsiders. Yet in great measure it was not any evil intentions of the colonizers but the great changes which these institutions themselves imposed upon Africans which re- sulted in African discontent under colonial rule.

In the colonies, African nationalists could blame "imperialism" for the mass discontent that accompanied change, and could channel frustration into the independence campaign. Liberian and Ethiopian leaders have no such luxury. Both William Tubman and Haile Selassie, knowing that modernization is inevitable, have tried to promote change only gradually and in small doses. They rightly fear that, just as happened in the African colonies, accelerating change will sweep them and the traditional ruling groups they represent from power. Indeed, a change of leadership may well be the long-term result of bringing still largely undeveloped Ethiopia and Liberia into step with the twentieth century.

PROBLEMS

1. Why, in your opinion, have Liberia and Ethiopia lagged behind some other African countries in their social, economic, and political development? Are they more stable than other African countries?

2. The United States has since 1944 contributed more than $100 million in foreign aid to Liberia. Assuming that most of this aid goes to the Americo-Liberian community, do you think the money is well spent? How could American aid best be used in Liberia? Would you give aid to Ethiopia to be used at the discretion of Emperor Haile Selassie?

3. Try to find examples of great Ethiopian religious art and make up an exhibit. How does Ethiopian art resemble the Christian paintings and illuminated manuscripts and architecture of medieval Europe?

4. Why did the Ethiopian Empire and its traditions survive, while the empires of the West African sudan (Ghana, Mali, Songhai) did not? Did Christianity in Ethiopia make a difference?

5. Is Liberia's settler problem like that of Kenya, Algeria, and South Africa? How does it differ? What are the prospects for the future?

READING SUGGESTIONS

Liberia

W. A. Hance, "Liberia," in *African Economic Development,* Harper & Row, 1958.

Gus Liebenow, "Liberia," in Gwendolen Carter (ed.), *African One-party States*, Cornell University Press, 1962.

E. J. Yancy, *The Republic of Liberia*, G. Allen (London), 1959.

Ethiopia

Ernst W. Luther, *Ethiopia Today*, Stanford University Press, 1959.

Alan Moorehead, *The Blue Nile*, Dell, paper.

Leonard Mosley, *Haile Selassie*, Weidenfeld (London), 1964.

Thomas Pakenham, *The Mountains of Rasselas*, Weidenfeld (London), 1959.

chapter 12

SOUTH AFRICA

When a man loves, he seeks no power, and
therefore he has power. I see only one hope
for our country, and that is when white
men and black men, desiring neither
power nor money, but desiring only the
good of the country, come together to work
for it.

He was grave and silent, and then he
said sombrely, I have one great fear in
my heart, that one day when they are
turned to loving, they will find we are
turned to hating.

ALAN PATON,
Msimangu to Kumalo, in
Cry the Beloved Country

Net Vir Blankes: For Whites Only

Endowed with great mineral resources and with a temperate climate
and much good soil, South Africa is a
rich country. Building on this wealth, it
has become in the last decade the fore-
most industrial country in Africa.

Prosperity and economic growth
should have begun to transform colonial
South Africa, with its sharp distinctions
between white rulers and black Africans, into a modern society with equal
political rights and more opportunities for those who did not have the
good fortune to be born with a white
skin. Instead, the opposite has happened. Impelled by a stern and intolerant Calvinist heritage and by an image
of themselves as the Chosen People, the
Afrikaners—white South Africans descended from early Dutch and other
European settlers—have taken control
of the South African government and
are using it to enforce racial inequality
and discrimination in every aspect of
human life. The result is the policy of
total separation of the races—*apartheid*.

While South African whites live very
well indeed, the black man is the victim
of a police state no less oppressive than
Hitler's Germany or Stalin's Russia. At
any time, he can be jailed, fired, or ordered to move from his home. He is denied modern education, a good job, and
the right to vote. He must live in a segregated "African location," carry a pass
book, stay out of "white areas" after
curfew, and bow and scrape to any white
man who condescends to greet him.

The implications of *apartheid* reach
far beyond South Africa's borders. Independent African nations have declared their intention to liberate South
Africa's 12 million nonwhites, by force
if necessary. Communists, hoping to incite and control a South African revolution, and ever eager to damage the
United States by propaganda, condemn
South Africa as an outpost of "western imperialism." The United States and
Britain, repelled by racism and oppression and not wanting to poison relations
with other African and Asian countries,
have formally condemned *apartheid* as
well, while hoping that South African

182

Hundreds of thousands of South Africa's blacks have been forcibly resettled in huge "locations" far from their city homes and their jobs. This community protests eviction. *(Information Service of South Africa.)*

whites will change their policies. All recognize South Africa as a threat to world peace, and as a possible cold war battleground.

There Are No South Africans

South Africa is a patchwork of races, languages, and cultures—a mosaic of distinct peoples. The five main groups of people who live in South Africa are the Afrikaners, Africans, Coloureds, English, and Indians. These are general groups, and each can be further broken down by language, culture, religion, or region.

The Afrikaners

When the Dutch first came to the Cape of Good Hope in 1652 they brought settlers to man the port and to raise fresh fruit and vegetables to supply the sailors of Dutch East India Company trading ships. Many of these settlers were sturdy folk who pushed on into the interior seeking land to farm. Over the years the original Dutch settlers were joined by others—French Huguenots (Protestants) fleeing persecution at home, Germans, and Scots.

In the course of three centuries these early immigrants have merged to form a unique and thoroughly African white community. The names of their families —Marais, Roux, du Toit, Murray, van Wyx, Bekker, Strauss—reflect their European heritage, yet the very name "Afrikaner" means African. The Afrikaner religion is the Calvinism of the Dutch Reformed Church, a faith as stern and intolerant as that similar faith of the first New England Puritans. Their language, Afrikaans, shows the effects of 300 years of African isolation on the original Dutch.

Some South African Words

Language often tells us much about a people, and Afrikaans is particularly expressive.

apartheid	A word coined to describe segregation. It means literally "separateness," with connotations of cleanliness and purity resulting from separation.	*kwela*	A popular dance and musical style, African in origin.
Boer	Originally "farmer," from the Dutch. Now used pejoratively to refer to Afrikaners.	*laager*	Camp. The *laager* was originally the circle of wagons drawn up by Afrikaner pioneers stopped for the night—in the manner of American pioneers in the West.
dorp	A small village, rural hamlet.	*trek*	A trip, migration.
Kaffir	A derogatory term for a black African. Used in the same superior-inferior sense as the word "nigger" in America.	*tsotsi*	A young black hoodlum.
		veld	The open South African plains or prairie.
Koelie	An Indian. From the word "coolie" used in English.	*voortrekker*	A Boer pioneer. Throughout their history, Boers pressed north across the veld in search of new land.
kraal	The enclosure in which cattle are kept. The *kraal* is the center of an African village, and *"kraal"* can mean "village." The word is the same as our "corral"—both originally from the Spanish.	*volk*	"People" as in German ("volkswagen"). To an Afrikaner, *"volk"* means a nation with its own separate and distinct tradition, culture, and historical destiny.

The Afrikaners were first called Boers, which means "farmers" in Dutch. Today, Afrikaners are the farmers of the platteland (flatland, or countryside) to the north, where their homes dot the veld of the Transvaal and the Orange Free State, the country opened up by their pioneer ancestors (see Chapter 4). Afrikaners also farm in the Cape Province and in Natal, side by side with many English-speaking farmers.

Since the establishment of the Union of South Africa in 1910, the growth of the gold and diamond mines of the Witwatersrand, the Free State, and Kimberley, and the spurt of manufacturing industry in the last decade, many Afrikaners, like rural people in other lands, have been forced off the farms into the towns. Here they found themselves competing for skilled jobs with immigrants from Britain and for unskilled jobs with black Africans. As with immigrants to the cities elsewhere—to the American cities around 1900 and to cities in Africa after World War II, for example—political machines and city bosses sprang up to cater to the needs of city Afrikaners, who were uneasy and insecure in their new, competitive surroundings. But while in America the machines and the bosses won favor and power by satisfying the material and welfare needs of the new groups, in South Africa they found it easier to cater to emotional needs and fan the flames of Afrikaner prejudice against the black men competing for jobs.

Classification of South African Peoples

African, *Bantu*	Black Bantu-speaking Negro.
Coloured	Person of mixed race, usually with European as well as African forebears.
Indian, *Asian*	South African of Indian origin.
White	South African of white origin. "European" often used as a synonym.

Boer and Briton

For many years the great conflict in South Africa was not between white and black, but between the Afrikaners and the English. Through the nineteenth century British settlers, and the soldiers and officials of Her Majesty Queen Victoria's government, hounded the Boers across the veld, until the "Century of Wrong" ended in the Anglo-Boer War of 1899–1902 (see Chapter 4). With the Peace of Vereeniging the Boers laid down their arms, moved to the towns to become Afrikaners, and changed their weapons from guns to ballots. The Afrikaner victory was won half a century later, in 1948, when the Purified (Afrikaner) Nationalists under Daniel François Malan swept Jan Smuts, and the cooperation with the British for which he stood, into oblivion. After victory, revenge came in 1960, when a referendum of only the whites (there are almost twice as many Afrikaners as English) voted by a small majority to withdraw South Africa from the British Commonwealth and become a republic. This triumph avenged the "Century of Wrong" and soothed the resentment felt when English South Africans spoke of "home" and meant England, and Afrikaners had to salute the hated Union Jack and stand at attention to "The Queen," the equally despised anthem of the British conqueror.

During all these years the crucial relationship between black and white was brushed aside as "the Native problem." In South Africa of course only black people are Natives. Others born there, Afrikaners and English, are called "Europeans" or, lately, "whites."

The Chosen People

The Afrikaners, despite their white skins and their European heritage, are, as their name implies, an African people. Unpopular as they are in the rest of the continent, they have no homeland elsewhere in the world. They see themselves as a small, isolated nation which has somehow survived through danger and persecution. They consider South Africa their own country and feel that it is their birthright to govern. Afrikaner policy, the *apartheid* policy of the ruling Nationalist Party, has as its end the preservation of the Afrikaner *volk* and its religion and language and culture, and the continued domination of South Africa by Afrikaners.

English South Africans

It is typical of this group that no handy name has ever been given them. The English South Africans are essentially those whites who are not Afrikaners and who speak English, not Afrikaans. While most are of British descent, the many Jewish South Africans, immigrants from Eastern Europe, form another minority.

The earliest British settlers came to the Eastern Province in the year 1820. The steady trickle of British immigrants became a torrent during the rushes to the diamond fields of Kimberley and the gold fields of the Witwatersrand in the late nineteenth century, and during the rush to the new industrial towns after World War I. Since their first arrival the English have been traders, miners, and businessmen as well as farmers. The mining companies, the banks, the real estate and insurance companies, manufacturing and commerce, the professions—all

SOUTH AFRICA

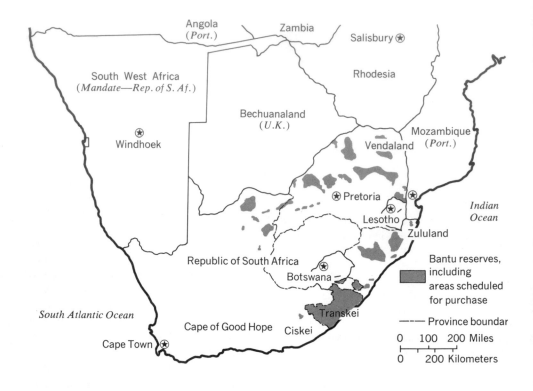

are still mainly in the hands of English South Africans. None of the English are poor, and some, in the wealthy suburbs of Cape Town and Johannesburg, are very rich indeed. The English have developed South Africa; they have built a vigorous and dynamic economy in mining, manufacturing, and commerce which is without equal in Africa and which has one of the fastest growth rates in the world today. They have done so with the aid of a very poorly paid African and Afrikaner labor force.

Unfortunately, the English South Africans sacrificed important principles in their pursuit of profit. They have not participated fully in South African politics—clearly their responsibility as by far the best-educated and most highly trained group—and have consequently lost control to the Afrikaner Nationalists. Far worse, some have developed an indifference to the suffering, poverty,

disease, and discrimination which are the lot of the Africans. Today the English South Africans are paying the price of their commercial dedication and moral casualness. More and more they are being dragged into the *laager* (camp) of the Afrikaner Nationalists, who reject all the liberal and democratic values of the English heritage.

South African whites, Afrikaner and English, seem to have made their peace with the Africa they know. They now confront together what used to be called "the Native problem," but what is now referred to—in a nervous undertone—simply as "the future."

The Africans

Three of four South Africans are blacks who speak Bantu languages. The three main groups of black South Africans, each numbering well over three million, are the Sotho, Xhosa, and Zulu.

A Zulu *kraal*. The circular enclosure protects the cattle at night. *(Information Service of South Africa.)*

These peoples, like Africans all over the continent, are adapting their way of life to a new age.

From the time of the first white settlers, conflict between the whites and the Africans was almost inevitable. Despite all other differences, both Africans and whites were farmers seeking land for cattle and corn. Each group was migrating toward the other in search of new land, Africans to the south from central Africa and whites north from the Cape. The Africans were the losers, cut down by the rifles of Boer pioneers and the muskets of British soldiers, their chiefs deported to remote islands in the Atlantic and Indian Oceans, their priests (called witch doctors by white South Africans) humiliated.

Like the American Indians, Africans were confined to "Native reserves." Agents of the white men, called Native commissioners, were brought in to rule, taxes were imposed and had to be paid, and labor recruiters came to draw African men away from their *kraal* (village) to the mines and big cities—experiences so well described in Peter Lanham's *Blanket Boy's Moon*. The first migrants to the towns came toward the

end of the nineteenth century, and the migration has been increasing ever since. In 1920, 40 percent of African men were peasant farmers. In 1960, only 3 percent were!

Today South Africa is divided into three areas: the "Native reserves" created by the Land Act of 1913 (13 percent of the country), the "urban areas," and the areas owned by white farmers. In each of these three areas there are more blacks than whites. In the case of the reserves and the white farms, where Africans do most of the farm work, this is not surprising. That the cities hold more blacks than whites, however, spells out some uncomfortable facts for white supremacists. It means that black South Africans are part and parcel of the new industrial economy, that they are producers and consumers of manufactured goods, that they are no longer tribesmen satisfied with a tribal way of life. It means that black and white depend on each other, and that modern South Africa could not exist without both groups.

The black communities of South Africa's cities are thoroughly urban. Many Africans have been in the towns for generations and cannot even speak an African language; others, although recently moved from the country, are from families that have known missionaries, teachers, and traders for 150 years. In the African townships of Johannesburg, South Africa's largest city and mining and commercial center, Africans are businessmen, teachers, doctors, gangsters, clerks, and bums. Nightclubs, jazzbands, *shebeens* (illegal drinking houses—the word is Irish), clubs, discussion groups, exhibitions of painting and sculpture, gangfights, and police raids make "Goli"—as Africans call Johannesburg, "the city of gold"— one among the great and vital cities of the world. Yet Africans are not permitted to take books from the Johannes-

burg library, cannot walk into a restaurant for a cup of coffee, may not buy a house in a "white" area, must carry a "pass," cannot vote, and are subject everywhere and all the time to insult and humiliation because they do not have white skins.

The Coloureds

"Coloured" is the official name given to the many persons of mixed origin in South Africa—those who are not white, yet who are obviously not black African (Bantu) or Indian (Asian) either. A number of groups, each having its special culture and traditions, are included in this catchall category. The main Coloured community, in the western part of the Cape Province, sprang from early

The skyscrapers of Johannesburg rise beyond the mine dumps. *(Information Service of South Africa.)*

SOUTH AFRICA
Population

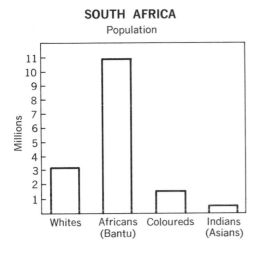

contacts between whites and Hottentots (the Hottentots are a non-Bantu people closely related to the Bushmen described in Chapter 1) and a few African and Malay slaves. This Cape Coloured people numbers nearly a million, speaks Afrikaans, attends the Dutch Reformed Church, and regards itself as closer to the whites than to the black Africans.

In the days of the Dutch East India Company, Malays were brought to South Africa to work. Their descendants still live close to Cape Town. Although they now speak Afrikaans, these Cape Malays maintain their Moslem faith, continue to earn a living as traders and craftsmen, and remain proud of their independent and industrious heritage.

In all the towns and in the countless *dorps* (small villages) of the countryside are isolated Coloured communities, whose people are descended from intermarriages and associations between white and black Africans.

Coloureds speak Afrikaans and English, dress, eat, live, and work in the same way as whites, go to the Christian churches so highly valued by white South Africans, and generally are identical in their way of life to their "racially pure" half-brothers. Yet the Coloureds are treated differently simply because all four of their grandparents were not

pure white; they are forced to live in separate areas, confined to lower-status jobs, educated at inferior schools and colleges, permitted to vote only for whites (not for Coloureds), and encouraged to worship in segregated churches. This situation is made ridiculous by the fact that perhaps a quarter of the "pure-blooded" whites have nonwhite forebears.

Given the fact that South Africa was to be run on the basis of "race," the officials had to decide who belonged to what "race." Race, in the case of an individual person, is neither a scientific idea nor an exact one. To classify individuals as belonging to one race or another, as the South African Nationalists have done, is an arbitrary procedure without scientific merit. In the case of a pitch-black African and a lily-white Afrikaner classification was not too difficult. Such cases, however, are the exception rather than the rule. Many children of "Coloured" parents look "white," and many children of "white" parents look "Coloured."

The government set up a Race Classification Board and decreed that every person in the country had to be registered and classified. If there was any question about the "race" of a person, the board was to decide. And decide it did, peering at applicants' ears and nostrils and hair and fingernails for physical signs of nonwhite ancestry.

The Indians

During the nineteenth century, English farmers began to grow sugar cane near Durban in the subtropical climate of Natal province. For this enterprise labor was needed—men who could be paid little or nothing to work long hours. The Zulu, the Africans of the region, had not yet been conquered and were certainly in no mood to put aside the warrior's spear. Teeming India, then a British colony, seemed the answer, and under an arrangement with the British

Colonial Office thousands of poor Indians were recruited as indentured laborers. Indenture usually meant that the Indian had to work at negligible pay for twenty years for the employer who brought him from India. After serving their time, the Indians could become full and equal citizens. (Indenture is an old system. Many of the first American settlers were English debtors and criminals brought as indentured laborers to the New World.)

As in most things colonial, the practice was rather different from the theory. In South Africa Indians were denied the vote, met discrimination in industry and the civil service, and were left without power in any attempt to gain social equality or economic opportunity. Many became traders, while the less fortunate ended up as waiters or laundrymen, or remained as laborers on the farms. In recent years a few Indians have become professional men—teachers, lawyers, doctors—and many have prospered as retailers and wholesalers. A large number, however, remain poor, more than half living below what is officially called in South Africa the "poverty datum line" (about $45 a month for a family of four).

There are today nearly half a million Indians in South Africa, most of them residents of several generations. Although they came to work and to build the country they are denied jobs, the vote, and social equality. Now officially classed as "Asians" (a nonexact "race" if ever there was one; Japanese, by comparison, are "honorary whites," because South Africa carries on a valuable trade with Japan), the Indians are being walled off from other South African groups by laws passed in the name of *apartheid*.

South African Life

A cross section of South African life, say on a Saturday afternoon, would reveal a country of great variety and great vitality. If it were winter, you might hear on the radio the play-by-play of a rugby match between two Cape Town teams (Border and Boland, for example), with a crowd of 30,000 whites cheering themselves hysterical. In the Transkei—largest of the Native reserves—a crowd of Xhosa tribesmen with painted faces and red blankets would be drinking "kaffir beer" and preparing to joust with sticks, while in a nearby *dorp* the local African minister prepared his sermon for the next day. In Johannesburg's northern suburbs, where great houses on acres of land are separated by tall, cool trees, a game

Johannesburg's labor force waits in line for a bus. (*Wide World Photos.*)

might be in progress on a private tennis court, with tea and drinks served by a gray-haired African "boy," immaculately clothed to his white gloves. In the nearby African townships black intellectuals, well-educated, articulate, bitterly frustrated, might gather at a favorite *shebeen,* while out in the platteland English and Afrikaner farmers supervised their African workers at the end of a long week. At one of the government's "tribal colleges" for Africans, say at the Turfloop College for the Sotho, young and inexperienced students would be trying to reconcile their new knowledge with what was happening in South Africa.

Life in Cape Town, Johannesburg, Durban is like sophisticated urban living anywhere. Plays, concerts, ballets, nightclubs, movies are all there for the taking, if you have money and if you are white. *Apartheid* is everywhere; yet it had its exceptions, and these exceptions endure until today despite all the government could do to eliminate them. At the University of Witwatersrand in Johannesburg, African and Indian faces were seen at concerts and plays; in the northern suburbs and in the built-up apartment section of Hillbrow parties were often attended by Africans and whites together.

Mixing, however, is nowadays largely limited to private contacts and friendships between some of the students, artists, and authors of all races. Between most members of different South African groups there is a vast abyss, a psychological wall which prevents anything more than orders from being communicated or understood. In the little *dorps* of the platteland, in the suburban housing developments, on the farms, in the offices, in factories and mines, nonwhites are not regarded by the whites as equals and are not spoken to or treated as such. South African whites have little understanding of what the nonwhites feel, think, believe, want, and need.

The vitality as well as the cruelty of South African life is revealed by the burst of creative writing (in English) by black South Africans. There are important and moving white writers, such as Nadine Gordimer and Alan Paton (*Cry, the Beloved Country, Hope for South Africa*). Yet only through the writing of black African authors can we see South Africa as blacks must live in it. Their viewpoint is best reflected in autobiography, such as Bloke Modisane's *Blame Me on History,* Todd Mashikiza's *Chocolates for My Wife,* and Ezekiel Mphahlele's *Down Second Avenue.*

White South Africans are simply not aware of the fact that they themselves, like most human beings elsewhere, are mediocre, and that all that distinguishes them from their black counterparts is privilege—privilege expressed both in custom and in the law of the land. They are certainly not aware of the existence, let alone the qualities of mind and character, of men like Mphahlele, Mashikiza, Modisane, or Thami Mhilambiso, a former vice-president of the National Union of South African Students recently imprisoned by the government.

Apartheid: Theory and Practice

In theory, *apartheid* is a complex blueprint for the future envisioned by racists such as Prime Minister Hendrik Verwoerd. Under ideal *apartheid,* each race would have its own homeland and would develop its own pure language and culture and religion in its own way, completely separated from and uncontaminated by the others.

For every theorist, however, there are thousands of ordinary folk who take a much less complex and academic view. The cruder (and more common) idea of *apartheid* is expressed in such slogans as *"Meer skop en minder kos vir die kaffer"* ("More kicks and less food for the niggers") and *"Die kaffer op sy plek en die koelie uit die land uit"* ("The nigger in his place and the coolies [Indians] out of the country"). Africans, Indians, and Coloureds in South Africa must face this attitude every day.

Is Separation Possible?

Shortly after it came to power in 1948 the Nationalist government asked a group of leading Afrikaner scholars to study the possibility of imposing partition on South Africa, with the Africans confined to the Native reserves, to be called Bantustans, and the whites in the rest of the country. The findings of the Tomlinson Commission, released in 1955 after several years of study, are of profound importance.

If present trends continued, the commission reported, by the year 2000 the larger "white areas" would contain 6 million whites and 15 million blacks. If the government prohibited further migration of Africans to the cities and instead developed industries in the Bantustans, there would still be in the year 2000 as many blacks as whites in the white areas—not to mention 4 million Coloureds and 1½ million Indians!

No sooner had the Nationalist government read the report than it decided to shelve it, for the facts of life it contained were very unpleasant. Real *apartheid* would mean personal sacrifice by whites. Whites would lose their cheap domestic servants. They would have to do the menial and unpleasant work now done by Africans. Much capital would be necessary to develop the Bantustans so that they could support the African population, and the money needed would have to come out of white pockets in the form of higher taxes. Clearly, the Nationalists had been voted into office to preserve white supremacy, not to impose taxes for the benefits of blacks.

The Alternative

The situation, then, is this: Total territorial partition (complete segregation or ideal *apartheid*) is impossible —utterly and completely out of the question. Everyone from Prime Minister Verwoerd on down recognized this fact. The alternative is repression of the nonwhites by force and by law. At present, the Nationalists are trying to keep the lid on the pot by suppressing all of the men and women—white and black—who oppose racial discrimination.

Long before the Nationalists came to power segregation was established custom and the law of the land. After the 1948 election the screws were tightened, sharply and painfully. In the sixteen years since, new laws have poured out in an ever-swelling flow. The restrictions are felt in every nook and cranny of private and personal life. They involve continual harassment of ordinary individuals, and the attempt to enforce them is rapidly turning South Africa into a police state. Some of the apartheid laws are summarized on pages 193 and 194; they speak for themselves.

The Afrikaner Nationalists are imposing a caste system on an industrial, developed country in the modern age. So far they have been eminently successful.

Parties and Politics

South Africa is theoretically a democracy—for whites only. Although they together are four-fifths of the population, Africans, Indians, and Coloureds have no vote. This basic fact must be kept in mind in any discussion of South African politics.

The Nationalists

In 1933, at the height of the Great Depression, Generals Jan Smuts and James Hertzog formed a coalition government of both English and Afrikaners to meet the economic crisis. Only a small group of extreme Afrikaner Nationalists refused to join this new "United Party." At the time, these men—Malan, Strijdom, Swart, Verwoerd—were unknowns, extremists, a small faction. During World War II many of them supported Adolf Hitler's Nazis and cheered victories of the Third Reich.

Some of the Apartheid Laws

Before 1948

1911   *Mines and Works Act*
All but whites prevented from becoming skilled or white-collar workers in the mines. Official job discrimination.

1913   *Land Act*
South Africa divided between Africans and whites. Native reserves set at 13 percent of the country; only whites could own land in the other 87 percent.

1923   *Urban Areas Act*
Africans forced to live in segregated "locations" in the towns.

1924,   *Industrial Conciliation Acts*
1937   Africans prohibited from forming labor unions. Workers' benefits limited to whites.

1936   *Natives Representation Act*
Africans no longer allowed to vote in the Cape Province.

After 1948

1950   *Immorality Act*
Sexual association between whites and nonwhites a criminal offense.

1950   *Population Registration Act*
Every man, woman, and child to be officially classified as White, Coloured, Asian, or Bantu.

1950   *Group Areas Act*
Amended many times, this law aims at making South Africa a gigantic jigsaw puzzle of perfectly segregated areas. The towns are to be "pure white," with others consigned to remote communities to be available as labor is needed. Known as the "Ghetto Act."

1950   *Suppression of Communism Act*
A misleading title. Anyone advocating action for *any* political or social or economic change can be "deemed" a "Communist" by officials and punished. In effect makes protest illegal.

1951   *Bantu Authorities Act*
African tribal chiefs, including leaders of the "self-governing" Bantustans, to be controlled by the government.

1953   *Reservation of Separate Amenities Act*
Segregation of public accommodations, including post offices and park benches.

1953   *Bantu Education Act*
Education of Africans put under government control. Missionary schools forced to close.

1953   *Public Safety Act*
Gives the government power to declare a state of emergency in any part of the country, under which it could suspend most laws and rule by decree.

1957   *Native Laws Amendment Act*
Limits freedom of assembly and association. No white school, club, or hospital may admit an African without official permission. Officials may prohibit any gathering in a white area which is to be attended by an African, including private parties and religious services.

1959   *Extension of University Education Act*
All universities closed to nonwhites. "Tribal colleges" set up for Africans. In effect prevents Africans from getting a modern college education.

1960   *Promotion of Bantu Self-Government Act*
Abolishes the last "Native representatives" in the South African Parliament and firms up the Bantustan system.

1960   *Illegal Organizations Act*
Working for the goals of the African National Congress or the Pan-Africanist Congress made a criminal offense. In 1961 thirteen Africans were convicted for working for "the establishment of the rule of law in South Africa" and "universal suffrage in South Africa."

Some of the Apartheid Laws; continued

1962	*Sabotage Act* Violence against the state pun- ishable by death.	1963	*Publications and Entertain- ments Act* Censorship tightened and ex- tended.
		1963	*Bantu Laws Amendment Act* All Africans assigned by tribe to a particular Bantustan, or tribal homeland. They may be deported from "white areas" (including all cities) for any reason, regardless of previous residence, job, or family.
1963	*Ninety-Day Detention Act* Police can imprison individ- uals indefinitely without ex- planation or formal charge or trial, and interrogate them. Has led to police brutality in many cases.		

All this changed when the Nationalists under Daniel François Malan won control of the South African Parliament, with a minority of the votes cast, in the 1948 election. In every election since, the Nationalists have increased their proportion of seats in Parliament, and can now claim a majority of votes in support of their policy.

Now firmly in power, the Afrikaners control the army, navy, air force, and police, and dominate the government from clerks to ministers. Knowing that it must back up its rule by force, the Nationalist government has vastly strengthened the armed forces, organized a secret police, and encouraged all white citizens to join militia units against a possible African uprising. Many whites spend Sunday mornings at rifle practice.

The Nationalists claim to represent and embody the spirit and the destiny of the Afrikaner *volk* (people, nation). Youth groups, women's groups, intellectuals of the Afrikaans-speaking universities, the Dutch Reformed Church, the South African police—all are linked to the Nationalist Party. The capstone of the Afrikaners' organization is a secret society called the Broederbond (brotherhood), which includes most high government officials, ministers of the Dutch Reformed Church, leading Afrikaner professors, and Afrikaner leaders from other walks of life. The Broederbond has been called the real ruler of South Africa.

The Legal Opposition

A number of white parties have opposed the Nationalists. The largest (and the least vigorous) of these is the United Party founded by Field Marshal Smuts. It is a "me-too" party, opposing the extremism of the Nationalists but not white supremacy as such. The United Party represents the more moderate Afrikaners, the great mining companies, most middle-class English South Africans in the cities, and English farmers in Natal and the Eastern Cape Province. In the Afrikaner areas —the Orange Free State, the Transvaal, much of the Cape—the Nationalists dominate.

In recent years a small part of the English community has tried to propose a solution to South Africa's problems through the Liberal Party, led by Alan Paton. The Liberals have become more liberal in their policy, and now propose the abolition of all *apartheid* laws and the right to vote for adults of all races. As a result, white members have left the party and Africans have joined, so that there are now far more black Liberals than white.

The Progressive Party is small, supported by a few business and professional men and academics. Its policy is limited desegregation, particularly in business and industry. While in the United States the Progressives would seem out of date, in South Africa they are rampantly liberal.

African Parties

One of the oldest political organizations in South Africa is the African National Congress (ANC). For thirty years, ANC was a cautious organization led by lawyers, doctors, and chiefs, eager for reform but also anxious to work with the government. Then in 1943 Anton Lembede, who died too soon to use his many talents, founded the African National Congress Youth League and forged a vigorous policy of protest and action against discrimination.

Other groups soon joined the opposition. The ANC's closest ally was the Indian Congress, which traced its origin to the Natal Indian Congress founded in 1894 by a young lawyer named Mohandas Gandhi. The Coloured People's Congress, nonwhite labor unions, and a small group of whites came in to form the Congress Alliance, which published the famous Freedom Charter in 1955.

The Congress Alliance included known Communists (mainly white!), and many African nationalists were liberals who refused to work with them. In addition, a more extreme group opposed cooperation with whites in general and white Communists in particular. These "Africanists" soon left the ANC to form the rival Pan-Africanist Congress (PAC).

The Failure of Resistance

Following the successful example of Gandhi in India, the ANC and the Indian Congress in the early 1950's planned a campaign of passive resistance to the *apartheid* laws. They announced that wave after wave of volunteers would break minor laws and seek arrest and imprisonment until the jails were crammed to the limit and the government forced to change its policy. The Nationalists' answer was immediate and effective: Passive resistance (what Gandhi had called *satyagraha*) would be punished by a severe combination of fines, flogging, and imprisonment. The

In protest against the Sharpeville shootings, Africans in Johannesburg burn their hated pass books. *(Wide World Photos.)*

campaign collapsed. Leaders of the ANC and the Indian Congress realized that Afrikaner hatred of colored skins ran too deep to be altered by that appeal to conscience which is the basis of *satyagraha*.

In 1956 came the bombshell when the government arrested 156 anti*apartheid* leaders on charges of high treason. For five years the treason trial dragged on, as the courts threw out indictment after indictment brought by the government. Finally, long after their health, family life, and businesses had been ruined, the accused were found *not guilty* and set free.

In 1959 the Pan-Africanist Congress was formed under the leadership of Robert Sobukwe, a reserved and strong man in his thirties. The PAC spurned cooperation with whites, and prepared for extreme action. In March 1960, PAC announced a mass demonstration. Leaders were to burn their

passes—hated symbol of inferiority—
and then report to the nearest police
station requesting arrest.

At the little town of Sharpeville a
crowd of men, women, and children
gathered in front of the police station.
The police panicked and opened fire on
the crowd with machine guns. Nearly a
hundred were killed, and hundreds more
were wounded—most of them shot in
the back as they fled to escape the
gunfire.

The Sharpeville massacre hit the front
pages of the world's press, bringing
South Africa once again to world attention. The government proclaimed a state
of emergency. Within weeks both the
Pan-Africanists and the African National Congress were outlawed, and
thousands were held without trial or
charge. Since that time, other organizations have been banned and thousands
of Indians, Africans, and whites imprisoned.

After the Sharpeville massacre and
the effective outlawing of all organized
opposition, violence remained the only
means of protest against *apartheid*. Between 1960 and 1964 three underground
sabotage groups were formed. One,
called Umkonto we Sizwe (The Spear of
the Nation), was led by Nelson Man-
dela. Another group was Poqo (Alone).
A third was ARM, the African Resistance Movement. These groups, as sabo-
teurs go, were amateur. They were
easily penetrated by African police informers, and their leaders arrested,
tried, and sentenced to long prison
terms. Violent protest, at least for the
time being, has been crushed.

Just before the outbreak of violence
and sabotage in 1962, the former president of the banned African National
Congress, Chief Albert Luthuli, now
confined to a reserve under the Suppression of Communism Act, received
the Nobel Peace Prize for his efforts to
bring about a peaceful solution in South
Africa. While the Nobel Prize is a fit-
ting tribute to a great man, it is both
tragic and ironic that Luthuli so clearly
failed, through no fault of his own, to
find a nonviolent answer to South
Africa's problems.

The Economy and the Africans

South Africa is a boom country. With
the important exception of oil, everything needed for modern industry and
modern living can now be grown, made,
or mined in South Africa. While the
country still depends on its amazing
wealth of minerals, new factories are
springing up by the hundreds to manufacture everything from steel to lip-
stick. American, British, and European
corporations are pouring investments
into South Africa to maintain the boom.
On the farms and plantations, South
African farmers grow enough to feed
the country, and export corn, wool, and
fruits.

The Treasure House

Just beyond the skyscrapers of Johannesburg rise huge piles of gleaming
white sand—the mine dumps of the
Witwatersrand. More than two miles
under the surface of the veld, thousands
of African miners work in extreme heat
and humidity to bring the gold-bearing
ore to the surface.

Since gold was first discovered on the
Rand in 1886 it has been the backbone
of South Africa's economy. Other industries have grown up to provide
machinery and chemicals for the mines.
Gold, as South Africa's main export,
assures it a stable and secure position
in world trade and finance. Nor is this
all. When run through a delicate electro-
chemical process (called ion exchange),
tons of the gold-bearing ore release a
few grains of that most precious of
atomic age metals, uranium. South
Africa now produces about three-fifths
of the West's gold, and sells uranium
under contract to Britain and the
United States.

Almost a century after Cecil Rhodes
made his fortune in the diamond fields

PRODUCTS AND RESOURCES OF SOUTH AFRICA

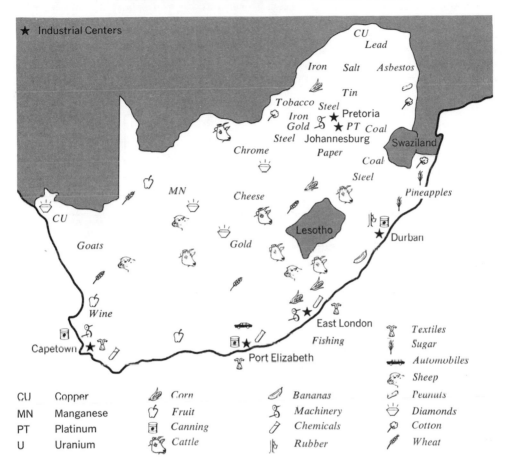

★ Industrial Centers

CU
Lead
Iron Salt *Asbestos*
Tin
Tobacco Steel
Iron ★ Pretoria
Gold ★ PT *Coal*
Steel Johannesburg
Chrome *Paper*
Coal
Swaziland
Steel
MN *Cheese* *Pineapples*
CU Lesotho
Durban
Goats *Gold*
Wine
East London
Fishing
Capetown ★
Port Elizabeth

CU	Copper	Corn	Bananas
MN	Manganese	*Fruit*	*Machinery*
PT	Platinum	*Canning*	*Chemicals*
U	Uranium	*Cattle*	*Rubber*

Textiles
Sugar
Automobiles
Sheep
Peanuts
Diamonds
Cotton
Wheat

SECTORS OF THE SOUTH AFRICAN ECONOMY

(Contribution to national income) 1962-63

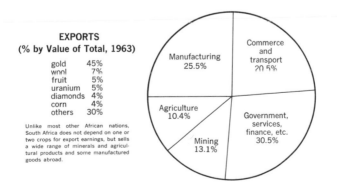

EXPORTS
(% by Value of Total, 1963)

gold	45%
wool	7%
fruit	5%
uranium	5%
diamonds	4%
corn	4%
others	30%

Unlike most other African nations, South Africa does not depend on one or two crops for export earnings, but sells a wide range of minerals and agricultural products and some manufactured goods abroad.

Manufacturing 25.5%
Commerce and transport 20.5%
Agriculture 10.4%
Government, services, finance, etc. 30.5%
Mining 13.1%

of Kimberley (see Chapter 4), diamond mines in South and South-West Africa continue to yield riches. Most of the diamond mines are owned by the De Beers Company, once the financial empire of Cecil Rhodes and now controlled by Harry Oppenheimer. De Beers is one of the world's giant corporations, with mining and other interests in Congo, Tanganyika, Portguese Africa, and Zambia.

In addition to gold, diamonds, and uranium for export, South Africa has coal, iron ore, manganese, copper, chrome, and fifty-odd other minerals, and is one of the few lucky countries with all the resources needed for iron and steel production and manufacturing industry.

Manufacturing

Beginning with the demand for goods of all kinds during World War II, South African industry has grown by leaps and bounds. It now produces both consumer goods (food, textiles, paper) and industrial and military goods such as steel, chemicals, and machinery. Many South African plants use the most up-to-date technology.

The main industrial center, making steel, machinery, and chemicals, is Johannesburg and the Rand. Durban, the largest port, has sugar refineries and oil refineries, fertilizers, paper, and chemicals. Around Cape Town, the fruits and vegetables of the surrounding farms are canned, preserved, or distilled into liquor. Cape Town is also the textile center, and most of the Cape Coloureds work in textile mills.

Foreign companies have invested heavily in South African industry. To take just one example, Chrysler, Ford, General Motors, British Motors, and Volkswagen all assemble cars in South Africa.

The Farms

On South African back roads there are still rundown farms where an Afri-

kaner and his wife, with a black African servant or two, plant a few acres of corn and manage to scrape along. As in

EXHIBIT 1

SOME STATISTICS ON SOUTH AFRICA

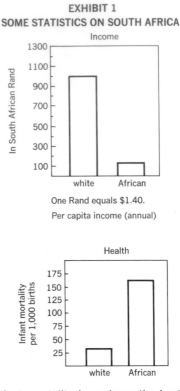

One Rand equals $1.40.

Per capita income (annual)

Infant mortality is perhaps the best indicator of overall health standards.

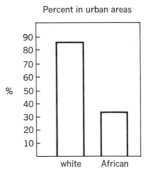

While a smaller proportion of Africans live in the towns, the total number is greater than the number of whites. Many more Africans, not included here, work in the mines and factories most of the year but are considered to "live" in the Native Reserves.

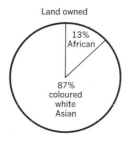

Land owned

13% African

87% coloured white Asian

Of the 87 percent not owned by Africans, practically all is owned by whites.

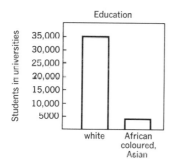

Education

Students in universities

35,000
30,000
25,000
20,000
15,000
10,000
5000

white   African coloured, Asian

the United States, however, large farms worked by machinery and growing crops for city markets are becoming the rule. South Africa produces all varieties of food for the home market—meat, milk, fruits and vegetables, grain, sugar— and exports large amounts of corn, wool, and fruits, mainly to Britain, Europe, and Japan.

Does the African Fit In?

On the farms, in the mines, on the assembly lines, in the homes of whites, manual work is done by Africans. By law, Africans are prevented from getting jobs higher than foreman in most industries. The few Africans in white-collar jobs are paid far less than whites for the same work.

Africans cannot organize labor unions or strike for better conditions or higher pay. A worker may not, in many cases, quit his job without permission, and if he is unemployed he may be ordered back to a "tribal area."

African workers on white farms have perhaps the worst of it. They cannot leave without official permission, are paid very little, and are sometimes badly treated by their employer. Africans not wanted in the towns are sometimes assigned by the police to work on a farm for a certain time—a form of forced labor.

South Africa's defenders point out that black Africans have a higher standard of living there than in any other African country. This is not only untrue but also misleading. The many African city dwellers have modern tastes and want the same things that whites take for granted—electricity, plumbing, and a balanced diet. They are by no means comparable with the peasant farmers in tribal villages that make up about 90 percent of the population (and the standard-of-living statistic) elsewhere in Africa.

The better comparison is between whites and blacks in South Africa. On the average, an African worker makes about one-eighth as much as a white— and pays the same prices. A progressive firm in South Africa now pays its workers perhaps $2.50 per day. Others pay much less (although they often provide housing and meals in company barracks), and Africans on the white farms make practically nothing at all.

The Economy versus Apartheid

As the economy grows, the need for labor, particularly *skilled* labor, grows with it. If South Africa is to continue to prosper, more and more Africans will have to be trained as mechanics and machine tool operators at the very least. This prospect is in direct contrast to the *apartheid* vision of Africans living a tribal, peasant life far from the white cities.

Industry also requires a *market*— someone to buy the goods produced. South Africa's 3½ million whites (about the population of Chicago) are not enough. And if Africans, Indians, and Coloureds are to buy more and better products, they must have more money and higher wages. This does not bode well for *apartheid* either.

South Africa's big businessmen, including Harry Oppenheimer as well as leaders of the United Party, recognize this contradiction between *apartheid* and prosperity. So far their opposition has been halfhearted, but it may grow if profits begin to lag. *Apartheid* will certainly become harder and harder to enforce as economic growth brings white and nonwhite into ever-greater economic dependence on one another.

A World Problem

As long as white supremacy is the keynote of South African policy, so long will that country remain a source of division and hatred in the world. Asians and Africans have long since served notice that white domination of the world is at an end, and Africans are determined to end it in South Africa.

Apart from the morality or immorality of *apartheid*, the feeling of African solidarity (see Chapter 14), and concern for the dignity of other human beings, there is the crucial factor of pride. African and Asian leaders see the humiliation of Africans under white rule as an insult to themselves. So long as South African whites are able to dominate a much larger number of Africans and Asians, the much-vaunted independence of African and Asian countries must appear to be a delicate plant, fragile to the touch and sensitive to heat.

We have seen what men and women in South Africa are doing in opposition to *apartheid*—and how they have so far failed. What is happening abroad?

The United Nations

The issue of South African racial policies was first raised in the UN by India and Pakistan in 1947. With independence, African countries have since taken over the assault. The African and Asian countries, now with support from both the United States and the Soviet Union, have passed resolutions condemning *apartheid* in the strongest terms in the General Assembly. Resolutions, however, have little effect. South African spokesmen claim that the UN concern is intervention in the affairs of a member country and therefore a violation of the UN Charter. UN committees established to investigate *apartheid* have repeatedly been turned away from South Africa.

The General Assembly has recently called upon UN members to invoke sanctions against South Africa. (Sanctions are punishment short of war or violence, such as breaking off diplomatic relations or refusing to trade with the punished nation.) Sanctions can be very effective in bringing a country to heel, but the main difficulty lies in enforcing them, as the United States found out when it was unable to stop its closest ally, Britain, from selling buses to Cuba.

Independent African Action

In their Organization of African Unity (see Chapter 14), the African nations have urged a course of action just short of violence, including refusal to trade with or be part of any international organization (such as the International Labor Organization and other UN agencies) that includes South Africa. Effective African action is not really possible, however. Trade is small. African countries have neither the economic power nor the firepower to stand up to South Africa's well-equipped army, navy, and air force. In addition, South Africa is protected from guerilla attack by the belt of white-controlled states to the north—the Portuguese colonies and Rhodesia.

The United States Position

While publicly condemning *apartheid* in the UN and elsewhere, the United States has been very reluctant to take action against South Africa. American diplomats fervently hope that South

African whites will reverse their policies and make concessions to Negro equality and freedom for all, but at the moment this seems to be little more than wishful thinking. The reluctance to take action is understandable. Britain and America are South Africa's main trading partners, and Americans have invested over half a billion dollars in the country. White South Africans share our European cultural heritage. The South African government is fanatically anti-Communist, and in the eyes of at least some people this makes up for its bitterly anti-Negro practices.

Everyone, then, has an interest in South Africa, whether it is racial hatred or pride, monetary gain or loss, political expediency or humanitarian concern. South Africa's problems show signs of becoming a critical world issue. Years of contention and strife lie ahead, involving South Africans and many others.

PROBLEMS

1. By whom, and by what means, could the policy of *apartheid* be changed? (Try to think of all possibilities.) Which way do you consider to be the best? Which is the most unlikely?

2. One can sympathize with the situation (if not the policy) of the Afrikaners who feel themselves threatened by a black African community three times as large as the white. Write a speech presenting the Afrikaner point of view, explaining how the South African situation came about and defending *apartheid* in theory.

3. What is the meaning of the phrase "There are no South Africans"? Will (a) rigid enforcement of *apartheid* and (b) economic growth tend to create more "South Africans" or fewer?

4. Low wages for African workers make it possible for South African businessmen (and foreign investors) to earn high profits. This money can then be reinvested in new factories, which yield further profits. What is the *economic* limitation on this growth process based on low wages? Can it continue indefinitely? What is the American business attitude, pioneered by Henry Ford and others, relating wages and business prosperity?

5. The *apartheid* laws were passed and the police enforcement of them sanctioned by a freely elected parliament after full public debate. Was this a democratic process?

READING SUGGESTIONS

Mary Benson, *The African Patriots,* Faber and Faber (London), 1963.

Brian Bunting, *The Rise of the South African Reich,* Penguin, paper.

Trevor Huddleston, *Naught for Your Comfort,* Macmillan, paper.

Peter Lanham, *Blanket Boy's Moon,* Crowell, 1953.

Leo Marquard, *The Peoples and Politics of South Africa,* Oxford University Press (London), paper.

Ezekiel Mphahlele, *Down Second Avenue*, Faber & Faber (London), 1959.

Alan Paton, *Cry, the Beloved Country*, Scribner, paper.

Edward Roux, *Time Longer than Rope*, University of Wisconsin Press, 1963.

Chapter 13

MEN OF POWER

You are the protector of the children,
of the oppressed.

—*Song in praise of
Sékou Touré, President of
Guinea*

African leaders have great personal power over their countries and their countrymen, far more power than an American President. The same man is usually both head of state and the leader of the single ruling political party. In most matters his word becomes law. This power of the leader, based on his party organization or national army and on his popularity with the common people, strikes most Africans as being quite proper and natural.

To the illiterate and uneducated majority of Africans, the leader is a living symbol of the new nation and its government. His portrait adorns posters, coins, and stamps to remind the people that they are not Ashanti, Masai, or Lunda, but Ghanaian, Kenyan, or Congolese. African leaders are seldom directly blamed for unpopular policies (such as Kwame Nkrumah's decision to cut down cocoa trees to stop root disease) or injustice or corruption on the part of officials.

In their effort to build nations, the new leaders make practical use of Afri-

can tradition to win support. They wear the robes of a great traditional chief when they appear to make a speech in parliament or greet visitors from abroad. Animals are offered as sacrifices to the leader. Potions are mixed to protect him from harm. Exaggerated tales of his power and prowess make the leader a hero, the chosen of the gods, a man not to be questioned or challenged by ordinary men.

The Politician Becomes a Statesman

Today's African leaders rose to power as organizers and politicians in the rough-and-tumble campaign of anticolonial nationalism (see Chapter 8). They won the right to lead by being able to hypnotize an African crowd with fire-breathing orations about imperialism, by inspiring loyalty to the cause of independence among party workers, by making shrewd political deals with rivals and associates, and by successfully negotiating with colonial officials. To bargain for independence took great political skill, for any nationalist leader who tried to compromise was tagged as an "imperialist stooge" by his rivals and was doomed to political obscurity. The trick, as Tom Mboya of Kenya has put it, was to sound like a black dragon ready to swallow any white colonialist on sight, while at the same time negotiating discreetly, using the unspoken threat of violence by a mass of passionately aroused followers to twist the arm of the colonial administration. This strategy, with minor variations, was successful and led to peaceful independence everywhere in Africa except Rhodesia, South Africa, Algeria, and the Portuguese colonies (see Chapter 9).

The abilities that bring a nationalist politician to the top—fiery oratory, a magnetic personality, organizing skill, toughness in negotiating — are not necessarily the qualities of a responsible and successful statesman. A prime minister or president must do more than inspire people to defiance and agitation; he must persuade them to work hard. He must deal with other nations in the rest of Africa and around the world. He must understand such complicated matters as taxation and finance, allocation of investments under the national development plan, and administration of teachers, technicians, and bureaucrats on the government payroll. Even those leaders who were most successful as politicians have had their troubles trying to administer a country and its economy. Senegal's economic plans have foundered as a result of rivalry between planning officials and the conservative

---

In Praise of Nkrumah

These verses were written in praise of Kwame Nkrumah by a Ghanaian high school student and were printed in the *Accra Evening News,* the newspaper published by Nkrumah and his Convention People's Party. There is a clearly Christian influence in the poem—a hymn putting Nkrumah in the place of the Messiah, in the tradition of African political leaders who were regarded as divinely chosen.

> O revered, beloved son of Africa
> O great Redeemer of Africa
> Thy wisdom has wrought things many and wonderful
> Thou seemest a Saviour come from God
> O, before we were in darkness;
> But thy beam did give us light
>
> O great thinker, great sage of today
> O thou humble man, who was destined
> To spring from the depths of obscurity
> To redeem us, a repressed people
> Suffering, sorrowful, hypochondriac
> O, we accord thee our sincere gratitude
>
> At Lincoln University, in America
> O, a miserable, studious life lived thou
> O, a humble, penurious soul
> Yearning after hidden knowledge
> Thy lofty aspirations have brought us all and sundry
> The joy of freedom
>
> Thou whose name is enshrined in Africa
> Now we are assured that, with thee,
> No unhappy divisions or dissensions
> Will tear asunder our cherished continent
> O, humble Africa is grateful to you,
> Thou votary of Freedom and unity.

Julius Nyerere. (*David R. Giltrow.*)

underground leaders, for they are denied the experience of serving in government that most leaders of French and British colonies gained just before independence.

Four African Leaders

Julius Nyerere of Tanzania (1922–   )

Julius Nyerere is President of Tanzania and the leader of Tanganyika's one and only political party, the Tanganyika African National Union (TANU). Today, after a smooth transition to independence, Nyerere attempts to cope with the problems of what is even by African standards a poor and backward country. Most who know Nyerere consider him up to the job.

Like many other prominent Africans, Nyerere was the son of a chief, and, like most of today's African leaders, he was educated by missionaries. Nyerere followed the now well-worn path from a tribal background through Christian schooling to a university diploma. From Makerere College in Uganda, Nyerere went on to study in Europe, and returned in 1952 to a job as a teacher near Tanganyika's port and capital city of Dar es Salaam (which means "haven of peace" in Arabic).

Nyerere soon entered politics. He joined the Tanganyika Africa Association, a cultural group with heavy political overtones, became president, and quickly changed its name to Tanganyika African National Union and its purpose to winning independence. He married a girl from a different tribe, thus proving that he was a Tanganyikan nationalist. To organize votes and party workers for TANU in the back country, Nyerere, traveling in a jeep over bumpy roads, spent many weeks visiting village after village. Wherever he stopped the theme of his message to the people was Tanganyikan national unity and the coexistence of whites, blacks, and Indians as equal citizens. In Tanganyika's 1960

backers of President Léopold Senghor. Fulbert Youlou was deposed as President of the Congo Republic (Brazzaville) when he could not cope with the problem of finding jobs for the thousands of migrants pouring from the villages into the capital. On the other hand, Julius Nyerere of Tanganyika and Habib Bourguiba of Tunisia were not flamboyant political leaders, but both have accomplished much as heads of state.

There is another kind of political leader in Africa: the revolutionary. In Algeria before independence, and in the Portuguese colonies and South Africa today, the African leader is an outlaw, working in secret to organize cells and arm guerilla fighters for revolution. These underground organizers are very different from the popular leaders of mass parties who elsewhere were voted into office, and they are often unrecognized both at home and abroad, until the revolution they planned begins in earnest. The transition to power and responsibility is even more difficult for the election TANU won seventy of seventy-one seats, and when independence followed in 1961 Nyerere was acclaimed President.

The Zanzibar episode of January 1964 demonstrated Nyerere's shrewd political judgment and his ability to find solutions to messy problems. In Zanzibar, just off Tanganyika's coast, a disorganized rebel government came to power during days of violence. While Western newspapers reported the presence of Chinese Communist and Cuban advisers, under headlines "The Cuba of Africa," Nyerere kept calm counsel, waited, and negotiated with Zanzibar leader Sheikh Obeid Karume. A Tanganyika police force was dispatched to the island. A few weeks later, fear and confusion died away when Nyerere announced the political union of Tanganyika and Zanzibar—now called Tanzania.

This example of a solution achieved through unity and compromise shows Nyerere's practical approach to African problems. He has advocated an East African Federation to overcome the partition of Africa into countries so small and so poor that they cannot muster the resources for development. Nyerere knows that freedom of criticism and opposition is necessary for good government, but he has decided that only government by a single party can unite Tanzania's Africans and successfully carry out his ambitious development program. Rather than making the few Europeans and the well-to-do Indian shopkeepers and sisal plantation owners scapegoats for African frustrations, Tanzania is pledged to cooperation between the races. Above all, Nyerere is aware that the toughest problems are those that come after independence. His slogan for Tanganyika was *"Uhuru na kazi"*—"Freedom *and work.*" Nyerere is highly respected by other African leaders, and his counsels carry great weight at inter-African conferences.

In foreign policy, Nyerere has offended the United States by accepting Chinese Communist aid and allowing the Chinese to operate freely in Tanzania. In fact, however, Nyerere is his own—and Tanzania's—master. Chinese leaders, who scented an easy political conquest, were stunned when Nyerere refused to support the Chinese line and sternly advocated real neutralism (see Chapter 18 for general African views of the cold war). More aid comes from the West than from the East, and the handful of Chinese military instructors are outnumbered by Canadians and Israelis.

Nyerere's current slogan for Tanzania is *"Uhuru na moja"*—"Freedom and unity." While Tanzania is a single-party state (see Chapter 17), freedom of speech and opinion has been upheld. In hotly contested elections in December 1965, several Cabinet ministers lost their seats in Parliament. Nyerere has shown that he values individual freedom and wishes to achieve progress through cooperation rather than dictatorship.

Léopold Senghor of Senegal (1907–   )

Léopold Senghor is the outstanding example of the cultured and sophisticated French-trained African intellectual. The French set out to turn Africans into Frenchmen, and they succeeded with a chosen few. Senghor, however, remained an African in his attitudes and his purpose, performing the difficult feat of becoming a nationalist politician after deep involvement with the French, an accomplishment shared by Félix Houphouet-Boigny of Ivory Coast.

Senghor is scholar and poet as well as politician and statesman. Enrolled by his landowner father in a missionary school in the cosmopolitan West African city of Dakar, he was considered so brilliant by his teachers that they sent him to Paris on scholarship. During the 1930's he remained a professor in France, deeply involved in writing

Léopold Senghor. (*Embassy of the Republic of Senegal.*)

poetry and in the intellectual circles of Paris. Senghor's work is now considered among the best French poetry of this century (see Chapter 15).

As happened to many other Africans, great and humble, war swept Senghor into a different life. In 1940, he was drafted into the French Army and was captured by the Germans during the invasion of France. In a Nazi prison camp Senghor discovered his political talents, organizing resistance to the Germans. Allowed to return to occupied France, he joined the Resistance against the Nazis and pondered the meaning of his experiences.

At war's end, Senghor finally returned home to get himself elected Senegalese deputy to the French Parliament, where he served until 1959. For Africans of the French Empire, French politics and African politics were two sides of the same coin. The African territories were represented in the French National Assembly, and the African deputies were consulted by the colonial officials in Paris when an African matter came up.

Senghor bid for power at home by opposing the political machine of the famous Lamine Gueye that had run Senegal from the city of Dakar. Like Nyerere, Senghor toured the dusty villages, persuading influential *marabouts* (Moslem religious leaders) and village elders to back him against the Dakar machine. Equally at home in the literary salons of Paris and in the villages of Senegal, Senghor built his own political machine from the *marabouts* and the prosperous peanut farmers, who delivered the vote that returned him year after year to his seat in Paris. He was easily elected President of Senegal and is now an African elder statesman.

With his lifelong immersion in French ways, continued close economic and cultural ties with France mean a lot to Senghor. He follows a moderate economic and social policy, giving free rein to the peanut farmers and small businessmen, and relying on the conservative *marabouts* to bring in the vote. Confronted with strong opposition from development-minded bureaucrats and Marxist students, Senghor has, like other African political leaders, suppressed it. Senghor's lifelong friend and ally Mamadou Dia was sentenced to life imprisonment for organizing a *coup d'état* after opposing Senghor's economic policy. The radical Party of African Independence (PAI) has been outlawed.

Like other African countries, Senegal faces a long battle with poverty and economic stagnation, and, in spite of French aid, has made little progress so far.

Sékou Touré of Guinea (1922–   )

Sékou Touré's independent ideas and strength of character have made him a national hero and strong leader. Seven hard years as Guinea's President have aged and perhaps mellowed this still-young man, who, perhaps more than any other African leader, is a symbol of

The politician becomes an administrator: Sékou Touré at work. (*Republic of Guinea, Four Years of Independence and Liberty.*)

African independence. Touré is dedicated to raising the standard of living in his poverty-stricken country, and is eager to use all the power of his government to reach this goal. Yet even economic development must, if necessary, be sacrificed to true and complete national independence.

Touré represents the self-made man, the African leader who worked his way to the top without the advantages of much formal schooling or education abroad. His parents were peasants of the village of Faranah in northern Guinea. Guineans believe that he is descended (as he may well be) from the famous Samory Touré, the Guinean national hero who successfully fought the French Army for nearly twenty years at the end of the nineteenth century.

From a Moslem religious primary school, Touré went to a French technical school, from which he was expelled for leading a student strike against the authorities. He finally earned a high school diploma through correspondence courses and worked as a clerk in the post office department of the French colonial administration. He early became a labor organizer and by dint of forceful per-

sonality and hard work rose in 1948 to the leadership of the big Guinean labor union, the CGT (Confédération Générale du Travail). At this time labor unions in French Africa were influenced by French Communists, and Touré began to talk of a Marxist solution to the African problem of poverty.

In 1953 a successful general strike of seventy-six days established the Guinean labor union as leader in the campaign for independence. Touré, the orator and organizer, became a hero of legendary proportions. Elected to the French National Assembly, he was prevented by a hostile administration from taking his seat in Paris. Next time he was elected again, and by 1957 Touré was head of Guinea's territorial assembly—obviously slated to become the first President of Guinea.

Touré rejected the idea of the French Community (see Chapter 9) from its proposal in 1958. Complete independence and nothing less was to him the only solution compatible with African dignity and self-respect. When French President de Gaulle came to Guinea to promote the Community, Touré told him at a public meeting that "we prefer poverty in liberty to riches in slavery." The Guinea voters, awed by Touré and mobilized by his well-oiled political machine, the Democratic Party of Guinea, voted 97 percent against the French Community. When De Gaulle cut off aid and pulled out his administrators and all their equipment, including even electric light fixtures and telephone wires, President Touré quickly asked first the United States (which refused in deference to De Gaulle) and then the Soviet Union for help. Yet in 1961 the Russians learned what De Gaulle had found in 1958—that Touré would not tolerate any outside attempts to dominate his country. Touré spoke publicly of an "Eastern plot" against Guinea, and within a few days most Russian advisers were gone (see Chapter 18). Western politicians began to see that

Touré's fiery revolutionary language did not make him a Communist or a puppet of the Soviets.

As in other African countries, independence in Guinea has run afoul of international economics and the problems of state-run economic enterprise. The Guinean franc, a separate national currency (the other countries of ex-French Africa remained tied to the French monetary zone), declined drastically in value, causing inflation, smuggling, and loss of trade. State-run stores failed because of inefficient management. Touré has been forced to rethink his idealistic conception of total political and economic independence.

Touré's concern is with the needs of his people and with the methods he feels will best answer those needs. The tightly organized PDG (Democratic Party of Guinea), led by Touré and close followers, influences every side of life in Guinea and allows no opposition or interference. Like most other African leaders, Touré believes that political

Kwame Nkrumah addresses the United Nations General Assembly. (*United Nations.*)

wrangling will only hold back the "fundamental revolution" which must transform Africa.

Kwame Nkrumah of Ghana (1909–   )

In 1965, at the age of fifty-six, Kwame Nkrumah was probably the most famous African. Nkrumah was the first President of the first independent black African nation, Ghana. As the man who organized and led the successful Convention People's Party (CPP) and who developed the tactics of "positive action," Nkrumah set the example for other African leaders. African intellectuals admire Nkrumah's constant efforts to unite the more than thirty nations of independent Africa.

In Ghana, Nkrumah was idolized by millions and hated by many—his political rivals and those who resented the meteoric career of the poor boy from the coastal strip. Nkrumah was Father of His Country, Life Chairman of the Convention People's Party, Life President of Ghana, Osagyefo (Redeemer, or Great and Glorious Leader), the smiling face on postage stamps, the marble statue in front of the Ghana parliament building, and the hero of countless poems, songs, and hymns.

The first thoughts of African nationalism stirred Nkrumah when he was a student in Accra. In the *African Morning Post* Nkrumah read the bitterly anticolonial editorials of Nnamdi Azikiwe, a Nigerian who was later to lead the nationalist campaign in that country. By the time "Zik" left Gold Coast for Nigeria in 1937, his nationalist spirit had been thoroughly absorbed by the young reader. Azikiwe had studied in America, and Nkrumah determined to follow in his footsteps.

In 1935 Nkrumah arrived in New York on his way to begin undergraduate studies at Lincoln University in Pennsylvania. In America Nkrumah had one major problem: money. Born poor, he had arrived with about $200 in his pocket, not enough to pay even a single semester's tuition. Library work and waiting on tables pulled him through the school term, but summers were another problem. With millions of Americans out of work in those years of depression, work for a Negro African student was hard to find. After hawking fish on Harlem street corners and laboring in a soap factory, Nkrumah signed on board ship, where he was quickly demoted from waiter to pot washer. The future president eventually was promoted to bellhop and continued to work the high seas during summer vacations until he graduated from Lincoln University in 1939.

As a Negro, Nkrumah was, of course, not shielded from discrimination while studying and later teaching in the United States. As with so many African students and statesmen since, segregation left scars. His comment, and his experience, might have been that of countless other Africans:

> When I compared this racial segregation with the modernity and advancement of the country it made my heart sink.
> I well remember my first experience of active racialism below the Mason-Dixon line. I was travelling by bus on one of my lecture tours from Philadelphia to Washington and the bus stopped en route at Baltimore for the passengers to refresh themselves. I was parched from thirst and I entered the refreshment room at the terminal and asked the white American waiter if I could have a drink of water. He frowned and looked down his nose at me as if I was something unclean. "The place for you, my man, is the spittoon outside," he declared as he dismissed me from his sight. I was so shocked that I could not move. I just stood and stared at him for I could not bring myself to believe that anyone could refuse a man a drink of water because his skin happened to be a different color.

Nkrumah stayed on in America until 1945. He taught philosophy and Negro history at Lincoln, worked the midnight-to-8 A.M. graveyard shift in a shipyard, and preached on Sundays in a Philadelphia Negro storefront church. During these years Nkrumah read hungrily. He read Marcus Garvey and reveled in the fervor of Garvey's Negro nationalism (see Chapter 7). Above all he read Marx and Lenin and became bitterly opposed not only to actual colonial rule but also to the economic exploitation which went with it. Today Nkrumah describes himself as a Christian and a Marxist, and claims that the two complement one another.

Nkrumah's American years left him with wide experience, ideas, and an education. After he left his rise was spectacular. His next stop was England, where Nkrumah made his reputation as an energetic and competent political leader. He was one of the leading organizers of the Pan-African conference held late in 1945 in Manchester (see Chapter 9). The young unknowns of the conference were dispatched to the four corners of the earth to carry their urgent message of national revival, but Nkrumah stayed on in London to organize and coordinate the growing movement. For the next two years he was the center of a whirlwind of meetings, petitions, and visits—all aimed at promoting African independence. He traveled to Paris to meet French-speaking African leaders such as Senghor and Houphouet-Boigny, edited newspapers and journals, and organized Negro workers in Britain.

In 1947 African politicians in Gold Coast were looking for a vigorous and capable organizer. They asked Nkrumah to serve as manager of their party, the United Gold Coast Convention. Although the UGCC was a party of chiefs, merchants, lawyers, and doctors, of whom Nkrumah was deeply suspicious, he nevertheless took the job. Back in Ghana, it did not take long for his energy and dash to make him the hero of the African rank and file, and in a time of mounting discontent Nkrumah was clearly the man whom the masses would follow.

Nkrumah broke with the conservative leaders by pushing for a mass campaign of civil disobedience against the Gold Coast government. He set up his own organization, the Convention People's Party (CPP), in 1949, and immediately began his campaign of "positive action." Mass meetings drew the crowds to the Accra Arena. The *Accra Evening News*, Nkrumah's party newspaper, lashed out at the colonial rulers. The demand of the CPP was clear and simple: "Self-government NOW!" Nkrumah's tactics were equally clear: complete noncooperation with all Europeans, whether as employers (a strike), merchants (a boycott), or police (protest demonstrations, and rallies). The campaign was a success, and Kwame Nkrumah and his colleagues were soon in prison awaiting trial. In court Nkrumah proudly agreed that he had tried to force the British administration to change its policies.

The British soon gave way. For the first time, elected African representatives would be a majority of the Gold Coast Legislative Council. Elections were held in February 1951. Nkrumah, still sitting in jail, was elected to represent Accra. Carried from the jail by a cheering crowd, Kwame Nkrumah was from that day the acknowledged leader of his country.

As head of the majority party, Nkrumah became Leader of Government Business. He soon began to feel the responsibilities of office—the need for compromise with colonial officials and the unpopular but necessary action of opposing demands made by fellow Africans. Few trained Africans could be found to replace the English agricultural extension workers, accountants, and other experts, so Nkrumah had to make do with the old officials, even though many were bitterly opposed to independence for Gold Coast and were less than enthusiastic about working for Nkrumah.

Swollen-shoot disease, which was attacking the cocoa trees on which the Gold Coast economy depended, nearly toppled Nkrumah's administration at its start. The only thing that could be done was to bring the sick trees down. African cocoa farmers were naturally enraged when colonial officials turned up on their farms with axes and proceeded to cut down their source of income. Threats and protests poured into Nkrumah's office. In spite of the outcry the Leader of Government Business ordered the sick trees felled.

Nkrumah was in a touchy position. He had to keep pushing for "Independence NOW!" or be devoured by more extreme opponents. Fortunately for Nkrumah, the British were prepared to see Gold Coast become an independent country. On March 6, 1957, the first black African nation took the name of the great and ancient West African empire, Ghana. Kwame Nkrumah had become the first African Negro to lead his country to independence.

This was the high point of Nkrumah's career. He was soon to discover, as the leaders in other countries of Africa have all discovered, that with "independence" the names may change but the faces never do. The mass of the people is still poverty-stricken, diseased, ignorant, and apathetic. The new rulers—black Africans—replace the old, but they confront the same problems and use, often enough, the same methods of ruling: police harassment of political opponents, censorship, restrictions and bans on movement and meetings, imprisonment, and executions. In fact, the new rulers have fewer resources of skills, money, and experience than the old. Even their black skins often turn out to be less of an advantage than many had thought.

It was Kwame Nkrumah's misfortune as well as his triumph that he was the first, for it was Nkrumah's rule in Ghana which revealed that independence would be no honeymoon. When Nkrumah reacted swiftly and often harshly to put down opposition, he aroused dismay and then hostility in Europe and America, where many had believed, perhaps more innocently than the African nationalists themselves, that all would be milk and honey after independence. Nkrumah's own sensitivity caused him to lash back at the hostile Western press, and the rebukes continued in a vicious circle.

The Convention People's Party extended its control over Ghana. The Young Pioneers, CPP's youth group, gave the many unemployed roughnecks hanging around the new towns something to do. After a longshoremen's strike at the port of Secondi-Tokoradi was put down by government troops in 1961, the once-strong labor unions became a mere satellite of the party. Newspapers were censored. Opposition leaders of the UGCC, a small but vocal faction, and of the National Liberation Movement, the party of the powerful Ashanti tribe, were jailed. Under a Preventive Detention Act the government could imprison without trial anyone considered dangerous.

All this repression was carried out by Nkrumah in the name of national unity—a dubious reason for depriving any man anywhere of life or liberty. Yet while Nkrumah's regime was hard on several hundred political opponents, it could not be accused of such outrages as the massacre of the Tutsi in Rwanda, the uprooting of whole peoples in the brutal warfare of Congo, or the beatings and shootings in Zanzibar. Nkrumah's aim was clearly to preserve his own position in power, which, like that of other African leaders, teetered on the edge of political rivalry, tribal conflict, and economic stagnation.

Then, suddenly, over the 6 A.M. Accra radio news on February 25, 1966, it was all over. Lieutenant Colonel Emmanuel Kotoka went on the air to announce that "The myth surrounding Kwame Nkrumah has been broken." Kotoka's troops had marched into Accra during the night, and General Joseph Ankrah, Army Chief of Staff until fired by Nkrumah in August 1965, was heading an army *junta* that had taken over the country. (See Chapter 17 for an explanation of the coup.) At the moment of the coup Nkrumah himself was high in the air, flying toward Peking on a peace mission aimed at resolving the conflict in Vietnam. His embarrassed Chinese hosts were forced to break the news after parading Nkrumah with banners and cheering crowds through the streets of Peking.

The final act left diplomats gasping. Just a week after the army takeover in Ghana Sékou Touré announced that Kwame Nkrumah would become President of *Guinea,* equal to Touré himself. As the confusion cleared, it appeared that Touré had handed his deposed colleague an honorary Presidency which could be a soapbox and a springboard for Nkrumah's comeback. Even apart from the fact that Nkrumah has not been elected by the people of Guinea (this may come), Nkrumah does not even speak Guinea's official language, French. Does the power of an African leader—and the principle of Pan-African solidarity (see Chapter 15)—extend to offering a national Presidency to deposed friends?

Future histories may indeed give Kwame Nkrumah pride of place as the father of African independence. And perhaps Kwame Nkrumah will even now continue to play a leading part in African affairs.

Shattered Idols

In this chapter the men who won independence—and ruled after—have held the limelight. Yet in 1965–66—the Year of the Generals—no less than seven African armies (see Chapter 17, table on page 274) have swept their independence leaders off their pedestals, shattering statues, myths, and the personal power of the fallen rulers. In the two potentially most powerful states of black Africa, Congo and Nigeria (see Chapter 10), generals replaced a clique of politicians assailed for corruption, lavish living at public expense, and weakness in coping with the crucial conflict of regions and tribes. Even more important, however, were two military take-overs that were totally unexpected. Two of the heroes of "revolutionary" Africa, who drew cheering crowds with radical rhetoric and who ruled through a single political party loyal to themselves— Ahmed Ben Bella of Algeria and Kwame Nkrumah of Ghana—were quickly, efficiently, and ignominiously sent packing from power by a small number of soldiers.

In Algeria and Ghana, the generals said a major cause of their revolt was the excessive "cult of personality" built up around the deposed leader. Algeria's General Boumedienne has shunned publicity and makes a point of ruling through a council in which he is first among equals. Ghana's General Ankrah announced that one-man rule would never again be allowed in his country. The famous statue of Kwame Nkrumah, larger than life in front of Ghana's Parliament House, was smashed by rioters, and children were photographed among the ruins.

Leadership and Progress

African leaders differ widely in personality, in background, and in their methods of rule. They do, however, share certain goals. The first of these is the material progress of their country and its people. Progress, to African leaders, means adequate nourishment and more cash for the African masses. But it also means the sinews—and the trappings— of a modern nation: a steel industry, a disciplined and well-equipped army, an airline. The other goal is secure independence and political stability. African leaders disagree widely over the meaning of independence; Sékou Touré believes that continued close ties to France or any foreign power would compromise his revolutionary ideals, while Léopold Senghor and Félix Houphouet-Boigny of Ivory Coast are eager to continue close cooperation with France after independence. In internal policy, all African leaders naturally desire to see their own regimes remain in control. Some, like Nkrumah, were willing to rely on arbitrary and authoritarian methods; others, like Nyerere, have been less willing. All seek to enlist the voluntary support and participation of their people in the task of nation building.

The outstanding quality of African leaders is in fact this ability to command support and loyalty from party (or army) comrades and from the people as a whole. The measure of progress that each leader is able to achieve depends to a great extent on his success in inspiring men to action.

PROBLEMS

1. What qualities of character and personality should an African leader have to govern well? How do these differ from the qualities of a good American political leader? How would you explain the differences in terms of the different problems which African and American leaders face?

2. From books, articles, and newspapers find out what you can about an African leader not covered in this chapter and write a thumbnail biography. (Suggestions: Nnamdi Azikiwe, Haile Selassie, Gamal Abdel Nasser, Ahmed Ben Bella, Habib Bourguiba, Jomo Kenyatta, Kenneth Kuanda, Félix Houphouet-Boigny, Joseph Mobutu, to mention a few.) Do

you think that your man has done a good job as a political leader or head of government? What are his contributions, and what mistakes has he made?

4. Read carefully the poem in praise of Kwame Nkrumah on page 204. Why are African leaders held in such high esteem by ordinary Africans? Is hero worship of the leader *necessary* for stable government in Africa? What are the dangers of carrying the dependence on a single leader too far?

5. How might the next generation of African leaders—those educated and brought into politics and government after independence—differ from the men now in power?

6. If you were to plan a program to educate future African leaders in the United States, what would it include? How would you manage the problem of race discrimination? Would you set up special courses for the Africans, or include them in classes designed for American students? To what kinds of schools would you send them? What courses would you **recommend**?

READING SUGGESTIONS

Nnamdi Azikiwe, *Zik: The Writings of Nnamdi Azikiwe*, Cambridge University Press (London), paper.

George Delf, *Jomo Kenyatta*, Doubleday, 1961.

Rolf Italiaander, *The New Leaders of Africa*, Prentice-Hall, 1961.

Kenneth Kaunda, *Zambia Shall Be Free*, Heinemann (London), 1962.

Thomas Melady, *Profiles of New African Leaders*, Macmillan, 1961.

Leonard Mosley, *Haile Selassie: The Conquering Lion*, Weidenfeld (London), 1964.

Gamal Abdel Nasser, *Egypt's Liberation*, Public Affairs Press, 1955.

Kwame Nkrumah, *Ghana* (an autobiography), Nelson, 1957.

Alan Rake, *Tom Mboya*, Doubleday, 1962.

Paul Sigmund (ed.), *The Ideologies of the Developing Nations*, Praeger, paper.

Reference

Ronald Segal, *Political Africa*, Praeger, 1961.

part four
THE SEARCH FOR UNITY:
Pan-Africanism and Negritude

For the past half-century Africans have been seeking a common bond. This search has deep meaning, for it is the effort of Africans to find out who they are. Is there any such thing as an "African" at all?

The search has been made along two lines. Two generations of African poets and writers have sought the common bond in African culture. Writers have expressed their belief in "Negritude," or "Negro-ness," a quality of the spirit that unites men of black skin. They contend that the history of slavery and suffering which Negroes share has created a deep psychological kinship among them. Other writers, less emotional, explore the meaning of the great changes in colonial Africa and try to fit the rich folklore of African peoples into its new setting. As in other countries during times of great change, African writing is more than "art for art's sake"; it is an effort to explore changing society and point a way toward a better future.

The second line of search is the Pan-African movement: the effort of African national leaders to promote peace, economic cooperation, and political union in Africa, and to assert the African personality in world affairs. Some leaders, like Kwame Nkrumah, want a united Africa like the United States that will bring all African countries under a single flag. Most other leaders wish to begin slowly. While these men often quarrel, and are still groping, all agree that the African nations must work together. Pan-Africanism has been made real to the extent of their cooperation.

PART FOUR:

The Search for Unity:

Pan-Africanism and Negritude

chapter 14

ONE AFRICA... OR MANY?

We must all hang together, else we shall all hang separately.

—BENJAMIN FRANKLIN,
to the Continental Congress, 1776

Pan-Africanism—the belief in African unity—was born with the twentieth century, in the year 1900. In the sixty-odd years since, it has swept over Africa and aroused the passions of politicians and their followers from Cape to Cairo. The Pan-African idea first stirred in the minds of American Negroes, West Indians, and African students in the European capitals of colonial empires, and was not known to the mass of Africans in their villages. With the African students and politicians who returned home to clamor for independence after World War II, and with the postwar boom that brought millions of Africans to the new towns, the Pan-African idea took root in Africa as well.

What does "Pan-Africanism" mean? "Pan" means "all"; the Pantheon of ancient Rome was the temple of all the gods, and Pan-American is an airline serving all the Americas. "Pan-Africanism," then, is at bottom the idea of an "all-Africa," a united Africa.

The underlying force that has given the Pan-African movement its wide and great support is the idea that Africans, and particularly Negro Africans, despite their many tribes, languages, and religions, and their division into many colonies, are one people. And their being one people means that Africans share a common fate, a single historical destiny. Such a belief is not right or wrong. If it is believed and acted upon by Africans, the Pan African idea will in fact shape Africa's future.

Does Pan-Africanism mean an Africa united under a single government? This question was debated by the students and intellectuals in the years before World War II, and is still being argued today. The vision of a single great African state ruling the whole continent is enticing, but is it practical or possible? The realization of such a goal would at least have to await the coming of independence and majority rule to Southern Africa. Often citing the example of the Thirteen Colonies, which had united after a similar struggle to overthrow colonial rule nearly two hundred years before, English-speaking African leaders, and a few French-speaking ones, accepted the goal of political unity.

Yet the African case was very different from the American. Unlike the Thirteen Colonies, the African colonies each waged a separate campaign for independence and built national organizations to do it. Africa, divided among many colonial rulers, had no equivalent of the Continental Congress or the Continental Army that waged America's war for independence. Independence came almost haphazardly, piece by piece, over many years. Now the problem is to unite independent nations, many with strong national governments and leaders jealous of their new authority.

Pan-Africanism could mean something different. As an exciting, arousing slogan it could unite Africans seeking independence in many parts of the continent and become a symbol of the unity of black men everywhere. The idea of Pan-Africanism has brought about cooperation between African governments, parties, labor unions, student groups, and womens' and youth organizations. There is, as yet, no Pan-Africa, but Pan-African cooperation is real and will certainly continue.

Back to Africa: From Manchester to Accra (1945–1958)

The Pan-African movement came to life at the Manchester, England, meeting of 1945 (see Chapter 8), when workers, students, and politicians of Africa came to meet the exiled intellectuals who had been working for African independence for more than a generation. Pan-Africanism became a rallying cry of the mounting nationalist campaign in Africa.

During these same few eventful years another great change occurred, a change which gave the new African leaders important international allies. This change was the new independence of the countries of Asia. In countries such as Indonesia, Pakistan, India, Burma, and Ceylon, leaders of nations molded by colonial rule replaced the colonial government after the war—a pattern to be repeated in Africa a few years later.

The world community suddenly became much larger, with many more nations clamoring for public attention and new respect. At the same time the world became much smaller as the volume and speed of transport, travel, and communications vastly increased. Nationalists in the African colonies watched the course of events in Asia eagerly, and welcomed support for their demands for reform and independence from such new nations as India and Indonesia.

The Pan-African movement soon became part of the larger current of cooperation between the newly independent, nonwhite peoples. As early as 1947 an Asian conference met in New Delhi, and in 1950 an Arab-Asian bloc was formed at the United Nations. While the bloc included two Arab African countries, Egypt and Libya, no black African country took part. (Today more than thirty African countries are members of the United Nations.)

These first attempts at international cooperation among the new nations led to the now-famous meeting at Bandung, Indonesia, which was called by Indonesia's President Sukarno in 1955. Delegates from twenty-five countries, representing more than half the people of the world (Communist China was there) attended. The only African countries represented were Ethiopia and Egypt, while a single delegation from the Gold Coast (which became independent Ghana in 1957) spoke for all of black Africa. The Afro-Asian conference met to "promote cooperation among the nations of Africa and Asia" and to "consider the position of the people of Africa and Asia in today's world." Independence from colonial rule was the theme, and the Bandung program stressed the "sovereignty and territorial integrity of all nations" and the "equality of all races and all nations."

The impact of the Bandung conference on Africa's nationalist leaders was tremendous. For the first time in modern history leaders of free and independent nonwhite peoples had met to discuss the changing face of the world and their place in it. The very fact of such a meeting was an occasion for rejoicing by those who had been under the spell of European rule for generations. In the years that followed, nationalists continually cited resolutions taken at Bandung and quoted speeches made there. Asian and African independence, Bandung seemed to say, was a fact, irrefutable and inevitable; while the nonwhite nations might be poor and socially backward, they were the political equals of their former colonial rulers. The new attitude was that of self-confidence and, above all, self-respect.

In 1957, two years after the Bandung meeting, Ghana became the first black African nation to win independence. Others would surely follow. The need for cooperation between African nations would soon be a reality.

First Steps: 1958–1960

The Accra Conference

At the celebrations marking Ghanaian independence, Prime Minister Habib Bourguiba of Tunisia suggested to Ghana's new Prime Minister Nkrumah that a conference of independent African states be called. There were nine independent African states at the time— Ghana, Tunisia, Morocco, Egypt, Ethiopia, Liberia, Sudan, South Africa, and Libya. All agreed to meet in Accra in April 1958, with the exception of South Africa, whose white supremacist government wanted no part of an anticolonial nationalist gathering.

The Accra conference, called to plot an African course toward the future, thrust leaders of a new Africa before the eyes of their own people and drew world attention. The confident tone of the meeting foreshadowed a strong "African personality" to come. A journalist described the opening of the conference:

Promptly at 9:30 A.M. the leaders of the delegations enter the Assembly Chamber. A minute later Dr. Nkrumah, quietly and without any preliminaries, declares the conference opened. "I recognize," he says, "the leader of the Ethiopian delegation." Prince Sahle-Selassie Haile-Selassie, son of the Emperor of Ethiopia, walks fumblingly to the rostrum set against the splendor of a large green and yellow kente cloth embroidered with Ghanian flags. He is short, shy, and olive-skinned; his hair stands up like a schoolboy's. His speech shows his English public school training.

Kwame Nkrumah followed with these remarks to the delegates:

This is a memorable gathering. It is the first time in history that representatives of independent sovereign states in Africa are meeting together with the aim of forging closer links of friendship, brotherhood, cooperation, and solidarity between them. What is the purpose of this historic conference? We are here to know ourselves and to exchange views on matters of common interest; to explore ways and means of consolidating and safe-guarding our hard-won independence; to strengthen the economic and cultural ties between our countries; to find workable arrangements for helping our brothers still languishing under colonial rule; to examine the central problem which dominates the world today, namely the problem of how to secure peace.

This statement by Nkrumah is a good summary of the hopes and purposes shared by African leaders.

Then the conference got down to issues and took a stand on the major problems that troubled the sleep of African nationalists. The Algerian war must end with full Algerian independence. France must not test atomic weapons in the Sahara. South Africa must reverse its racist policy of *apartheid* and give full voice to its black majority. All the African colonies must be free. The conference also defined Africa's place in international affairs. African countries pledged support for a strong United Nations, vowed a campaign for an end to colonialism everywhere, and proclaimed "that a distinctive African personality will play its part in cooperation with other peace-loving nations to further the cause of peace" (see Chapter 18 for Africa's role in world politics). The African nations at the Accra conference largely succeeded in uniting on the issues that concerned them most.

The All-African Peoples Conference

Another kind of African meeting took place in December 1958, again in Accra. This was a meeting of African nationalists still waging their struggle for independence; of politicians not yet statesmen. The atmosphere was electric with the hope of a general breakthrough to independence, more tense and less formal than the earlier meeting of African states. As a black South African journalist watched:

Dr. Nkrumah spots the Turkish ambassador in London next to me. What an electric smile of recognition as the premier waves his hand. So spontaneous. As Tom Mboya later ushers him on to the rostrum, with his arm around the premier while they whisper to each other, I realize all the more that this is Africa—an Africa with a totally different sense of convention from that of the West. All during the speech the feeling of self-confidence that Dr. Nkrumah inspires does not escape me. I look at his ministers and am struck by the same self-confident and bold, dignified facial features that characterize the

Ghanaian of today. At close quarters you find it isn't conceit; it's something beautiful against the background of colonialism and all the servility it demands.

As might be expected from its membership of nationalist leaders on the threshold of independence, the All-African Peoples Conference was a hotbed of anticolonial oratory. The conference met three times, moving after the founding meeting in Ghana in 1958 to Tunisia in 1960 and Cairo in 1961. At each successive meeting the accusations grew more impatient. At the first conference it was declared that "the All-African Peoples Conference vehemently condemns colonialism and imperialism in whatever shape or form these evils are perpetuated."

In a crescendo of enthusiasm and fervor, the second conference declared that:

[It] bows before the martyrs fallen in the course of the glorious struggle against the forces of slavery and colonialist oppression; notes with satisfaction the progress, across the whole of Africa, of the historic movement towards liberation; and emphasizes joyfully the fact of the African peoples becoming conscious of their personality and their strength.

The third conference, in Cairo in 1961, was the high point of the revolutionary tirade. Listen to these ringing words denouncing things white and Western: "Contemptuous of the role of the negative United Nations in the struggle for African Liberation . . . Whereas the existence of British rule over Central Africa is nothing but an accident of history . . ."

By 1961, of course, most African countries had achieved the status of independent nations, and their leaders had moved on to meetings of heads of state. The All-African Peoples Conference, which may never meet again, had become the mouthpiece of the more radical leaders, and many of its views were no longer shared by men in power. Yet Westerners would do well to heed the strong current of bitterness and resentment that runs deep in the minds of more than a few educated Africans.

Years of Division: 1960–1963

In 1960 the Pan-African movement ran into a storm which nearly broke up the whole attempt at cooperation. The time of troubles lasted for nearly three years before it evaporated in the relative tranquillity of the historic May 1963 meeting at Addis Ababa, when thirty African heads of state came together to form the Organization of African Unity. In these years African leaders seemed to spend more time in the air and in conference halls than they did at home. They formed and re-formed groups whose names roll off the tongue in glorious confusion—the African and Malagasy Union (UAM), Pan-Africa Freedom Movement of East, Central, and South Africa (PAFMECSA), Brazzaville bloc, Casablanca bloc, Monrovia bloc. Amid the dissension, observers too hastily saw a split between pro-Western and pro-Communist leaders, and assumed that the cold war was moving into Africa. What really had happened?

In 1960 and 1961 the former French colonies left the French Community and struck out on their own as independent countries. Where there had been eight African states to meet at Accra in 1958, and thirteen at a second meeting at Addis Ababa in 1960, within months there were more than twenty-five (see

Presidents (left to right) Keita of Mali, Nkrumah of Ghana, and Touré of Guinea at Conakry in 1960. The three West African leaders proclaimed a Ghana-Guinea-Mali Union, which they hoped would form the nucleus for a United States of Africa. The union proved premature. *(Republic of Guinea, Four Years of Independence and Liberty.)*

chart on page 141). The newcomers wanted their ideas to be heard, and the growth in numbers strained the time, resources, and ability of the African leaders.

The new African states were French-speaking and had a Pan-African tradition different from that of the English-speaking Africans. The drive for political unity of the English-speaking Africans, begun by the American W. E. B. DuBois and carried on by men like the West Indian George Padmore, Kenya's Jomo Kenyatta, and Kwame Nkrumah, met an equally strong current of cultural Pan-Africanism, expressed as the idea of "Negritude" (see Chapter 15), among the French-speakers. Many of the French-speaking leaders such as Félix Houphouet-Boigny of Ivory Coast and Léopold Senghor of Senegal felt close kinship with France and French culture, and were still reluctant to put all their eggs in the African basket.

When the French Community broke up in 1960, both France and its former black African colonies wanted to maintain close relations. Cooperation with English-speaking leaders, notably Nkrumah, as well as with the Maghreb countries and Egypt was not to take place. Two separate groups formed.

Brazzaville: December 1960

Three matters concerned the former French black African countries. At the top of the list was the war in Algeria, which dragged on and on, poisoning the air between Frenchmen and Africans. Houphouet-Boigny of Ivory Coast wanted to arrange a compromise acceptable to France as well as Algeria, and thought that the former French black African countries could act as mediator. Another issue was Mauretania, the large swath of desert at the western end of the Sahara. Was Mauretania a separate country, or was it part of Morocco, as Moroccan sultans had claimed since their invasion of Songhai in 1591 (see Chapter 2)? Finally, no African leader

could ignore the political storm raging over the Congo (see Chapter 10), where the continued secession of Katanga and the downfall of Prime Minister Lumumba had thrown the African states and the United Nations itself into tumult and confusion.

Twelve former French colonies sent delegations to the famous meeting at Brazzaville in December 1960: Senegal, Upper Volta, Niger, Dahomey, Ivory Coast, Chad, Gabon, Central African Republic, Malagasy, Mauretania, Cameroun, and the Congo Republic (former French Congo, capital Brazzaville). They agreed to cooperate for economic development but rejected the idea of a united government. The political tone was pro-West, and the twelve countries urged an end to the Algerian war because it might bring Communist intervention in Africa.

The Brazzaville group changed its name in 1961 to the African and Malagasy Union (in French the Union Africaine et Malgâche, or UAM). The UAM remains pro-French; its members have become African associates of the European Common Market and have signed a military treaty backed by the French Army. The UAM countries have pooled resources for an airline, Air Afrique, and have a single postal and communications network.

Because these exclusively French-speaking countries accepted close military and economic treaties with France, and because they have been reluctant to dissolve their bloc within the present Organization of African Unity (see end of this chapter), they have been accused of being French satellites by other African leaders who roundly condemn French "neocolonialism" ("neo" means "new" or, in this case, "continued") in Africa. When French paratroops were flown overnight to Gabon to suppress a popular revolt in December 1963 against pro-French President Leon Mba, a leader heartily disliked by many Gabonese,

French neocolonialism seemed quite real.

Casablanca: January 1961

In July 1960, the Congo disaster (see Chapter 10) burst upon the African leaders without warning. Congo's fall to anarchy and violence, and the warring political factions that in August and September sprang up like weeds, threatened to bring the cold war to Africa and menaced the neighboring countries. In any event, Congo was a blot on the record of African competence and ability.

The Casablanca conference met as a reaction to the Congo events and the formation of the Brazzaville bloc. Morocco, enraged by Brazzaville's support for a separate Mauretania, called the meeting. The countries represented were Guinea, Mali, Egypt, Ghana, Morocco, Libya, and the Algerian rebel government. These were, in Western eyes, the "radicals" of Africa. However, it must be admitted that some of these countries had quite legitimate reasons to be anti-West: Egypt had been invaded by Israel, Britain, and France in 1956; the French had tried to wreck Guinea's economy when they pulled out in 1958; and Algerians were being killed daily fighting the French Army. Events since have shown that while several of the Casablanca countries were at the time quite anti-Western, not one of them had any intention of becoming a Communist satellite (see Chapter 18).

On the all-important Congo question (see Chapter 10), the Casablanca group came out squarely for Patrice Lumumba, because he was the elected and legitimate Prime Minister, although they were disturbed by his emotional, even irrational behavior. After Lumumba's murder in Katanga, most of the Casablanca countries wanted to send guns and soldiers to the "Lumumbist" government in Stanleyville headed by Antoine Gizenga and backed by the Communist bloc. As anti-Western feeling reached fever pitch, Kwame Nkrumah stepped in with cool words and insisted that the Casablanca countries continue to back the United Nations' efforts in Congo. Fortunately, he was heeded.

The Casablanca meeting expressed its views on other issues too. In return for Egyptian support for his Congo resolution, Nkrumah had to accept an Egyptian resolution calling Israel "an instrument in the service of imperialism." (Words to the contrary, Ghana, like Ivory Coast, Tanzania, and many other black African countries, keeps right on trading with Israel and receiving Israeli help on development projects.) Mauretania was of course condemned for existing, and the French were denounced for testing atomic bombs in the Sahara and for continuing the fruitless and devastating war against the Algerian guerillas, whose government was represented at the conference.

Casablanca was the high point of North African, and particularly Egyptian, influence in the Pan-African movement. Egypt's President Nasser had worked vigorously to become a leader of the African as well as the Arab nations. As more and more black African countries became independent, the center of gravity naturally shifted south of the Sahara. Some black African leaders, while admiring President Nasser's efforts to build a strong and independent Egypt (though not his policy toward Israel), regarded his African ambitions suspiciously. The proper African role of Egypt—a geographic and cultural bridge between Africa and the Arab Middle East, and a country with a long Western tradition as well—remains an interesting and important question.

Monrovia: May 1961

Hot on the heels of the Casablanca meeting, African leaders with a more easygoing attitude toward the problems plaguing Africa joined forces. President Tubman of Liberia invited all the

Haile Selassie, Emperor of Ethiopia, greets Kwame Nkrumah at the African Summit Conference in Addis Ababa in May 1963. The African leaders went on to create the Organization of African Unity. *(Wide World Photos.)*

African nations to Monrovia in May 1961. The Brazzaville group (the former French colonies except Guinea and Mali) joined Liberia, Nigeria, Somalia, Sierra Leone, Togo, Ethiopia, and Libya (which switched sides), but the Casablanca countries of Ghana, Guinea, Mali, Morocco, and Egypt refused to come. The tone of the Monrovia conference was mild, and neither Congo nor Algeria seemed to trouble the delegates much, in direct contrast to the strident radical tone of Casablanca. The split between the radicals at Casablanca and the moderates at Monrovia was official, and seemed to be widening. Through 1961 and 1962 journalists and politicians mused on the meaning of the African split. Some tried to dub the Monrovia nations "pro-West" and the Casablanca

group "left-leaning" or "pro-Communist." Many thought the split would be permanent.

The Organization of African Unity: Addis Ababa, May 1963

The newspaper commentators, as they so often are, were wrong. The dispute had been over issues and tactics, not principles. With the 1963 lull in the Congo crisis, with the coming of independence to Algeria after seven years of war, and with all but the southern tip of the continent now under African rule, the split evaporated. African leaders were determined not to allow their continent to be divided. When sober thought revealed the problems facing a poor, backward Africa in the whirlwind of social and technological revolution, all the African leaders came together to discuss the problems of African unity and to set up a new organization in which to work.

Haile Selassie, the organizer and host and the traditional Emperor of an African nation independent for more than a thousand years, spoke to the assembled heads of state at the African summit conference at Addis Ababa:

> The commentators of 1963 speak, in discussing Africa, of the Monrovia States, the Brazzaville Group, the Casablanca Powers, and many more. Let us put an end to these terms. What we require is a single African organization through which Africa's single voice may be heard, within which Africa's problems may be studied and resolved.

Haile Selassie's proposal was welcomed by all thirty African leaders present, and the upshot was the new Organization of African Unity.

Established in a burst of cooperative enthusiasm, the OAU has had both ups and downs since 1963. Of the committees and commissions set up by the OAU (see chart on page 228) for the organization of the OAU), the Conciliation Commission helped settle the border dispute between Morocco and Algeria and the Liberation Committee at Dar es Salaam has channeled aid to guerillas in Angola and Mozambique and to refugees from South Africa. On the other hand, the African states continue to disagree, sometimes violently, over other issues. In spite of their disagreements, however, no African state or bloc has left the OAU, and all remain pledged to the fundamental principle that African matters should be settled in an African framework (the OAU) by Africans alone.

The French-speaking Bloc

While all other groups, blocs, and unions dissolved into the OAU, the group of French-speaking black African states kept together. In February 1965 at Nouakchott, capital of Mauretania, leaders of thirteen countries (see list)

revived the old Brazzaville bloc under the new name of OCAM, the Organization Commune Africaine et Malgâche (Joint African-Malagasy Organization). Leaders of these ex-French colonies—most of them small, poor, and sparsely populated—apparently feel a common bond based on their French language and culture and their continued close ties to France, but they insist that OCAM can exist as a special group without violating the spirit of African unity. The OCAM states are part of the African group at the United Nations and welcome programs for African economic cooperation such as the proposed combined West African steel industry.

The OCAM States

Cameroun
Central African Republic
Chad
Congo (Brazzaville)
Dahomey
Gabon
Ivory Coast
Malagasy Republic (Madagascar)
Niger
Senegal
Togo
Upper Volta

OCAM includes all the countries of former French West and Equatorial Africa with the exception of Guinea and Mali, plus Madagascar. Mauretania dropped out shortly after the group was formed.

Congo Again

The 1964–1965 Congo rebellion was the first real test for the new Pan-African spirit. The second annual African summit conference was held in Cairo in July 1964 as the Congo rebels were sweeping victoriously through eastern Congo toward Stanleyville. Moise Tshombe, without doubt the most unpopular man in Africa after his stint as leader of the Katanga secession (see Chapter 10), had just been named Premier of Congo. His rebel adversaries

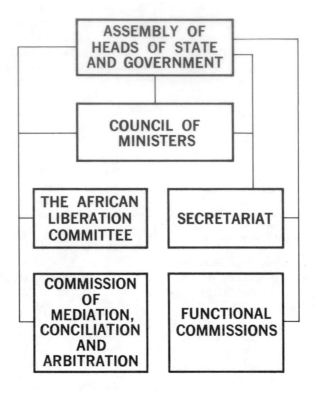

Exhibit 2
The Organization of African Unity

The OAU has been in existence for only a short time, and its procedures, lines of authority, and patterns of operation are by no means clearly set. The Heads of State are clearly able to make decisions, for they personally hold effective power in the nations of Africa, and to a lesser extent this is true of the Council of (Foreign) Ministers as well. The African Liberation Committee at Dar es Salaam has become quite active politically in its support for independence movements in the Portuguese colonies, Rhodesia, and South Africa. Perhaps the most difficult job, and potentially the most rewarding and constructive, has fallen to the Commission of Mediation set up to settle disputes between African states by peaceful means. This group has had some success in dealing with the Morocco-Algeria and Somalia-Ethiopia border problems. The Secretariat is an unknown quantity, and most of the commissions set up to coordinate African planning in the various fields of government activity have barely begun to function.

claimed to carry the torch of Patrice Lumumba, Congo's martyr. Tshombe was barred from the OAU summit meeting (although Nigeria protested that the OAU Charter prohibited black-balling legal African governments). In October another conference, this time of all nonaligned nations, was held in Cairo. Tshombe went. He was met at the airport by Egyptian police, who took him away and locked him up in a villa far from the scene of the meeting. Tshombe finally returned in a rage to Leopoldville, an African pariah.

At a special September 1964 session the OAU created a commission headed by President Jomo Kenyatta of Kenya to resolve the Congo crisis. Although Kenyatta's group tried long and hard to get Tshombe and the rebel leaders to sit down together and call off the bloodshed, the warring Congolese politicians refused to meet and the OAU effort failed.

During December of 1964 several African states of the old Casablanca group began to aid the rebels, who by then were losing to government forces. Guns were shipped from Egypt. Algeria threatened to send veteran officers to match the white mercenaries hired by Tshombe, and observers reported Ghanaian planes carrying sup-

plies as well. In reaction, when the conservative French-speaking states met to form OCAM, they decided to offer diplomatic support and even troops to Tshombe. Fortunately the rebellion was put down before the revolutionary and conservative groups could trade blows. The whole incident, however, showed how fragile African unity can be when confronted with an African crisis of major proportions.

Liberation

The slogan around which Pan-Africans now rally is the liberation of Southern Africa. On this, all African leaders are agreed; there can be no compromise with white-minority domination. Every effort must be made to drive

Liberation Movements in Southern Africa

Country	Party	Leader(s)	Situation, Tactics
Angola	Union of the Peoples of Angola (UPA)	Holden Roberto	Waging guerilla war in Angola; recognized by the OAU as the Revolutionary Government of Angola in Exile (GRAE) in Leopoldville
	People's Movement for the Liberation of Angola (MPLA)	Mario de Andrade Agostinho Neto	Exile politics in various African capitals
Mozambique	Front for the Liberation of Mozambique (FRELIMO)	Eduardo Mondlane	Began guerilla war in 1965; based in Tanzania
	Democratic National Union of Mozambique (UDENAMO)		Based in Tanzania
Rhodesia	Zimbabwe African National Union (ZANU)	Joshua Nkomo	Suppressed; Nkomo restricted
	Zimbabwe African People's Union (ZAPU)	Ndabaningi Sithole	Suppressed; Sithole in prison
South Africa	African Nationalist Congress	Albert Luthuli Nelson Mandela	Suppressed
	Pan-Africanist Congress	Robert Sobukwe Potlako Leballo	Suppressed; many members imprisoned for sabotage

the Portuguese from Angola and Mozambique, to break white-settler rule in
Rhodesia, and somehow to finally be-
seige the fortress of white-racist South
Africa. Angolan guerillas are being
trained by Algerian veterans, and guns
and dynamite are being sent into Angola and Mozambique through Congo
and Tanzania. The OAU Liberation
Committee in Dar es Salaam channels
money to black nationalists in the
south. At the United Nations African
spokesmen are trying to organize a
world boycott of South African goods—
an almost impossible task.

A United States of Africa?

For many years, in private and in his
speeches and books, Kwame Nkrumah
consistently urged a union government
for Africa. He argued that small African nations must combine their meager
resources and coordinate their economic
planning under a single government if
they are to raise living standards—a
rise every African leader has promised
his people. The fact that African countries are today a jumble of tribes, languages, and cultures makes it urgent
that they be united now, before African
peasants come to feel strongly about national rivalries and develop national
rather than African patriotism. Surely
a war between, say, Guinea and Liberia
would be silly if not tragic. *Now* is the
time to bring African countries into a
greater whole.

The great majority at Addis Ababa
and at Cairo in 1964 disagreed. Unity
must come slowly, they argued, with
each small effort at cooperation building
trust and confidence for the next, big-
ger step. Practical economic efforts at

cooperation such as joint airlines, elimi-
nation of tariffs across African borders,
and joint campaigns to wipe out malaria
and the tsetse fly must be worked out
gradually, by trial and error. These are
the views of the majority.

African Unity?

Pan-Africa may yet come about, although it may take generations to become a reality greater than the paper
on which resolutions and signatures
rest. But Pan-Africa is not inevitable.
We have looked at some of the issues
which divide the African states as well
as at the goals they have in common.
National feelings may harden. The real
test of Pan-Africanism today is whether
the spirit of unity can settle such deeply felt and troublesome disputes as the
border war between Ethiopia and Somalia, the rebellion in southern Sudan,
or the rivalry between competing nationalist movements in Rhodesia, Angola, and Mozambique. The Charter of
African Unity signed by the thirty African heads of state at Addis Ababa em-
braces African unity as a goal, but at the
same time declares African states independent of one another and free to do as
they please. The unity that does exist
depends wholly on the voluntary cooperation of more than thirty individual
African leaders and their governments,
parties, and peoples. Most African
leaders have difficulty holding their own
countries together against the divisive
forces of race, language, religion, region, and tribe. Why should the uniting
of these turbulent countries be all that
easy?

_____

PROBLEMS

1. Campaigners for a united Africa under a single government often point to the United States as a country that succeeded in merging many parts into a single nation. What advantages did the American Founding Fathers have that African leaders do not have? How many campaigns for independence took place in the Thirteen Colonies? In Africa? How many languages and peoples were there? Did the Thirteen Colonies have their own united government *before* independence? In what ways does Africa have the beginnings of a united government now?

2. As African countries build their own schools and factories, and plan their own economic progress, will the chances for unity increase or decrease? Do you agree with African countries that insist on economic cooperation between African countries before political union? Would you favor a single African army capable of keeping the peace in Africa and of handling situations like the Congo violence?

3. Are many Africans concerned about what happens at the meetings of African leaders? Would the life of an African peasant be much changed by the formation of a United States of Africa? Would leaders of small countries such as Hastings Banda of Malawi or Ould Daddah of Mauretania want a united Africa? What would happen to national politicians?

4. Draft a short constitution for an African Union. How should it differ from the United States Constitution?

5. Draw a map of Africa showing combinations of countries which you think could fruitfully be united. Geography, economy, and colonial background are all important. Add a note explaining your choices.

READING SUGGESTIONS

Colin Legum, *Pan-Africanism,* revised edition, Praeger, paper.

Kwame Nkrumah, *Africa Must Unite,* Heinemann (London), 1963.

chapter 15
AFRICAN VOICES

In every living thing ... there is a passion for dignity ... a determination to be oneself.

We do not object to the learning of European culture—how can one reject the music of Handel or Bach or the words of Wordsworth ... but at the same time we have much that is rich and good to share with the European too ...

—E. M. DENRAH
*of Ghana, at Georgetown
University, August 1961*

There have been many changes in Africa in the last 100 years, most of them—at least the most obvious—political and economic. There have been other changes less obvious, often unnoticed, and hardly ever talked about—but nonetheless very important. Power and profit were not the only values learned by Africans from Europeans: African culture too has changed. Poetry and prose, the fine arts, and music from the West have enriched cultures already wealthy with epics, folk tales, songs, and dances.

In most parts of the African continent the tales of heroes and gods, myths and epics and tragedies, were passed on from generation to generation around evening firesides, and in many little villages this is still so. But what of the new Africa, the educated, the literate, the sophisticated, and the "been-to's"—those who have "been to" England, France, or the United States? These men and women wanted poems, plays, novels, and essays to explain the turbu-

lence of Africa and the specific physical surroundings and emotional climate in which they live. In literature, as in politics, Africa has begun to give its own answer. For more than sixty years, in all parts of Africa and in Europe and America, educated Africans have been writing in European languages and Western literary forms to express their ideas.

American Negro Revival

In the 1920's in the United States, Negro poets began to reflect the rising hopes of their people in a new Negro poetry. Men such as James Weldon Johnson, Countee Cullen, Langston Hughes, and Claud McKay spoke for the new Negro with a voice of pride in their race and bitter rebellion against segregation and discrimination. In a deeply moving sonnet, Claud McKay recalled the lost Negro heritage and the imposed exile of Negroes whose forebears had come unwillingly from Africa long ago:

Outcast

For the dim regions whence my fathers came
My spirit, bondaged by the body, longs,
Words felt, but never heard, my lips would frame;
My soul would sing forgotten jungle songs.
I would go back to darkness and to peace.
But the great Western world holds me in fee.

And I may never hope for full release
While to its alien Gods I bend my knee.
Something in me is lost, forever lost,
Some vital thing has gone out of my heart,
And I must walk the way of life a ghost,
Among the sons of earth, a thing apart.
For I was born, far from my native clime,
Under the white man's menace, out of time.

Peter Abrahams, now a famous novelist, grew up in the slums of the South African city of Johannesburg in the dreary years of the 1930's. In his autobiography, *Tell Freedom*, Abrahams gives a graphic account of how the words of poets carry ideas around the world. Through a stroke of great good fortune, young Peter was hired as a file clerk at $1.50 per week. In the office library he came across a volume of poetry called *The New Negro*, where he read Countee Cullen, Claud McKay, and Langston Hughes. Hughes's lines

> I'm looking for a house
> In the world
> Where the white shadows
> Will not fall

opened up new vistas for the slum boy:

> In the months that followed, I spent nearly all my spare time in the library of the Bantu Men's Social Centre. I read every one of the books on the shelf marked "American Negro Literature." I became a nationalist, a colour nationalist through the writings of men and women who lived a world away from me. To them I owe a great debt for crystallising my vague yearnings to write and for showing me the long dream was attainable.

Peter Abrahams is only one of many Africans who has been inspired by the first New World stirrings of the Negro voice. The debt of Africa to Negro Americans remains, in this as in so many other things.

The Caribbean Heritage

From the time of Columbus the little islands scattered over the Caribbean Sea served as slave markets and sugar plantations under the rule of Britain, France, or Spain. The Negroes who were brought to these islands as slaves left behind in Africa their homes, their customs, even their names.

In 1794 the slaves of Haiti, under their great revolutionary leader, Toussaint L'Ouverture, rose against their French masters and overthrew them. As has often happened in other lands, an artistic revival took place as a celebration of freedom regained. Haiti was followed by Cuba, which became free of Spain in 1898 following the Spanish-American War. In Spanish and in French, Caribbean Negroes began to write poetry, trying to explain to the world and to themselves their strange situation as black men who for generations had lost all touch with the motherland, Africa, but who were not, could not be, and did not want to be Frenchmen or Spaniards.

The most famous of the Afro-Cuban writers, as they came to be called, was Nicolas Guillen. Guillen wrote in the 1920's, just as the American Negro revival was beginning in the slums of New York City's Harlem. His lament is as old as Africa:

Have I not got an ancestor of night
With a large black mark
(blacker than the skin)
A large mark
written with a whip?
Have I not got an ancestor
From Mandingo, the Congo, Dahomey?

The theme of the homeless people was continued by the Haitian Jacques Roumain, who in his poem "Guinea" described a legendary homeland where all the Negro peoples gathered after death. Another Haitian, Regnor Bernard, praised the glories of ancient Africa, destroyed by slavery and conquest:

African Dusk

The Pharoahs are troubled
    at the heart of the Pyramids:
and Africa no longer is:
Neither its temples,
nor its mysteries,
for the priests are dead
for the traders in Negroes have come.

These Caribbean writers were in revolt against their inferior position in a society which could never quite accept fully a man who was not white; in revolt against the past suffering and enslavement of the Negro peoples; in revolt against colonial rule in Africa; in revolt against their own shame at being black.

Negritude

In the 1930's in Paris three young Negro students were drawn together. They discussed art, life, the European world around them. But always they came back to the problem that plagued them: What was their position as black men, well-educated and fluent in their adopted tongue, in the European country which had adopted them? What was their place in French civilization? These three, who had followed the path of *assimilation* to the bitter end, found there not the promised acceptance but only doubt and uncertainty. Thus it was that Aimé Césaire of Martinique, Leon Damas of French Guiana, and Léopold Senghor

of Senegal came to evolve "Negritude" —a word, a slogan, a myth.

Negritude—literally, "Negro-ness"— meant positive pride and self-respect in being Negro and African. Negritude glorified the Negro and his African way of life, and broke the spell of inferiority which had so long afflicted Africans wherever they were touched by the European world.

Aimé Césaire

The first of the group to put pen to paper was Aimé Césaire, the most revolutionary and the most defiant. Césaire's first recognized work was a long poem called *Thoughts of a Return to My Native Land (Cahiers d'un Retour au Pays Natale)*. When in the late 1940's Césaire's poem caught the attention of the French literary world it gained international repute overnight. A strident and unsettling voice broke over restless empires:

Hurray for those who never invented
    anything
for those who never explored anything
for those who never conquered anything
hurray for joy
hurray for love
hurray for the pain of incarnate tears!

And later, coining the word "Negritude":

My negritude is no deaf stone that
    reflects the noise of the day
My negritude is no spot on the dead eye
    of the earth
My negritude is no tower and no
    cathedral
It dives into the red flesh of the soil
It dives into the flowing flesh of the sky
Piercing the weight of oppression with
    its sweet patience.

Léopold Senghor

The most famous of the three poets is Léopold Senghor, now President of Senegal (his biography is in Chapter 13). Senghor's poetry is the purest and the most lyric, and is probably the best. Senghor evokes not bitterness but beauty:

Black Woman

Naked black woman
Dressed in your color of life, your figure of beauty!
I grew up in your shade; your soft hands blindfolded me.
And now in midsummer and at noon I discover you, Promised Land, from
    the top of a high sunbaked pass
And your beauty strikes my heart like the lightning flash of an eagle.

Naked obscure woman
Fruit ripe as firm flesh, dark raptures of black wine, mouth which makes
    mine lyrical
Savanna of clear horizons, savanna trembling at the warm caresses of the
    east wind
Carved drum, stretched drum rumbling under the Conqueror's fingers
Your deep contralto voice is the sacred song of the Beloved.

Naked obscure woman
Oil unruffled by any breath, calm oil on the athlete's thighs, on the thighs
    of the Mali princes
Gazelle with divine wrists and ankles, pearls are stars on the night of your
    skin
Witty delights, red-gold reflections on your wet skin shimmering
In the shade of your hair my sorrow brightens in the approaching suns of
    your eyes.

Naked black woman
I sing your passing beauty, form I fix in eternity,
Before jealous fate turns you to ashes to nourish the roots of life.

Césaire and Senghor assert that Negroes have certain qualities of the spirit which are far more valuable than the mere ability to create, to build, or to conquer. These qualities of the Negro are not qualities of doing but of being. In this ability to be happy, to be strong, and to remain untouched by degradation and humiliation lies the Negro's greatness and humanity.

Bitter Voices

Other French-speaking poets often lost touch with reality and became extreme in their glorification of the Negro and his cause. Leon Damas had written as early as 1937:

Do they really dare to treat me as white
While I aspire to be nothing but negro
and while they are looting my Africa?

In his effort to separate white from black, Damas's poetry becomes sheer froth:

The white will never be negro
for beauty is negro
and negro is wisdom
for endurance is negro
and negro is courage . . .

In 1939 Leon Damas's poems were seized and burned by the French police —a pathetic effort to destroy an idea.

This deeply committed, emotional, unreasoning tone reached its artistic height in the poetry of David Diop, who died in an air crash off Dakar before he had found time to become a great poet. The closing lines of his poem "Listen Comrades" sound like the impassioned war cry of a man goaded beyond endurance:

Listen comrades of the struggling centuries
To the keen clamour of the Negro from Africa to the Americas
It is the sign of the dawn
The sign of brotherhood which comes to nourish the dreams of men.

And when David Diop condemns the "assimilated" black man, the Negro who has sold out to the whites, his tone becomes acid with contempt. These are savage lines:

The Renegade

My brother you flash your teeth in response to every hypocrisy
My brother with gold-rimmed glasses
You give your master a blue-eyed faithful look
My poor brother in immaculate evening dress
Screaming and whispering and pleading in the parlors of condescension
We pity you
Your country's burning sun is nothing but a shadow
On your serene "civilized" brow
And the thought of your grandfather's hut
Brings blushes to your face that is bleached
By years of humiliation and bad conscience
And while you trample on the bitter red soil of Africa
Let these words of anguish keep time with your restless step—
Oh! I am lonely so lonely here.

Stirring as it is, this poem is politics as much as art. Much Negro African writing in French has suffered because it concerned politics—the immediate problems of colonialism and the place of the Negro—rather than striving for greater understanding of human beings.

Mongo Beti, of Cameroun, is a bitter voice in prose. The novels of Beti are like his country—stark, assertive, violent, sensual, and passionately anticolonial. Probably his best work is *The Poor Christ of Bomba* (*Le Pauvre Christ du Bomba*), which has unfortunately not yet been translated into English. This novel describes the failure of a missionary's efforts in Africa. It reflects the growing impatience of Africans with the self-righteous bossiness of many Europeans who refuse to recognize that religion must be part and parcel of life's activities, not just memorization of the gospels or the aping of European Christianity's social codes. Yet the value of Beti's writing is that he shows people as human beings, not as white men or black.

A Down-to-earth Writer

Other French-speaking novelists write as if the whole colonial era were but a ripple on the waters, a mere brush stroke on the African canvas. One of these is Camara Laye, who has written of his childhood in Kouroussa, a village in Guinea near the source of the Niger River, where his father was a craftsman in metals. While a penniless student, Laye found himself working on the assembly line in a French automobile factory, and during this time was able to reflect on his fabulous youth. The result was a serene and nostalgic autobiography, *L'Enfant Noir*, well translated into English as *The Dark Child*.

The complete absence of that bitterness which almost consumes poets like David Diop distinguishes Laye from many fellow writers. Born and brought up in a healthy, active, and self-sufficient African community, and at home with the traditions of his native land, Laye did not need slogans like "Negritude." David Diop, on the other hand, was born, raised, and educated in France. He returned to an adopted Africa only as a grown man, and to an Africa—the down-to-earth village Africa of Camara Laye—which he perhaps did not understand.

Camara Laye has written a second novel, *The Radiance of the King* (*Le Regard du Roi*). This is the story of a renegade white man in a Negro kingdom whose strange experiences are

sometimes painful and often hilarious. *The Radiance of the King* is quite different from *The Dark Child;* both are major works in modern African literature.

English-speaking Africans

African writing in English is more recent and less emotional. Its poetry is not on a par with that of the writers in French.

The Nigerians: African Renaissance?

In English-speaking Africa, the hotbed of artistic activity today is Nigeria. Nigerian playwrights, poets, novelists, painters, and sculptors flourish in vigorous competition. This artistic explosion is the product of the last decade. Before that Nigeria and the other West African countries were as silent as tombs.

One of the first Nigerian novels was Cyprian Ekwensi's *People of the City,* a racy account of life and politics in the Nigerian capital of Lagos. Although it is not great art, *People of the City* is entertaining reading. Nigerian artists recently began the project of making it into Nigeria's first film, but were stopped by the Nigerian government, which feared that the reputation of African politicians would suffer a severe blow. This case dramatically brought to light an important issue in Africa today: What should be the relationship between the independent artist and the government, especially where both are uncertain of their direction? As for *People of the City,* it seems a pity to lose what could be a rambunctious, riotous movie.

Nigeria has produced another controversial writer, Amos Tutuola, who writes the kind of English which makes sticklers for grammar weep in their sleep. Tutuola has attracted tremendous attention in English and American literary circles. He has written many books, including *The Palm-Wine Drinkard* and *My Life in the Bush of Ghosts,* all packed with swift-moving events about absurd, frightening, and impossible creatures and places. His first work, *The Palm-Wine Drinkard,* opens with these lines:

> I was a palm wine drinkard since I was a boy of ten years of age. I had no other work more than to drink palm wine in my life ... My father got eight children and I was the eldest among them, all the rest were hard workers, but I myself was an expert palm wine drinkard. I was drinking palm wine from morning till night and from night till morning. By that time I could not drink ordinary water at all except palm wine.

While grammarians struggle to straighten out his syntax, Tutuola's imagination runs riot with Yoruba folk tales and legends. Rumor has it that he wrote *The Palm-Wine Drinkard* in three days.

The most serious of the modern Nigerian novelists is Chinua Achebe. His first book, *Things Fall Apart,* tries to explain the reaction of Africans to the onsweep of colonial rule. In his second novel, *No Longer at Ease,* Achebe tackles a major African problem (see Chapter 6): the uncomfortable transition from the traditional African village to the new life of the city, from the old values to new desires. One later novel is the prize-winning *Arrow of God.* Achebe has a high standing with critics and fellow writers alike.

Nigerians are writing poetry as well. Christopher Okigbo's poems are difficult but rewarding. Another poet, Wole Soyinka, writes biting satire about his own countrymen, as well as about his former colonial rulers. Listen to his description of an African student in London:

> My dignity is sown
> Into the lining of a three piece suit.
> Stiff, and with the whiteness which
> Out-Europes Europe.

One of the men who has made Nigeria a center for African writing and art is

Ulli Beier, a German who has made Nigeria his home. Beier edits and publishes *Black Orpheus,* a journal of Nigerian poetry and art, and has coedited an important little volume called *Modern Poetry from Africa.* Ulli Beier is a new kind of European, a man who can sincerely adopt the ways of a new African country, who can work *with,* not *for* or *over,* Africans, and who comes as an immigrant, not as a conqueror or ruler.

The South Africans: The Fruit of Injustice

In South Africa Africans have been in close touch with whites for many decades. Here *apartheid* and the growth of bitterness between the races have naturally left their marks on African writing.

In the early days, before harshness and brutality had poisoned daily life in the southern part of the continent, South Africa's first writers were lyric and romantic. The first black man to turn out a novel in English was Thomas Mofolo, who wrote at a remote mission station deep in the veld. Mofolo's two novels hark back to the past. One is about Chaka, the Zulu King who brushed aside custom and constitution to become a ruthless conqueror (see Chapter 4). The other is an allegory about good and evil, where a bold prince carries off a young maiden from a harsh world to a fairyland. When Mofolo finally left the veld for the new industrial cities, he found a different and bitter way of life. He never wrote again.

After World War II a new wave of South African writing began. Since then there has been an unending stream of protest literature—realistic, bitter, and sometimes, understandably, full of deep self-pity. The new writers were men who had fought their way up in the tumble-down shantytowns of Johannesburg, Durban, and Cape Town, men who had overcome poverty, ignorance, crime, and color to get an education and to sharpen their skills as writers. They wrote as they lived, passionately and in a hurry, against deadlines and for immediate results.

This was the era of the first African jazz, of gang wars and American movies, all played out in the poverty-stricken "locations" and "townships" of the South African cities. It was also the time when the white supremacy of Jan Smuts was replaced by the harsher doctrine of *apartheid,* when police raids became more frequent and more vicious, when whole settlements of black Africans were uprooted and thousands of men and women were taken from their homes to languish in the jails of a powerful but frightened government. It all added up to a fast-moving life, steeped in violence, cynical, bitter, and impassioned, a maze of contradictions and impossibilities. One of the most fascinating accounts of the South African underworld of educated black men is *Drum,* written by Anthony Sampson, an Englishman who came to know and befriend many black South Africans.

The life that Sampson saw was the life that Ezekiel Mphahlele, Bloke Modiasane, Lewis Nkosi, and many others lived. They wrote short stories, essays, and sketches, and their works appeared in newspapers and journals such as *The Purple Renoster* ("rhinoceros" in Afrikaans), a university magazine; *Fighting Talk,* a political monthly; and *Drum,* a mass-circulation magazine.

So far, Ezekiel Mphahlele is the only one of these writers to have written more than one full-length book. His autobiography, *Down Second Avenue,* shows how for years he lived under *apartheid* until he was no longer able to stand the insults constantly directed against him because his skin was the wrong color. Like Mphahlele, other black South Africans have been able to write at length only in exile. Todd Matshikiza, in *Chocolates for My Wife,* and Bloke Modisane, in *Blame Me on History,* recount their own experiences and those of their families and their friends and their people. These books are a mixture of autobiography, political comment, and anecdotes, and they make interesting and moving reading.

J. Arthur Maimane, a Johannesburg journalist now in London, has written a short short story, called "The Homecoming," just one page on the back of the last issue of *Fighting Talk* before it was banned by the South African government. "The Homecoming" tells about a man who was arrested in the streets of Johannesburg for not carrying a pass, kept for seventeen months on a Boer farm which uses prison labor for digging potatoes, and then dumped, a broken, exhausted shell, on the streets of Johannesburg, only to be immediately rearrested for not carrying a pass. The story opens with these lines:

> He climbed slowly over the steel side of the lorry, holding on with shaking, skinny, festering hands. He placed one naked, cracked, and swollen foot carefully on the dawn-cool tarmac near the side of the street. He was bringing the other as carefully down when the lorry jerked forward and away with its high-piled potatoes. He landed on his face in the street, then rolled into the gutter.

It closes just sixteen paragraphs later with this description of his arrest by white policemen:

> "We'll have to fumigate the bloody car afterwards!" His voice was impersonally disgusted. He opened the back door of the car. They grabbed the man gingerly around his skinny arms and heaved him up. "Throw him on the floor, Hannes. He'll mess up the seats." Three doors slammed in quick succession. The engine roared and the big car shot forward, horn blowing stridently.

Todd Matshikiza is both writer and composer. He wrote the score for *King Kong*, a musical with an all-African cast about a heavyweight boxing champion who became a legendary figure in the African townships. King Kong was a giant of a man, tough and ruthless, a bully and a braggart, and he captured the imagination of the country. When he was charged with murder for stabbing his girl friend in a fit of rage, King Kong pleaded guilty and asked for the death sentence, but was sentenced to twelve years' hard labor instead. A rebel to the last, King Kong gave his own answer, drowning himself in a huge dam on the prison farm where he was working.

Matshikiza's autobiographical sketch is called *Chocolates for My Wife*. The excerpt given here explains how the book got its title. Matshikiza was waiting for the special bus which took performers home from rehearsals of *King Kong* when he was accosted by six white policemen:

> ... "Where's your pass?"
> I released one hand from the large box and whipped out of my inside pocket the little blue cards printed, "Bearer ... is a member of the *King Kong* cast. Members of the South African Police are kindly asked to allow him to go home after rehearsals which usually stop about one o'clock A.M. Thank You."
> "Oh God, this is one of the *King Kong* kaffirs. Okay an' what's that you got in the parcel, jong?"
> "It's choc'lat's, baas, choc'lat's for my wife. I jus' got them now from a friend."
> "Oho, Jesus, Piet, listen to this one. Of all my night shifts I never met a baboon like this one." They gathered around me.
> "Please, baas, don't break the box."
> "Ha, ha, ha . . . caw . . . caw . . . caw, ha, ha, ha" until they split their sides with laughter. "The monkey got choc'lat's for his wife . . . ." They laughed into their big police van and their echo drifted into the night, echoing long after they had gone.
> "The maid is now called wife, caw, caw, caw, and choc'lat's for her!"

Dennis Brutus is a young South African writer who has been a teacher, a sports instructor, and most recently a student at Witwatersrand University. In 1963 Brutus was a leader in the campaign to have South Africa barred from the Olympic Games until black South Africans are allowed to compete for places on the Olympic team. On his way to a meeting of the Olympic organization, Brutus was seized in Mozambique by Portuguese police and returned as a prisoner to South Africa. In Johannesburg Brutus tried to escape through the crowded city streets, but was gunned down by the police. He pulled through from the brink of death and, having served years in prison, has escaped to the freedom of London.

These two short poems of Brutus are rich in imagery yet precise. They have the ring of nobility and bespeak the deep sadness of a man whose country is not free.

Erosion-Transkei

Under green drapes the stars scream,
red wounds wail soundlessly,
begging for assuaging, satiation;
warm life dribbles seawards with the streams.

Dear my land, open for my possessing,
ravaged and dumbly submissive to our will,
in curves and uplands my sensual delight
mounts, and mixed with fury is amassing

torrents tumescent with love and pain.
Deep-dark and rich, with deceptive calmness
time and landscape flow to new horizons—
in anguished impatience await the quickening rains.

Nightsong-City

Sleep well, my love, sleep well:
the harbor lights gaze over restless docks,
police cars cockroach through the tunnel streets;

from the shanties creaking iron sheets
violence like a bug-infested rug is tossed
and fear is imminent as sound in the wind-swung bell;

the long day's anger pants from sand and rocks;
but for this breathing night at least
my land, my love, sleep well.

An Unfinished Chapter

All over the continent Africa's writing is like its people—tumultuous, in ferment, expressing new urges and desires. This chapter has touched only a small part of a great and many-sided enterprise. We have not mentioned any of the writers of the Maghreb, in the Arab land, where novels and short stories are appearing in French and Arabic. We have not mentioned the East Africans, or the white South Africans, Afrikaans and English. We have not explored the journals, the conferences, and the societies which bring together African writers and artists so that they may learn from one another and go forward together. Another book would have to be written to do justice to the subject.

PROBLEMS

1. One of the great debates in Africa today concerns languages. Should poets and novelists write in French and English, or in African languages? What specific practical problems might plague an African who wanted to earn his living as a writer, publishing in an African tongue?

2. What audience are African writers writing for? As more Africans learn to read and have time to read, how do you think African writing will change? If you were going to write a book for African city dwellers to enjoy, what would you write about?

3. The *form* in which an idea is expressed eventually affects the thinking of the writer. In what ways might the use of the novel and particularly the essay—two Western literary forms—change the way Africans think and reason?

4. Compare some of the poems in this chapter with those of an American poet—for example, Longfellow or Walt Whitman or Robert Frost. How do the themes of the poems differ? Which are more forceful? Which, in your opinion, are better poetry?

READING SUGGESTIONS: A SELECTION FROM AFRICAN LITERATURE

Poetry

Ulli Beier and Gerald Moore (ed.), *Modern Poetry from Africa*, Penguin, paper.

Langston Hughes (ed.), *An African Treasury*, Pyramid, paper.

Books

Peter Abrahams, *Tell Freedom*, Knopf, 1954.

———, *A Wreath for Udomo*, Knopf, 1956.

Chinua Achebe, *Things Fall Apart*, Obolensky, 1959.

———, *No Longer at Ease*, Obolensky, 1961.

Mongo Beti, *Mission to Kala*, Heinemann (London), 1964.

Aimé Césaire, *Cahier d'un Retour au Pays Natale*, Bordas (Paris), 1947.

John Pepper Clark, *Song of a Goat*, Mbari (Ibadan), 1961.

Cyprian Ekwensi, *People of the City*, Dakars (London), 1954.

———, *Jagua Nana*, Hutchinson (London), 1961.

Camara Laye, *The Dark Child*, Noonday Press, 1954.

———, *The Radiance of the King*, Collins (London), 1956.

Bloke Modisane, *Blame Me on History*, Thomas & Hudson (London), 1963.

Ezekial Mphahlele, *Down Second Avenue*, Faber & Faber (London), 1959.

————, *The African Image,* Faber & Faber (London), 1962.

Lewis Nkosi, *Home and Exile,* Longmans (London), 1966.

Christopher Okigbo, *Heavensgate,* Mbari (Ibadan), 1962.

Amos Tutuola, *The Palm-Wine Drinkard,* Faber & Faber (London), 1952.

————, *My Life in the Bush of Ghosts,* Grove Press, 1954.

Criticism and Comment

Ulli Beier, *African Mud Sculpture,* Cambridge University Press (London), 1963.

Gerald Moore, *Seven African Writers,* Oxford University Press (London), 1962.

Journals and Magazines

Black Orpheus, Nigeria.

The New African (South African, published in London).

Présence Africaine, Paris.

Transition, Uganda.

part five
PROBLEMS OF INDEPENDENCE

Most Africans are still peasants who live in mud or grass huts and eat what food they grow. They sell their surplus to pay taxes and maybe, in a good year, have enough left over to buy a few yards of cloth or a steel-bladed axe. Only one of five Africans has ever lived in a city. Most of the others live according to tribal custom. Very few can read or write. Although most African babies now survive to be adults, they are underfed and continually sick.

Where can new nations get the money to build roads, schools, and hospitals? When will Africans be able to afford bicycles, sewing machines, and houses of brick or cement? Who will build the factories, manage the businesses, and repair the machines that Africa must have to prosper? How can farmers learn to break age-old habits and take up crop rotation and contour plowing? Who will satisfy the universal clamor of the young for education?

As one African country after another declared its independence, observers shook their heads and wondered, "Are African countries really capable of governing themselves?" What they meant was, "Can African countries govern themselves *well?*" Can the new nations remain peaceful and orderly without suppressing the freedom of their citizens? Can they survive cold war politics and preserve their independence in a peaceful continent? Can the new nations, endangered by tribal rivalries and split by divisions of language, culture, and religion, survive as nations at all?

As African leaders always knew and as most Africans are now finding out, independence is a beginning, not an end. It raises far more questions than it answers. The crowds shouting *"Uhuru"* disperse, the banners demanding "Self-government NOW" are folded and put away. The excitement is over, but the work has only begun.

PART FIVE:

Problems
of Independence

chapter 16

UHURU NA KAZI...
THE PROBLEM OF DEVELOPMENT

Uhuru na kazi—Freedom and work.

*—Slogan of the Tanganyika
African National Union*

Amelioration of the conditions of life is
the only true meaning independence
can have.

—PATRICE LUMUMBA

African leaders rose to power and African nations to independence on a whirlwind of change. Now these new men of power must tame that whirlwind and bend it to the task of creating harmony and abundance. The new slogan for the long hard pull toward prosperity is *"Uhuru na kazi"—Freedom and work."*

African nations do not begin with a clean slate. Most depend on the export economies built and still largely run by Europeans. Most are poor in resources and lack not only industries but the roads, railroads, and electric power that make industries possible. While African economies remain backward, social change goes on, wrenching African peasants from their villages, their tiny farms, their chiefs and priests and kinfolk, and pulling them into city slums where life is just as miserable and frustrating after independence as before. The education brought first by missionaries and later by colonial governments has awakened many Africans to the possibility of being rich, of enjoying health, newspapers, automobiles, and air conditioning, and educated Africans are impatient to reach the promised land of abundance.

Economic Development

The most difficult problem facing African leaders is a problem of economics: How can they raise the standard of living of their people? Every people in the world—Americans, Russians, Cubans, Indians, and Europeans—agrees that having enough to eat, a firm roof under which to sleep, and eventually a car and a television set is a good thing. There is no debate about the need to make 250 million poor Africans less poor. The problem is finding out how it can be done.

Agriculture

In Africa perhaps four of every five people are peasants who eat what they grow and buy very little from others. The peasant's own labor and the labor of his wife, plus an iron hoe, are often

Unloading cargo from surfboats at Accra. Thirty thousand tons every month come ashore here in this backbreaking and inefficient way. The crate is full of beer— one of Africa's major imports. (*United Nations.*)

have to find out how many cameras he could sell once they were produced. If there was no demand for the cameras because only a very few people had the money to buy them, there would be no reason for the American to invest his capital in Ethiopia. Yet new factories, and capital investment, are just what African countries need most to become modern, industrial, and rich. The poverty of the peasants is a vicious circle.

For many years colonial officials thought that use of farm machinery and modern agricultural techniques would automatically make African farms produce twice as much. Today's African leaders, after many colonial failures, are not so sure. With the help of Western economists and agricultural experts Africans are seeking new solutions to this basic problem of agricultural productivity. In East Africa the best way to supply the meat that most Africans lack in their diets may be to "farm" the wild animals of Africa by keeping herds of antelopes and zebra! Perhaps large amounts of fertilizer will

his only tools. The tropical laterite soils that nourish his grain and roots are poor compared with the rich black earth of the Ukraine or the American prairie. The peasant's land usually belongs not to him but to his village, and if he improves the land it may be given to a neighbor next growing season. Lack of tools, seeds, and fertilizer, poor soil, and community ownership of land all help make African farming unproductive and inefficient.

There is more to the problem of African agriculture than the simple fact that peasants produce little and are therefore poor. Because they do not sell their crops to others, most Africans have no money to spend. Why, then, should investors and businessmen put up factories to make things that no one can buy? If an American wanted to go into partnership with an Ethiopian to make cameras in Ethiopia, he would

PER CAPITA INCOME:

Africa Compared
with the World

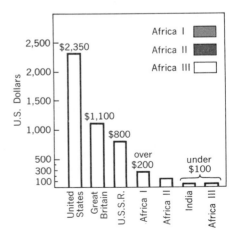

INCOME PER CAPITA

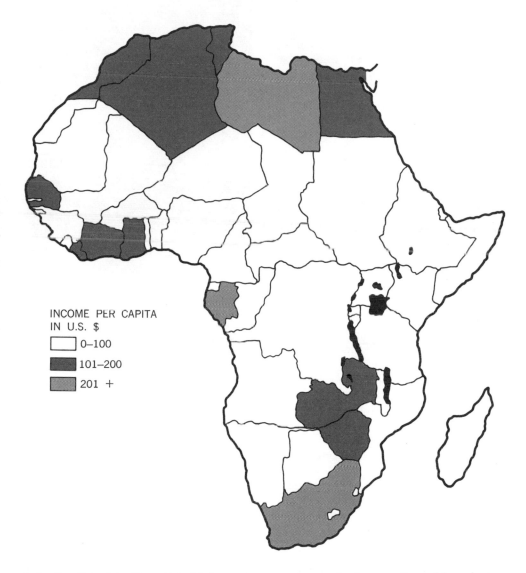

INCOME PER CAPITA
IN U.S. $

- 0–100
- 101–200
- 201 +

help the thin laterite soils which are so vulnerable to erosion and which lose their richness so quickly. The serious study of African farming problems is only beginning, and the agricultural problem may be the toughest of all to solve.

Industry

Most people in the world, and most educated Africans, think of economic progress in terms of smoking factory chimneys, railroad cars loaded with coal and iron ore, and assembly lines that mass-produce automobiles or tractors. Economic progress means the growth of industry, and economic development means industrialization.

South of the Sahara, only white-ruled South Africa is a modern industrial country. Under General Nasser's regime, Egypt has pressed forward with ambitious plans for new factories—some of which, like textile, have worked well while others, like automobile, have not. Algeria's infant industries were badly hurt by the Algerian war and lost most of their skilled workers when the French *colons* left in 1962. During the economic boom of the 1950's, Congo began to make such common consumer goods as shoes, beer, packaged food, cigarettes, lumber, and cement. In most other independent black African countries there are very few industries.

Skills

Industries must have skilled workers. A very ordinary advertisement in the *New York Times* of June 2, 1963, asked for "experienced machine shop grinders. Must be capable of set-up for internal and external surfaces. Knowledge of machine shop practices desired." The company that submitted this notice probably expected ten suitable applicants that day. Yet there are probably fewer than 100 such men in all Africa! Africa badly needs men trained to do industrial work, not only engineers and scientists and business managers but machinists, electricians, riveters, foremen, and mechanics.

African workers must be trained from scratch. Workers in Gabon, hired

Tanganyikan mechanics learn their trade. (*White Fathers.*)

as construction laborers, have to be taught how to climb a ladder and use a wheelbarrow. A lawn mower can be a strange and dangerous machine. The problem is not lack of ability but lack of experience with even the most primitive tools and machines. Once taught, African workers manage without trouble. A Lancashire, England, man who manages a textile factory in South Africa claims that in six months African men and women fresh from the *kraals* (as African villages are called) are as good workers as his English employees, whose families have been in the mills for generations.

Labor

Most African workers want to return to their home villages for two or three months each year to tend the crops and to see their families, who are often left behind. As far as the company is concerned, the worker who leaves may never return to his job, and often he never does come back. The result is that in Africa new men must be trained

Dinka tribesmen gather kenaf, a local fiber, in southern Sudan. The operation is more akin to the Stone Age than to the twentieth century. (*United Nations.*)

LITERACY

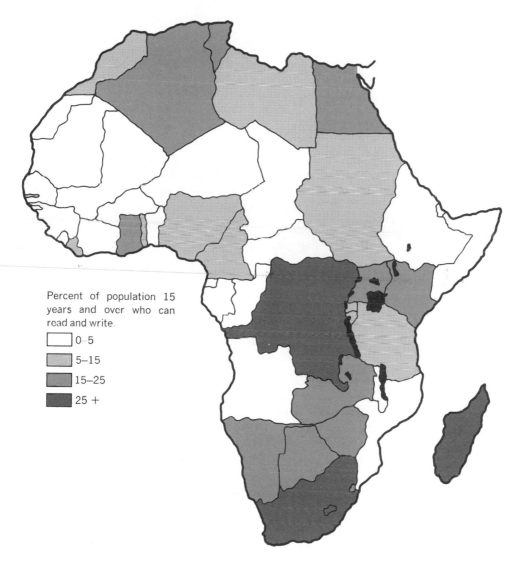

Percent of population 15
years and over who can
read and write.

- ☐ 0–5
- ☐ 5–15
- ☐ 15–25
- ■ 25 +

every year or two to do a job, which is expensive for the company and makes the operation less efficient. This will change when and if conditions of living in the towns and at the mines become attractive enough to hold the workers, and when there is room for the worker's family and pay enough to feed them.

Transport

Africa still has few roads and railways, and needs more badly. Nigeria, with the largest population in Africa, is a good example. Nigeria's two railroads run a parallel course from the north to the coast, one on each side of the Niger River. In eighty years of colonial rule the British never built a bridge across the Niger, and today this is a priority project in the Nigerian development plan. Traveling in Nigeria is a hazardous business. In Lagos, the capital, covered trucks wait to haul passengers to Ibadan or Kano, each

LITERACY:

AFRICA COMPARED WITH THE WORLD

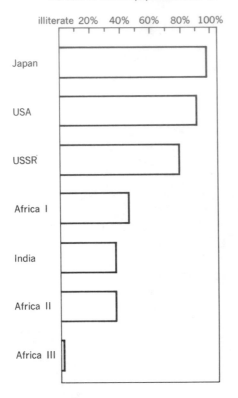

Percent of literate population over 15

	illiterate 20% 40% 60% 80% 100%
Japan	
USA	
USSR	
Africa I	
India	
Africa II	
Africa III	

ride begins, over unpaved roads at breakneck (for that kind of road) speed, weaving from side to side to avoid the potholes and the onrushing "mammy wagons" from the other direction. Passengers are relieved to arrive safely.

The situation in many other African countries is worse—no transportation at all, except Shank's pony.

Power

Another problem is power, the electric power that drives modern machinery. During the past fifty years the United States has built coal- and water-based power plants to make enough electricity for every American factory and home. Most African nations have not yet begun this long-term, costly, and all-important project. The Kariba Dam in Southern Rhodesia, Ghana's Volta River Project, and the planned Nigerian dam across the Niger River at Kainji will provide some hydroelectric power for those countries. Egypt's high dam at Aswân, on the upper Nile, will be completed in 1968. The mines and copper-smelting plants of Congo's

Road building near Dar es Salaam. Mud and undergrowth make African road construction a formidable task. (*World Bank.*)

truck owned by someone who makes a living driving from town to town. As Peter Abrahams tells us:

These "mammy trucks" are the principal carriers of the country. They carry passengers as well as produce and go hurtling across the countryside with little regard for life or limb. Each truck has its own distinctive slogan, such as: Repent for Death is Round the Corner, or Enter Without Hope, or The Last Ride, or If It Must It Will. My own favorite, and I travelled in this truck, pleaded, Not Today O Lord Not Today.

Agents scour the streets looking for passengers. When the truck is full, the

A motor train in the Sahara. One diesel pulls five trailers. This huge vehicle is used by the Algerian subsidiary of the French Petroleum Company. (*White Fathers.*)

Kariba hydroelectric project on the Zambezi River. Rhodesia is on the right bank of the river, Zambia on the left. The dam is 420 feet high and has created the world's largest man-made lake. Kariba power supplies both Rhodesia and the Zambia Copperbelt. (*World Bank.*)

Katanga province run on power from dams built by Belgian companies on the Congo River.

While Africa lacks power now, the future could be different. Africa's rivers could produce more hydroelectric power than any other continent. The Congo River and its tributaries hold half of Africa's potential water power resources, and one-eighth of the world's.

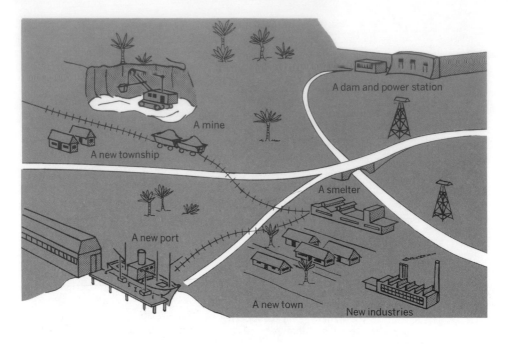

A dam and power station

A mine

A new township

A smelter

A new port

A new town

New industries

Exhibit 3
Volta River Project

This schematic drawing shows all the elements that go into Volta. The smelter will make aluminum from bauxite mined nearby. The Volta dam will provide power. A harbor is being built at Tema, which is rapidly becoming the country's major port. In addition to the dam and the port, power lines, a railroad to carry the ore from mine to plant, roads, and a town for the factory workers are needed. The cost of all the *infrastructure*—which must be in place before the bauxite mine and aluminum plant can operate—shows why African development is so expensive.

Capital

No country can build industry without machines or the money to buy them. The money, and the machines, are called *capital* by economists, and the process of getting them is called *capital formation*.

There are three main ways for a country to get capital. The first is by foreign investment. Foreigners with money can be persuaded to build factories, to employ African workers, and to teach Africans the mechanical and business skills needed to run the enterprise—all in the hope of gaining a profit. African leaders of newly inde-

pendent countries have not had an easy time attracting foreign businessmen with money to invest. Investors are wary of political troubles and suspect nationalist politicians of hostility to foreign business. In fact, African leaders are torn between their great need for capital and their great desire to be complete masters of their countries' economies. Foreign companies are welcome if, like the aluminum companies in Ghana and the French oil companies in the Algerian Sahara, they agree to train Africans and to pay a large share of the profits to the African government. Investors seeking to profit by hauling raw materials out of Africa, without putting anything back in, are likely to get the cold shoulder.

The most popular way to raise capital in Africa is by foreign aid—either loans or, better yet, outright gifts. Aid from the United Nations or the World Bank is most popular because Africans feel that this aid has no political strings attached. Aid from the United States or the Soviet Union is regarded with suspicion. Yet African governments need capital so badly that most would probably accept aid from the devil himself if necessary.

The third way to raise capital is by taxing the people at home. The Soviet Union under Stalin built factories by taxing Russian peasants and workers very heavily. Russian housewives waited hours to buy a loaf of bread, and families were crowded two to a room. The discontent of the people was repressed by secret police, forced labor camps, and work laws so harsh that a man could be shot for coming late to the job. Such repression of the people is a prospect which few African leaders can face, and they are committed to less-drastic methods.

Neither Europe, the United States, nor the Soviet Union is now willing to pay for the industrialization of Africa, and the United Nations doesn't have the money. So the factories and tractors will have to be bought with money raised at home. Unfortunately, little money can be raised by taxing people who earn less than $100 a year. Since African peasants who grow barely enough for themselves cannot be taxed of money they don't have, the burden will fall on the cash-crop farmers, shopkeepers, and office workers. Taxes are just as unpopular in Africa as in the United States. African leaders who want quick industrial development will have a hard time persuading their people to make the necessary sacrifices, for every dollar spent on machines and factories means a dollar less for someone to spend on food or clothes or consumer goods such as radios or gasoline or beer.

Entrepreneurs

Besides technical skills, African countries need men with business skills, including the courage and daring to take risks. Called *entrepreneurs* by economists, such men organize a business, large or small, by bringing together the materials, the workers, and the machines needed to produce something and sell it. In West Africa many traditional tribal cultures, like that of the Ibo (see Chapter 1), develop entrepreneurs, for these cultures were based on trade. In Ghana, Nigeria, Ivory Coast, Uganda, and Ethiopia Africans have bought land and turned it to growing crops such as coffee or cocoa or cotton to be sold for profit, which is entrepreneurship in agriculture. In East Africa, where most small businessmen —owners of bicycle repair shops or country village general stores—are Indians, it is hard for an African to get into business. Aggressiveness, industriousness, and acumen in business are a matter of culture, part of the psychological revolution still to come in Africa. The shortage of these qualities, in business, finance, and manufacturing, is one of Africa's greatest economic problems.

Trade

African leaders say that formal political independence is only the first step toward real independence. This real independence, in their view, requires breaking the stranglehold of export trade in just one or two products which limits each country's economy. Today, African countries cannot survive, let alone prosper, without trading African raw materials and crops for manufactured goods made abroad. Only when African countries can make their own spare parts, gasoline, clothing, cement, and a hundred other things will they feel securely independent.

URBANIZATION

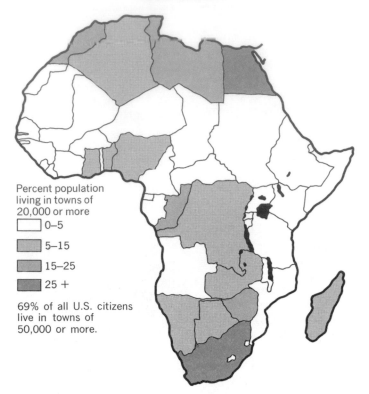

Percent population
living in towns of
20,000 or more

☐ 0–5

■ 5–15

■ 15–25

■ 25 +

69% of all U.S. citizens
live in towns of
50,000 or more.

In addition, Africans are worried because the prices of the cotton and cocoa and coffee that they produce seem to be getting lower in relation to the prices of the machinery and tools and electrical equipment that they must buy in Europe or America. An economist would call this, from the African point of view, a decline in the *terms of trade*, meaning that where one bale of cotton, for example, was worth three radios one year, the same bale of cotton would be worth only two radios the next. African cotton growers in Sudan don't like this any better than American cotton growers in Alabama, who are faced with exactly the same problem. But Africans can do little about it until they produce their own radios. Many are inclined to think that the industrial countries are plotting and conspiring to keep them forever poor and forever backward.

In colonial times most African products were naturally sold in the European country which ruled the colony. In the French and Portuguese colonies import taxes were imposed which in effect required the Africans to buy from France or Portugal, even though products made in the United States or Germany or Japan were cheaper. In return, the colonial country paid a little more for African products from their own colonies.

These restricted patterns of trade are breaking down slowly in the years after independence. Peanuts from Senegal are still cheaper in France than peanuts from Nigeria.

Population

In many parts of Africa the population is increasing at its fastest possible rate. For every African today, there will probably be two Africans twenty years from now! This means that in twenty years African countries will need twice as many schools, twice as many houses, twice as many doctors, nurses, and hospitals, twice as many factories, jobs, and machines—just to keep up the present low standards! Most important, Africa will need twice as much food, and in crowded places like Algeria, Kenya, or Eastern Nigeria new ways will have to be found to grow more food on the little available land. An exploding population adds a great burden to the already-staggering problems of development in many African countries, and African statesmen are seeking ways to stem the high birth rate before it leads to catastrophe.

Public Needs

The need for public services grows as Africans stream from the villages to the cities. City people, in Africa as in America, require clinics, schools, proper houses, clean water, lighted streets, cheap public transportation, and a host of other expensive improvements. For example, the cost of building a sewer system for a large city is tremendous, greater than the total yearly budget of many African countries. Social welfare projects require engineers to plan them, skilled workmen to build them, and doctors, teachers, managers, and electricians to keep them operating. Money and trained men, and large quantities of both, are desperately needed. In the slums of some African cities, more than a thousand people must share a single water tap! Before they became the government, African leaders could blame such miserable conditions on "colonial exploitation." They can't pass the buck now.

The problem is so vast, and the need so great and so pressing, that little progress is being made. All the while, city Africans are demanding more and more frequently the basic conveniences which they regard as due to them. For the new African leaders, the problem is how to enlist the people themselves in the work of improvement: digging ditches, building, contributing more of their tiny incomes for city taxes. *"Uhuru na kazi"* means that Africans must work with their leaders to pull themselves from poverty and the slums by their own bootstraps.

African Socialism?

Africans turn naturally to government to guide the nation through all the problems of development. Perhaps because almost all African leaders—the men to whom workers and villagers will listen—are in government, only government can provide strong leadership. Since African leaders feel that they cannot afford to waste any of their scarce resources—capital and trained men—they try to organize everything around a government plan for economic development. This conviction that in

Water is scarce on Africa's dusty plains. Water taps are rare and a treat. (*World Bank*.)

Even with the roof and walls not yet up, this Congo school is packed with
eager pupils. Education is both the key to modernization for African countries and the road to a good job with status and high pay for individual
Africans. *(Wide World Photos.)*

Exhibit 4
The Nigerian National Development Plan (1962-1968)

Most African governments draw up a plan for economic development. The
plan usually covers a four- or five-year period and sets goals for everything
from production of shoes to the number of children in school. As in the Nigeria
plan shown here, many African countries are counting on foreign aid to help
meet the costs.

Total cost: $1,900,000,000. This is about 1/60 of the United States budget for a
single year.

Revenue—where the money is expected to come from:

	%	*Millions of dollars*
Assumed foreign aid!	48	919
From taxes	39	740
Unknown!	9	174
Underspending!	3	67
	99	1900

Expenditures—where the money will go:

	%	Millions of dollars
A. Economic Development		
1. Transportation	21.4	412
2. Electricity: This includes the Niger River dam at Kainji, which is the cornerstone of the whole plan.	15.1	287
3. Agriculture.	13.6	258
4. Industry: This includes a steel mill and an oil refinery.	13.4	254
5. Telephone system	4.4	83
6. Water supply	3.5	63
	71.4	1,357
B. Social Welfare		
1. Education	10.3	196
2. Health	2.5	48
3. Village improvements	6.2	118
4. Other	9.5	181
	28.5	543
	100.0	1,900

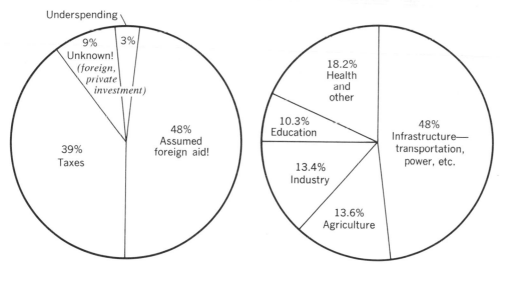

REVENUE

Underspending 3%

9% Unknown! *(foreign, private investment)*

48% Assumed foreign aid!

39% Taxes

EXPENDITURE

18.2% Health and other

10.3% Education

13.4% Industry

13.6% Agriculture

48% Infrastructure— transportation, power, etc.

In the first year of the Nigerian plan, results were slow and somewhat discouraging. Yet most of the public projects were begun, and private investors continued to pour money into Nigeria. The United States has agreed to build the Kainji dam. We may not know the lasting result of this ambitious program and others like it for ten or twenty years!

Africa governments must act to sweep away poverty and get the country moving toward prosperity is called "socialism" by African leaders. "African socialism" is an idea popular with the people, and almost all African leaders call themselves "socialists."

Most Americans look with hostility on anything that carries the label "socialist." "Socialism," meaning an economy run by government, seems to contradict the spirit of individual effort and self-reliance that gave America the world's highest standard of living. In the name of "National Socialism," Hitler killed millions of Jews and plunged the world into war. In the name of "Bolshevik Socialism," Stalin ruled Russia by the terror of his dread secret police and kept both bread and freedom from the Russian people. Americans are rightly suspicious of the doctrine of "socialism," just as most people everywhere are suspicious of universal panaceas and utopian solutions.

African experience has been far different. In traditional village Africa the tribal chief, who was often ruler, high priest, and head of the family all rolled into one, distributed the land and the. crops and provided the beer and meat on feast days. Under colonial rule the British District Officer or French Commandant collected the taxes, built the roads, and hired the villagers to work in faraway cities or mines. Colonial governments regulated the conditions under which Africans worked on European mines or plantations, and sponsored the missionaries who built schools and hospitals. In fact, colonial Africa was much more a government-run, planned economy than a product of free enterprise. This was especially true in the French and Portuguese colonies and in the Belgian Congo. By giving a leading part to government, today's African leaders continue in the ways they have inherited from their African and European forerunners.

A second reason for "African socialism" is that most of the few educated and skilled Africans are in government. In colonial Africa, government jobs had the most prestige and the highest salary. Later, the nationalist political parties, which now control the governments of Africa, drew in all the young men with talent for leadership. As a result, most capable men with an enterprising spirit are now government officials, and most young Africans with education and ambition aspire to government careers.

Finally, African leaders believe that government planning is the fairest way to progress. In theory at least, "socialism" means that the benefits of change will be spread among all the people. The catch is, of course, that the government officials and politicians who do the planing may take most of the benefits for themselves. Critics point to the shiny cars and palatial mansions of some African leaders, which are in stark contrast to the shacks of their barefoot people.

"African socialism" is not a doctrine at all, and it has no single definition. The fact is that different leaders and African countries will follow whatever economic policy they think will bring the most benefit, with government directing the work. If the government did not try to plan for economic development, most educated citizens of African countries would feel that their leaders were not doing a good job.

A Story

For several years, the government of Guinea tried to manage all retail trade, including even small shops and neighborhood markets. The market women of Guinea, who for many years were President Sékou Touré's strongest backers, began to grumble. The supply of goods went down, and prices went up. There was talk of bad administration and of corruption in high places. In December

1963, the government stores were closed, and business was given back to the market women, who have been known to *always* make a profit. The real point here is that even the most "socialist" of African governments will do what works best, rather than relying on any abstract doctrine.

Summary

Political independence is only a step toward the goal of growth and progress. Freedom from poverty, freedom from sickness, and the chance to be educated are what really matter to Africans, once their own flag and government hold sway. Political independence was the easiest hurdle as well as the first, for the problems of economic development are far more subtle and far more difficult to master. How can a poor country build factories, grow more food, and pay for teachers, mechanics, surgeons, water pipes, policemen, and electric lights on the public streets? Not even the world's greatest economists are sure of the answer, for much depends on the people who must do the job. Each African country must now grope ahead with its own meager resources, each learning from the successes and the failures of the others.

Development means the day when telephone calls from one African capital to the next need not be routed through London or Paris, when it will be possible to drive across Africa on a paved road, and when Africans need not rely on the London *Economist*, *Le Figaro* of Paris, or the *New York Times* for their news of the world. Seen this way, development is necessary for true independence.

PROBLEMS

1. Development means many things. Specifically it means to:
   a. Build transportation and communications—roads, railroads, airports, telephones
   b. Try to get farmers to grow more food
   c. Build factories to make steel and machines for other factories to use; economists call this production of *capital goods*
   d. Build factories to make shoes, clothes, umbrellas, and flashlights for people to buy and use—*consumer goods* production
   e. Teach everyone to read and write, and get all the children into school
   f. Train mechanics, surveyors, teachers, engineers, doctors, and businessmen
   g. Clear out city slums and build houses with plumbing and electricity

   In what order would you do these things, and why? This is the most difficult planning problem that African businessmen, planners, and officials face. Remember that all of these projects cost money, and that the African countries have very little to spend.

2. Draw up a development plan for your school or community for the next five years, trying to meet the needs it will face in that time. What kind of information is needed to draw up a development plan for a country? Planning in an African country, or anywhere, for that matter, is basically

the same: It requires estimates of population, materials available, skilled workers and specialists, and money. Do African planners have accurate information about these items?

3. In independent African countries, foreigners still own the mines and few factories. What would happen if, for example, the new government of Zambia took over the Copperbelt mines of the Anglo-American mining trust? Would this be a wise move from the economic point of view? What kind of arrangement would best satisfy both the Africans' desire to control their own natural resources and economy and the foreign investors' desire to profit from their investment?

READING SUGGESTIONS

Africa Report, special issue on "African Socialism," May 1963.

Peter Gould, *Africa: Continent of Change* (section on economic and social problems), Wadsworth, 1961.

William M. H. Hailey, *An African Survey,* Oxford University Press (London), 1956.

W. A. Hance, *African Economic Development,* Harper & Row, 1958.

Elspeth Huxley, *A New Earth,* Morrow, 1960.

George Kimble, *Tropical Africa,* 2 volumes, Twentieth Century Fund, paper.

Statistical Reference

United Nations, *Economic Survey of Africa since 1950,* 1959.

chapter 17

WHO SHALL GOVERN?

Liberty is a slow fruit. It comes, like religion, for short periods and in rare conditions, as if awaiting a culture of the race which shall make it organic and permanent.

—RALPH WALDO EMERSON,
"The Emancipation Proclamation"

The Party State

In the history of politics, the twentieth century is the age of the party state. In the European world the supposedly God-given right of kings to rule was thrust aside by the men of the eighteenth-century Enlightenment — Locke, Voltaire, Rousseau, Thomas Paine, and Thomas Jefferson. This revolution in the European world took place in the name of individual liberty and constitutional democracy, expressed in our nation's Declaration of Independence and Constitution. In Asia and Africa, on the other hand, the decaying traditional regimes of monarchs, tribal chiefs, feudal warlords, and rich men crumbled only in our century. The idea that gave power and inspiration to the new revolutionary generation was not individual freedom but nationalism. Nationalism meant national independence for those countries under colonial rule. It also was, and is, the desire to eliminate poverty, ignorance, and disease.

In the countries of the twentieth-century nationalist revolution, the revolution has usually been led and won by a single national political party and its leader (for the African details, see Chapters 8 and 9). And just as the European revolution of an earlier age produced its characteristic form of government—constitutional democracy—so the revolution of party and leader in Asia and Africa today has produced its characteristic form of government: the party state.

All but a few of the African countries are now ruled by a single nationalist political party. One result has been that in nation after new nation the government, in the usual sense of legislature, courts, laws, and police, has become an instrument of the party and its leaders. The party does not hesitate to use both the law and physical force to gain its

Entrance to Uganda's parliament. In African countries, the government is the most important institution and merits the most extravagant buildings. *(Damon Kletzian.)*

ends; the terror of Stalin's Communist Party in Russia and the brutality of Hitler's Nazis in Germany were only the extremes of a more general trend. Yet a party state need not be a dictatorship. The other extreme is India, which has been ruled by the Congress Party of Gandhi and Nehru since independence, yet is a true democracy. How much freedom to allow the individual citizen is a decision which the leaders of the new nations must make.

A party state, in Africa or elsewhere, is not hard to identify. In the first place, the party has a leader, a national hero who has led his people to the glorious triumph of independence or victory over the tyrants of the old regime. Lenin was worshiped after his death. Mao Tse-tung and Kwame Nkrumah have been worshiped during their lifetimes.

In a party state, the party controls all other organizations—labor unions, student groups, even women's clubs and boy scouts. To be promoted, to succeed, a young man must gain the favor of party officials, and usually must become a party member.

To the party falls the task of teaching "the masses" what they must do to make their country strong and rich.

The party makes all the important choices. Not independent businessmen but party officials in high government jobs manage the nation's economy. While local party members and interested citizens may have some limited chance to voice their opinions and complaints, only the party organization can act. Decisions are made at the top and carried out by party officials under orders from their superiors in the party hierarchy, which extends from local party committees up to the leader himself.

Most of this description could also apply to countries where the army rather than the party rules. Like the party, the army is a single organization directing many sides of national activity through government. Like the party, the army sees itself as torchbearer of the modern nation's destiny. While little as yet can be said about those African military regimes which sprang up like weeds in 1965–1966 (see below), one example is Egypt, where under Nasser's leadership military rule and the party state have become one and the same.

Why the Party State in Africa?

To win independence, the Africans of each country had to form a united front against the colonial government. The young African politicians who led the nationalist campaign brought together groups of followers wherever they could in the cities and the villages, and organized these groups into a single united political party. This single party and its leader were naturally accepted by the great majority of Africans as the rightful voice of the people, with the right to govern after independence.

In the last years of colonial rule, the British and French made efforts to educate African leaders in the complicated ways of Western democratic government. Africans sat on local councils, district councils, legislative councils, executive councils—councils of every shape and variety. At independence, each country was given a constitution, an elected parliament, independent courts and judges, guarantees of individual liberties, and other trappings of Western democracy. Yet all this was artificial and often hollow. The reality of African politics remained the strong, organized mass party and the deeply rooted African tradition of strong leaders and government by men, not laws. In Nigeria and a few other countries Western democracy stuck, at least for a time, because it seemed the best way to keep the country together. In the great ma-

Youngsters march to celebrate the anniversary of Congo independence. In every country youth groups are a key part of the government's campaign to build loyalty to the new state. (*United Nations.*)

jority of new African states the single party quickly emerged as the sole ruler of the nation.

African Governments 1966

Country	Leader(s)	Political Party(s)
1. One-party States:		
Cameroun	Ahmadou Ahidjo	Cameroun Union (UC)
Chad	François Tombalbaye	Progressive Party of Chad
Congo (Brazzaville)	Alphonse Massamba-Debat Pascal Lissouba	National Revolutionary Movement (MNR)
Gabon	Leon Mba	Gabon Democratic Bloc (BDG)
Guinea	Sékou Touré	Democratic Party of Guinea (PDG)
Ivory Coast	Félix Houphouet-Boigny	Democratic Party of Ivory Coast (PDCI)

African Governments 1966 (continued)

Country	Leader(s)	Political Party(s)
Kenya	Jomo Kenyatta Tom Mboya	Kenya African National Union (KANU)
Liberia	William V. S. Tubman	True Whig Party
Malagasy Republic	Philibert Tsiranana	Social Democratic Party
Malawi	Hastings Banda	Malawi Congress Party
Mali	Modibo Keita	Soudan Union [Union Soudanaise]
Mauretania	Mokhtar Ould Daddah	Party of Mauretanian Unity (PRM)
Niger	Hamani Diori	Progressive Party of Niger (PPN)
Rwanda	Gregoire Kayibanda	Parmehutu (Party of Hutu Emancipation)
Senegal	Léopold Senghor	Senegal Progressive Union (UPS)
Sierra Leone	Albert Margai	Sierra Leone People's Party (SLPP)
Tanzania	Julius Nyerere	Tanganyika African National Union
Uganda	Milton Obote	Uganda People's Congress
Zambia	Kenneth Kaunda	United National Independence Party (UNIP)

2. Military Rule (civilian leaders and parties in brackets):

Algeria	Houari Boumedienne [Ahmed Ben Bella]	[National Liberation Front (FLN)]
Central African Republic	Jean Bokassa	[Movement for the Social Evolution of Black Africa (MESAN)]
Congo (Kinshasa)	Joseph Mobutu [Joseph Kasavubu]	[Bakongo Alliance (ABAKO)]
	[Moise Tshombe]	[National Congolese Confederation (CONACO)]
	[Christopher Gbenye]	[National Congolese Movement (Lumumba) (MNC/L)]
Dahomey	Christophe Soglo	[United Party of Dahomey]
Ghana	Joseph Ankrah [Kwame Nkrumah]	[Convention People's Party (CPP)]

African Governments 1966 (continued)

Country	Leader(s)	Political Party(s)
Nigeria	Yakubu Gowon	
	[Nnamdi Azikiwe]	[National Council of Nigerian Citizens (NCNC)]
	[Obafemi Awolowo]	[Action Group] [Northern People's Congress]
Togo	Nicholas Grunitzky	[Committee of Togolese Unity]
United Arab Republic	Gamal Abdel Nasser	
Upper Volta	Sangoule Lamizana	
	[Maurice Yameogo]	[Democratic Party of Volta]

3. Monarchies:

Country	Leader(s)	Political Party(s)
Burundi	Mwami Mwambutsa IV	Party of National Unity and Progress (UPRONA)
Ethiopia	Emperor Haile Selassie	none
Libya	King Idris I	none
Morocco	King Hassan II	Istiqlal

4. Multiparty States:

Country	Leader(s)	Political Party(s)
Botswana	Seretse Khama	Democratic Party
	Motsamai Mpho	People's Party
	Kgaleman Motsete	
	Philip Matante	
Gambia	David Jawara	People's Progressive Party (PPP)
	J. S. N'Jie	United Party
Lesotho	Chief Leabua Jonathan	National Party
	Ntsu Mokhehle	Congress Party
	Makalo Khaketla	Marematlou Freedom Party
Somalia	Aden Abdullah Osman	Somali Youth League
	Abdirizak Haji Hussein	Somali Youth League
	Abdirashid Ali Shermarke	Somali Youth League
	Sheikh Ali Giumale	Somali National Congress
Sudan	al-Khatim al-Khalifa	
	Sadiqq al-Mahdi	Umma Party
	Ismail al-Azhari	National Union Party
	Aggrey Jaden, William Deng	Sudan African National Union (SANU)

African Governments 1966 (continued)

Country	Leader(s)	Political Party(s)
5. White-minority Rule:		
South Africa	Balthazar Vorster [Albert Luthuli]	Nationalist Party [African National Congress]
	[Robert Sobukwe]	[Pan-Africanist Congress]
Rhodesia	Ian Smith [Joshua Nkomo]	Rhodesian Front [Zimbabwe African People's Union (ZAPU)]
	[Ndabaningi Sithole]	[Zimbabwe African National Union (ZANU)]
6. Colonies:		
Angola	(Portugal)	
Mozambique	(Portugal)	
Portuguese Guinea	(Portugal)	
Swaziland	(Britain)	
South-West Africa	(South Africa)	

Tribes and Nations: The Need for Unity

The trouble is, of course, that African countries were artificially created by Europeans during the scramble for Africa. From an African point of view, these "countries" were conglomerations of tribes which often had nothing in common.

Until Africans become patriots (i.e., loyal to all the many different peoples within a country) African countries are in danger of being torn apart by tribal rivalries and by power-seeking factions. Simply to hold the country together, African nations need a strong central government controlled by a single strong national party. This is practical policy, not abstract doctrine, and it is followed by such different leaders as Obote (Uganda), Tubman (Liberia), Nyerere (Tanganyika), and Touré (Guinea). Year after year of bloodshed between warring tribes and factions in Congo convinced many doubters that without strong central government many other African countries might suffer a similar fate.

Many African countries have been able to live with their tribal troubles without civil war, although they have curbed political liberty to do it. Kwame Nkrumah fought for years to beat down the powerful chiefs of the Ashanti Confederacy, in the end making all political parties other than his own illegal. In Nigeria each of the three original regions of the federation (see Chapter 10) was dominated by a single tribe: Hausa-Fulani in the North, Yoruba in the West, Ibo in the East. Chief Awolowo, leader of the Yoruba party, the Action Group, was accused in 1963 of trying to split the Western Region from Nigeria. Awolowo was convicted and imprisoned, although there was little firm evidence of a plot. Finally, growing tension between North and South resulted in the Nigerian Army takeover in January 1966.

EXAMPLES OF TRIBAL DIVISIONS

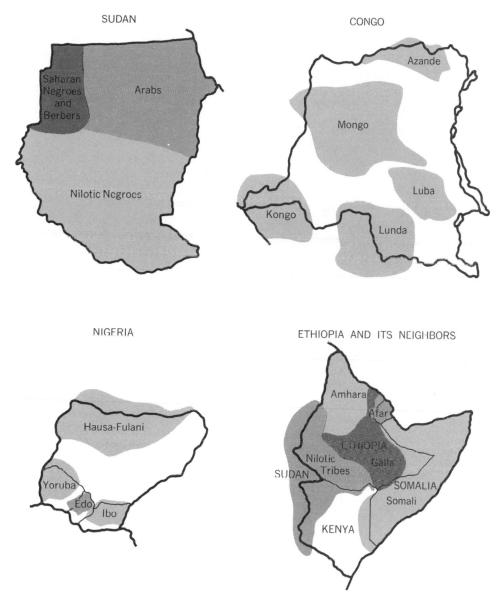

SUDAN

Saharan Negroes and Berbers

Arabs

Nilotic Negroes

CONGO

Azande

Mongo

Luba

Kongo

Lunda

NIGERIA

Hausa-Fulani

Yoruba

Edo

Ibo

ETHIOPIA AND ITS NEIGHBORS

Amhara

Afar

ETHIOPIA

Nilotic Tribes

Galla

SUDAN

SOMALIA

Somali

KENYA

Such troubles are by no means limited to West Africa. The Ganda people of Uganda, led by their Kabaka, Mutesa II, have threatened to establish a separate Ganda state, leaving the other smaller and poorer tribes of Uganda to fend for themselves. In the spring of 1966 Uganda Army troops attacked the Kabaka's palace in an effort by Prime Minister Obote to quell, once and for all, the Kabaka's power. In Sudan tribal troubles become racial ones. Sudan is clearly divided between the ruling Moslem Arab north and the Nilotic Negro south, where Nuer, Dinka, Shilluk, and Anuak tribesmen live in the swamps of

Mutesa V, Kabaka of Buganda and leader of the Kabaka Yekka Party. Traditional political groups, particularly the more advanced and organized ones such as the Ganda of Uganda, the Ashanti of Ghana, and the Fulani of Northern Nigeria, still command the loyalties of many Africans and must be taken into account by nationalist leaders. (*Uganda Information Service.*)

the upper Nile, still untouched by the modern world. In 1958 the tribesmen took up spears and bows against the Sudan government, only to be put down by modern weapons. Bloody skirmishes have occurred ever since. In early 1965 southern rebels claimed to control all but the major towns of the upper Nile. A peace conference in Khartoum in March found most southern leaders demanding secession. Fighting goes on, as today's Sudan government continues a conflict fought by the British in the 1890's and by Mohammed Ali's Turks before that (see Chapter 4).

The worst case of all is the tiny central African country of Rwanda, where a bloody civil war has raged since independence in 1961. Cattle-herding Tutsi warriors, who had been overlords of the Hutu peasants before independence, fled the country but continued to raid across the border from neighboring Congo and from Burundi, where the Tutsi have remained in power. The Hutu have retaliated by the massacre of thousands of Tutsi left in Rwanda.

These are only examples. Every country in Africa has to cope with the

The gate at the entrance to parliament carries the emblems of Uganda's provinces, which are based on tribal kingdoms. Like other African countries, Uganda wrestles with the problem of welding many African peoples into a single nation (*Damon Kletzian.*)

A Rwandan soldier guards the hydroelectric plant at Taruka. Civil war between the Tutsi and Hutu peoples has racked Rwanda since independence. African governments find that force is essential to hold power and achieve stability. (*United Nations.*)

problem of binding different peoples into a single nation.

The other side of the coin is that many African peoples were split by colonial boundaries. The Ewe people were reunited when British Togoland became part of Ghana. The Kongo are divided between Congo Brazzaville (former French), Congo Kinshasa (former Belgian), and Angola, where many support the revolt against the Portuguese colonial government. The division of the Somali people between northern Kenya, eastern Ethiopia, and Somalia may lead to war on the Horn of Africa. The Somali government has threatened more than once to take drastic measures against Ethiopia and Kenya, and border skirmishes are frequent. The problem of divided peoples will continue to test the ability of African leaders and governments to live in peace with one another.

Most African statesmen are committed to keeping the present boundaries, arbitrary as they are. This tacit agreement to leave things as they are is both wise and responsible, for any wholesale attempt to redraw boundaries and reshuffle nations would open a Pandora's box of border warfare, political

feuding, and ill will between African nations that would poison Africa for many years. President Nyerere of Tanganyika said in 1963:

> The boundaries which divide African nations are so nonsensical that without our sense of unity they would be a cause of friction. We have no alternative but to start from the position which we inherited after the colonial partition of Africa. For us to start making claims on each other's territory would be to play into the hands of those who wish to keep Africa weak.

Another way of looking at the problem of national unity in Africa is to think in terms of language and culture. African leaders cannot rely on the strong ties of common language (habits of thought) or culture (habits of behavior) which bind together Germans, Russians, Chinese, or Englishmen. In Africa the colonial language—French, English, or Portuguese—remains the language of government, business, higher education, and diplomacy. Only Egypt and the Maghreb countries—Libya, Tunisia, Algeria, and Morocco—have a unifying Arab Moslem culture and Arabic language.

Without the help of patriotic loyalty, in countries without common language or culture, African leaders must rely on their nationalist parties and on the personal loyalty of their followers to keep their countries together. The party flag becomes the national flag. The party leader becomes president or prime minister—the human embodiment of the new nation's past struggles, present plans, and hopes for the future. When the voluntary ties of personal and party loyalty are not enough, few African leaders hesitate to use the power of government, including the law, the courts, and the police, in the interest of national unity. In the minds of African leaders, opposition to the party, to the government and its policies, or to the leaders themselves becomes treason against the nation or, worse still, against the idea of the nation.

In much of West Africa, Islam has been important in politics as well as being the dominant religion for 500 years. The Prayer of Ramadan finds President Touré of Guinea (front row, second from left) among the worshipers. (Note the phonograph beside the leader's prayer rug.) *(Republic of Guinea, Four Years of Independence and Liberty.)*

Pitfalls

One-party rule in Africa fails to solve many of the problems it sets out to solve, and creates a few new problems besides. The first of these is the transfer of power—how to change leaders—both at the top and throughout the party ranks. Once a strong nationalist party has established itself, it cannot be dislodged peacefully. All government jobs, impor-

tant and not so important, are held by party members. The party machine turns out the vote in city and village to give party candidates huge majorities. In the official one-party states, only party members can get on the ballot at all. Once out of favor with the party, a politician has no chance of being elected or appointed to any responsible position. Unless the loser is one of those few Africans fortunate enough to have professional training as a doctor, scholar, or engineer, he is simply out of work.

One consequence is the resort to violence: the only way left to the "outs." Nigeria's Prime Minister Balewa and two regional premiers were killed by army plotters in January 1966. Assassins with guns and homemade bombs attacked Kwame Nkrumah several times. In 1960 Patrice Lumumba of Congo was killed in Katanga, which was then under the rule of Lumumba's rival, Moise Tshombe. Mamadou Dia of Senegal is now in jail for allegedly plotting to overthrow the government. All this is of course a vicious circle: The more violent the opposition, the less likely that the ruling party—or army government —will allow any political freedom, which drives the opposition to further violence. The problem of changing government leadership without violence will continue to grow in Africa.

A second African problem that will become more acute might be called the "difference of the generations." Most of the men in top jobs today were young politicians or recent university graduates during the independence campaign of the 1950's. These men, now entrenched in power, will grow old in their jobs over twenty, thirty, even forty years, frustrating the ever-increasing number of new graduates from African and foreign universities who are eager for advancement. The newcomers often lack the passionate commitment to revolutionary struggle which sustained the present leaders through the independence campaign. On the other hand, they are often more concerned with getting on with the job of economic development and are often ready to experiment with radical economic solutions. Will the young men get their chance within the party and the government, or will they too be forced into violent opposition?

A final pitfall is the potential lack of constructive criticism of government policy. National leaders flushed with "victory over imperialism" tend to think they are on the right side of history— both morally and politically. Add to this the fact that in a nation run by a single bureaucracy—the party organization— the bosses get their information mainly from subordinates seeking favor who tell them what they want to hear, and not necessarily what's wrong and needs to be changed. Lack of criticism can lead to a mental hardening of the arteries, an unwillingness to move with the times or to accept disagreeable facts. Particularly in economic development—where problems respect no political ideology, radical or conservative— the results can be disastrous.

African Army: The Road to Power?

In many African countries, the army is the only organized group capable of challenging the party which rules. In colonial days, the army was a small force led by European officers and was used to put down tribal wars and nationalist riots. While both French and British African troops fought in two world wars, African regiments were on the whole poorly trained and lacked discipline. Since independence, African soldiers have resented low pay scales and the continued presence of European officers as their commanders. This situation offers African armies a strong incentive to revolt, and the fact that they have arms offers them a good chance of success.

The danger of army takeover is strongest where the civilian government —the party—is weak. In the summer of 1963 the popular President of Togo, Sylvanus Olympio, was murdered, and in the days that followed army officers stepped into power. In January 1964 an adventurer named John Okello and a few hundred toughs overthrew the government of Zanzibar, which had been independent less than two months. Days later, African regiments in Kenya, Tan-

Military Takeovers in Africa

Year	Country	Military Leader	Ousted Leader
1952	Egypt	Colonel Mohammed Naguib Colonel Gamal Abdel Nasser	King Farouk
1958	Sudan	General Ibrahim Abboud	Prime Minister Ahmed Ismail al-Azhari
1960	Congo	Colonel Joseph Mobutu	Prime Minister Patrice Lumumba
1963	Togo	Nicholas Grunitzky	President Sylvanus Olympio
1963	Dahomey	Colonel Christophe Soglo	President Hubert Maga
1965	Algeria	General Houari Boumedienne	President Ahmed Ben Bella
1965	Congo	General Joseph Mobutu	President Joseph Kasavubu
1965	Dahomey	Colonel Christophe Soglo	President Souron Migan Apithy Vice-president Justin Ahomadegbe
1966	Central African Republic	Colonel Jean Bokassa	President David Dacko
1966	Upper Volta	Colonel Sangoule Lamizana	President Maurice Yameogo
1966	Nigeria	General T. U. Aguiyi-Ironsi Colonel Yakubu Gowon	President Nnamdi Azikiwe Prime Minister Tafawa Balewa Sir Ahmadu Bello, Sardauna of Sokoto
1966	Ghana	General Joseph Ankrah	President Kwame Nkrumah

ganyika, and Uganda mutinied against their governments and their British officers, throwing East Africa into a week of rioting and uncertainty. The mutiny ended only when British troops were flown in at the request of Prime Ministers Kenyatta (Kenya) and Obote (Uganda) and President Nyerere of Tanganyika. And it was an army mutiny that began all the trouble in Congo in 1960.

The point is that however few and badly trained they may be, soldiers can easily upset the precarious situation in many African countries, as Africa's recent history all too clearly shows.

The Year of the Generals

In later histories, 1965–1966 may be known as the Year of the Generals. Between June 1965 and February 1966 no less than seven African governments were overthrown by their armies, with the shock of each takeover following the last like firecrackers on a single fuse.

The overthrow of Algeria's Ahmed Ben Bella in June 1965, which surprised everyone, set the style. Ben Bella had waged a long and successful campaign, often with the help of the army, to eliminate his rivals for power. The Algerian National Liberation Front (FLN) was both army and party, and the army, hardened by long years of war against France, was one of the most powerful forces in all Africa. Algeria's new leader, General Houari Boumedienne, will also rule through the FLN organization, after replacing Ben Bella men in key positions with his own supporters.

Army rule is nothing new in Moslem Africa. Gamal Abdel Nasser was an army colonel, and his 1952 revolution was an army coup. Egypt has been under military rule ever since. In Sudan, the shoe was recently on the other foot. Army rule under General Ibrahim Abboud was overthrown in October 1964 by a campaign of strikes and demonstrations, and Sudan is now governed by a coalition of moderate civilian political parties.

The year's next takeover, in Congo in November 1965, brought more relief than astonishment. The leader was General Joseph Mobutu, who had done the same thing before, in 1960, to seal the downfall of Prime Minister Patrice Lumumba (see Chapter 10). This time Mobutu's coup was a response to ineffective government by feuding politicians but was designed to be more permanent. Mobutu announced that he would rule for five years in an effort to pull his torn country together.

With the new year, the soldiers began in earnest. On New Year's Day David Dacko of the Central African Republic lost his Presidency to Colonel Jean Bokassa, and a scant two days later Maurice Yameogo of Upper Volta lost his. Both these leaders of small, dry, poor countries seemed almost glad to let the army try to rule for a while.

The next two takeovers, however, were of the greatest importance. On January 15–16 a colonels' plot and army takeover in Nigeria (see Chapter 10) swept parliament and politicians from power and the quarrelsome and hostile regions off the Nigerian map, although even the soldiers are not immune to the deep tribal resentments which no change of government can erase. The last of the series, in Ghana, was the biggest shock of all.

Ghana: End of a Party State

Africa was rocked in February 1966 by the news that Kwame Nkrumah and his Convention People's Party had been swept from power by Ghana's army. Nkrumah himself was flying to Peking to talk with the Chinese about Vietnam, and only Nkrumah's small palace guard put up a fight. The ease with which Nkrumah and the party were booted out shocked those Africans and others who had come to believe that the single-party state ensured stable government.

Why the army takeover? No doubt most students and educated Ghanaians resented Nkrumah's cult of personality, his suppression of free speech and all opposition. No doubt bureaucrats felt the government was wasting money on political payoffs and on propaganda, while the price of cocoa dropped and the nation's finances went from bad to worse. No doubt inflation was thinning paychecks, and unemployment—the social curse of Africa's cities—was increasing. Perhaps a few nationalists resented Nkrumah's Marxist talk and his reliance on Russian and Chinese advisers. But the immediate cause was Nkrumah's efforts to undermine the independence of the army itself, as he had earlier brought the labor unions, the bureaucracy, and the universities under party control. In August the popular army Chief of Staff, General Ankrah, was fired by Nkrumah. Officers were sent to the Soviet Union for training, breaking the British monopoly. Nkrumah's "Own Guard," a special force, was trained and advised by Russian officers; and Chinese instructors had begun to set up a "people's militia" under party, not army, control. It was either Nkrumah or the army, and taking the occasion of Nkrumah's trip to China, army troops marched into Accra the night of February 25, 1966.

One of the first decrees of the generals outlawed the instrument of

Nkrumah's rule, the Convention People's Party. No one rose to defend it. Perhaps the CPP, model of the single mass party, had fallen prey to corruption, laziness, and the all-too-easy sin of commanding the people without listening to them.

The new military regime made attractive promises—a return to constitutional and democratic government; the eventual encouragement of free speech and political opposition. A new constitution will require separation of powers between the parliament, the Cabinet, and the courts. Above all, under Kwame Nkrumah's long shadow, one-man rule will not be allowed again.

Combined with the planeloads of Russian and Chinese technicians and advisers thrown out of the country, such talk was music to American and British ears, and will result in aid to Ghana from the West. The army, however, is in power. A change of leadership will not by itself create national unity in Ghana, satisfy students or bureaucrats, or raise the rock-bottom world market price of cocoa. These are the problems which require, in the opinion of African leaders, a single directing national authority—if not the party, then the army. Constitutional democracy is not yet in sight.

Reformers—or Caudillos?

African nationalist party leaders rightly fear the army as a threat to the political stability of their countries and to their own positions in power. In some African situations, however, the army claims to be the organized group best able to create a sense of national purpose and to promote economic development— in fact, to do what a nationalist political party tries to do. The Egyptian Army made the successful Egyptian revolution, and the recent army takeovers in Algeria, Congo, and Nigeria were justified on a platform of "pulling the country together" and "getting it moving."

The generals now in power claim to be a new breed of African leader. The style is impersonal, businesslike, and more concerned with results at home than with publicity at home or abroad. Revolutionary oratory, world diplomacy, and political wrangling can only get in the way of national development and construction. Squandering the nation's treasure on Cadillacs or mansions—as in Congo and Nigeria—or on imposing but needless symbols of national prestige—such as the $20 million conference hall built in Accra for just one week's use by the Organization of African Unity—is, say the generals, out.

But only results will count. Reaction against old leaders is no guarantee that the new regime will be an improvement. Will the generals really apply their energy and succeed in providing schools, jobs, goods to eat, wear, and use, a sense of personal freedom and dignity? Will they be able to reach peasants and slum dwellers, and enlist their cooperative efforts? Or do these takeovers signal a bleak future of African power grabs, Latin-American-caudillo-style, in which leaders and governments are here today, gone tomorrow depending on who has the guns—and in which rivals for power pay little attention to the people's needs and the people's will?

African Government in Practice

African societies are a mass of peasants and city slum dwellers with a thin layer of intellectuals and politicians on top. Whatever theory of government the politicians may have has little meaning for the ordinary poor and illiterate African. No telephones, few roads, and the self-sufficiency of isolated villages where the people eat the food they grow make control of how people live and work by government or party officials virtually impossible. Total control of society, which the Communist version of the party state represents, *is* impossible in Africa because African countries are simply not organized.

While African countries cannot easily be made into totalitarian dictatorships, they probably cannot be Western-style democracies either. Africa lacks a middle class, which is another way of saying that it has no large numbers of people with opinions on public issues such as taxes or education, or groups to express those opinions. Until many more Africans are educated and have regular jobs as workers in factories or offices, African countries will not have the informed and active citizens necessary to make Western-style democracy work.

In this situation, the political party and government officials not only run the country (the control aspect of government) but also provide a channel for public opinion and a way for the people to make their wishes known to the leaders (the representative aspect). The party also provides the services that people need. It runs schools for illiterate adults. It acts as an insurance company, giving from party funds pensions for widows and relief for the sick. It supervises the construction of badly needed houses or even more badly needed drainage ditches. Party committees are in touch with local needs and complaints, even when local Africans are not able to write letters asking for help or improvement. Local party officials have in many ways taken over the authority of traditional chiefs. Just as the authority of the chief was personal and immediate, party officials on the spot can also intervene to settle local quarrels and direct local jobs.

Tanganyika's version of the war on poverty shows how African leaders use their political parties as the instrument of revolutionary change. Village Development Committees (VDCs) run by the local officials of TANU (the Tanganyika African National Union) have been formed to persuade tradition-bound villagers to improve their lot by their own efforts. The committees will direct road building, start local schools, and attempt to shift local farming to profitable cash crops. TANU looks for cooperation and participation from Tanganyikan peasants. The party will not—and probably cannot—carry through such an ambitious program by coercion. Clearly, however, the party, as in other African countries, sees itself as the force pulling all Tanganyika into the twentieth century.

The Rights of the Citizen

Perhaps because Europeans in Africa seldom practiced it, the Western tradition of individual freedom has not taken root in Africa. African governments care little for political liberty when it gets in the way of what the government wants to do. Ghana, the first black African country to become independent, was also the first to pass a preventive detention act. Many other countries have followed suit. Under a preventive detention act, political opponents of the government may be imprisoned without trial for long periods. In other cases, newspapers are censored or forced by the party leaders to publish false information favorable to the government. In some countries, the ominous growth of a secret police and a network of spies and informers has followed establishment of a party state.

Today, with few, perhaps temporary, exceptions, African governments show an equal disregard for civil liberties. Opposition is put down as firmly in "conservative" Ivory Coast or "moderate" Tunisia as in "radical" Guinea. In Egypt, President Nasser's enemies, Communists and monarchists alike, have been in jail for years. In South Africa a thousand people are arrested every day for "crimes" such as moving from one town to another or changing jobs without permission. In Tanganyika labor leaders have been imprisoned, newspapers banned, and editors deported. The Chief Justice of the Ghana High Court was deposed in 1963 by President Nkrumah after he refused to convict one of Nkrumah's rivals without evidence that the prisoner had done anything illegal. Guinean students were beaten up by toughs of Sékou Touré's Democratic Party of Guinea when they dared to criticize the government—for not being radical enough!

The reply of African leaders to criticism of their harsh laws and their disregard for civil liberty is that their shaky countries must be protected by whatever means necessary. Stability is vital, while imported Western notions of political freedom are not. Opposition parties and leaders, African governments claim, are not merely criticizing the present government but are working for its overthrow. If opposition remained free to inflame tribal rebellion, to incite mobs and soldiers to revolt, African countries would soon disintegrate. To American and European liberals who worked for African independence and who now disapprove of the African policies, African leaders point out that colonial governments used the same kind of repressive laws and police rule to govern effectively. Granting the element of truth in these arguments, is suppression of criticism and opposition and disregard for individual rights still justified?

African Democracy?

African one-party governments claim to represent the people. They claim to be democratic governments because they work for the interests of the whole nation, rather than a particular social class or economic group. They claim that even though there is only one ruling party, the government is democratic because the party is itself democratic. Any African with talent can join the party and express his views in it regardless of his background or his beliefs. In the extreme case, in Guinea, every citizen is by law a member of the ruling party, Sékou Touré's PDG.

Yet ordinary citizens and even local party members have little say about government policy, which is made by the handful of top leaders and passed down to be put into action by local officials. Organized opposition to present leaders and their party is prohibited in most African countries, and in many, public criticism of government policy in the press or in speeches is suppressed. Individual rights are not sacred, and may at any time be overridden if the government feels its rule is threatened.

Some Americans are uncomfortable about the lack of constitutional democracy and individual liberty in Africa. Yet such democracy is a fragile plant that has only rarely taken deep root. Constitutional democracy requires a set of accepted ground rules—a constitution written in actions and beliefs as well as in words. It requires that the voters be educated and informed about politics and government. It requires a sense of national loyalty greater than divisions of region, race, or culture, as the United States learned from its terrible Civil War. Above all, it requires a respect for "the rule of laws, not of men," and the rejection of violence as a way to solve national problems. None of these conditions is present in Africa today.

African leaders make no apologies for their style of government. They justify their policy of strong leadership and no opposition with the facts of life in Africa—tribal and regional conflicts, the crying need to put an end to poverty, the widespread lack of education. African leaders claim that their way is the best way to advance the condition of their people.

PROBLEMS

1. Are African leaders attached to any theory of government? Do they believe that the consent and support of the people are necessary to good government? Always?

2. Any politician's first concern is to keep himself in office. What methods do African leaders use to keep power? Will these methods, in your opinion, be successful in the long run? What other methods are possible for African leaders, given African conditions?

3. Politics in Africa means the activities of a very small group of educated people. How would you expect the style of politics and government to change as more people become educated? What may happen if the present leaders refuse to make changes?

4. Would most ordinary Africans prefer a one-party state or a number of competing parties? Why? How is the influence of African custom and tradition important in today's African politics?

5. If you were an African leader, what steps would you take to bring about a feeling of national loyalty among the people? What kind of government would best enable you to carry out these steps?

6. Find a sample in a newspaper or magazine of a public opinion poll taken in the United States. Make up a similar poll to test the attitudes of the Africans of a particular African country. How might the questions and answers differ?

READING SUGGESTIONS

Chief H. O. Davies, *Nigeria: The Prospects for Democracy,* Weidenfeld (London), 1961.

Peter Gould, *Africa: Continent of Change* (selections on politics), Wadsworth, 1961.

Tom Mboya, "The Party System and Democracy in Africa," *Foreign Affairs,* July 1963.

Kwame Nkrumah, *I Speak of Freedom,* Praeger, 1961.

Paul Sigmund (ed.), *Ideologies of the Developing Nations,* Praeger, paper.

Reference

Thomas Hodgkin, *African Political Parties,* Penguin, 1961.

chapter 18

INTERNATIONAL ISSUES...
AFRICA AND THE UNITED STATES

Communism is not the way for Africa.

—SEKOU TOURE,
President of Guinea

We seek two results; first, that truly independent nations shall emerge on the world scene; and, second, that each nation will be permitted to fashion, out of its own culture and its own ambitions, the kind of modern society it wants.

This will not be a victory of the United States over the Soviet Union. It will not be a victory of capitalism over socialism. What this victory involves, in the end, is the assertion by nations of their right to independence and by men and women of their right to freedom as they understand it.

—WALT W. ROSTOW,
U. S. Department of State

African nations must become truly independent of foreign influence. At the same time, African nations need help from abroad to back up that independence with strong economies. Above all, the cold war must be kept out of Africa. These are goals on which African leaders agree.

Behind this agreement lies the strong conviction that the unique African Personality must be recognized throughout the world and taken into account by both the West and the Communist powers. Yet African leaders realize that African nations are very weak by traditional standards. If Africa is to be heard, African nations must speak as one.

The African voice in world affairs is the voice of a handful of men. Most African peasants have never seen a globe, or even a map of their own country. Only the politicians, government officials, business and professional men, and the students know anything about the world beyond their town or village. Of this small group, only the tiny minority who hold top government jobs can really influence their country's foreign policy. Africa's appearance on the international stage is the work and the worry of these few African leaders.

Neutralism

African nations call themselves "neutral" in world affairs. In American newspapers a neutral is any country that takes neither a Communist nor a Western position in the cold war. This description is accurate as far as it goes, but can be very misleading. The cold war is not very important to African leaders. Many of them, rightly or wrongly, regard it as an irresponsible and dangerous competition in bomb building. Just as the United States would try to stay out of a war in Angola, Somalia, or Kashmir, Africans would hate to watch the skies turn radioactive as the result of a white man's quarrel in Berlin or Cuba. African nations together support disarmament and a strong United Nations to keep the peace.

EXHIBIT 5 TOTAL U.S. AID TO AFRICA

AID TO AFRICA COMPARED WITH OTHER WORLD AREAS

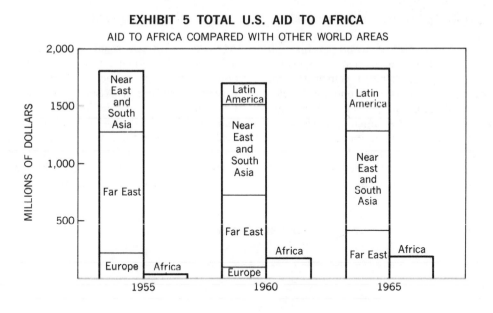

Countries Receiving Most Aid in Order*

1962	*1964*	*1966*
U.A.R. (Egypt)	U.A.R. (Egypt)	Ethiopia
Congo (Leopoldville)	Algeria	Congo (Kinshasa)
Ghana	Nigeria	U.A.R. (Egypt)
Morocco	Tunisia	Nigeria
Tunisia	Congo (Leopoldville)	Tunisia
Nigeria	Morocco	Sudan
Somalia	Liberia	Liberia

Total United States Aid Given to All African Countries
(In millions of $)

Country	Total since 1945	1961 through 1964	1966
Algeria	145.8	143.6	—
Congo	257.7	275.7	34
Ethiopia	96.9	58.7	35
Ghana	90.1	87.4	6
Guinea	46.5	42.7	6
Liberia	88.2	65.2	8
Libya	137.8	43.2	—
Morocco	449.3	254.7	8
Nigeria	111.0	105.2	23
Somalia	34.1	25.3	4
Sudan	68.2	24.1	17
Tunisia	390.5	255.3	17
U.A.R. (Egypt)	884.0	637.1	33
East African countries	76.9	70.6	8
French-speaking West and Equatorial Africa	80.1	78.7	42
Other countries	140.0	89.1	

---

* The aid given the U.A.R. and Algeria has been wheat shipped under the Food
For Peace program (P.L. 480).

Active participation in the cold war on either side is strictly taboo. Taking sides could pit Africans against one another, blocking African cooperation and diverting African countries from the primary task of economic development. Taking sides means military alliances and bases manned by foreign soldiers, and gives outsiders, whether Chinese, Russian, French, or American, a chance to erode the precious independence of African nations.

Foreign Aid

African countries must have outside help to build schools, roads, factories, and laboratories. Speeches condemning foreign meddling in African affairs do not erase the need for foreign capital and technical asistance, and most African leaders know this. At the same time, African leaders want foreign aid to come without "strings." No African politician in his right mind will accept

AID PROGRAMS

In 1965, every independent country on the continent except South Africa was getting some help from the United States.

Foreign aid is a happy event. Here Nigerian Minister of Finance Chief Okotie-Eboh (with feather in hat) signs a World Bank loan at the Bank's Washington headquarters. The loan is being used to improve and extend Nigeria's railroad lines. (*World Bank.*)

foreign aid or agree to a foreign business investment if he suspects that the independence of his country might in any way be diminished. The result is the paradoxical combination of the harsh word and the outstretched palm, the "keep off" plus "help me" attitude that irritates many Americans—and Russians. When forced to accept "entangling alliances" (Thomas Jefferson's phrase) along with aid, African leaders usually choose to reject the aid.

The United Nations

The United Nations provides African statesmen, diplomats, and propagandists opportunities that they find nowhere else. From the speaker's platform of the General Assembly Africans continually proclaim passionate opposition to colonialism and explain their need for foreign aid. The potential audience is the whole world, represented by the United Nations delegates of every nation and newsmen from every nation.

Besides its value as a soapbox, the United Nations is economical and convenient. Most African countries are too poor to maintain diplomats anywhere except in a few major world capitals: Paris, London, Washington, Moscow, and perhaps Peking or New Delhi. Yet through its United Nations delegation in New York such countries as Mali, Malawi, and Rwanda can keep in close touch with other African governments.

The United Nations General Assembly is the only place in the world where the weak and poor African nations have influence in proportion to their numbers. In the General Assembly, each country has one vote. Thirty-seven independent African countries (excluding South Africa), with a combined population only a little larger than that of the United States, can outvote the United States thirty-seven to one.

African Issues Before the United Nations

In the years after World War II, the UN gave newly independent anticolonial countries such as India and Indonesia a chance to criticize strongly colonial rule in Africa. African nationalists were invited to New York to press their demands, and such leaders as Julius Nyerere made their reputations speaking for independence at the United Nations. The anticolonial campaign has tapered off with the flood tide of African nationalist success after 1959.

The Algerian war was publicized mainly at the United Nations. Year after year the General Assembly voted to discuss Algeria over strong French objections, and year after year more details of the "dirty war" (a French phrase) came to light. Algerian rebels of the National Liberation Front (FLN) came to address the General

Moise Tshombe, then President of secessionist Katanga, lays a wreath on the coffin of Dag Hammarskjöld in September 1961. Hammarskjöld, seeking reconciliation in Congo, died in a mysterious plane crash. (*Wide World Photos.*)

Assembly, and French delegates walked out in protest.

The Congo crisis of 1960–1962 (see Chapter 10) proved beyond doubt the usefulness of the United Nations and its importance to African leaders. The United Nations intervened at the request of the Congo government itself, with the support of all other African nations. Tunisia, Ghana, Guinea, Ethiopia, Sudan, Morocco, the United Arab Republic, and Nigeria contributed troops to the United Nations army in Congo.

African issues before the United Nations in 1965 were Rhodesia, the Angola and Mozambique rebellions against Portuguese colonial rule, and racial discrimination in South Africa—the biggest issue of all.

Africa and Europe

Independence has not meant the end of European influence in Africa. African nations still must export cash crops and minerals. Patterns of trade change slowly, and most exports still go to the former colonial ruler. The great companies, such as Unilever (Lever Brothers soaps on your grocery shelf) in Nigeria, the Anglo-American mining trust in Zambia (Northern Rhodesia), and Union Minière in Congo carry on business as usual under African governments. French companies are only beginning to exploit the oil and iron ore in the still largely unprospected Sahara.

Relations between Britain and its former colonies have been generally friendly and cooperative. All of Britain's former African colonies have joined the British Commonwealth, which is an informal organization for consultation on trade and political issues.

France has tried to extend its economic influence in Africa through the European Common Market. The Treaty of Rome, which established the Common Market in 1957, allowed African countries to become "associate members" with trade privileges. In July

1963 all the former French (except Guinea) and Belgian colonies and Somalia signed an agreement with the Common Market that will send $780 million in aid to the African countries between 1963 and 1968. France now spends a far higher proportion of its total national income on foreign aid than the United States (2½ percent for France, less than 1 percent for the United States). Almost all this French aid goes to Africa.

Ghana, Guinea, and other African countries which are excluded from the Common Market and do not receive French aid have protested the French policy, calling it neocolonialism. They claim that it divides African countries and makes economic cooperation within Africa difficult. Some have accused the French of continuing to tamper with African independence. In February 1964 President Mba of Gabon was threatened by a revolt. The same day French paratroops landed in Libreville, the capital, and restored Mba to power. Yet the African leaders of these former French colonies benefit from French aid, and refuse to bite the hand that feeds them.

Europe is represented in Africa by many thousands of doctors, teachers, engineers, skilled workers, and civil servants who remained after independence to work for European companies and African governments. These trained men are absolutely vital to the countries they serve, and will be needed for at least a generation.

The European and African elites are united by a common culture. The men who now rule in Africa were educated in Europe, speak to one another in European languages, and have adopted a "European" way of life. Every African high school student learns English or French. Yet the "Europeanized" Africans, the present upper class, are a tiny minority. They will be swept aside by men who never experienced colonial rule.

The rise of the first "African generation" will bring many important changes in Africa.

Communism in Africa?

What do we mean by "communism"? "Communism" and "Communist" are words that frighten many Americans. All too often, any anti-American attitudes and actions are automatically called "communism," and then dismissed as matters too dreadful to think about. Such blindness can be very dangerous in Africa, and will help no one but the Communists.

Whether a country is in fact Communist or not depends on two different questions. In internal policy, is it a totalitarian state without individual freedom or private enterprise, governed by men who believe in the ideas of Marx and Lenin? In foreign policy, does the country follow a Communist line and, if so, which line—Chinese, Russian, Cuban, or Yugoslav?

Fortunately these questions are not too difficult to answer for the Africa of 1967. Most African countries are ruled by a single political party, and many African leaders believe in government control of the economy (see Chapters 16 and 17). Almost every African resident and prime minister calls himself and his country "socialist," which sounds suspiciously like "Communist" to Americans who value economic free enterprise. Yet none of these countries represses and regiments its citizens to anywhere near the degree that Russians were repressed by Stalin or Chinese are today regimented by Mao Tse-tung. All African countries, including the "socialist" ones, encourage the enterprise of their citizens and some private business investment from America and Europe. Not even Sékou Touré or Kwame Nkrumah could call himself a disciple of Communist ideas. All African countries follow the independent African policy of neutrality in the cold war, and not

Ghanaians demonstrate against white rule and *apartheid* in South Africa following Kwame Nkrumah's call for a boycott of South African goods. These villagers brandish rifles in a modern war dance. (*Wide World Photos*.)

one could in 1966 be called a Communist satellite.

Communism has as yet failed to take root in Africa in spite of the efforts of the Soviet Union, and more lately China. What have these efforts been? Why have they failed? Can they eventually succeed?

Communists in Africa

Most African leaders are fully aware that both the Soviet Union and China would like to see African countries fall under communism. But the one thing that African leaders will not tolerate is foreign interference. Communist efforts have so far failed because they have been directly pitted against the steamroller of African nationalism.

In the one-party states, including Guinea, Mali, and the United Arab Republic (Egypt), the Communist Party is illegal. President Nasser of Egypt imprisoned hundreds of Egyptian Communists when he took power in 1952. Most of them are still in jail.

The strongest Communist movement on the whole continent is in South Africa, where Communists are trying to lead the fight against *apartheid*. When it was founded in the 1920's the South African Communist Party, like most things South African, was segregated—whites only. Since those early days the Communists have changed their tactics several times, although their stated goal of a Communist dictatorship has never changed. In recent years Communists have worked with and in the African National Congress of Nobel Peace Prize winner Albert Luthuli. The Suppression of Communism Act passed by the South African government in 1950 drove Communists and African nationalists together by calling almost any protest against the South African regime "communism." Yet even with all the help that the South African government has given Communists in their effort to dominate protest against *apartheid*, African nationalists are still in control.

Elsewhere in Africa homegrown Communists are few and their influence small. The chances of a Communist takeover in African countries by peaceful means are very slim. If African nations are plunged into civil war as in Congo or into war against each other, Communists' chances will improve greatly. This is what present African leaders fear most.

Shades of Red

Russian and Chinese policies in Africa are now very different. Although the conflict between the Chinese and the Russians became public only in 1963, the differences are clear. The Chinese have inherited the tradition of violent revolution. They will try to install African Communists as rulers of full-fledged African Communist states, and will supply guns and money to Communists —or anyone else, for that matter—plotting revolution. Southern Africa may soon be a major target. The Soviets, on the other hand, are trying to win friends among present African leaders. Soviet policies have aimed at influencing such leaders as Nasser, Touré, Ben Bella of Algeria, and Modibo Keita of Mali, in the hope that they will support the Soviet side in the cold war.

Propaganda

Three issues are stressed in Communist propaganda. The first is "colonialism" or "imperialism." Since 1945, at the United Nations and in the world press, the Soviet Union has joined in the chorus of condemnation of colonialism in an effort to win favor with nationalists in Africa and Asia. The Soviet attack often twisted the truth to extend the accusation of "imperialism" to the United States.

With the passing of colonial rule a lot of wind has been taken out of Communist sails. Particularly disturbing to the Soviets and their allies is the active cooperation after independence between Britain and France on the one hand and the new African nations on the other— which is denounced as "neocolonialism." Soviet propaganda supports the Angolan revolt against Portugal and continues to stress *apartheid* and exploitation in South Africa. Communists never miss a chance to point out that Portugal and the United States are military allies in NATO, or that American "international monopoly capitalists" have invested millions of dollars in South African industry.

The second propaganda point made by Communists concerns economic development. The growth of Russia from a backward peasant country to a world power in forty years of Communist rule is held up as a shining example to all underdeveloped countries. African students and officials, eager to achieve their dream of building modern industrial nations from scratch in a few short years, are brought to Russia to inspect model factories and farms, schools and hospitals. What the African delegations on these very guided tours miss is the terrible human cost of such growth, which in Stalin's time (the 1930's and '40's) deprived Russians of houses, clothes, and even food, and which was carried out under a police regime that sent millions of Russians to Siberian labor camps and kept the people in a state of terror.

China has also used this "development" line and has been praised by some Africans as an example of a very backward country that succeeded in pulling itself up by its own bootstraps. Communist propaganda of course exaggerates Soviet and Chinese success, ignoring both the terror and hardship and the disastrous Communist failures in agriculture.

Finally, propagandists claim that communism is color-blind. Men like President Nkrumah, who slept in subways and park benches while a student in the United States in the 1930's, have been tremendously impressed by such propaganda. The Chinese in particular push the race issue, and never fail to point out that they—unlike the Russians —are not white.

A Demonstration in Red Square

African university students of today are the African leaders of tomorrow. No one knows this better than the Communists, who make great efforts to win favor among idealistic students. In Accra, Conakry, Nairobi, Cairo, and many other African capitals Communist bookstores sell the wares of Moscow's Foreign Languages Publishing House, an enterprise run by the Agitation and Propaganda Department of the Soviet Communist Party. These books present the Communist point of view on every subject from America to Zoology. They are sold at low prices and are often the only books that eager and curious African students can afford.

More and more African students have been brought to Moscow, Peking, and Eastern European universities. Moscow's special school for African and Asian students has been renamed Lumumba University to win African favor. African students in Moscow are favored with high living allowances and all expenses paid, which presumably makes the rigid academic control and forced diet of Marxism-Leninism less tedious.

Yet African students have been no end of trouble to the Russians. Many have returned from Bulgaria and Russia protesting racial discrimination. In December 1963 a Ghanaian student died mysteriously near Moscow. His friends at Lumumba University claimed he had been murdered. Hundreds of African students protested at the gates of the Kremlin in Red Square, the first demonstration against the Soviet government in Red Square in forty-five years of Communist rule. Many Africans have since left Russia to pursue their studies in West Germany. The experience of African students seems to be that com-

munism looks much better from a distance than at close range. Among African educators the saying goes, if you want a good capitalist send your man to Moscow, and if you want a flaming radical, let him study in the United States!

Aid

Since 1957 foreign aid and trade agreements have been an important part of the Soviet drive for influence in Asia, Africa, and Latin America. Through 1963 the Russians had spent about a billion dollars in Africa. In addition the Soviets—and particularly the Chinese— are usually quite willing to ship arms to Africa whenever they see a chance to encourage the warfare and chaos that may open the way for communism. The classic case is Congo, where Communist arms originally sent to Egypt were used by Congolese rebel bands.

Most economic aid has gone to Guinea, Mali, Algeria, and Egypt, which were the countries considered most vulnerable to communism. The Soviet aid program has made mistakes. Two hundred outboard motors were sent to Mali, which is a landlocked country with almost no water. Guinea, where the average temperature is above 80 degrees, was given a shipment of snowplows—presumably to be used for bulldozing!

Egypt's high dam at Aswân, on the upper Nile, is the most impressive of all Soviet projects. The dam will be 350 feet high and 2 miles long, and will create a lake stretching 300 miles downstream across the Sudan border. When finished in 1968 Aswân will provide cheap power for Egyptian industry and will control the floodwaters of the Nile, making year-round farming possible in the rich Nile Delta. Aswân will cost the Soviet Union $400 million.

President Nasser of Egypt has made it quite clear that he regards Aswân as an engineering agreement, and nothing more. The 1,500 Soviet engineers and technicians working on the dam have been told to stay away from Egyptians. Publicity about Aswân has put a feather in the Russian cap. Yet Egyptian Communists are still in jail, and Nasser remains firmly neutral.

Guinea and Elsewhere

The fate of Soviet efforts in Guinea is a good example of Communist inexperience and clumsiness in Africa. When France and Guinea quarreled in 1958 (see Chapter 9) conditions seemed ideal for the Communists. Sékou Touré was known to admire the ideas of Marx and Lenin, and had repeatedly said that a "socialist" society was the best. Touré's Democratic Party of Guinea (PDG) had local cells throughout the country and could quickly be converted into an instrument of Communist rule.

When the French pulled out, Touré was willing to accept desperately needed aid from any source. While the United States remained aloof in deference to France, the Russians quickly offered help. For three years, Guinea and the Soviet Union cooperated smoothly, in what seemed to be a spirit of mutual admiration. Hundreds of Soviet bloc technicians and advisers (including Soviet intelligence agents) poured into Guinea. Guinea leaned more and more toward the Soviet position on international issues. When in the fall of 1961 a radio transmitter called "The Voice of the Revolution" was put up by the Russians on a mountaintop near Conakry, the capital, Russians and Americans who thought in terms of the cold war alone were respectively ready to welcome and to write off Guinea as a Communist satellite.

They were wrong. A few weeks later, Sékou Touré exposed to his countrymen an "Eastern plot" against Guinean independence and sent the Russians packing. Communist technicians, advisers, and propagandists left as quickly as the French had left just two years before.

Most aid to Guinea now comes from the West, half of it from the United States. Guinea recently signed an agreement with the United States government to protect American investments there, including the big aluminum refinery at Fria, which is a joint French-American venture.

What made Sékou Touré steer his country away from the Communist bloc? It seems safe to say that like other African leaders Touré means what he says about both independence and neutrality. If Communists give aid as a contribution to national welfare and independence, it will be accepted gladly. But if there is any hint of subversion that threatens independence, out go the foreigners, Communist or not.

Frustrated elsewhere, both the Soviets and the Chinese may now be concentrating on East Africa, while preparing for possible developments in brooding Southern Africa. In 1963 the Soviet Union promised to equip 20,000 Somali soldiers. The Somalis claim desert regions of Ethiopia (American-armed) and Kenya (British-armed), where Somali nomads graze their cattle. Border fighting lasted through 1963 and 1964, but other African states have put pressure on the Ethiopians and Somalis to keep the issue in the background. Wherever there is the likelihood of war between African states, there is the danger of the cold war—which nobody in Africa wants.

The Kenya incident of spring 1965 is another case in point. Kenya politician Oginga Odinga, thought to be sympathetic to Communist goals, seemed to be gaining a hold over Kenya's ruling nationalist party, the Kenya African National Union. He was running the party school—staffed in part with Russian lecturers—set up to train Kenya's next generation of leaders, and he had recently visited both Moscow and Peking. Rumors of a coup against Kenya's revered—and aging—leader Jomo Kenyatta spread.

When a Soviet ship carrying arms entered the harbor at Mombasa, the stage was set. Perhaps no one need have worried. Kenya's government sent the ship on its way without unloading the "aid," on the marvelous diplomatic pretext that the arms were obsolete. Immediately Oginga Odinga's headquarters were raided by Kenyatta's men, who claimed to uncover hidden guns and explosives. Parliament fired Oginga Odinga as head of the party school, and "Mzee" (old man) Kenyatta remains in the saddle.

African Attitudes Toward the United States

What determines the attitudes of Africans toward the United States? Our policy toward "colonialism"? Our democratic way of government? Our tailfins, rockets, and skyscrapers? The number of dollars of foreign aid given to African countries? The answer is that all these factors fade when compared with one real issue in African minds—the issue of Negro equality in America.

Every time a Negro home is stoned in Philadelphia or a Freedom Riders' bus is left burning by the Alabama roadside, Africans know it. The African press picks up and reports every racial incident reported in our own newspapers. In Africa, American racial incidents are news. The reports reach beyond the educated Africans to the city laborers, the market women, the messenger boys. Even the illiterate know, for photographs of white policemen clubbing demonstrators in Birmingham or dragging them into police vans in Harlem are more eloquent than words.

For African leaders, discrimination in the United States is often real and personal. After a Nigerian diplomat had been thrown out of a Virginia restaurant in 1960, the National Council of

Asian and African students demonstrate at the United States embassy in Moscow in November 1964 against the Belgian-American paratroop drop to rescue hostages held by the Congo rebels at Stanleyville. The sign at right reads, "Freedom for the People of Congo." (*Wide World Photos.*)

Nigerian Citizens, Nigeria's leading nationalist party, called the United States "a country devoid of respect for human dignity; a country with a completely bankrupt racial policy; a country which still lives in the dark ages; [which] has no claim to leadership of free men."

Many African leaders are aware, when thinking abstractly, that the United States government cannot immediately push racial equality on segregationist Americans by force. Successful Negro protest has impressed Africans with the fact that American democracy provides a peaceful way to remedy injustice. Yet Africans continue to think of America as a white man's country, somewhat hypocritical in its talk of "freedom" and "human dignity."

Another cause of African hostility toward the United States might be summed up as fear of America as the world's greatest military and economic power. The use of American planes to drop Belgian paratroops on Stanleyville in November 1964 (see Chapter 10) provoked violent denunciations from even "moderate" African nations in spite of the mission's stated and ostensible humanitarian purpose of rescuing civilians held hostage by the Congo rebels. American military intervention in the Dominican Republic (April 1965) and the war in Vietnam lead Africans to fear that it may be their turn next to play unwelcome host to the Marines.

Africans are annoyed with what they consider American obsession with the cold war. Time and again, Africans explain that they have their own "African Personality," their own political traditions, and their own interests which are not those of either the East or the West. They fear that America—like Russia or China—will try to push small and poor African countries into taking sides in the cold war and thus keep them weak and divided through fighting one another.

Finally, African leaders strongly committed to "liberation" of Southern Africa fear that America will stay neutral or even aid Rhodesia, Portugal, and South Africa in preserving white supremacy. They point out that Portugal is an American ally in NATO and that Americans hold large financial investments in big mining companies and industry in South Africa. Convinced that liberation is the only morally just policy and is necessary to the dignity of *all* Africans, African statesmen have said quite plainly that they will judge the United States mainly according to its policy on Southern Africa.

All this is not to say that Africans are totally or even generally hostile to the United States. On the contrary, they hope that their fears will be disproved and that American military and economic power will be used to bring peace, development, and justice in Africa.

United States African Policy

In the minds of most American politicians Africa was, until the mid-1950's, a large lump of empty space. France, Britain, Belgium, and Portugal—all members of the NATO alliance for European defense against the Soviet Union—assured the United States that all was well, that African independence was many years away, and that Americans should leave African matters to the Europeans. In the United States Department of State, African affairs were handled by the Bureau of European Affairs!

As the nationalist movement gained momentum the United States was caught on the horns of a dilemma. On the one hand, the Europeans were necessary allies. Most Americans agreed that Africans had to guarantee "orderly" and "responsible" government to merit their independence. On the other hand, America's own anticolonial traditions and sentiments, harking back to the American Revolution, favored the African side. Unable to choose, the United States sat on the fence during the crucial decade of the 1950's. A 1953 speech by an Assistant Secretary of State is a model of equivocation. He began by saying:

> The clock of history cannot be turned back. Alien rule over dependent peoples must be replaced as rapidly as possible by self-determination. Of this there can be no question.

This was music to African ears. Yet the speaker went on to say:

> Premature independence for these peoples would not serve the interests of the United States nor the interests of the dependent peoples themselves.

These words had a strangely colonial ring, and were music to European ears.

In 1956, with Morocco and Tunisia already independent and Ghana about to become the first black African nation, the Suez Canal crisis finally forced the United States to take sides. Egypt seized the canal in July. In October, Israel attacked Egypt, and British and French troops invaded Egypt "to protect the canal." The issue went immediately to the UN. The United States sided with the Asian and African countries against the invasion, and in doing so finally took a clear stand for African independence.

The State Department began to realize that it would be greatly to American advantage to have African governments approving of the United States. Aid programs were begun. Official pronouncements began to drop the "dangers of premature independence" line. In the words of Secretary of State John Foster Dulles, the United States began to "rejoice at the current evolution."

When John F. Kennedy became President in 1960, American policy was revised. African posts were no longer considered the end of the road for diplomats unfit for promotion. The Peace Corps (see below), welcomed by African governments, sent young American volunteers to many African countries. Aid more than doubled between 1960 and 1964.

Congo's collapse in 1960 (see Chapter 10) was the real test of the new African policy. For the first time, the United States became deeply involved in African affairs. When the Congo government asked the United Nations to send troops to restore order, the United States voted for the resolution in the Security Council. United Nations troops and equipment were ferried in American planes to Leopoldville, and American supplies sustained the blue-helmeted United Nations troops, including troops of many African countries. During the Congo crisis African leaders saw that the United States could be a constructive force in Africa, and America won the praise of even that most militant of nationalists, President Nkrumah. United States backing for the unity of Congo and for the United Nations was compared with the clumsy Soviet attempts to destroy the United Nations operation and plunge Congo into civil war.

Southern Africa Tangle

The avowed intention of independent African governments to establish ma-

jority rule in Southern Africa is the current problem for the United States. In practice this means guerilla war against Portugal in Angola and Mozambique, and any kind of pressure, such as economic boycott or refusal of landing rights to airplanes, that can be brought against South Africa. Portugal is an American ally in NATO. On the other hand, Americans have little use for the Portuguese dictatorship of Salazar or for Portugal's backward colonial policies. In the United Nations the United States sides with the Africans against Portugal, although in mild terms.

South Africa could become one of the world's biggest headaches, and one of America's major problems abroad. American investments in South Africa now amount to more than half a billion dollars. South Africa is and will remain the economic heart of Southern Africa —a region of tremendous strategic and military importance.

Some Americans feel that the United States should support the present Afrikaner Nationalist government in spite of its repressive racist policies. They stress that the South African government is anti-Communist and that American investors in South Africa may lose their money if black South Africans succeed in breaking white rule. Most Africans would reply that while South Africa is anti-Communist, so was Hitler, and that a police state cannot be justified on any terms. Since it is only a matter of time before black Africans come to power, they argue, the United States should break its ties with South Africa and be ready to accept black African rule. If the United States continues to support white South Africa, the black revolution may be led and provisioned by Communists.

The United States officially opposes the *apartheid* policy that separates black from white in South Africa. When in March 1960 South African police killed sixty-nine unarmed African demonstrators and wounded one hundred seventy-eight, the State Department made the American position quite clear:

> The United States deplores violence in all its forms and hopes the African people of South Africa will be able to obtain redress for legitimate grievances by peaceful means. While the United States as a matter of practice does not ordinarily comment on the internal affairs of governments with which it enjoys normal relations it cannot help but regret the tragic loss of life resulting from the measures taken against the demonstrators in South Africa.

This is extremely strong language for diplomats. A month later, Henry Cabot Lodge spoke for the United States at the United Nations:

> We appeal once again to the government of the Union of South Africa that it reconsider policies which prevent people of certain races from enjoying their God-given rights and freedoms.

The United States hopes the bloody racial war predicted by so many for South Africa can be averted. Yet unless South African whites have a change of heart, America may be forced to choose between racism and the lasting ill will of Africans on the one hand, and a race war on the other.

The unilateral declaration of independence (called UDI) by white-ruled Rhodesia in November 1965 brought a new—though long-expected—crisis to Southern Africa. The United States has supported the British policy of eventual black majority rule in Rhodesia (population: 4 million Africans; 220,000 whites) and has backed up the British government of Harold Wilson in trying to bring the white-supremacist regime in Salisbury to heel by means short of war. With Britain, the United States has severed trade and financial relations and plans to airlift copper out of neighboring Zambia if the Rhodesians cut Zambia's rail link with the sea. Both Western powers hoped to avert the threat of African armies marching on Salisbury, with the inevitable Rhodesian counteraction of blowing up the magnificent Kariba Dam, which powers the Zambian Copperbelt. Zambia, caught in the jaws of the situation, quite naturally does not want its economy blown to bits, however sympathetic Zambian President Kaunda remains to the cause of African majority rule in Rhodesia. African states have threatened war if diplomatic pressure fails to put down the rebellious settlers. By the time this book is in print readers may decide for themselves whether Western policy has met successfully its first real test in Southern Africa.

American Aid

American officials (including the last four Presidents), scholars, and many businessmen have believed that American dollars used to help the economic development of other nations are well spent. African nations came late to the aid scramble, and Africa has received less than any other area of the world. In 1966 less than one United States aid dollar of every eight went to Africa. At the high point of American aid, in 1963, more than half a billion dollars of aid represented about two American dollars spent on every African man, woman, and child. As the new nations presented plans and projects for economic development, the amount of aid to Africa increased fivefold in the five years after 1958.

Like other countries, the United States plays favorites in giving aid. Ethiopia, which takes a sizable chunk of Soviet aid as well as American, has a large United States military communications center hidden away in its mountains. Liberia, with its historical ties to the United States, is a perennial favorite in Washington. American grants keep the mineral-rich Congo barely on its feet. A recent favorite has been Nigeria, the key nation of West Africa. With American help, Nigeria will hopefully become an example of de-

velopment under a government that en-
courages private enterprise.

In 1963, the development projects
paid for by United States aid dollars
included Ethiopian highways, a teacher-
training college in Mali, dams for hydroelectric power in Liberia, and tractors
for Tunisia. For several years the American Food for Peace program has fed
Egyptians and kept Algerians from
starvation following the disruption of
the Algerian war.

Investment

In spite of some encouragement from
new African governments, American
business has been slow to invest in
Africa. The pronouncements of "African socialism" and all the oratory about
imperialists who seize raw materials
and profits from a defenseless Africa
have discouraged businessmen. Most
American investment has gone to South
Africa, Liberia, and the Rhodesian
(now Zambian) Copperbelt, rather than
to countries ruled by African nationalists. Americans own a substantial por-
tion of Africa's oil wells and mines, and
share in such giant European companies
as Union Minière of Katanga and the
great mining trust of Zambia, which is
part of the financial empire of South
African tycoon Harry Oppenheimer.

American investment has not gone
into industries which produce goods for
African workers and housewives to use,
nor has American private investment
supported economic development plans.
A significant exception is Ghana's Volta
River dam and aluminum project. The
Kaiser and Reynolds Aluminum Companies are building an aluminum refinery at Tema. The plant will use
Ghanaian ore and power from the Volta
River dam now under construction.
Profits will be shared between Ghana
and the American investors. American
managers and engineers will train
Ghanaians to take over the plant after
a number of years. If it works out, other
similar projects may follow.

Labor

American labor has strong ties with
African workers through the International Confederation of Free Trade
Unions (ICFTU). The ICFTU with the
help of the American AFL-CIO has
built a school at Kampala, Uganda, to
train the future leaders of a democratic
African labor movement. The AFL-CIO
took a pro-African and anticolonial
stand throughout the campaign for independence, and has persuaded many
African labor leaders—a key group—to
look favorably toward America.

Youth and the Universities

The number of young Africans studying in the United States doubled between 1958 and 1962, and is still increasing rapidly. Twice as many Africans
study in America as in Russia. However, most young Africans abroad are
still in Europe. These students are tomorrow's African leaders, who by the
time they are thirty will be high officials
at home. The attitudes they form as
students are critical. Unfortunately
discrimination and poverty are still the
rule for African students in America.
Instead of seeing the friendly and pleasant side of American life, many Africans return home embittered as well as
educated.

Americans in Africa

The largest group of Americans in
Africa are the 3,000 missionaries serving Africans in churches, schools, and
hospitals. As new African governments
build government schools, the great importance and contribution of missionaries to Africa will probably decline,
although many are choosing to stay on
and teach as employees of the new governments.

Universities are springing up in city
after African city, to train African
teachers, engineers, businessmen, and
government officials. Through exchange
programs with American universities,
and by direct recruiting, more and more
American professors are serving on

Sargent Shriver, then head of the Peace Corps, on tour as President Kennedy's special envoy to Africa in 1961. Here he rides with Sékou Touré. *(Republic of Guinea, Four Years of Independence and Liberty.)*

African university faculties. While the number is small, their importance is great, for their ideas go directly to future African leaders.

In 1961 President Kennedy offered young Americans a new and challenging way to serve their country: the Peace Corps. Fifteen hundred Peace Corps volunteers are in Africa, and seventeen hundred more are in training to go. The volunteers have served as surveyors in Tanganyika, agricultural extension workers in villages in Guinea and Nigeria, and teachers in these and most other African countries. The volunteers are not officials but individuals working both for African development and for better understanding between the United States and their African host countries.

Do Africans and Americans Share Common Goals?

Africans are trying to pull their countries toward prosperity and toward peace and unity. Modern Africans are

Exhibit 6
The Peace Corps in Africa

After Latin America, Africa takes more Peace Corps volunteers than any other area of the world.

Where they are		*What they do*	
Nigeria	759	Teaching	2,810 (80%)
Ethiopia	725	Village Improve.	208 (6%)
Liberia	468	Construction	182 (5%)
Sierra Leone	244	Health	165 (4½%)
Tanganyika	209	Agriculture	105 (3%)
Ghana	200	Law & Gov't	
Cameroons	155	Administration	52 (1½%)
Nyasaland	153		
Senegal	112		
Somalia	74		
Gabon	70		
Togo	59		
Guinea	52		
Ivory Coast	51		
Niger	51		
Others	138		

aroused and active people. They have recently rejected the benevolent rule of colonial supremacy. They want to achieve their own goals and make their own mistakes in their own African way. Americans share this spirit of independence and self-help.

During the lifetime of today's young people events will determine the success or failure of the twin African aims of economic progress and African unity. There will be times of peace and times of violence, successful efforts and disappointments, and a great deal of change and turbulence. The danger is that the pressure of events will blind Americans and Africans to their common beliefs and hopes.

An independent and stable African community of developing nations is the fervent wish of African leaders. This is also in the practical interest of the United States.

PROBLEMS

1. If you were to travel to Africa during your next vacation, how would you answer questions which Africans would be sure to put to you about the struggle for Negro rights in the United States? List the points you would try to make to an inquiring and perhaps hostile African student.

2. Collect clippings about events in Africa. What kind of news about Africa gets into American newspapers? Are Americans who read newspapers likely to think of Africa as a continent of peaceful progress? Are they likely to have an understanding of the problems faced by African leaders?

3. Find out what you can about *one* African crisis (examples: Rhodesia, the Somali-Ethiopia border war, the Angola rebellion, *apartheid* in South Africa). Draw up what you think would be a fair solution, and try to

justify it. What should the United States attitude be? Should the United States take any action?

4. What would be the likely attitude of a conference of African leaders toward: (a) a Chinese Communist offer to train an African army to fight for the "liberation" of South Africa, on the condition that its officers be Chinese Communists; (b) an American plan to keep all weapons out of Africa except those requested by the Organization of African Unity; (c) a joint proposal of Britain, France, and Germany to supply a huge sum in foreign aid if African countries agree to accept aid from no one else.

5. Do you think communism will be a greater threat to Africa in the future? What circumstances would make it easier for Soviet or Chinese Communists to gain influence?

6. Make a rough map of the world as African leaders might see it, by drawing each continent in a size proportionate to its importance to Africa. Draw a similar map to show the American world view, and compare them. Is United States attention to Africa and Africa's attention to the United States likely to increase in the future? Why?

READING SUGGESTIONS

American Assembly, *The United States and Africa* (Chapter 1, Chapter 3, Appendix), Praeger, paper.

Harold R. Isaacs, *Emergent Americans*, Day, 1962.

Louis E. Lomax, *The Reluctant African*, Harper & Row, 1960.

Vernon McKay, *Africa in World Politics*, Harper & Row, 1963.

Sylvanus Olympio, "African Problems in the Cold War," *Foreign Affairs*, October 1961.

Philip Quigg (ed.), *Africa: A Foreign Affairs Reader*, Praeger, paper.

INDEX

ABAKO Party, 156; *see also* Kasavubu, Joseph
AFL-CIO, 294
ARM (African Resistance Movement), 196
Abboud, Ibrahim, 136, 275
Aborigines Rights' Protection Society, 116
Abrahams, Peter, 120, 139, 233, 252
Accra, Ghana, *see* Ghana
Accra Conference (1958), 221-22
Accra Evening News, 203, 211
Achebe, Chinua, 237
Achmed, Mohammed, *see* Mahdi
Action Group, 105, 164-65, 268; *see also* Nigeria
Addis Ababa, 177, 178, 179, 223, 227; *see also* Ethiopia
Addis Ababa Conference (1963), 126-27
Adoula, Cyril, 158-60; *see also* Congo (ex-Belgian)
Advisory councils, *see* Great Britain, colonial policies
Afonso, 43
African and Malagasy Union (UAM), 223, 224
African Association, 51
African churches, 112-14
African National Congress (ANC), 115, 146, 193, 195, 196, 286; *see also* South Africa, parties and politics
African Orthodox Church, 110
"African personality," 280, 291; *see also* Pan-Africanism *and* Negritude
African prophets, 112-14
Africanus, Leo, 34
Afrikaners, 59-60, 63, 145-46, 182-85, 194; *see also* South Africa
Afro-Asian Conference, *see* Bandung Conference
Age-set system, 14-15; *see also* Masai people
Agriculture: modern, 85-86, 88-90, 198-99, 247-49, chart, 88; traditional, 12, 56
Aguiyi-Ironsi, J. T. U., 166
Ahidjo, Ahmadou, 145
Aid, foreign, 167, 206, 276, 290: countries receiving most aid, 281; from Europe, 285; Nigerian National Development Plan, 258; to raise capital, 255; from Soviet Union, 288; US aid programs, 281, chart, 228, 293-94
Air Afrique, 224
Akintola, S. E., 165-66; *see also* Nigeria
Algeria: French occupation, 64, 68, 82, 91; independence and after, 213, 226, 229, 250, 275; people, 19-20; war, 128-29, 131, 205, 222, 224, 284
Algiers, Dey of, 64
Ali, Hassan Ben, 38-39
Ali, Mohammed, 54, 134
Ali, Sonni, 34
All-African Peoples' Conference (1958), 143, 221-22
Allahi, Khalifa Abd, 60
Almoravids, 18; *see also* Islam
Alooma, Mai Idris, 35
Aluminum, 84-85; *see also* Volta River Project
Alumini Associations, 115
Alvarez, Francisco, 176-77
American Colonization Society, 171; *see also* Liberia
Americo-Liberians, 170-74
Amhara people, 178; *see also* Ethiopia
Ancestor worship, *see* Religion
Anglo-American Mining Trust, 284
Anglo-Boer War, *see* Boer War
Anglo-Egyptian Sudan, 67, 69; *see also* Great Britain *and* Sudan
Angola: colonialism in, 68, 84, 128; illiteracy rate, 95; liberation movements, 144, 229; Portuguese labor policies, 90-91; school systems, 95
Ankrah, Joseph, 212-13, 275
Anti-colonialism, defined, 119
Apartheid, *see* South Africa, race policy
Arabs: culture, 19-20, 33-34, 271; expansion, 18, 32, 176; modern nationalism, 130-31, 135; trade, 7, 35, 38-39, 48-49, 54, 154
Arabi, Ahmed, 66
Army, rule by, 264; chart, 266; Ghana, 212-13; military takeovers (chart), 274; Nigeria, 166, 168; Year of the Generals, 274-76
Art, 7; *see also* Literature *and* Arabs, culture

WITHDRAWN